Elder Law

Elder Law

Evolving European Perspectives

Edited by

Ann Numhauser-Henning

Faculty of Law, Lund University, Sweden

Edward Elgar
PUBLISHING

Cheltenham, UK • Northampton, MA, USA

Published by
Edward Elgar Publishing Limited
The Lypiatts
15 Lansdown Road
Cheltenham
Glos GL50 2JA
UK

Edward Elgar Publishing, Inc.
William Pratt House
9 Dewey Court
Northampton
Massachusetts 01060
USA

A catalogue record for this book
is available from the British Library

Library of Congress Control Number: 2016953931

This book is available electronically in the **Elgar**online
Law subject collection
DOI 10.4337/9781785369094

MIX
Paper from
responsible sources
FSC® C013056
FSC
www.fsc.org

ISBN 978 1 78536 908 7 (cased)
ISBN 978 1 78536 909 4 (eBook)

Typeset by Columns Design XML Ltd, Reading
Printed and bound in Great Britain by TJ International Ltd, Padstow

Contents

Contributors

Martina Axmin is a doctoral candidate in EU law at the Faculty of Law, Lund University, Sweden. She is a member of the Norma Elder Law Research Environment. Axmin's research examines the free movement of the elderly and their access to cross-border healthcare in the EU. The research project highlights the tension between the guarantee of free movement on the one hand, and on the other the autonomy of the Member States and their right to organize their healthcare systems.

Alysia Blackham is Senior Lecturer at Melbourne Law School at the University of Melbourne. Her research focuses on the intersection of employment law, equality law and public law, using empirical evidence to cast new light on legal problems. A monograph based on Blackham's PhD thesis, entitled *Extending Working Life for Older Workers: Age Discrimination Law, Policy and Practice*, was published by Hart Publishing 2016. She is a guest researcher in the Norma Elder Law Research Environment.

Cécile Brokelind is Professor of Business Law at the Department of Business Law, School of Economics and Management, Lund University. She is an active researcher on EU tax law (income tax) and focuses on cross-border mobility issues, specifically international tax law dealing with tax incentives and protectionism for domestic tax bases used to finance welfare, and incompatibility of these practices with EU tax law or double tax treaties. Brokelind's research sheds light on this conflict in several areas, such as the tax treatment of pensions. She is a guest researcher in the Norma Elder Law Research Environment.

Judy Fudge has been Professor at Kent Law School, University of Kent, since 2013. She began her academic career at Osgoode Hall Law School in 1987, and in 2006 she became Lansdowne Chair and Professor at the Faculty of Law at the University of Victoria, Canada. Her research interests are employment and labour law, feminist approaches to law, and the political economy of law. She has written widely on Canadian labour law, labour rights as human rights, and atypical and precarious work. Fudge was elected fellow of the Royal Society of Canada in 2013 for her contribution to labour law scholarship. Fudge is a guest researcher in the Norma Research Programme.

Emma Holm is Doctor of Private Law (LLD) at the Faculty of Law, Lund University and a member of the Norma Research Programme since 1998. Her research mainly concerns EU law and social security law (Regulation (EC) No. 883/2004), in particular benefits relating to families. More recently, her research has also focused on the rules on free movement of EU citizens and the specific situation of elderly migrants. She participates in the European Commission's Network for Free Movement of Workers and Social Security Coordination (FreSsco).

Andreas Inghammar is Associate Professor in Business Law and Head of the Department of Business Law at the School of Economics and Management, Lund University. His research primarily covers comparative and national aspects of labour law, focusing on employment law and disability discrimination law and, most recently, on the legal situation of undocumented migrant workers under international, EU and national provisions. Inghammar has been a Visiting Professor at Pannasastra University of Cambodia during 2015/16 and was previously a visiting researcher at the University of Warwick in the United Kingdom, and the Institute for Labour Law, University of Göttingen, Germany. He is a long-standing member of the Norma Research Programme.

Jenny Julén Votinius is Associate Professor in Private Law at the Faculty of Law, Lund University. She has been a member of the Norma Research Programme since 1997. She specializes in Swedish and EU labour law, and her research spans over the areas of non-discrimination law and work-family balance, youth employment, the discourse on social and interpersonal skills, and the intersection of age with other grounds for discrimination. Her work is characterized by an interdisciplinary approach, integrating perspectives from social science and political philosophy. She has wide experience of labour law research in comparative and international settings, including participation in projects for the International Labour Organization (ILO) and ongoing research within the European Network for Labour Law and Crisis Studies (INLACRIS), financed by the European Commission. In 2014, she was a senior visiting scholar at Berkeley Law School, University of California.

Mirjam Katzin is a doctoral candidate in social welfare law at Lund University and a member of the Norma Elder Law Research Environment since 2013. Her project focuses on different aspects of the privatization of elder care and the shifting responsibility for older people, as part of a larger conflict in society regarding the future of the Scandinavian welfare state.

Miriam Kullmann is Assistant Professor at the Faculty of Law, Maastricht University and a researcher at the Faculty of Law, Leiden University. She defended her PhD thesis on the 'Enforcement of Labour Law in Cross-Border Situations' at Radboud University Nijmegen (The Netherlands) in April 2015. Her research focuses on EU employment law and policy and its interplay with national employment laws and policies, particularly addressing issues on and around the ageing of the workforce. Kullmann is a guest researcher in the Norma Elder Law Research Environment.

Titti Mattsson is Professor of Public Law at the Faculty of Law, Lund University and a long-standing member of the Norma Research Programme. She has written on issues concerning the legal and social position of children and youth. Several of her projects have dealt with different rights for foster children and youth in residential care. Another field of research for Mattsson involves issues related to government. She has published widely in monographs, anthologies and journals. She is an expert adviser for the Child Ombudsman of Sweden, and a member of several national and international research networks in the field of social law. Her project within the Norma Elder Law Research Environment, 'Active Ageing for All?', examines older people's legal position in healthcare and social services.

Per Norberg is Assistant Professor of Private Law at the Faculty of Law, Lund University and a long-standing member of the Norma Research Programme. Norberg's research is directed towards the conflict between market functional values and social values in law. He has worked with labour law, housing law and gender equality law, and is currently working with social security law as well. He is a member of the European Commission's Network of Legal Experts on Discrimination and is involved in the steering group of a network of lawyers and economists interested in wage discrimination.

Ann Numhauser-Henning is Professor of Private Law at the Faculty of Law, Lund University and the former Pro-Vice-Chancellor. She has been head of the Norma Research Programme since its start in 1996 and initiated the Norma Elder Law Research Environment in 2012. She has written widely on labour law, especially employment law and non-discrimination law. A more recent field for her research is social security law in a European integration perspective. She is a member of the

European Commission's Network of Legal Experts on Equal Treatment between Men and Women.

Hanna Pettersson is Doctor of Private Law at the Faculty of Law, Lund University. She is a member of the Norma Research Programme and has been a postdoctoral researcher in the Norma Elder Law Research Environment 2013–15. Her research is within employment law, social security law, and critical legal studies. Petterson's doctoral thesis, published in 2012, concerns discrimination of part-time and fixed-term employees. She is currently working on a project concerning legal perceptions of ageing and its relevance for working life.

Eva Ryrstedt is Professor of Private Law at the Faculty of Law, Lund University. The focus of her research is family law and the interface between social welfare law and family law. She is a long-standing member of the Norma Research Programme and participates in the Norma Elder Law Research Environment, where her research is aimed at civil rights of the elderly in a family law setting. Ryrstedt often works comparatively, and has taken a special interest in the Nordic countries, England and Australia. She participates in comparative and international research collaborations, and has published her research results in monographs and anthologies, as well as in international and national journals.

Mia Rönnmar is Professor of Private Law and Dean of the Faculty of Law, Lund University. She has been a member of the Norma Research Programme since its start in 1996. She has written widely on Swedish, EU and comparative labour law and industrial relations. She is President-Elect of the International Labour and Employment Relations Association (ILERA), and has been a visiting researcher at a number of institutions, including Sydney Law School, the European University Institute and the London School of Economics. She is the former Editor-in-Chief of the International Journal of Comparative Labour Law and Industrial Relations and a member of editorial boards of several journals in the fields of labour law and industrial relations.

Kirk Scott is Professor of Economic History at Lund University, Sweden and guest researcher in demography at the Stockholm University Demographic Unit. His research lies primarily in the intersection between immigrant integration and demography, with focuses on labour market integration in general, and its impact on demographic behaviour in particular. Parallel with these studies, Scott has become increasingly interested in the economic impacts of population ageing, and potential policy answers to the challenges caused by an ageing population. Scott is a past president of the Swedish Demographic Association and the Nordic

Demographic Association, and served as Dean of the European Doctoral School of Demography 2009–11.

Elsa Trolle Önnerfors is Associate Professor in Legal History at the Faculty of Law, Lund University. Trolle Önnerfors is a legal historian, specializing in family law history and inheritance law history. Her dissertation focused on the Swedish law of wills in the seventeenth century. She also has a great interest in family law of today, and has written on inheritance law of both past and present. She is now part of the Norma Elder Law Research Environment.

Carin Ulander-Wänman is Associate Professor in Labour Law and a senior lecturer at Umeå University, Sweden. Her research projects concern European employment policy and the regulation of the Swedish labour market in law and collective agreements. Her ongoing research focuses on employees' skills development in existing employment. She is a guest researcher in the Norma Elder Law Research Environment.

Ania Zbyszewska is Assistant Professor at the University of Warwick Law School, United Kingdom. She researches regulation of work and labour markets, and is particularly interested in their gender dimensions. Her work also examines the dynamic interactions between law and politics in multilevel governance contexts such as the EU and under conditions of political-economic and social change. Author of *Gendering European Working Time Regimes* (2016), she has published articles in international journals and has contributed to several book collections. Dr Zbyszewska is a guest researcher within the Norma Elder Law Research Environment.

Preface

This book aims to introduce the area of elder law in a European setting and, more specifically, how it has been understood and developed within the Norma Elder Law Research Environment since the programme's start. The Norma Elder Law Research Environment was founded at the Law Faculty of Lund University, Sweden, in response to the increased presence of 'ageing concerns' detected in EU policies and EU law at the turn of the millennium – developments that reflected growing concern about demographical ageing and its consequences. Given the magnitude of these concerns and their character of a long-term global challenge, elder law as a notion – and even more so as a legal discipline – so far has occupied a surprisingly modest position in the European context. In the context of the Norma Elder Law Research Environment the studies cover 'everyday life' legal structures in terms of work, family, housing and complementary welfare structures, factors which are all intrinsically interrelated with each other and also with general societal developments. The programme has focused on the structural implications of certain legal and societal solutions related to ageing at the macro or institutional level, and is characterized by its understanding of the elderly as a contextualized concept, ultimately determined by the specific area and problems concerned.

The contributors to this book include members of the Norma Elder Law Research Environment as well as invited guests – well-known and prestigious scholars as well as upcoming and promising young researchers. They have all worked together to amalgamate the results and consequences of their studies in an attempt to deepen our understanding of legal and other conditions affecting ageing individuals in our society. The analysis has been further developed by means of continuous internal seminars in the winter of 2015/16, culminating with the Norma Research Programme Twentieth Anniversary Workshop 'Researching Legal Development within the Social Dimension', held in Lund from 10 to 11 March 2016. As editor I am deeply indebted to all the authors and grateful for the effort and enthusiasm that they have put into the project. I also want to thank the funders of the Norma Elder Law Research Environment – Ragnar Söderberg's Foundation, the Marianne and Marcus Wallenberg

Foundation and the Faculty of Law at Lund University – for their generous contributions. Finally, I would like to thank PhD student Martina Axmin for assisting me in the editing process.

Ann Numhauser-Henning
Lund, June 2016

Publications on elder law within the Norma Elder Law Research Environment

Martina Axmin, 'Health care – a right without borders also for the elderly?' in Ann Numhauser-Henning (ed.), *Introduction to the Norma Elder Law Research Environment – Different Approaches to Elder Law* (The Norma Research Programme, Faculty of Law, Lund University 2013)

Alysia Blackham, 'Addressing the ageing workforce: a critical examination of legal policy objectives and values in the United Kingdom' (2016) Ageing and Society (forthcoming)

Helene Brodin and Titti Mattsson, 'Lägst ned på skalan? Hälso- och sjukvårdens bemötande av äldre kvinnor som migrerat till Sverige' (2014) 21(3–4) Socialvetenskaplig Tidskrift 372

Linus Broström, Mats Johansson and Titti Mattsson, 'Registrering av beslutsoförmögna för forskning, statistik och systematiskt förbättringsarbete' (2014) 3 Förvaltningsrättslig Tidskrift 369

Judy Fudge and Ania Zbyszewska, 'An intersectional approach to age discrimination in the European Union: bridging dignity and distribution?' in Ann Numhauser-Henning and Mia Rönnmar (eds), *Age Discrimination and Labour Law, Comparative and Conceptual Perspectives in the EU and Beyond* (Kluwer Law International 2015)

Emma Holm, 'Pensions on the move' in Ann Numhauser-Henning (ed.), *Introduction to the Norma Elder Law Research Environment – Different Approaches to Elder Law* (The Norma Research Programme, Faculty of Law, Lund University 2013)

Emma Holm, 'Fri rörlighet och tillgång till sociala förmåner för icke-förvärvsaktiva – har unionsmedborgarskapet kommit till vägs ände?' (2015) 2 Förvaltningsrättslig Tidskrift 225

Jenny Julén Votinius, 'Intersections of age and gender' in Ann Numhauser-Henning (ed.), *Introduction to the Norma Elder Law Research Environment – Different Approaches to Elder Law* (The Norma Research Programme, Faculty of Law, Lund University 2013)

Jenny Julén Votinius, 'Age discrimination and labour law in Sweden' in Ann Numhauser-Henning and Mia Rönnmar (eds), *Age Discrimination and Labour Law, Comparative and Conceptual Perspectives in the EU and Beyond* (Kluwer Law International 2015)

Jenny Julén Votinius, 'Intersectionality as a tool for analysing age and gender in labour law' in Simonetta Manfredi and Lucy Vickers (eds), *Challenges of Active Ageing* (Palgrave Macmillan 2016)

Håkan Jönsson and Titti Mattsson (eds), 'Special Issue – Likvärdighet och äldreomsorg' (2014) 21 3–4 Socialvetenskaplig Tidskrift

Mirjam Katzin, 'Citizens as customers – social rights and the marketization of elder care' in Ann Numhauser-Henning (ed.), *Introduction to the Norma Elder Law Research Environment – Different Approaches to Elder Law* (The Norma Research Programme, Faculty of Law, Lund University 2013)

Mirjam Katzin, 'Tillbaka till familjen: privat och offentligt ansvar i den svenska äldreomsorgen' (2014) 2 Retfaerd 37

Mirjam Katzin, 'Valfrihet istället för jämlikhet – förändrade målsättningar för äldreomsorgspolitiken?' (2014) 21(3–4) Socialvetenskaplig Tidskrift 310

Miriam Kullmann, 'Extending working life: the Dutch government's response' (2016) 1 European Labour Law Journal

Titti Mattsson, 'Rätten att få åldras tillsammans – en fråga om skälig levnadsnivå' (2012) Blendow Lexnova Expertkommentar

Titti Mattsson, 'A right to active ageing for all? On the status of the elderly in social services and health care' in Ann Numhauser-Henning (ed.), *Introduction to the Norma Elder Law Research Environment – Different Approaches to Elder Law* (The Norma Research Programme, Faculty of Law, Lund University 2013)

Titti Mattsson, 'National ombudsman for the elderly: a solution for a more responsive welfare state?' (2013) 142(3) Retfaerd 9

Titti Mattsson, 'Registrering av äldre patienter för kvalitetsutveckling och forskning' (2013) Blendow Lexnova Expertkommentar

Titti Mattsson, 'Patient safety at odds with patient privacy? The case of national and regional quality registries for incapacitated elderly in Sweden' (2014) (Special issue IV EAHL Conference) Lex Medicinae 69

Titti Mattsson, 'Collecting data for quality improvement and research in Swedish health care, and the individual patient's right and ability to protect their privacy' The International Journal of Technology Policy and Law Pages (forthcoming)

Titti Mattsson, 'E-government for the distribution of public services in Sweden: privatization, vulnerability and social responsibility reshaped' in Martha Albertson Fineman, Ulrika Andersson and Titti Mattsson (eds), *Privatization, Vulnerability, and Social Responsibility: A Comparative Perspective* (Routledge 2017)

Titti Mattsson, '"Participation" for all? Challenges and tools for realizing the goal for vulnerable people with focus on health services' in Marlies Hesselman, Antenor Hallo de Wolf and Brigit Toebes (eds), *Socio-Economic Rights in Essential Public Services Provision* (Routledge Press 2016)

Per Norberg, 'Sickness Insurance Reform and the Elderly' in Ann Numhauser-Henning (ed.), *Introduction to the Norma Elder Law Research Environment – Different Approaches to Elder Law* (The Norma Research Programme, Faculty of Law, Lund University 2013)

Per Norberg, 'Hem eller vårdplats – hur behandlas personer med omsorgsbehov i hyreslagstiftningen?' (2014) 21(3–4) Socialvetenskaplig Tidskrift 350

Ann Numhauser-Henning, 'Om avgång i samband med pension och åldersdiskriminering' in Birgitta Nyström, Örjan Edström and Jonas Malmberg (eds), *Nedslag i den nya arbetsrätten* (Liber 2012)

Ann Numhauser-Henning, 'Age discrimination and compulsory retirement' in Ann Numhauser-Henning (ed.), *Introduction to the Norma Elder*

Law Research Environment – Different Approaches to Elder Law (The Norma Research Programme, Faculty of Law, Lund University 2013)

Ann Numhauser-Henning, 'Äldrerätt – ett nytt forskningsfält inför stora utmaningar' in Aslak Syse and others (eds), *Velferd og rettferd, Festskrift til Asbjörn Kjönstad 70 år* (Gyldendal Juridisk 2013)

Ann Numhauser-Henning, 'An introduction to elder law and the Norma Elder Law Research Environment' (2013) 3 Eur J of Soc L

Ann Numhauser-Henning, 'An introduction to elder law and the Norma Elder Law Research Environment: age discrimination and compulsory retirement' in Ann Numhauser-Henning (ed.), *Introduction to the Norma Elder Law Research Environment Different Approaches to Elder Law* (The Norma Research Programme, Faculty of Law, Lund University 2013)

Ann Numhauser-Henning, 'Introduction to the Norma Elder Law Research Environment Different approaches to elder law' in Ann Numhauser-Henning (ed.), *Introduction to the Norma Elder Law Research Environment – Different Approaches to Elder Law* (The Norma Research Programme, Faculty of Law, Lund University 2013)

Ann Numhauser-Henning, 'Labour law in a greying labour market – in need of a reconceptualisation of work and pension norms, the position of older workers in labour law' (2013) 4(2) Eur Lab L J 84

Ann Numhauser-Henning, 'The EU ban on age-discrimination and older workers: potentials and pitfalls' (2013) 29(4) IJCLLIR 391

Ann Numhauser-Henning, 'La prohibición de la UE contra la discriminación por edad y el papel de los agentes sociales' (2014) *El derecho a la negociación colectiva, Liber Amicorum Profesor Antonio Ojeda Avilés* (Junta de Andalucia 2014)

Ann Numhauser-Henning, 'Labour law in a greying labour market – in need of a reconceptualisation of work and pension norms' in Steven Willborn and Alan Neal (eds), *Yearbook of Comparative Labour Law Scholarship* (Lancaster House 2015)

Ann Numhauser-Henning, 'Labour law, pension norms and the EU ban on age discrimination: towards ultimate flexibilization?' in Ann

Numhauser-Henning and Mia Rönnmar (eds), *Age Discrimination and Labour Law, Comparative and Conceptual Perspectives in the EU and Beyond* (Kluwer Law International 2015)

Ann Numhauser-Henning and Mia Rönnmar, 'Compulsory retirement and age discrimination – the Swedish Hörnfeldt case put in perspective' in Patrik Lindskoug and others (eds), *Essays in Honour of Michael Bogdan* (Juristförlaget i Lund 2013)

Ann Numhauser-Henning and Mia Rönnmar (eds), *Age Discrimination and Labour Law, Comparative and Conceptual Perspectives in the EU and Beyond* (Kluwer Law International 2015)

Ann Numhauser-Henning and Mia Rönnmar, 'Concluding discussion' in Ann Numhauser-Henning and Mia Rönnmar (eds), *Age Discrimination and Labour Law, Comparative and Conceptual Perspectives in the EU and Beyond* (Kluwer Law International 2015)

Ann Numhauser-Henning and Mia Rönnmar, 'Introduction' in Ann Numhauser-Henning and Mia Rönnmar (eds), *Age Discrimination and Labour Law, Comparative and Conceptual Perspectives in the EU and Beyond* (Kluwer Law International 2015)

Ann Numhauser-Henning and Mia Rönnmar, 'Age discrimination and labour law in a comparative perspective' in Laura Carlson, Örjan Edström and Birgitta Nyström (eds), *Globalisation, Fragmentation, Labour and Employment Law – A Swedish Perspective* (Iustus 2016)

Ann Numhauser-Henning and Mia Rönnmar, 'Age discrimination law and social partners and collective bargaining' in Bernhard Johann Mulder et al. (eds), *Sui generis – Festskrift til Stein Evju* (Universitetsforlaget Oslo 2016)

Hanna Pettersson, 'Challenge or opportunity? Perceptions of ageing in labour law and social security law' in Ann Numhauser-Henning (ed.), *Introduction to the Norma Elder Law Research Environment – Different Approaches to Elder Law* (The Norma Research Programme, Faculty of Law, Lund University 2013)

Hanna Pettersson, 'Döden – en privatsak? Socialförsäkringsrättsliga perspektiv på ansvarsfördelning vid närståendevård' (manuscript)

Hanna Pettersson, 'Managing the ageing population: Swedish legal approaches to older workers in the 1970s and the 2010s' (manuscript)

Eva Ryrstedt, 'Civil rights of the elderly in a family law setting' in Ann Numhauser-Henning (ed.), *Introduction to the Norma Elder Law Research Environment – Different Approaches to Elder Law* (The Norma Research Programme, Faculty of Law, Lund University 2013)

Eva Ryrstedt, 'Får jag inte bestämma något själv? En studie av kvarstående beslutanderätt hos dementa äldre' (2014) 21(3–4) Socialvetenskaplig Tidskrift 328

Eva Ryrstedt, 'Dementa äldre personer; vem ska bestämma?' (2016) 1 Tidskrift utgiven av Juridiska Föreningen i Finland 179

Mia Rönnmar, 'Protection of established position, social protection and the legal situation of the elderly in the European Union' in Mia Rönnmar and Ann Numhauser-Henning (eds), *Normative Patterns and Legal Developments in the Social Dimension of the EU* (Hart Publishing 2013)

Mia Rönnmar, 'Flexicurity and the legal position of the elderly' in Ann Numhauser-Henning (ed.), *Introduction to the Norma Elder Law Research Environment – Different Approaches to Elder Law* (The Norma Research Programme, Faculty of Law, Lund University 2013)

Mia Rönnmar, *Intergenerational Bargaining in Sweden.* Report for the project iNGenBar (2014)

Mia Rönnmar 'Age discrimination and labour law: a comparative analysis' in Ann Numhauser-Henning and Mia Rönnmar (eds), *Age Discrimination and Labour Law, Comparative and Conceptual Perspectives in the EU and Beyond* (Kluwer Law International 2015)

Mia Rönnmar, 'Elder Law' (2015) September/Oktober Recht der Arbeit 305

Mia Rönnmar, *Older Workers and 'Stayers' in the Swedish Labour Market: An Analysis of the Legal Framework* (Report for the project 'Towards sustainable ageing: a life course perspective' funded by the Kamprad Family Foundation 2016)

Beryl Ter Haar and Mia Rönnmar, *Intergenerational Bargaining, EU Age Discrimination Law and EU Policies – and Integrated Analysis*, Report for the project iNGenBar (2014)

Carin Ulander-Wänman, 'Swedish collective agreements and employers' willingness to hire and retain older workers in employment' (2016) 6(2) Nordic Journal of Working Life Studies 61–79

Carin Ulander-Wänman, 'The Swedish occupational pension scheme ITP2 – a limiting factor for older employees' employability?' (manuscript)

Ania Zbyszewska, 'Active aging through employment: a critical feminist perspective on Polish policy' (2016) Int J Comp Lab Law and Indus Relations (forthcoming)

Table of cases

COUNCIL OF EUROPE

EUROPEAN UNION

NATIONAL COURTS

Canada

Sweden

Supreme Court

Labour Court

United Kingdom

United States

PART I

Introduction

1. Introduction

Ann Numhauser-Henning

1. INTRODUCTION[1]

The aim of this book is to introduce the research area of elder law in a European setting, and more specifically how this field has been understood and developed within the Norma Elder Law Research Environment since the programme's start in 2012. Contributors to this book include scholars within this research environment but also invited guests. The book offers an innovative and important interdisciplinary approach to the analysis of legal developments in the European setting from a multitude of theoretical and legal-substantive perspectives. Thus this introductory part (Chapters 1 and 2) is followed by one on conceptual and theoretical perspectives (Chapters 3–6), and the book then continues with a part on different elements of elder law (Chapters 7–15).

This introductory chapter starts out by providing a brief background on ageing society in a European Union (EU) policy development perspective (Section 1.1) and continues with an introduction to studies on law and ageing in the setting of the Norma Research Programme (Section 1.2). The interrelations between the different contributions are then thematized and related more generally to a variety of relevant concepts and perspectives. An established theoretical approach within the Norma Research Programme is the late Anna Christensen's theory of law as normative patterns in a normative field, as described in Section 1.2, and throughout this chapter I relate to the legal developments elaborated upon in the different chapters in the terms of normative patterns. The chapter is organized in parallel with the different parts of the book – that is, conceptual and theoretical perspectives (Section 2) and elements of elder law (Section 3), and finishing with some concluding remarks (Section 4).

[1] This work was carried out within the Norma Elder Law Research Environment (www.jur.lu.se/elderlaw) funded by Ragnar Söderberg's Foundation and the Marianne and Marcus Wallenberg Foundation.

1.1 An Ageing European Society

Demographic ageing is one of the major challenges for the future. In recent decades the EU has carefully monitored the implications of an ageing population. The fifth ageing report, entitled *The 2015 Ageing Report. Economic and Budgetary Projections for the 28 EU Member States (2013–2060)*,[2] starts out by stating that 'Europe is "turning increasingly grey" in the coming decades' and that 'the Commission, as well as the European Council, have already recognized the need to tackle resolutely the impact of ageing populations on the European Social Models'.[3] Due to the interrelated dynamics of fertility, life expectancy and migration, demographics in the EU Member States will change significantly by 2060. The overall population will increase slightly by 2050 (526 million as compared to today's 507 million), only to decline slightly thereafter (523 million). At the same time, the demographic old-age dependency ratio (people aged 65 or above relative to those aged 15–64) will double – from 27.8 per cent to 50.1 per cent. Labour-market participation rates are projected to rise – especially among those in the 50+ group – due to women's integration and the expected impact of pension reforms. Nevertheless, labour supply will decline, despite the expected rise in employment rates and migration flows, and already by 2023 the number of employed will begin to diminish. Throughout the projected period, labour productivity growth is assumed to be the sole source of the still-projected gross domestic product (GDP) growth (1.4 per cent). These developments pose a massive challenge for public finances and especially so regarding pensions, healthcare and long-term care. Pension expenditure is expected to grow until about 2040, when it begins to decline due to both pension reforms and significantly lower pensions. Nevertheless it must be noted that the differences in this respect among EU Member States are considerable.

In light of these trends, the EU declared 2012 'The Year of Active Ageing and Solidarity between Generations'.[4] This declaration was accompanied by 'Guiding Principles for Active Ageing and Solidarity between Generations' in terms of employment, participation in society, and independent living. The EU's overall ambitions are expressed in the

---

[2] European Economy 3/2015 (Luxembourg Publications Office of the European Union 2015).

[3] Ibid 1.

[4] Decision No. 940/2011/EU, 14 September 2011, OJ 23.09.2011, No. 246/5.

Europe 2020 Strategy, promoting a healthy and active ageing population as a way to achieve social cohesion and higher productivity.[5]

These strategies find support in the EU Treaty provisions. The Lisbon Treaty now cites solidarity between generations as one of the Union's objectives (Article 3.3 Treaty of the European Union (TEU)) and the EU Charter of Fundamental Rights (CFR) apostrophizes (in Article 25) the rights of the elderly to lead a life of dignity and independence and to participate in social and cultural life. Article 34.1 of the CFR mentions social security and social assistance in the case of old age and Article 15 of the CFR refers more generally to the right to work. Non-discrimination is also an important tool for these strategies – Article 21 of the CFR bans discrimination, among other grounds on age – prohibitions that have received a more detailed expression at secondary law level in the Employment Equality Directive 2000/78/EC.[6]

In Chapter 2, 'Demographic developments and economic challenges in an ageing Europe', Kirk Scott provides us with a deepened understanding of the demographic transition leading to an ageing society. The 'first population ageing', which took place towards the end of agrarian society, was driven by a combination of mortality decline and related fertility decline, and was mostly beneficial to society. The 'second population ageing', on the other hand – characterized more by longevity than fertility decline and thus an ageing society – is indeed troublesome. A key issue is the increasing old-age dependency ratio, also referred to above, with its implied reallocation of capital to the elderly. Scott discusses potential solutions to this challenge in terms of increases in fertility, immigration and/or tax bases. Prospects are not looking so good, though. Increased fertility raises the economic burden over the short and medium terms, whereas immigration has a 'snowball character' in the long run – increasing the ageing population while (originally often high) fertility rates are adjusted. Moreover, there simply are not enough potential immigrants to solve the EU's – and less so the world's – ageing problem. Increasing already high taxes is not an obvious remedy for the EU internal market – and is even less so for a global one. One way of increasing tax revenue, however, is to increase the number of hours worked in an overall perspective. In this regard Europe is trailing far behind both the United States (US) and Japan. There are also the

[5] Commission Communication, Europe 2020, *A strategy for smart, sustainable and inclusive growth*, COM(2010) 2020 final. See also the Commission's Communication *Taking stock of the Europe 2020 strategy for smart, sustainable and inclusive growth*, COM(2014) 130 final.

[6] OJ 2000 L 303/16.

potential positive effects, according to Scott, of 'the second demographic dividend', with allusion to the accumulated wealth among an ageing population, which can be transformed into asset income through investment. Notwithstanding these possible effects, the challenges to address will vary considerably between countries. Whereas Europe, generally speaking, is far worse off than the US with its higher fertility rates, there are also huge differences among the EU Member States.

Finally, some additional words on immigration and population ageing in the EU perspective are worthwhile here. In abstract terms, immigration is a poor solution to the looming challenge of an ageing society. However, given that Europe is currently experiencing unprecedented inflows of asylum seekers and immigrants, the potential of this influx in terms of decreasing the old-age dependency ratio – in both the short and the longer run – must not be underestimated. For the coming decades, migration will be a focal point of both politics and social challenges in the EU perspective, and any 'pros' in this development deserve to be highlighted.

1.2 Law and Ageing in the Setting of the Norma Research Programme

Despite growing concern regarding ageing society, elder law as a concept – and even more so as a legal discipline – still has a surprisingly modest presence in the European context.[7] Given the increased presence of 'ageing concerns' in EU policies and, eventually EU law, it was only natural for the Norma Research Programme at the Law Faculty at Lund University – of which the Norma Elder Law Research Environment is a part – to take an interest in this area of law. The Norma Research Programme as such started out some 20 years ago when Sweden became a member of the EU, with the aim of studying 'normative development within the social dimension in an EU integration perspective'. We understand the *social dimension* to mean 'everyday life' legal structures in terms of work, family, housing and complementary welfare structures, intrinsically interrelated both with each other and general societal developments. Research is conducted within a multidisciplinary legal science framework, including labour law, social security law, family law, housing law, social law, competition law, EU law and comparative law, and also encompasses legal theory. Moreover, a major characteristic for the Norma

---

[7] Cf, however, A Evrard and C Lacour, 'A European approach to developing the field of law and ageing' in I Doron and A Soden (eds), *Beyond Elder Law* (Springer 2012), arguing for this new research area in the terms of 'Law and Ageing'.

Research Programme right from the start was 'a social science approach' to law, applying an external and a structural/functionalist perspective to the studies of law with a view to deepening understanding of law and legal developments in the social dimension.[8]

The legal challenges implied by ageing society can thus be said to constitute a core area of studies in the more general perspective of the Norma Research Programme – as an intrinsic part of societal developments. In addition, given the importance of social welfare structures in the EU (and Sweden!),[9] it was natural to establish elder law in Europe as a new area of research in response to an ageing society as such, as well as the strategies (legal and others) that go with it. This implies a specific interest in the structural implications of certain legal and societal solutions related to ageing at the macro or institutional level. Initial focus areas of the Norma Elder Law Research Environment were thus expressed in terms of legal empowerment of elderly workers, elderly citizens and elderly migrants – all in line with EU policy statements regarding key areas in relation to a greying Europe. Increased labour-market integration is thus a crucial element of active ageing strategies; active citizenship is an important element in effectuating the right to live in dignity and independence; and migration and internal market mobility are fundamental concerns in relation to the increasing dependency ratio and reversing decreases in the labour force.

Who, then, are these old or elderly people? There is no obvious answer. The social sciences offer many different categorizations.[10] In the Norma Elder Law Research Environment – aiming at a deepened understanding of normative developments in view of societal developments more generally – age has to be understood as a contextualized concept. The group of people relevant for a certain study is thus best defined by taking into consideration the area and problems concerned. In relation to the labour market, an 'older' worker in the EU is considered to be in his/her fifties or older.[11] Acceptance of the idea that the critical period with regard to old age and employment begins in the early part of the end of a person's working life is reflected in EU policies on active

---

[8] See further A Numhauser-Henning and M Rönnmar (eds), *Fifteen Years with the Norma Research Programme, Anniversary Volume* (Lund University 2010).

[9] Cf the EU as a 'Social Market Economy', Article 3.3 TEU.

[10] Cf for instance, V L Bengtson, D Gans, N M Putney and M Silverstein, *Handbook of Theories of Aging* (2nd edn, Springer 2009).

[11] Cf however, the US and Age Discrimination in Employment Act, now covering all workers over the age of 40.

ageing and in the age discrimination cases of the Court of Justice of the European Union (CJEU), which mainly concern employees from the age of just above 50 years of age and older. In regard to pensions, 65 is frequently understood as the 'normal' pensionable age. In relation to dementia and questions of autonomy/independence, we usually deal with individuals of a considerably higher age. Even so I have referred only to one notion so far: the chronological conceptualization of ageing. In a more empirically oriented article about important factors for extending working life, Kerstin Nilsson identifies three additional conceptualizations of ageing, which are sometimes clustered as 'functional ageing': biological ageing, social ageing and mental/cognitive ageing, to be discussed in a nine-factor work environment perspective.[12] In other words, a contextualized understanding of age is necessary, because age is also 'a constructed, contested and differentiated social relationship'.[13] In such an approach, the broad setting of 'everyday life' legal structures in the Norma Research Programme is especially valuable; in addition, in the light of Fineman's vulnerability theory it has been suggested that ageing is more a part of life than a distinct group of (older) persons.[14]

As noted earlier, one established theoretical approach in the Norma Research Programme is the late Anna Christensen's theory of law as normative patterns in a normative field.[15] Christensen's theory is based on the thesis that different basic normative patterns can be distinguished in the multitude of legal norms – much like in a drawing by Escher[16] or as Hofstadter has depicted human thinking.[17] Up to this point, analysis of law in the social dimension has identified some crucial basic normative patterns within this area of law, and these patterns underlie every legal system; they are a part of the cultural values upon which society is built.

[12] K Nilsson, 'Conceptualisation of ageing in relation to factors of importance for extending working life – A review' (2016) Scand J of Public Health 1–16.

[13] Judy Fudge on gender, in J Fudge, 'From women and labour law to putting gender and law to work' in M Davies and V Munro (eds), *The Ashgate Research Companion to Feminist Legal Theory* (Ashgate 2012).

[14] Mattsson and Katzin, Chapter 5 in this book.

[15] See further A Numhauser-Henning, 'Understanding law as normative patterns in a normative field' in A Numhauser-Henning and M Rönnmar (eds), *Normative Patterns and Legal Development in the Social Dimension of the EU* (Hart Publishing 2013), with further references to (among others) Christensen.

[16] Maurits Cornelis Escher (1898–1972) was born in the Netherlands and became widely known for, among other things, his symmetry drawings.

[17] D Hofstadter, *Metamagical Themas: Questing for the Essence of Mind and Patterns* (Basic Books 1985).

Among these important basic patterns present in the normative field within the social dimension are, on the one hand, the rights of ownership and the freedom of contract, which together form the market functional pattern, and on the other hand, protection of established position – the right to one's possessions, or for instance, security of employment and the principle of replacement of lost earnings. A third basic normative pattern is just distribution, a distributive pattern related to social justice and solidarity. As social life is quite complex, these normative patterns do not make up the 'hierarchical legal system' we frequently imagine.[18] Instead, these patterns are put into play in a normative field as determined by different basic patterns, which also act as normative poles. The 'origin' of the patterns differs according to the values they are set to protect, and thus, typically speaking, tension exists between different patterns. Societal change is what creates the 'attraction' between the poles over time, and thus also legal change. Changes in the underlying conditions of production provide explanations for the movements in the normative field. These developments also account for the resurrection of basic normative patterns in new legal contexts – new or different normative fields, such as the normative field of social security law complementing that of labour law. Thus the protection of the established position has taken the form of employment protection in the field of labour law, only to emerge as replacement of lost earnings in the field of social security law. The basic normative patterns all represent enduring and legitimate normative conceptions in society, and it is the task of legislators and courts to balance these conceptions within the framework of law. As is reflected throughout this book, this theoretical approach proper has not yet been applied to any larger extent in studies within the Norma Elder Law Research Environment.[19] In a working paper, however, Numhauser-Henning has reflected on retirement in these terms[20] and she has also elaborated on the CJEU's case law in terms of the protection of

---

18 Cf Christensen who argues that '[l]egal theory … has been trapped in that Kelsean dream about a consistent, hierarchical system. This eternal arranging and rearranging of the different parts of the assembly of norms in order to make them fit into a system seldom brings about any new insight.' A Christensen, 'Polycentricity and normative patterns' in H Petersen and H Zahle (eds), *Legal Polycentricity: Consequences of Pluralism in Law* (Dartmouth Publishing 1995).

19 See the list of publications at the beginning of this book.

20 A Numhauser-Henning, *Kort normativ reflektion kring avgång med pension* (selected works working paper 2012), available at http://works.bepress.com/lundlaw and www.jur.lu.se/elderlaw.

established position, established rights or legitimate expectations.[21] Rönnmar, too, has written about the protection of established position and the elderly in an EU perspective.[22] I return to legal developments in terms of normative patterns throughout this introductory chapter.

Elder law as described in American doctrine is about a mainly applied or practice-oriented approach characterized by concepts such as 'counselling'. Professor Lawrence Frolik, with a background from the Pittsburgh School of Law as well as the University of Nebraska and Harvard Law School, and one of the founders of elder law as a separate discipline, wrote a fundamental article about the early developments of elder law for the 1993 inaugural issue of the Elder Law Journal.[23] In the article, Frolik describes elder law as a product, on the one hand, of the legal profession's shift towards specialization, and on the other the increasingly inclusive and pragmatic nature of legal education (with admission of more women and second-career students) in combination with the needs of an increasing elderly population. These developments 'explain' the applicative perspective in elder law as developed in the US. In another article – ten years later – Frolik again examines elder law.[24] Although Frolik here describes the broadening of elder law to 'late life legal planning', the applicative character of elder law as a professional 'practice' is still evident.[25]

Frolik also points, however, to the development of legal science as such towards 'law as social science rather than a self-contained doctrinal

[21] For a Swedish version see A Numhauser-Henning, 'Noteringar om Skydd för Etablerad Position – ett normativt grundmönster' in A H Persson and L Ryberg-Welander, *Festskrift till Catharina Calleman, I rättens utkanter* (Iustus 2014). See also A Numhauser-Henning, *Annotations on Protection of Established Position – A Basic Normative Pattern* (selected works working paper 2013), available at http://works.bepress.com/lundlaw and www.jur.lu.se/elderlaw.

[22] M Rönnmar, 'Protection of established position, social protection and the legal situation of the elderly in the European Union' in A Numhauser-Henning and M Rönnmar (eds), *Normative Patterns and Legal Development in the Social Dimension of the EU* (Hart Publishing 2013).

[23] L Frolik, 'The developing field of elder law: A historical perspective' (1993) 1 Elder L J 2.

[24] L Frolik, 'The developing field of elder law redux: Ten years after' (2002) 10 Elder L J 1.

[25] See also L Frolik, 'Later life legal planning' in I Doron (ed.), *Theories on Law and Ageing: The Jurisprudence of Elder Law* (Springer 2009). The National Academy of Elder Law Attorneys (NAELA) was founded in 1988 and had in 1993 already more than 2,000 members.

entity'.[26] Elder law shifted focus from the needs of the elderly as a social group to specific legal problems – linking to sociology, gerontology, geriatrics, political science, and economics. Israel Doron, Professor of Law at Haifa University, Israel, has argued for law and ageing in the terms of jurisprudential gerontology.[27] Already in 1978, gerontologist Elias S Cohen referred to legal analysis as too important to be ignored by gerontologists.[28] Despite this, mainstream social gerontology has continued to pay little attention to legal developments in the field of ageing.[29] Doron ascribes this to the utterly legal-positivist approach developed in early elder law, which made the field 'just another application of law, without any unique theoretical perspective, thus making it relevant mostly to lawyers working with older clients' and labels this 'the Positivist-Professional Approach', defined by the clients to be served or the areas relevant (the 'content-specific' approach), in both cases standing 'jurisprudentially speaking, on existing ground'.[30] He then describes subsequent elder law developments in terms of monist and pluralist approaches to law and ageing. Among the monist approaches he identifies the later-life planning approach,[31] the law and economics approach,[32] the therapeutic jurisprudence approach[33] and the feminist ethic of care approach.[34] The pluralist approach to ageing – the multi-dimensional model of elder law – was developed by Doron himself through a number of publications in later years.[35]

No doubt, a deepened understanding of law in the context of ageing offers important additional knowledge to our understanding of ageing in

---

26 Frolik (1993), above n 23, 15.

27 I Doron, 'Elder law: Current issues and future frontiers' (2006) Eur J on Ageing 3 60–66; and I Doron, 'Jurisprudential Gerontology: Theorizing the relationships between law and aging' in Bengtson et al. (2009), above n 10.

28 E S Cohen, 'Editorial: Law and aging, lawyers and gerontologists' (1978) 18 Gerontologist 229.

29 Doron (2009), above n 27, 644.

30 Ibid.

31 Cf Frolik (2002), above n 24.

32 Cf R Posner, *Aging and Old Age* (University of Chicago Press 1995).

33 Cf D Wexler, *Therapeutic Jurisprudence: The Law as a Therapeutic Agent* (Carolina Academic Press 1990) and B M Kapp, *The Law and Older Persons: Is Geriatric Jurisprudence Therapeutic?* (Carolina Academic Press 2003).

34 Cf C Gilligan, *In a Different Voice: Psychological Theory and Women's Development* (Harvard University Press 1982); R Korzec, 'A feminist view of American elder law' (1997) 28 U Tol L Rev 547–61.

35 I Doron, 'A multi-dimensional model of elder law' in I Doron (ed.), *Theories on Law and Ageing: The Jurisprudence of Elder Law* (Springer 2009).

its social and political context. This book offers an innovative and important interdisciplinary approach to the analysis of legal developments in the European setting from a multitude of theoretical and legal-substantive perspectives.

2. CONCEPTUAL AND THEORETICAL PERSPECTIVES

In Chapter 3, 'Dignity, disadvantage, and age: putting constitutional and fundamental rights to work for older workers', Judy Fudge introduces the case law of the Supreme Court of Canada (SCC) concerning claims of employment-related discrimination brought by older workers and compares this with case law of the CJEU. Fudge argues in terms of constitutional/fundamental rights for older workers, which no doubt is correct with regard to Canada and the EU. Canada is a federal state; complicated legal regulation exists at constitutional level in the Canadian Charter of Rights and Freedoms and some 14 human rights statutes at provincial/territorial jurisdiction level – all of these concerning age. In the EU, at Treaty level, there are open-ended guarantees of equality rights on the basis of age, interrelating to Member State constitutional rights. The interesting conclusion of Fudge is that despite very different constitutional architectures and anti-discrimination instruments in Canada and the EU, the SCC's and CJEU's approaches to resolving employment discrimination claims brought by older workers are virtually the same. 'Both defer to political authorities and social partners when it comes to justifying mandatory retirement policies in order to achieve employment and labour market goals, and they look to the same set of features – the age of retirement, the availability of pension income, the existence of a collective agreement – to determine whether the policy is reasonably necessary.'[36] She also draws our attention to the fact that neither of the courts really considers the adequacy of pension income in the individual case.

In this context, one aspect may be worth noting: despite the fact that age discrimination (generally speaking) holds a more uncertain status in constitutional and international human rights law – and that as yet there is no international convention proper on the rights of old people – national apex courts have been willing to a certain extent to review the compatibility of age-based distinctions with constitutional guarantees of

[36] Fudge, Chapter 3 in this book.

equal treatment and non-discrimination more widely, precisely in such terms of 'a light touch proportionality test'.[37]

Fudge contributes in her chapter in an interesting way to discussions on the application of the proportionality principle in the case law of the CJEU, in that she distinguishes a threefold categorization of the Court: 'a light touch rationality approach' in cases of general mandatory retirement policies, 'a slightly higher level of scrutiny' regarding occupationally specific mandatory retirement policies and 'a stricter proportionality standard' to scrutinize public safety justifications and genuine occupational requirements. A strict standard of scrutiny is also applied in relation to employment benefits.[38]

In Chapter 4, 'The elder law individual versus societal dichotomy – a European perspective', Ann Numhauser-Henning elaborates on much of the same case law of the CJEU as does Fudge in Chapter 3, but now in an endeavour to illustrate the differences between US and EU application of age discrimination law. At the basis of this analysis is 'the weaker format' of the age discrimination ban – a characteristic which lies at the heart of Fudge's conclusion in Chapter 3 – in terms of a double bind.[39] On the one hand there is the 'human rights rationale' reflected in discrimination bans as a dignity defence at individual level; on the other is the scope for more instrumental interests at societal level, often resulting in the justification of age-related differential treatment in terms of ageing policies or age as a traditional social stratifier. Here, the continued acceptance of compulsory (or mandatory) retirement in the EU is regarded as an expression of this double bind and the traditional European welfare devices acceptance of the notion that 'in Europe, employment equality requires collectively imposed norms about the role

---

[37] C O'Cinneide, 'Constitutional and fundamental rights aspects of age discrimination' in A Numhauser-Henning and M Rönnmar (eds), *Age Discrimination and Labour Law, Comparative and Conceptual Perspectives in the EU and Beyond* (Kluwer Law International 2015).

[38] Cf M Schlachter, 'Mandatory retirement and age discrimination under EU law' (2011) Int J Comp Lab Law and Indus Relations 27; C Kilpatrick, 'The Court of Justice and labour law in 2010: A new EU discrimination law architecture' (2011) 40(3) Indus L J 280–301; and E Dewhurst, 'Intergenerational balance, mandatory retirement and age discrimination in Europe: How can the ECJ better support national courts in finding a balance between the generations?' (2013) 50 CML Rev 1333.

[39] Cf also Numhauser-Henning, Julén Votinius and Zbyszewska, Chapter 7 in this book.

of work in a person's life cycle'.[40] These practices stand in stark contrast with those of the US. Firstly, in the US the age discrimination ban is asymmetric, protecting only 40+ workers and leaving a significant amount of age-related differential treatment outside its scope. Secondly, US non-discrimination regulation is firmly rooted in the liberal tradition and the practice of mandatory retirement was abandoned long ago. What is recognized as 'the legal double helix' – hypothetically a parallel to the EU equality law 'double bind' – results in a hybrid norm of equal protection and substantive due process, working to reinforce the role of the individual and free choice in a pluralist market society. The EU acceptance of compulsory/mandatory retirement is argued as an ultimate defence of the conventional standard contract with its typical employment protection devices, and thus age as a social stratifier. As with Somek, this chapter also recognizes non-discrimination regulation's typical role as a neoliberal forerunner in the European perspective.[41] Here, the differences between the EU and the US are also put in the perspective of more general welfare developments in a quest of state welfare versus the market. A conclusion is that despite a European welfare state in flux, societal or collectively institutionalized solutions are still held in relatively high regard in the EU 'Social Market Economy'. The chapter can be read as a discussion on normative developments in terms of the market functional pattern. However, as indicated by its title, this chapter situates its discussion in terms of the elder law individual versus societal dichotomy – arguably an equivalent at a more organizational level of the value-related autonomy versus paternalism dichotomy.[42] No doubt, EU law represents a more paternalistic stand than US law – and this is not only reflected in its continued acceptance of compulsory retirement. It is argued, however, that 'autonomy and individual choice' – that is, a ban based on the human rights rationale – may well lead to increased vulnerability for certain groups, not least older persons.[43]

---

40 J C Suk, 'From antidiscrimination to equality: Stereotypes and the life cycle in the United States and Europe' (2012) 60 Am J Comp L 75.

41 A Somek, *Engineering Equality* (Oxford University Press 2011).

42 Cf Doron (2009), above n 35.

43 Cf also A Wiesbrock, 'Mandatory retirement in the EU and the US: The scope of protection against age discrimination in employment' (2013) 29(3) Int J Comp Lab Law and Indus Relations 305, arguing that in real life, US employer practices force employees to retire against their will despite legal differences.

'Vulnerability and ageing' is precisely the subject of Chapter 5, written by Titti Mattsson and Mirjam Katzin. This chapter contains a comprehensive presentation of American Law Professor Martha Albertson Fineman's 'vulnerability theory',[44] an important theory of reference for the Norma Elder Law Research Environment.[45] The authors place Fineman's theory in the borderland between critical theory and normative ethics of care, striving to transform the fundamental ideals of the law. They continue by identifying two central questions in Fineman's work: what does it mean to be human, and what does this say about how we should organize our society? According to this theory, vulnerability is a *universal* human condition, and also something that characterizes the relationship between the individual and the state – it is the state's obligation to guarantee the equality of opportunities and decent living conditions which follow from the idea of the equal value of all persons. This leads to an emphasis on the duty of society to provide the resources and institutions necessary to overcome the dependency and shortcomings thus characterizing human life, not only in old age.[46] Notwithstanding, vulnerability must not be equated with harm any more than age inevitably means loss of capacity – it also presents opportunities for innovation and growth, creativity and fulfilment. The authors conclude that 'the vulnerability theory has broad applicability for studies that focus [on] the significance of the institutional and organizational conditions in society that can create reasonable living conditions for older people'. It also problematizes the conceptualization of the elderly as a group. In its notion of old people as individuals and taking a more general approach to vulnerability, the theory helps us avoid unnecessary competition among different groups in a society of scarce resources.

This chapter also highlights the importance of Fineman's theory as a critique of liberal ideology and autonomy. As argued in Chapter 4, US reality – to a larger extent than the European reality – is based on the premise that individuals are responsible for their own welfare; it imposes expectations of self-sufficiency and independence on rich and poor, advantaged and disadvantaged alike – also with regard to the elderly. Vulnerability in this society is rather perceived as a result of 'poor choices' and lack of control. Fineman criticizes the idea of the autonomous subject in law and argues that vulnerability is a universal condition

---

[44] M Fineman, 'The vulnerable subject and the responsive state' (2010) 60(2) Emory L J 251.

[45] Cf Chapter 5, note 6.

[46] M Fineman, '"Elderly" as vulnerable: Rethinking the nature of individual and societal responsibility' (2012) 20(2) Elder L J 71–112.

positioned as the polar opposite of the liberal subject. She further argues that 'dependency', too, is universal and but a physical or developmental aspect of the human condition – not a failure on the part of the individual or the family (conceptualized as 'derivative dependent'). Dependency 'has been assumed to attach to the elderly as a group' and is also assigned to the private sphere in contrast to the liberal subject 'who dominates the public sphere'.[47] According to Fineman, the political subject must be developed in a more inclusive manner, placing 'the individual entirely within societal contexts by developing the relationships between vulnerability and resilience and societal institutions and resources'.[48] The conclusion is that '[a] vulnerability approach is an integrated approach to society, not one of either separate spheres or competing generations'.[49]

The idea of the universal character of vulnerability as the basis for state interventionism thus offers a way to confront claims that elder law is 'inherently paternalistic',[50] and thus confront the autonomy versus paternalism dichotomy referred to earlier. Fineman's argumentation – apart from reflecting current market hegemony and thus the market functionalist pattern in the US perspective – offers a basic argument for the societal approach in the individual versus societal dichotomy explored in Chapter 4.

In Chapter 6, 'Intergenerational aspects of elder law: conflict, solidarity – or ambivalence', Jenny Julén Votinius and Mia Rönnmar discuss ageing from a labour-market and industrial-relations perspective, precisely in the terms of competing generations. Whereas much of the legal scholarly debate regarding intergenerational aspects – mainly in environmental and constitutional law, respectively – has developed with frequent reference to forthcoming generations, or in a diachronic perspective, Julén Votinius and Rönnmar focus on the concept from the viewpoint of simultaneous but different generations, or the synchronic perspective. The introduction of intergenerational ambivalence – developed within the areas of sociology and social psychology – is argued as an important complement to the binary solidarity-conflict approach when it comes to the understanding of intergenerational conflict in elder law. In this area 'the intergenerational experience is not characterized only by conflict or solidarity, but rather by a complex coexistence of these two positions'. The 'solidarity, conflict and ambivalence model' acknowledges that in the

---

47 Fineman (2010), above n 44, 117.

48 Fineman (2012), above n 46, 139.

49 Ibid.

50 Cf I Doron (ed.), *Theories on Law and Ageing: The Jurisprudence of Elder Law* (Springer 2009) preface.

elder law area, people are 'involved in intergenerational relationships in three different capacities: as individuals, as part of families and personal relationships, and as members of the society … shaping different, and sometimes incompatible, attitudes and actions in intergenerational matters'. In law this materializes in three main ways: legal vagueness, contradictory legal norms and openly ambivalent legal norms.

These three manifestations of intergenerational ambivalence in elder law are then discussed with examples from the area of labour law and industrial relations. Vagueness is reflected in the perceived right to retire at a certain age, which is established in parallel with the perceived right to remain in employment without age-related restrictions, a vagueness said to open up for the influence of age-related stereotypes and misconceptions about the labour market. Intergenerational ambivalence thus also plays out in legal contradictions, such as age discrimination law, which in principle prohibits age differentials but – through exceptions – opens up for age as an important organizing principle in labour law, in the form of not only compulsory retirement but also seniority rules in dismissal and wage-setting (as these concepts are developed in Chapters 3 and 4). Complex intergenerational bargaining at collective level, finally, provides examples of acknowledgement of the impact of intergenerational ambivalence.

All in all, the synchronic perspective calls for a clarification of the actual interests at stake and the need for identifying conflicting interests that must be reconciled. Within the 'solidarity, conflict and ambivalence model' the notion of 'intergenerational solidarity' – at the heart of both EU policies and EU law – can be interpreted as supporting different normative solutions that are mutually incompatible, making it possible for legal science 'to embrace the complexities of intergenerational relations in elder law, while investigating the ambivalence permeating intergenerational issues and the implications of this ambivalence for this field of law'. The 'solidarity, conflict and ambivalence model'– in the perspective of the law as normative patterns theory – can be said to reflect the basic idea of this theory that different normative patterns, such as the market functional pattern but also the pattern of protection of established position and fair distribution patterns, are persistent over time and must be consistently balanced in the process of legislation and policy-making.

3. ELEMENTS OF ELDER LAW

3.1 Labour Market and Pensions

The third part of the book starts out with a set of chapters relating in the main to the labour market.

In Chapter 7, 'Equal treatment and age discrimination – inside and outside working life', Ann Numhauser-Henning, Jenny Julén Votinius and Ania Zbyszewska return to the weaker template of the EU age discrimination ban and its implications for older workers (compare Chapters 3 and 4). This weaker template thus manifests itself in the fact that direct age discrimination can also be justified, and draws upon both a wider uncertainty about its 'wrongness' when compared to other grounds and the societal/collective approach inherent to 'the double bind' that characterizes this ban. Age-based distinctions are thus not linked to historically embedded patterns of group subordination, and are said not to have a negative impact upon human dignity to the same degree as do distinctions based on archetypical non-discrimination grounds such as gender and race. In addition, age is still influential as a traditional social stratifier, as well as the focus of important social strategies. It is the duty of the CJEU – in its interpretation of Article 6.1 of the Employment Equality Directive – to balance these competing dignitarian and distributional concerns in its case law. This case law, as presented, reveals underlying, partly conflicting, human rights and economic rationales, and also turns out to be particularly problematic (albeit in very few cases hitherto) in situations of multiple or intersectional discrimination.

The chapter goes on to address age discrimination outside working life. In EU law we have not yet seen such a ban, but the work recently resumed to land the so-called Horizontal Directive. In Sweden, though, there is already an age discrimination ban in place covering social protection and healthcare. The analysis shows that there is a high likelihood that a broad scope for justification of continued differential treatment on the grounds of age will prevail, thus applying a double bind in this area of application as well, and creating a scope for the collective interest approach within a cost-effectiveness logic. To this we should add the tradition within social services/elder care of dealing with 65+ persons in terms of care and internal comparisons, rather than using concepts of traditional discrimination law in the liberal tradition (such as inclusion and equality) in comparison with more externalized categories. Such practices, the authors conclude, tend to undermine the potential effects of a ban on age discrimination in these new areas and maintain attitudes of paternalism and dependency.

Continued acceptance of compulsory retirement thus honours the traditional use of age as a social stratifier. Paternalistic as these practices may be, they may still be favourable to older workers, protecting them in relation to the ongoing precarization of both work and pensions. At the individual level, however, it is easy to see that this continued acceptance of compulsory retirement works to 'stereotype' the old-age individual in terms of ageism and dignity harm. Ageism is a multifaceted concept and is suggested to cover:

> negative or positive stereotypes, prejudices and/or discrimination against (or to the advantage of) elderly people on the basis of their chronological age or on the basis of a perception of them as being 'old' or 'elderly'. Ageism can be implicit or explicit and can be expressed on a micro-, meso- or macro-level.[51]

Discrimination – or discriminatory behaviour – is thus an integral part of the very definition of ageism. The concept is crucial to discrimination and may well cover both beneficial and negative differential treatment. At the same time, non-discrimination regulation is an important tool to come to terms with ageism from the legal point of view. In addition, what is beneficial for one group may well be detrimental to another. Not all ageing employees have benefitted from the standard employment contract and its implicit norm of mandatory retirement coupled with a standard pension. This is especially true for already weaker groups in the labour market, such as women and workers coming of age.

Dignity is thus also central to the concept of ageism and has been recognized as both a fundamental right in itself and the real basis of fundamental rights altogether – axiological to the equal rights of every person.[52] In addition, it has been said that 'strong[er], anti-discrimination laws specifically designed to protect older persons would send a social and political signal that rights and dignity in aging should be the norm'.[53] No doubt, however, differential treatment on the grounds of age cannot

---

51 T N Iversen, L Larsen and P E Solem, 'A conceptual analysis of ageism' (2009) 61(3) Nordic Psych 14, 15.

52 Cf Praesidium of the European Convention, *Explanations relating to the Charter of Fundamental Rights of the EU*, OJ C303/15, 14 December 2007.

53 L O Gostin and A Garsia, 'Governing for health as the world grows older: Healthy lifespans in aging societies' (2014) 22 Elder L J 111.

be fought successfully only at individual level and in terms of dignity if we want to come to terms with substantive inequalities in today's societies.[54]

In Chapter 8, 'The rationales of government action on ageing and the extension of working lives', Alysia Blackham, Miriam Kullmann, Hanna Pettersson and Ania Zbyszewska provide an integrated analysis of four different studies of governmental action in response to ageing European society in four Member States: the United Kingdom (UK), the Netherlands, Sweden and Poland. Despite the fact that the countries addressed differ significantly in the level of workforce engagement of older people and the measures required to address demographic ageing, all four countries are working actively to increase participation rates for older workers; the authors 'identify a neoliberal reform tendency, with an associated individualization of the risks of ageing' in these actions. Interventions are identified largely to fall into two categories: supply- or worker-side factors designed to incentivize individuals to remain active in the labour market and demand- or employer-side factors intended to boost demand for older workers. In Sweden, many of the measures directed towards managing employee behaviours and state responsibilities – such as training opportunities or managing the work environment – have become less of a focus than individual work capacity. The Dutch government has relied substantially on tax incentives for employers and tightening eligibility for social protection to promote longer working lives. In Poland, policy documents suggest a focus on responsibility shared by government, employers and employees, but many claim that this has not yet been borne out in practice. Instead, pension reforms focus on individual responsibility, and this is to be added to the discourse of employability. Finally the authors note that individual choice has turned out to have an especially strong position in UK policies, and that all four jurisdictions appear to have renewed focus on individual choice. The overall conclusion is that 'the rationale for managing ageing has largely relied on neoliberal ideas and conceptions of work and individual responsibility' in all four Member States. This, of course, brings us back to the apparent increasing hegemony of the market functionalist pattern – in Christensen's terms. However, the authors of this chapter question the

---

54 For a discussion of the area of sex and sexual harassment in terms of 'the dignity harm approach' and its tendency to perpetuate the invisibility of structural (and individual) oppression (of women) in society, see A Numhauser-Henning, 'Executive summary' in A Numhauser-Henning and S Laulom, *Harassment Related to Sex and Sexual Harassment Law in 33 European Countries* (Luxembourg Publications Office of the European Union 2013).

efficiency of this tendency, identifying said approaches as being highly fragmented and sometimes contradictory, and having only limited success in practice. Ageing society is too important a challenge to leave it at that!

In Chapter 9, 'Employment protection and older workers', Mia Rönnmar, Miriam Kullmann, Ann Numhauser-Henning and Carin Ulander-Wänman offer an analysis of the function, content and future challenges of employment protection from the perspective of older workers and a prolonged working life, with EU law and comparative European law as the focus. As already addressed in Chapter 4 in this book, employment protection is in a way characteristic for European labour law. Article 30 of the CFR now states that 'every worker has the right to protection against unjustified dismissal'. At any rate, employment regulation differs considerably between EU Member States, and the flexibilization of work – as well as austerity measures in the wake of economic crisis – is also known to be a characteristic of employment protection development, and 'flexicurity' is recognized as an important strategy for the EU. Here, the links between employment protection and flexible work – especially fixed-term work – and also compulsory retirement are explored, as well as more specific measures to prolong working life. Non-discrimination regulation at large, in the European perspective – in contrast with the case of the US, where an important function is to compensate for the employment-at-will doctrine – can be seen as an expression of the trend towards individualization and flexibilization of work.[55] Thus, the ban on age discrimination is identified to promote the further flexibilization of work in respect of the ageing individual, whereas compulsory retirement – justifying age differentials – can be seen as a defence for the standard employment contract, which typically also provides for seniority rules in redundancy situations, seniority wage-setting and the like. Here, upholding the ban on age discrimination is argued as a risk for weakening employment protection altogether. On the other hand, flexicurity strategies call for precisely a shift towards employability rather than employment protection. Issues such as lifelong learning and 'transition measures' for redundancy situations are addressed – also in terms of collective bargaining. A diversified approach is suggested to meet the needs of older workers – with 'not only traditional employment protection elements, but also investments in training and competence development aimed at enabling transitions and employability along with reasonable adjustments in work organization, working time and working environment'.

---

[55] Cf Somek (2011), above n 41.

Such a development can well be argued as representing resignation in the face of ongoing flexibilization or – if you prefer – marketization of work and labour law. It also reflects a parallel to the trend in governmental active ageing strategies as detected in Chapter 8. The flexicurity approach, as well as the discourse on employability, entails an augmentation of the employee's own responsibility for acquiring security, and thus a movement away from the protection of established position (employment protection) towards the market functional position.

Pensions and their long-term stability are crucial issues for ageing societies. In Chapter 10, 'Prolonged working life and flexible retirement in public and occupational pension schemes', Andreas Inghammar, Cécile Brokelind and Per Norberg present a view of the Swedish pension system. This chapter provides us with a multilayer investigation of the contents and coherence within and between the different pillars of this system – including the public pension scheme as well as the main occupational pension schemes – in relation to the overarching goal to prolong working life, eventually through flexibilization of retirement itself. It is important in an in-depth study to fully grasp the complexity of (most) pension systems, and analysis reveals the contradictions typically embedded in such systems. The Swedish public pension scheme was already adjusted to an ageing society through reform in the late 1990s, when the system was changed from a defined-benefit system to a defined-contributions system built on lifelong average earnings. The occupational pension scheme – consisting mainly of four major schemes covering about 90 per cent of Swedish employees – is also considered a reformed and basically solid system. Still, together with social security benefits and a range of tax incentives/disincentives, the system is far from coherent in relation to the goal of a prolonged working life. Some flexibility in relation to retirement age is characteristic for all parts of the system. However, various occupational pension schemes seem rather intended to stimulate premature retirement than a prolonged working life.[56] Some, for instance, do not imply further contributions after the age of 65 and, correspondingly, do not provide higher future benefits; this practice does not support a prolonged working life. Collectively agreed work-end solutions are designed in much the same way. Moreover, continued defined-benefits elements in various schemes, relating to the

[56] Cf also C Ulander-Wänman, 'Swedish collective agreements and employers' willingness to hire and retain older workers in employment' (2016) 6(2) Nordic J Working Life Studies 61–79 as well as C Ulander-Wänman, 'The Swedish occupational pension scheme ITP2 – A limiting factor for older employees' employability?' (manuscript).

last five years of employment, are a hindrance to adjustments in relation to 'a greying staff' in the form of changes in working time and/or accommodated work situations. Coherence could be significantly improved if the legislator and the social partners were to unite and enforce the idea of a delayed retirement age accommodating individual adjustments (including the case of a change of employers) to existing pension schemes, the opportunity to accrue pension rights at higher ages and coherent financial incentives in the form of taxation and the like. Social security schemes should also be adapted to higher retirement ages. Despite public pension reform, second-pillar occupational pensions as well as related systems on taxation and social security thus provide for features that disenable or at least reduce the full potential of the normative ambition to prolong working life – an ambition that is embedded in the general pension scheme.

At the EU level some attention has already been given to the difficulties encountered in occupational pension schemes, through the introduction of the Directive 2014/50/EU on minimum requirements for enhancing worker mobility between Member States by improving the acquisition and preservation of supplementary pension rights.[57] In the Directive, as in Chapter 11, 'Migrant pensioners – taxation and health-care issues in the EU', by Cécile Brokelind and Martina Axmin, focus is not only on transitions between employers but more specifically on mobility between Member States and how this relates to pension rules. Pension systems and mobility between the Member States are also addressed by the EU Regulation 883/2004 on the coordination of social security systems including pension rights.[58] Generally speaking, pension rights are fully exportable to other EU Member States and there are also very complex rules on competences/responsibilities when pension rights have been earned in two or more Member States. Nevertheless, the situation – especially for pensioners on a small pension – is still problematic in respect of mobility, because these pensioners risk being a burden on the host state's welfare system. This issue is addressed further in Chapter 13 in this book.[59] In contrast to pensions, taxes are neither coordinated nor harmonized at EU level. Instead, taxation is regulated at domestic level – sometimes, as far as pensions are concerned, in 'mysterious ways' – and also by quite complex bilateral (or multilateral) tax treaties with widely varying content. This chapter shows how both the

---

[57] OJ 2014 L 128/1.

[58] OJ 2004 L 166/1.

[59] Mattsson, Axmin and Holm, Chapter 13 in this book.

EU social security rules and Member State tax rules may hamper mobility and at best make up for an opaque system that is barely penetrable for the individual pensioner. With Sweden as the example, the study shows that pensioners migrating from an EU Member State to Sweden enjoy a limited right to Swedish welfare in terms of social security coverage, and the extent of their pension rights depends on their situation before migration. They may also face obstacles upon exit from their country of origin. A Swedish pensioner, leaving Sweden and becoming a non-resident, thus is liable to source taxation in Sweden (20 per cent SINK) on all their Swedish income – that is, pension. Add to this the varying effects of often bilateral tax treaties, interrelated with the tax system of the now-host country/country of residence. The conclusion is 'the lack of a common system and the need to identify the rules that apply. These factors render cross-border situations complicated and sometimes cause juridical double taxation; they can threaten social security coverage and trigger cash flow problems for mobile pensioners, in conflict with their legitimate expectations.' This chapter also deals with the specific coordination rules concerning healthcare – typically a crucial issue for the ageing individual – for the mobile pensioner. Generally speaking, irrespective of where the rights to pension were accumulated, migrant pensioners' access to healthcare in the EU is secured. However, the system does not provide any incentive to allow inbound pensioners who have no previous pension rights, as the host state cannot obtain any compensation from the state of emigration. This – together with the requirement of having comprehensive sickness insurance in the so-called Residence Directive[60] – may hinder mobility of pensioners in fragile economic situations.

The issues treated in the pension chapters, Chapters 10 and 11, reveal a strengthening of the market functional pattern in the wake of pension reform, where defined-benefit systems are replaced by defined-contribution schemes and where individual responsibility and choice are stimulated, both in relation to retirement decisions as such and in relation to pension benefits (including third-pillar savings pensions). This is also in line with the studies presented in Chapter 8 as described above. These chapters also reveal, however, that the market is not necessarily optimally stimulated by these systems in relation to mobility interests, whether in the form of transitional labour-market functioning or mobility within the

---

60 Directive 2004/38/EC on the right of citizens of the Union and their family members to move and reside freely within the territory of the Member States, OJ 2004 L 158/77.

EU internal market. Here, lingering defined-benefit occupational pension scheme solutions, in combination with poorly synchronized financial incentives, still protect the established position of groups of older workers, to the detriment of active ageing policies, and also stimulate bargained early work-end solutions. System complexity and opaqueness of regulations further inhibit market flexibility and mobility.

3.2 Social Welfare and Family

An ongoing strengthening of the market functional pattern, whether in terms of marketization and privatization or reflected as a weakened position of solidarity, is also the theme of the two chapters discussed in this section.

In Chapter 12, 'Legal approaches to private and public responsibilities for elder care', Hanna Pettersson and Mirjam Katzin examine the transference in recent decades in Sweden of care work performed, and responsibilities borne, from the public sector to the families and relatives of older people – as part of a trend towards the production and mediation of elder care by market mechanisms. After an overall description of the system, particular attention is given to the regulation concerning long-term family caregivers on the one hand, and on the other, short-term family caregivers from the 1970s onwards. The situation is one of ongoing negotiation of boundaries between public and private responsibilities as reflected in legislation and politico-legal discourse – perspectives influenced by prevailing ideologies and ideas about society, the individual and the family.

Family care for older people has increased in recent decades and has gained a new role in the Swedish elder care system. The political ambitions have changed since the 1970s when family care was supposed to gradually become redundant. This remained the goal in the 1980s, although strained public finances now emerged as a threat to the advancement of the welfare state. Still in the 1990s, long-term family care was only seen as a solution to temporary economic problems. More recently, an ideal of long-term family care as something positive and desirable has emerged as a discursive shift 'on two levels: on one is downsizing of elder care an answer to an economic crisis, and on the other is a changed view of the family and ideas about what should belong to the public and private sphere'. New legislation on support to family caregivers is part of a process in which family care, due to downsizing in the public care system, is becoming increasingly important and in fact less and less voluntary. However, this shift is not reflected in short-term family care legislation or case law, which rather reinforces the invisibility of care work performed by relatives and argues that this care work should be a public responsibility. The authors point here to the fact that 'the legal rules in question [on limited short-term social security benefits] have no direct potential to transform the division of care work between professionals and relatives'.

The gendered nature of family care work is also addressed. Whereas the association with femininity was recognized and articulated in the more optimistic reasoning of the 1980s, this perspective has become 'invisible' in later years, when discourse describing 'family caregiving as natural and families as unquestionably positive' legitimizes unjust structures and distribution of unpaid care work.

As developed elsewhere,[61] a strengthening of family responsibilities is, if you will, on the same side as individual responsibility in the individual versus societal dichotomy, and on the same side as neoliberal trends strengthening the market functional pattern. In this context, typically speaking, it also supports paternalism rather than autonomy, making the individual increasingly dependent on his or her relatives. To the extent that this development reflects a withdrawal of the welfare state, it also mirrors a downgrading of solidarity as distributive justice.

In Chapter 13, 'Perspectives on solidarity in social security, healthcare, and medical research', Titti Mattsson, Martina Axmin and Emma Holm study the coordination of social security and healthcare at the EU level in terms of the principle of solidarity and from the viewpoint of the older citizen. They also reflect on the function of the solidarity concept in relation to medical research. Solidarity (together with protection of the established position in terms of income replacement) has always been a basis for social security distributive concerns and thus is of the utmost importance for old people – because ageing is an immanent 'risk' of life. The principle of solidarity is essential to the notion of a Social Europe and is referred to in various objectives of the EU, such as the promotion of solidarity among Member States as well as among generations.[62] At the same time, solidarity is a term that broadly refers to unity and belonging between people or unity of a group or a nation based on a community of interests, objectives, and standards. The EU is striving to become such a unit of more or less inherent belonging, but it is clear that the Union has not yet succeeded in this endeavour. Quite the contrary: the authors demonstrate how the principle of solidarity – understood

---

61 See Numhauser-Henning, Chapter 4 in this book.

62 For intergenerational solidarity see further Julén Votinius and Rönnmar, Chapter 6 in this book.

from different facets – has actually declined in importance in recent times. Firstly, it is about the level of solidarity between the Member States in the EU from the internal market perspective. The introduction of a Union Citizenship following the Maastricht Treaty in 1993 undoubtedly added to the expectations of solidarity towards the citizens of other Member States, providing freedom of movement also to the non-economically active. Secondary legislation – the 2004/38 Residence Directive – has conditioned this right to free movement, in requirements that the individual must have comprehensive sickness insurance and will not become an unreasonable burden for the host state. Early case law accepted 'a certain degree of financial solidarity between nationals of a host Member State and nationals of other Member States, particularly if the difficulties which a beneficiary of the right of residence encounters are temporary'.[63] However, as described here, recent case law from the CJEU shows that there is a shift back to economic activity and self-sufficiency as a precondition for free movement and social benefits. Secondly, it is about solidarity within healthcare systems as such and how EU rules on cross-border healthcare challenge this principle. The worry here is that by putting the individual before the group, case law views of healthcare in kind as a question of free movement of services under the Treaty will undermine solidarity as understood within the competent state. EU law thus benefits those who have the resources to go abroad to receive healthcare and takes resources from vulnerable groups, such as the elderly. Thirdly, it is about the principle of solidarity as a basis for medical research involving human beings – of major importance for the ageing individual and his/her increasing need of medical care. Here, the ethical standard in terms of the solidarity principle is contested by the standards of integrity and patients' privacy rights. The EU integration process thus challenges the traditional conceptions of solidarity.

It is easy to interpret these developments, again, as an expression of a strengthening of the market functional pattern and the increased individualization that accompanies it. At first glance, the famous *Dano* case[64] simply adds to 'the shift back to economic activity and self-sufficiency as a pre-condition for free movement and social benefits'. The fact that it puts any economic activity – even in the form of minor employment – on a pedestal can be said to reinforce the market functional pattern even further.

---

63 *Grzelczyk* C-184/00 EU:C:2001:458, para 44.
64 *Dano* C-333/13 EU:C:2014:2358.

In Chapter 14, 'New legal conflicts in an old legal context: the law of inheritance and its challenges in the twenty-first century in the perspective of the ageing individual', Elsa Trolle Önnerfors discusses inheritance rights – of surviving spouses and cohabitants, of children and in relation to recent EU international civil law regulations on inheritance. Inheritance rights – and testamentary freedom – are issues intrinsically related to the autonomy or independence of the ageing individual, and pose a constant challenge for the legislator in balancing different interests and meeting the demands of contemporary society. As Trolle Önnerfors puts it: 'For a long time, the role of the family was to reproduce, provide for the family members and protect them in times of misfortune'. Now family is no longer a constant in one's life; longevity implies greater economic needs in old age and the risk of outliving one's savings, at the same time that survivors inherit later in life. Moreover (albeit to a varying degree), welfare structures have been put in place to protect the individual. What purpose and function should inheritance law have in the future? Here, and not surprisingly for this context, Trolle Önnerfors comes up with more good questions than answers. Do marriage and consanguinity still make the best basis for the right to inherit? Is there really a need for forced heirship today? Are the needs of minor and still-dependent children and the surviving spouse or partner of greater importance than the inheritance rights of adult children? Should perhaps social affinity and emotional ties be given greater importance, not only in society but also in the law? The conclusion is that there is a strong need for individuality – and increased flexibility – when it comes to laws of succession, and that with eventual increased self-determination comes an increased need for 'death planning'. In this – it seems – European elder law is closing in on US elder law as 'late life legal planning'.[65]

The elderly individual in a relational context is also the focus of Chapter 15, 'Dementia and autonomy', by Eva Ryrstedt. This chapter addresses the fact that with increased longevity follows a growing number of elderly individuals suffering from dementia. In light of existing international documents relevant to the rights applicable for persons suffering from dementia – and most prominently the UN Convention on the Rights of Persons with Disabilities – Ryrstedt discusses the shift from substituted to supported decision-making in relation to the requirements of both protection and autonomy for the elderly individual. The UN Convention thus provides, in its Article 3, for

---

[65] Frolik (2002), above n 24. See also Frolik, 'Later life legal planning' in Doron (2009), above n 50.

the right to autonomy; in Article 12(2) that persons with disabilities are to have legal capacity on the same grounds as other persons; and in Articles 16 and 17 the right to protection from exploitation, violence and abuse and the right to physical and mental integrity, respectively. These rights are not arranged in a hierarchy but must all be balanced in the process of application. One question that arises is this: to what extent must the need for protection entail a paternalistic view, or rather, how can protection be balanced against the right to autonomy? The wishes of a person suffering from dementia can thus be interpreted in the context of what is perceived to be in the best interest of the elderly person, established in an objective way. A less paternalistic approach is to allow for what Ryrstedt calls 'a subjective best-interest test', taking into account individual characteristics of a person's earlier life in combination with the possibility of harm. According to Ryrstedt, whereas doctrine traditionally seems to have advocated substituted – yet carefully monitored – decision-making, supported decision-making in this less paternalistic way could be the answer when balancing autonomy and protection. Incapacity is simply no longer a legitimate concept! Instead we are witnessing a shift from a focus on protection to a focus on autonomy, with supportive strategies bridging the gap. In this context Ryrstedt also raises the special problem of relatives in protective/supportive functions. Just as discussed in Chapter 14, families are no longer (and indeed it is not certain if they ever were) a closely knit unity of interests.

Both chapters in this section are argued in terms of increased individualization and autonomy in combination with a certain retreat from government – or societal – intervention. To this extent they mark a movement towards the market functional pattern and individual choice as a replacement of family-belonging, and thus institutionalized solidarity. The fact that the US in principle already recognizes the freedom of disposition by will – not upholding a statutory share of inheritance for children – may be interpreted as just another expression of the hegemony of the market functional pattern. In Sweden, for instance, which has far more welfare structures in place, doing away with the statutory share is still only a debated issue. The direction of change – increasingly responsibilizing individuals and families as welfare society withdraws – does not really advocate the abandonment of solidarity within families, but rather continued inheritance rights within families, if only the family had not developed beyond such traditional conceptions!

4. CONCLUDING REMARKS

As this book demonstrates, the challenges of demographical ageing as experienced in European society have played a significant role in the origins of the Norma Elder Law Research Environment. It may seem that in studies until this point, the threats implied by these developments are the centre of concern. No doubt, increased longevity is first and foremost a good thing, both in view of society and the ageing individual, implying undiscovered cultural, relational and also economic potentials. Still, it challenges the basis of many existing legal institutions.

Among the important gains of our studies are the multifaceted analysis of age discrimination law from the European perspective, first and foremost in a labour-market perspective but also in relation to current neoliberal trends and addressing intergenerational tension. This analysis was also broadened here to include the functioning of age discrimination regulations in other areas of society such as healthcare and long-term care. The intrinsic relation between employment regulation, modern/globalized labour markets and pensions was also the subject of in-depth studies – along with consideration of these aspects in a European mobility perspective. The concept of solidarity is another centre of concern, in an EU perspective and as the basis for social security and social services complementing wage society. Here, family relations come to the fore – both as an increasingly important basis for elder care and as a questionable basis for future inheritance law and supportive decision-making in regard to the 'oldest old'.

If we turn to Christensen's theory of law as normative patterns put into play in the normative fields of law introduced in Section 1.2, most studies presented in this book – and this is hardly astonishing – reveal a trend towards a strengthening of the market functional pattern. In this respect, it can be said, studies hitherto in the Norma Elder Law Research Environment confirm an earlier conclusion that not only do normative patterns 'move' between different normative fields; the boundaries between such fields – labour law, social security law and family law – are increasingly blurred or even 'amalgamated'.[66] The simultaneously weakened protection of established position and just distribution patterns has not yet received the same attention. However, the conclusion of the studies presented here, for instance in Chapter 8, is that the efficiency of this market functional trend is questionable, identifying governmental

[66] A Numhauser-Henning and M Rönnmar (eds), *Normative Patterns and Legal Development in the Social Dimension of the EU* (Hart Publishing 2013).

approaches hitherto in this direction as highly fragmented and also contradictory. Chapter 6 also identifies the current approach to elder strategies in an intergenerational perspective as not sufficiently embracing the complexities of intergenerational relations in the area of elder law, and recommends an 'ambivalence model'. Chapter 4, finally, questions the market functional approach in terms of 'autonomy and individual choice' as potentially leading to markedly increased vulnerability for certain groups, not least for older persons.

European elder law is thus only starting out and there is much research to be done – anything and everything in society deserves to be looked upon through the lens of the older person. It became clear already from the start of this introductory chapter that there is no well-defined area of study as concerns elder law. Age – and even more so old age – is ultimately defined by the problem being studied and its context. In addition, old age has many definitions – apart from the mere chronological perception – in these different settings, and these definitions change constantly as society develops; or, as Fudge writes, age is 'a constructed, contested and differentiated social relationship'.[67] Consistent 'boundary work' is thus part and parcel of the elder law field.

Moreover, the lack of a cohesive identity has been seen as a characteristic of the ageing individual, as his or her 'age-based identity is typically secondary to other, previously adopted identities such as those based on gender, family, religion, ethnicity, occupation and political affiliation'.[68] Whereas feminist elder law is already a fairly well-established area of studies, gendered perspectives remain a less extensively explored domain in the studies of the Norma Elder Law Research Environment. This of course should not be seen as a matter of principle but as a result of the project's relatively brief period of existence. The role of gender, both in regard to 'the privatization' of elder care in terms of increased family care and in relation to multiple and/or intersectional age discrimination, is touched upon in the studies referred to in this book and, no doubt, further studies into the normative realities of the ageing individual will reveal how elder law is another social construct of patriarchy.[69] In a migration perspective, the importance of ethnicity and religion also comes to the fore.

Another aspect of elder law not explored to any greater extent in this book is the classical 'counselling approach' of elder law. Although far

---

[67] Fudge (2012), above n 13.

[68] N Kohn, 'A civil rights approach to elder law' in I Doron and A Soden (eds), *Beyond Elder Law* (Springer 2012), 24.

[69] Gilligan (1982), above n 34, and Korzec (1997), above n 34.

from claiming that there is no obvious need for this approach in elder law, I do fear that elder law's counselling character may be growing in importance in the European perspective, mainly because the market functional pattern is growing stronger – and this is indeed a reality that is harder to embrace!

2. Demographic developments and economic challenges in an ageing Europe

Kirk Scott

1. INTRODUCTION[1]

Population ageing is one of the most important challenges facing the developed world during the next decades. While there also exist many other economic challenges to be surmounted, an inescapable fact is that the population age structure sets the ground rules within which any economic manoeuvring must occur. Regardless of what happens in the coming decades, we will be facing a reality in Europe where the share of the population above retirement age is increasing, and the relative size of the workforce is declining. Given this development, it does not require advanced mathematics to come to the conclusion that economic pressures related to the elderly will be mounting, and some solutions must be found to ensure that the standard of living which we have attained does not decline, and even continues to increase. This is not a trivial challenge, as we shall illustrate in this chapter.

To get an understanding of how the European population will change over the coming decades, we need only look at the changing percentage above age 65. In 2015, the share of the population over the age of 65 in the European Union was roughly 19 per cent. By 2050, this share is projected to increase to 28 per cent. This increase is, of course, different in different Member States. Sweden, which is currently one of the countries with the oldest population, will face a fairly modest increase from 19 to 23 per cent. Poland, on the other hand, will move from being one of the countries in Europe with the youngest population to one with

[1] The work was carried out within the framework funding of the Centre for Economic Demography, Lund University. Funding for the Centre is provided by the Swedish Research Council.

the oldest, with an increase from 15 to 30 per cent. Given the disparity of ageing patterns, this chapter focuses on one of the countries with the most beneficial age developments: Sweden. The reason for this is that the discussion of the challenges facing the least disadvantaged country should serve to underline the urgency and importance of dealing with population ageing in all countries, and especially those projected to age much more rapidly.

2. THE DEMOGRAPHIC TRANSITION

To understand the situation that Europe is in at the beginning of the twenty-first century, we must begin with an understanding of the demographic developments of the past several centuries. The concept of demographic transition has become a stylized fixture in any discussion of population growth and population dynamics during the nineteenth and twentieth centuries. From its initial formulation in 1945, no demographic concept has been so universally accepted.[2] The stages of the transition have been used to explain everything from population growth to economic development, and now we will use it to at least partially explain the process of population ageing currently taking place in the developed world. This chapter will discuss the impact of the transition process on both population growth and population ageing, with a focus on how these developments have differed in different European countries and under different welfare state regimes.

Fundamental to the demographic transition theory is the shift in demographic behaviour from an agrarian pattern to an industrial pattern. In the early periods, mortality and fertility levels were both high and characterized by considerable fluctuations. This is associated with a society where external threats to health and life are abundant, and exogenous shocks such as drought can lead to famine and increased mortality. In a similar manner, epidemics as well as persistent disease also led to high and fluctuating death rates. On the other hand, fertility levels were also affected both by mortality levels as well as economic insecurities leading to behaviour which directly impacted the number of children born – such as delaying marriage. High child mortality, coupled

[2] For a discussion of the origins of the demographic transition theory, see Kingsley Davis, 'World population in transition' (1945) 237 Annals Am Acad Pol & Soc Sc 1–11; and Frank Notestein, 'Population – The long view' in Theodore W Schultz (ed.), *Food for the World* (University of Chicago Press 1945).

with the need to have children as a form of old-age insurance, led to a necessity of having many children so that enough would survive to adulthood.

The next stage of the transition occurs with the beginning of a secular decline in mortality levels. The reasons for this decline vary depending on the period and context, but for Europe it has been posited that this decline coincided with a decline in the virility of infectious disease.[3] Other explanations have been that improvements in hygiene and nutrition were responsible,[4] but considerable evidence indicates that these declines in mortality began prior to any noticeable improvements in public hygiene. Regardless of the underlying reasons, during this period mortality began to decline, first for infants and children and then later for older individuals. During this early period of mortality decline fertility remained at the same high levels. This was largely caused by a delay in adjusting childbearing patterns to a new reality where mortality continued to decline, rather than returning to previous levels as it had in the past. One of the most noticeable points in this period is the unprecedented population growth caused by the increasing gap between the high fertility levels and declining mortality. For most Western countries, this development occurred largely during the late nineteenth and early twentieth centuries. Despite the fact that mortality was declining, the mean age of the population decreased during this period. This was due to the twin processes of continued high fertility and the fact that the initial mortality declines were concentrated at younger ages, leading to an unprecedented increase in the proportion of the population that were children.

3. AN AGEING SOCIETY

3.1 The First Population Ageing

Some time after the beginning of the initial mortality decline, fertility began to decline to lower levels. These processes are generally understood as an adjustment to the fact that lower mortality allows for families

---

[3] See Gunnar Fridlizius, 'The mortality decline in the first phase of the demographic transition: Swedish experiences' in T Bengtsson, G Frilizius and R Ohlsson (eds), *Pre-Industrial Population Change: The Mortality Decline and Short-Term Population Movements* (Almqvist and Wiksell International 1984).

[4] See Thomas McKeown, *The Role of Medicine: Dream, Mirage or Nemesis* (Princeton University Press 1979).

to have fewer children and still arrive at their target family size.[5] As this occurs, we see the first glimpses of population ageing, referred to as the *first population ageing.*[6] During this period the mean age of the population was increasing, driven by the fact that the successive birth cohorts were declining in size, leaving an increasing share of the population at older ages. While it may seem counter-intuitive, the first population ageing was not driven by individual ageing, but rather almost solely by fertility decline. Repeating a famous experiment by Ansley Coale[7] using modern data, we have shown that the age structure in Sweden in 2000 would have occurred in the absence of any increases in longevity during the twentieth century.[8] If the opposite had occurred, and we experienced no fertility decline, but examined only the effect of the mortality decline, then we see that the age pyramids would have looked very similar at the beginning and the end of the century. This counter-factual development is shown in Figure 2.1.

This first population ageing was, unlike the ageing process to come, beneficial in most societies. The decline in dependent children was not offset by increasing cohorts of elderly, which led to an increase in the size of the workforce relative to the non-working population. Any potential increases in the share above retirement age were more than offset by the speed of the fertility decline.

This beneficial age structure played a significant role in the rise of Western economies during the middle of the twentieth century. The period during the transition when fertility is declining without an equivalent rise in the old-age dependency ratio is referred to as the *first demographic dividend*, and marks a time when economies can grow rapidly due to the possibilities for capital deepening allowed by the declining dependency ratio freeing capital that was previously bound in non-productive uses.[9] It has been calculated that between one-fourth and one-third of the economic growth in East and Southeast Asia during the

---

5 See Notestein (1945), above n 2.

6 See Tommy Bengtsson and Kirk Scott, 'The ageing population' in Tommy Bengtsson (ed.), *Population Ageing – A Threat to the Welfare State* (Springer Verlag 2010).

7 See Ansley Coale, 'How the age distribution of a human population is determined' (Cold Spring Harbor Symposia on Quantitative Biology 22 1957).

8 See Bengtsson and Scott (2010), above n 6.

9 For a discussion of the potential economic benefits of the first demographic dividend, see David Bloom, David Canning and Jaypee Sevilla, *The Demographic Dividend: A New Perspective on the Economic Consequences of Population Change* (Rand Corporation 2003).

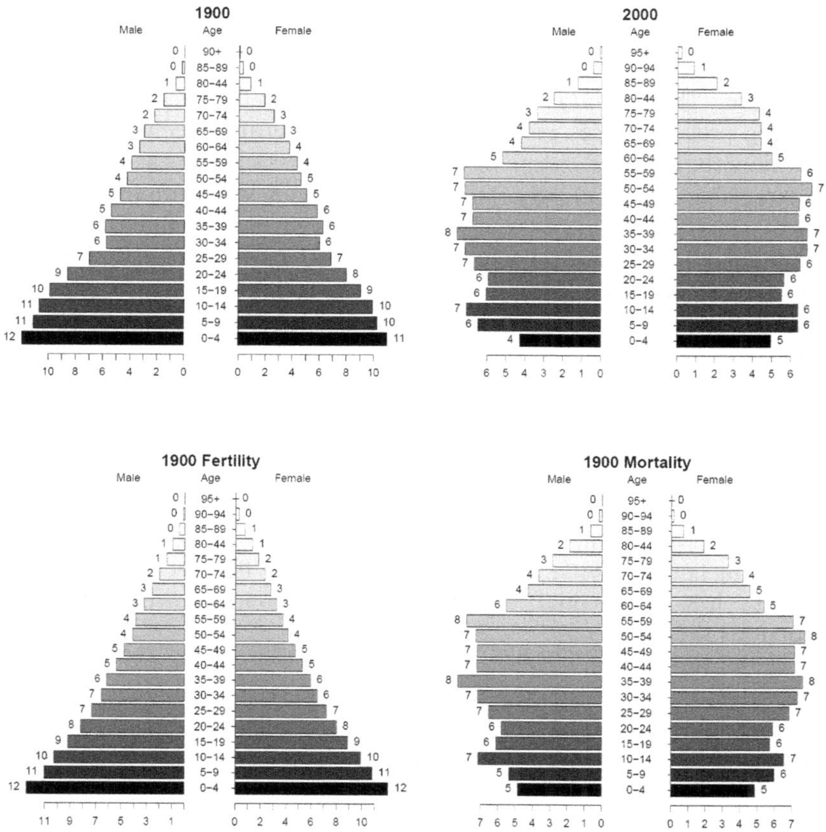

Source: Tommy Bengtsson and Kirk Scott, 'The Ageing Population' in Tommy Bengtsson (ed.), *Population Ageing – A Threat to the Welfare State* (Springer Verlag 2010).

Figure 2.1 Age structure in Sweden in 2000 compared to how it would have looked if fertility/mortality had remained constant at 1900 levels throughout the twentieth century (percentage of the population in each age interval, with females on the right, and males on the left)

last decades of the twentieth and first decade of the twenty-first centuries can be attributed to a beneficial age structure caused by this process.[10]

[10] See Andrew Mason 'Demographic dividends: The past, the present, and the future' in Andrew Mason and Mitoshi Yamaguchi (eds), *Population Change,*

3.2 The Second Population Ageing

As societies continue ageing, however, the process changes somewhat in character. The *second population ageing* refers to the period in which the ageing process ceases to be driven solely by fertility decline and begins to show the signs of an ageing society which is actually characterized by a large share being elderly. This situation begins when life expectancy at birth reaches a value of roughly 72 years, which is the point where additional increases in life expectancy lead to increases in longevity. Prior to a life expectancy of 72, increases in life expectancy are driven mostly by reductions in mortality at younger ages, which has a dampening effect on population ageing.[11] During this second population ageing, a relatively stable fertility rate and an increasing number of elderly lead to an increasing dependency ratio.[12]

This increasing dependency ratio is of a particularly negative character, since capital which was previously invested in workers must be reallocated to the elderly, who have a much higher consumption level than children. The resulting capital shallowing per worker will lead to declining productivity, *ceteris paribus*. Thus, the second population ageing has a potential to undermine economic growth patterns of previous decades.

In the rest of this chapter, we focus on how these developments may impact European countries, using the example of Sweden. Section 4 takes a look at the demographic processes which have led to population ageing. After this, Section 5 examines the extent to which ageing will be problematic through a discussion of the consumption and income patterns at different ages using the National Transfer Accounts (NTA) framework.[13] Section 6 explores possible solutions to the challenges brought

---

Labor Markets and Sustainable Growth: Towards a New Economic Paradigm (Elsevier Press 2007).

[11] See Ronald Lee, 'The formal demography of population aging, transfers, and the economic life cycle' in Linda Martin and Samuel Preston (eds), *The Demography of Aging* (National Academy Press 1994).

[12] See Lee, above n 11; Sam Preston, P Heuveline and M Guillot, *Demography. Measuring and Modeling Population Processes* (Blackwell 2001); Tommy Bengtsson and Kirk Scott, 'Population ageing and the future of the Swedish welfare state' (2011) 37 Pop Dev Rev Supplement; and Tommy Bengtsson and Kirk Scott, 'The world population in historical perspective', in R Burke, C Cooper and J Field (eds), *SAGE Handbook of Aging, Work and Society* (SAGE Publications 2013).

[13] See Ronald Lee and Andrew Mason, *Population Aging and the Generational Economy* (Edward Elgar Publishing 2011).

by population ageing. Following this, Section 7 discusses the possibility that the scenarios painted in this chapter will occur, and Section 8 concludes with a summary.

4. POPULATION AGEING IN A UNIVERSALISTIC WELFARE STATE

Sweden is the largest of the Nordic countries, and is well-known as a forerunner in demographic terms. Sweden was one of the first countries to experience population ageing, surpassing France as the most elderly country in the world by the mid-twentieth century. As seen in Figure 2.2, Sweden had a population structure in 1914 which is characteristic of agrarian countries, with a clear pyramid shape. The largest groups in society then were at very young ages, with fairly high mortality reducing the cohort sizes as they increased in age. By 2014 the situation was quite different, and Sweden had taken on a post-industrial population structure. Relatively low mortality levels at ages under 70, combined with constant or declining fertility levels, has led to an urn-shaped population structure, with small differences in size between cohorts.

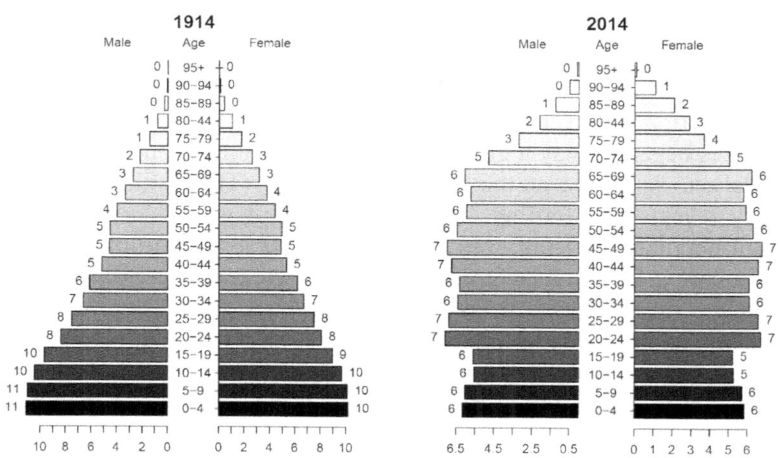

Source: Haodong Qi, *Live Longer, Work Longer? Evidence from Sweden's Ageing Population* (Media Tryck 2016).

Figure 2.2 Swedish population structure, 1914 and 2014

This ageing process moved fairly quickly in Sweden, at least from a sweeping historical perspective, but it moved very slowly in light of contemporary developments. Calculations of the speed of population ageing show that the rates are increasing.[14] For the case of Sweden it took 85 years for the share of the population over 65 years to increase from 7 per cent to 14 per cent, with the process beginning in 1890 and ending in 1975. Countries beginning their ageing process later have seen much faster developments. Japan, currently the most elderly nation in the world, reached 7 per cent of its population above 65 in 1970, and doubled this share by 1996 – only 26 years later. Thus, the rate at which countries are ageing is becoming increasingly compressed, with countries starting their ageing process now being expected to see extremely rapid shifts in age structure. Institutions will be faced with extreme difficulty adjusting to these new realities in such short periods of time.

Figure 2.3 shows the mean age of the population in Sweden during the past century. As we can see, the mean age has been increasing in an almost monotonic fashion, moving from just under 30 years in 1914 to roughly 40 years in 2014. This increase has been driven, as mentioned above, by a combination of increasing longevity and decreasing fertility. The extent to which the different components contributed to the increase is uneven throughout the period. Prior to 1950, all of the increase was driven by declining fertility, and during the following decades increasing longevity began to play a larger and larger role.

Figure 2.4 shows the increases in life expectancy at birth and decreases in total fertility rate, which are the causes of this increase in mean age of the population. The vertical dashed line shows the point where mortality decreases began to play a greater role in determining the mean age of the population. A glance at the total fertility rate (TFR) values, however, clearly reveals that fertility fluctuations have played a very substantial role in population ageing even after the start of longevity influences.

Comparing Figure 2.3 with Figure 2.4 it is clear how fertility works to adjust the mean age of the population, with age decreasing as fertility increases, and age increasing as fertility declines. This interplay between fertility and mortality is important in defining the mean age, but it is perhaps even more important in defining the impacts of population ageing on society at large.

---

14 See K G Kinsella and Y J Gist, *Older Workers, Retirement, and Pensions: A Comparative International Chartbook* (US Department of Commerce, Economics and Statistics Administration, Bureau of the Census 1995) and K G Kinsella and D R Phillips, 'Global aging: The challenge of success' (2005) 60(1) Pop Bulletin 5–42.

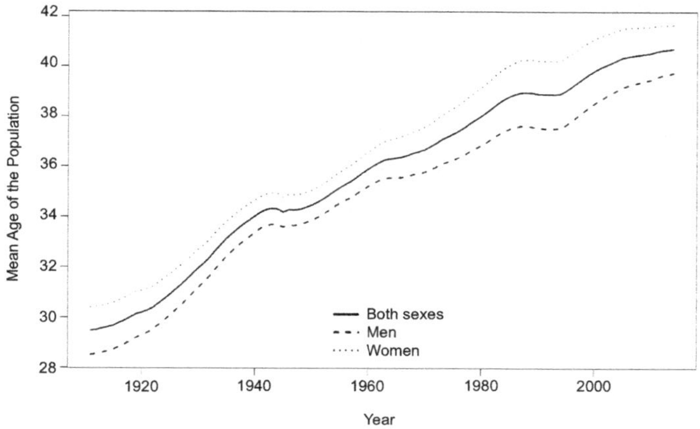

Source: Haodong Qi, *Live Longer, Work Longer? Evidence from Sweden's Ageing Population* (Media Tryck 2016).

Figure 2.3 Mean age of the Swedish population, 1914–2014

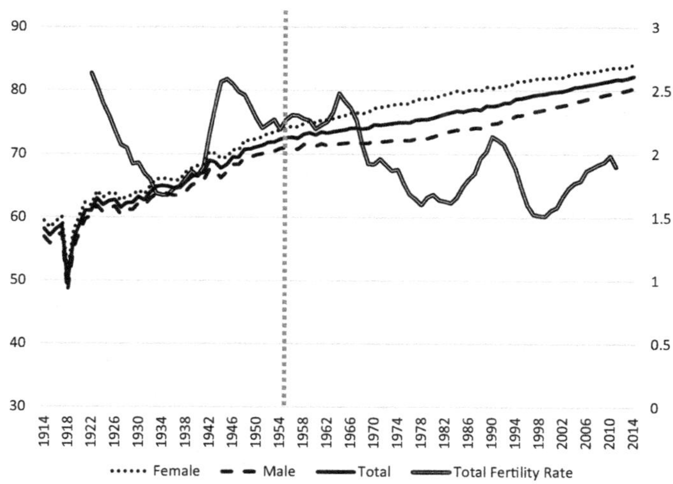

Source: Life expectancy: *Human Mortality Database*. University of California, Berkeley (USA) and Max Planck Institute for Demographic Research (Germany). Available at www.mortality.org or www.humanmortality.de. Total fertility rate: Statistics Sweden.

Figure 2.4 Swedish life expectancy at birth, 1914–2014, left axis and Swedish total fertility rate, right axis

5. THE CHALLENGE OF POPULATION AGEING

The mean age of a population is nothing more than an accounting figure. As hinted at above, the distribution of ages underlying the mean age is a much more important indicator of the seriousness of population ageing. The reason for this is found in the fact that individuals are not homogeneous throughout their life courses. Both countries with very young and those with very old populations display a high dependency ratio, which is the share of the non-working population relative to the working population.

Often, this dependency ratio is simply presented as a burden that the non-productive portion of society places on the workers. This is, however, often misleading. Young societies may have high dependency ratios, but they entail completely different costs than societies with older dependents. This section will discuss the unique economic challenges brought about by an ageing population.

In a simplistic view of society, all individuals consume roughly the same amount of resources. If this is the case, then there would be no need to differentiate between young or old regions, since a high share below working age and a high share above working age would have the same consequences on the resources required to support them. This is indeed the case in undeveloped countries without extensive state-provided social systems. In modern welfare states, however, the situation is very different depending on whether a country has a large share of children or a large share of elderly people.

Figure 2.5 shows the relationship between income and consumption across the life cycle for Sweden. It is evident here that the consumption attributed to the elderly is much higher than the consumption for the young. The age-specific consumption and income patterns in Figure 2.5 make it clear that there is a need to finance consumption at older ages when there is no significant income inflow. This distribution has been solved traditionally via intergenerational transfers, where the working population has financed the retirement of the elderly. This system works very well as long as the mean age of the producers is lower than the mean age of the consumers,[15] which has been the case until recently. As the population ages, however, the size of the working population shrinks relative to the elderly, and the economic pressure on each worker increases.

---

15 See W Brian Arthur and Geoffrey McNicoll, 'Samuelson, population and intergenerational transfers' (1978) Int Economic Rev 19.

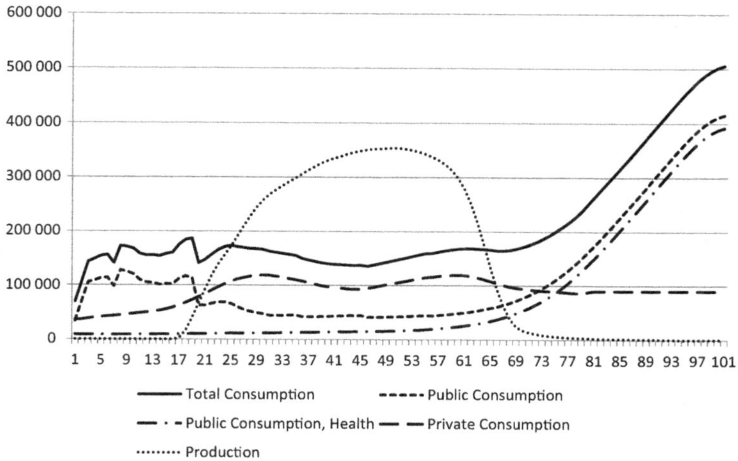

Source: C Forsell, D Hallberg, T Lindh and G Öberg, 'Intergenerational public and private sector redistribution in Sweden 2003' WP 2008:4 (Institute for Futures Studies 2008).

Figure 2.5 Relationship between production and consumption over the life course, 2003

The costs of traditional pay-as-you-go pension systems increase as the population ages, but this is not the greatest economic challenge. Pension systems can and have been reformed so that they become more closely linked to contributions during working life. The larger challenge comes from the fact that the fastest growing part of the population is in age groups where medical care costs are the highest. As seen in Figure 2.5, medical and care costs represent the majority of the costs associated with an ageing population, and these costs are largely financed in most developed countries though the tax bill.

If nothing is done to deal with population ageing, welfare states will face increasing difficulties in financing the growing costs associated with a larger elderly population. The potential answers to this challenge lie in one of two areas: either reduce the mean age of the population or find ways to more efficiently provide for the elderly. Barring either of these, the only result available is a reduction in standards of living. The next section will discuss several of the options that could help society overcome this challenge.

6. POTENTIAL SOLUTIONS TO POPULATION AGEING

6.1 Increase Fertility

Given the fact that one of the primary driving factors behind population ageing is fertility decline, an obvious way in which to reverse this trend is simply to *increase fertility*. Fertility in the Nordic countries is fairly high in a European sense, but still fluctuates around or slightly below the replacement level, which is 2.1 children per woman. Corresponding fertility rates for most other European countries are considerably lower.

Increasing fertility would, in the long run, counteract population ageing by increasing the sizes of the age cohorts entering working age. The problem with this approach is that increasing fertility actually *increases* the economic burden over the short and medium terms. The reason for this is that increased fertility leads, by definition, to an increased number of children. This increase in children increases the overall dependency ratio, leading to even more individuals who need to be supported by a relatively shrinking workforce. Additionally, childbearing removes women from the labour force during the period immediately surrounding the birth, and then removes both parents at varying times and to varying degrees to care for the child.

6.2 Encourage Immigration

One of the most popular solutions to population ageing discussed in media and by politicians is *immigration*. The idea is that the mean age of the population can be lowered by importing younger people. On the face of it, this idea is both appealing and reasonable. Labour immigrants tend to be young, with most being in the age range 25–35. An increase in migration would therefore naturally increase the size of the working-age population, which is exactly where the increase is most needed.

The immigrant solution, however, has several drawbacks that make it a very unlikely, if not impossible, solution. The primary drawback is that immigrants age as well. This implies that any immigration solution would take the character of a snowball, with increasing numbers of immigrants every year to account for the ageing native population as well as the ageing immigrant population. One argument against this snowball development is that immigrants have higher fertility levels, and will therefore contribute to an increase in the general fertility, and a deceleration of population ageing. The extent to which immigrants maintain high fertility in the destination country would then determine the extent to which they could serve as a brake for the ageing process. Studies show that, under the assumption that migrants adjust fertility, there is little overall impact of immigration on ageing.[16] Other studies, assuming maintained high levels of fertility, show a positive impact on the reduction of population ageing.[17]

Examination of immigrant fertility patterns in Sweden point to an assimilation towards native levels.[18] If this is the case, as we believe it to be, then the snowball effect will be required. The United Nations published a report in 2001 examining this potential for immigration to stop population ageing, and the numbers are staggering.[19] Assuming migrant fertility converges towards native rates, calculations show that the EU15 would require roughly 700 million immigrants between 1995 and 2050 to maintain a constant ratio of the working-age population to the population over 65.

Calculations made for the case of Sweden show that the reality lies somewhere between the two extremes.[20] If one erases the effects of migration to Sweden during the last 70 years of the twentieth century, in 2008 the population over the age of 65 would have been 20 per cent of the population instead of almost 18 per cent. This shows that immigration does slow population ageing somewhat, but that the effects are not enough to stop or reverse the process.

Even if immigrants did maintain high fertility, a vital assumption required for immigration to serve as a successful solution to the economic challenges of an ageing population is that they are successfully integrated into the labour market.[21] This is, unfortunately, an assumption that does not hold in most European countries, and as long as the integration situation remains unchanged, increasing immigration will lead to greater, not lower, strains on public finances.

---

16 See Robert Hartman and Thomas Espenshade, 'Can immigration slow U.S. population ageing?' (1994) 13 J Pol Anal Manag 759–69.

17 See S H Jonsson and M S Rendell 'The fertility contribution of Mexican immigration to the United States' (2014) 41(1) Demography 129–50.

18 See Gunnar Andersson, 'Childbearing after migration: Fertility patterns of foreign-born women in Sweden' (2004) 38(2) Int Mig Rev 747–74; and Gunnar Andersson and Kirk Scott 'Labour-market attachment and parenthood: The experience of immigrant women in Sweden' (2005) 59(1) Pop Studies 21–38.

19 See *Replacement Migration*, UN Publication ST/ESA/SER.A/206 (UN 2001).

20 See Bengtsson and Scott (2010), above n 6.

21 See David Coleman, 'Mass migration to Europe: Demographic salvation, essential labor or unwanted foreigners?' in A Messina (ed.), *West European Immigration and Immigrant Policy in the New Century* (Praeger 2002).

A final problem with the migration solution is competition. Population ageing is not only occurring in a single country or even a handful of countries. It is a global phenomenon. The sheer numbers of immigrants required, coupled with the number of countries requiring immigrants, leads to a situation where there are not enough immigrants in the world to solve this problem.

6.3 Increase the Tax Base

Another obvious solution for the financing of an elderly population is simply to increase the tax burden on the working population. Increasing taxes, however, is a difficult and dangerous means to finance an ageing society.[22] Most obviously, an increase in the income tax rate changes incentives to work, since the individual receives less money in their pocket for the same work. Less obviously, but perhaps more importantly, it is difficult to raise any taxes more than marginally in today's Europe. Given freedom of movement of capital and labour, increasing the tax burden could cause a migration of a portion of the tax base, thereby defeating the purpose of the increase, and potentially costing more than it brings in.

Another way to increase tax revenue, however, is simply to increase the number of hours worked. This is essentially the basis for extending the retirement age above 65. Increasing the retirement age has the dual benefit of increasing the amount of taxes an individual pays during the lifetime, as well as decreasing the number of years that an individual spends drawing pension benefits.[23] There is a downside to this, however. Not all individuals are able to work until the ages of 67 or 70. Individuals with physically demanding employment may quite simply be unable to continue in their chosen occupation. Future labour market retraining programmes should consider the need for occupation shifts during the lifetime, not only because some occupations are too physically demanding for employment at higher ages, but also because some occupations may disappear due to increasingly rapid technological development.[24]

---

22 See Åsa Hansson, 'In this world nothing is certain but death and taxes: Financing the elderly' in Tommy Bengtsson (ed.), *Population Ageing – A Threat to the Welfare State* (Springer Verlag 2010).

23 See Government Inquiry Report SOU 2011:05 *Högre pensionsålder – motiv för och emot* (Elanders 2012).

24 See CBRE 'Fast forward 2030: The future of work and the workplace' (2014), available at www.cbre.com/research-and-reports/future-of-work.

The number of hours worked can be increased without raising the retirement age. If one looks at the population in working ages, it quickly becomes obvious that there is room to increase hours worked within the framework of the working-age population. If we examine the number of weeks worked on average, the numbers show considerable room for improvement. Swedes, for example, worked on average 40.6 weeks in 2009, while Americans worked 44.2 weeks,[25] with other European countries falling somewhere in between. One of the prime reasons for these low numbers is sickness absence and other non-vacation absence. Efforts aimed at reducing this absence will result in fewer transfers to the workforce, and higher production levels.

There is also a non-insignificant portion of the population of working age which is not in gainful employment. For the case of Sweden, a European leader in labour force participation, the share of the working-age population actually employed was steady around 80 per cent until the recession of the 1990s, when the number declined to around 70 per cent, and has not recovered.[26] This implies that there is considerable room to move more people into employment, and therefore expand the tax base further.

This movement into work is not entirely simple, unfortunately. Employment must exist, and people must be willing and, perhaps most importantly, able to work. An examination of the situation in Denmark has shown that the gains possible by increasing the retirement age, and thereby effectively increasing hours worked by adding years to one's career, are greater than those attainable within other age groups.[27]

6.4 The Second Demographic Dividend

The first demographic dividend, caused by falling fertility without a significant increase in the number of elderly, was discussed above in the context of the first population ageing. The second population ageing is not without its positive sides, and one of the most promising is known as the *second* demographic dividend.[28] While the first dividend only worked when the numbers of elderly remained fairly constant, the second

---

[25] See 'OECD employment outlook: Tackling the jobs crisis' (OECD 2009).

[26] 'Inflationsrapport 2006/3, available at www.riksbank.se/Pagefolders/27926/2006_3_sve_ny.pdf (Riksbanken 2006).

[27] Arbejdsmarknadskommissionen, 'Velfærd kræver arbejde' (Schultz 2009).

[28] See Andrew Mason and Ronald Lee, 'Reform and support systems for the elderly in developing countries: Capturing the second demographic dividend' (2006) 62(2) Genus 11–35.

dividend is actually a function of the fact that ageing populations today have increasing shares of elderly.

While the elderly are largely unable to work for themselves, they do possess one quality that the working-age population does not: a long life behind them. The elderly are the one group in society which has had the longest time in which to accumulate wealth. This accumulated wealth can be transformed into asset income through investment, and thereby at least partially subsidize the costs associated with ageing. These investments can either be domestic, increasing capital available to production, and thereby hopefully also increasing productivity, which may also support the costs of population ageing. The investments can also be international, through investment in countries with younger populations, returning profits which again can subsidize the elderly.

7. WHAT WILL AN AGEING FUTURE ACTUALLY LOOK LIKE?

The potential developments discussed above will most likely *not* be an accurate representation of the future demographic situation. The reason for this is quite simple: we base our predictions either on current patterns or on some combination of current patterns and observed changes in patterns. Some patterns, however, are quite difficult to predict.

When it comes to the number of people over 65 in 2050 we have a fairly good idea of the maximum, since all of these individuals are alive today. Regarding the changing patterns of longevity, however, we are less certain. To predict the number of elderly in 2050 we must make assumptions concerning developments in old-age mortality over the next 35 years. A simple examination of past predictions of life expectancy give us strong reasons to question our accuracy at making such long-term predictions.

A comparison of projections made by a number of European statistical bureaus over the past decades to actual developments has shown that, on average, our predictions underestimate life expectancy by approximately two years only 15 years after the predictions were made, and by 25 years after the projections, the average error is 4.5 years.[29] This indicates that our projections of life expectancy are consistently too low, and that our estimations of the number of individuals surviving to higher ages in 2050

[29] See Chris Shaw, 'Fifty years of United Kingdom national population projections: How accurate have they been?' (2007) 128 Pop Trends 8–23.

will be considerably below the number who actually survive. This gives us exacerbating situation number one: we will have more elderly than we think.

Exacerbating situation number two is also related to uncertainty concerning future developments. We estimate future cost of an ageing society based upon observed consumption rates. While it is difficult to project how consumption will change in the future, it is possible to see how it has fluctuated in the past. The NTA project has estimated changes in age-specific consumption since 1985, and has found that the consumption patterns have changed dramatically over time, and that these shifts in consumption patterns have been almost universally towards *higher* consumption at older ages. This is not unexpected, since increasing longevity leads to an increasing incidence of disease; previously people died at younger ages, whereas increases in longevity lead to more people experiencing diseases and disabilities that did not afflict earlier generations due to early death.

Using the NTA figures, an estimation of the life-cycle deficit (LCD) can be calculated.[30] The LCD is a summing up of the costs and incomes at given ages across the life cycle, and represents the costs which cannot be funded through labour production. The left hand panel in Figure 2.6 shows the increases in LCD between 2015 and 2050 associated with population ageing given the consumption levels recorded for 2003, and the age structure projected in 2007 and the revised age structure projected in 2013. Here it is clear that a simple adjustment in population projections based on more realistic assumptions leads to a dramatic increase in costs. The right hand panel shows a similar situation, where we instead look at the changes in costs calculated using consumption patterns from different years. Here we examine the impact of the increase in consumption between 1995 and 2003. Again, using the later consumption patterns, we see a dramatic increase in costs.

Figure 2.6 graphically illustrates the problems we have in estimating future costs, and our tendency to underestimate both consumption and longevity. There is no reason to assume that we will see any change in either source of underestimation in the future.

[30] United Nations, National Transfer Accounts Manual: Measuring and Analysing the Generational Economy, United Nations: New York (2013).

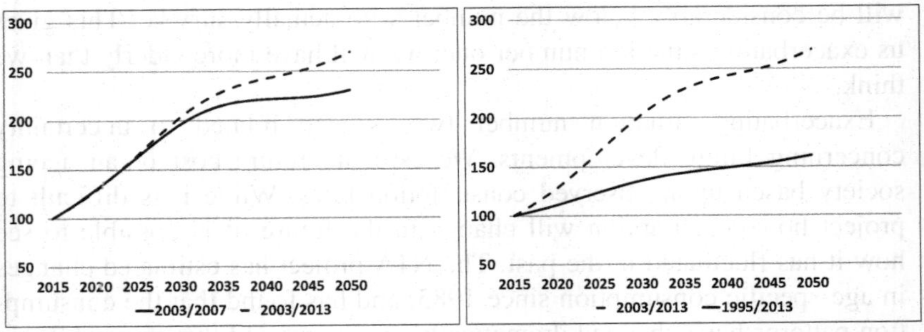

Figure 2.6 Changes in the life-cycle deficit given changes in assumptions

8. CONCLUSIONS

Population ageing is possibly the greatest challenge in the coming decades, not only for developed countries, but also for developing countries. The share over the age of 65 more than doubled in Europe over the past century, and will continue to increase. The worldwide share of the population over age 65 is projected roughly to double between 2015 and 2050. The challenge of supporting an increasing population which is no longer able to work will be the defining economic issue until at least 2050.

Population ageing is by no means a new issue, but the causes behind population ageing have changed over time. Initially, population ageing was caused by declining fertility, and this gave us the unusual situation of a relatively expanding workforce and allowed the phenomenal economic and social developments of the twentieth century. Today, we are experiencing the second population ageing, which is characterized by an increasing share of the population above 65, and a declining workforce.

The challenges caused by this second population ageing are many, and will define our future. Possible answers have been suggested, such as increasing fertility, encouraging immigration, raising taxes and increasing the number of hours worked. Of these, only increasing hours worked seems to have a straightforward application in ameliorating the economic threat of population ageing.

These challenges will not be spread evenly across nations, and not even similarly across developed nations. Some countries, such as the United States, will experience moderate challenges to ageing because of continued high fertility rates. All European countries will experience difficulties, but these challenges will also vary. Countries which have had very low fertility rates in recent decades, such as Germany and Italy, will experience rapidly growing financial difficulties associated with ageing. Other countries, such as Sweden, Norway and the United Kingdom, will face fewer and less dramatic challenges.

The fact that Sweden, our chosen case for this chapter, will experience great difficulties in financing an ageing population under current institutions highlights the seriousness of the issue. Sweden represents a 'best case' development, with most other European countries facing much more severe and rapidly encroaching threats. Unless these economic threats are dealt with appropriately, the welfare states built up in Europe since the Second World War will be in serious danger.

PART II

Conceptual and theoretical perspectives

3. Dignity, disadvantage, and age: putting constitutional and fundamental rights to work for older workers

Judy Fudge

Halvard Solness is to see about retiring now!
To make room for younger men!

Henrik Ibsen, *The Master Builder*

1. INTRODUCTION

Does constitutional human rights protection influence the interpretation of anti-discrimination instruments that prohibit discrimination on the basis of age in employment and occupation? If so, in what ways? In order to answer these questions, this chapter compares Canada and the European Union (EU) to see how the two 'constitutional' courts in these jurisdictions, the Supreme Court of Canada (SCC) and the Court of Justice of the European Union (CJEU), respectively, address claims of employment-related discrimination brought by older workers. Canada and the EU make a good comparison because they have very different approaches to the prohibition of age discrimination in both their constitutional guarantees of human rights and their specific anti-discrimination instruments. A key focus is how these courts treat claims that mandatory retirement policies are discriminatory on the basis of age.

The analysis begins by looking at the protection of age discrimination, the 'harm' that the prohibition of age discrimination in employment is designed to address, and the problems that age as a protected characteristic raise for a human rights approach in the context of mandatory retirement and employment-related benefits. Next, the key elements of the legal frameworks that prohibit discrimination against age in Canada and the EU are set out. The fourth section compares the jurisprudence of the two courts in relation to two types of age discrimination claims that are brought by older workers: those brought against mandatory retirement policies and claims against employment-related benefits to which older workers are not entitled on account of their advanced age. To conclude, I reflect on why, despite very different constitutional architecture and anti-discrimination instruments in Canada and the EU, the SCC's and CJEU's approach to resolving employment discrimination claims brought by older workers is virtually the same.

2. AGE DISCRIMINATION: RECONCILING DIGNITY AND DISTRIBUTION

Age is a ground of discrimination that is ontologically different from most other characteristics typically protected by equal treatment law.[1] Unlike other grounds, age is not associated with a history of subordination. Nor does it define a fixed group.[2] Every individual could experience age discrimination because each person has a specific age at a particular moment in time and, over a lifetime, will pass through different stages from birth, childhood, adolescence, adulthood and old age. Moreover, senescence is a fact of life, although it occurs at different rates and manifests in different ways for each individual.[3] But, like other grounds of discrimination, age has often been the basis for social stereotypes that are not rooted in reality and are used to justify the different, and detrimental, treatment of individuals simply on the basis of their age.

Welfare states have traditionally relied on age-based norms and cut-offs in shaping employment and social policy.[4] Age is seen as a 'neutral' marker for dealing with the complex problem of how to distribute social benefits entitlements and opportunities as individuals travel through the life course without requiring time-consuming and difficult individualized assessments for determining entitlement. Mandatory retirement policies,

---

1 Colm O'Cinneide, 'Constitutional and fundamental rights aspects of age discrimination' in Ann Numhauser-Henning and Mia Rönnmar (eds), *Age Discrimination and Labour Law: Comparative and Conceptual Perspectives in the EU and Beyond* (Kluwer Law International 2015) 51.

2 S Fredman, 'The age of equality' in S Fredman and S Spencer (eds), *Age as an Equality Issue: Legal and Policy Perspectives* (Hart 2003) 21.

3 B Hepple, 'Age as discrimination in employment' in S Fredman and S Spencer (eds), *Age as an Equality Issue: Legal and Policy Perspectives* (Hart 2003) 71.

4 D Schiek, 'Age discrimination before the ECJ – Conceptual and theoretical issues' (2011) 48 CML Rev 777, 781.

for example, have long served to redistribute labour market opportunities and, while directly discriminatory in practice, were (and often still are) justifiably regarded as a significant social achievement because they were coupled with the benefits of state and occupational pensions.

However, shaped in part by prevailing assumptions about what constitutes typical working-life trajectories and ideal workers, age-related distinctions can be harmful to older people who do not fit this normative model. Workplaces and labour processes have often been designed with a particular ideal worker in mind, with the result that those workers who fall outside the norm are excluded, even though it is possible to design these spaces and processes to accommodate a different normative worker.[5] Moreover, policies developed for older workers, such as mandatory retirement, were linked to a standard employment relationship that provided a host of benefits such as an occupational pension.[6] As this employment norm changes, the relevance and viability of policies associated with it – such as mandatory retirement – are being called into question.

Yet, the fact that age is different from other protected characteristics in anti-discrimination law and that it is a widely accepted social stratifier does not vitiate a human rights approach to challenging age-related injustice. As Bob Hepple noted, the starting point of all equality legislation is the right of individuals to autonomy, dignity and participation and 'the fact that there are different justifications for the various grounds of discrimination does not affect the basic principle'.[7] He claimed that the broad framework of the principle of equal treatment could accommodate specific justifications for age discrimination. The balancing of an individual worker's dignity against broader distributional concerns, which has been termed the 'double bind', is at the very heart of

---

5 Judy Fudge and Ania Zbyszewska, 'An intersectional approach to age discrimination in the European Union: Bridging dignity and distribution?' in Ann Numhauser-Henning and Mia Rönnmar (eds), *Age Discrimination and Labour Law: Comparative and Conceptual Perspectives in the EU and Beyond* (Kluwer Law International 2015).

6 See Numhauser-Henning, Julén Votinius and Zbyszewska, Chapter 7 in this book; Kendra Strauss, 'Equality, fair-mutualisation and the socialisation of risk and reward in European Pensions' in Nicola Countouris and Mark Freedland (eds), *Resocialising Europe in a Time of Crisis* (Cambridge University Press 2013).

7 Hepple (2003), above n 3, 71, 90.

decisions about permissible or prohibited differential treatment on the grounds of age.[8]

A human rights approach that emphasizes individual choice as a key component of individual dignity may, especially in an economic and business context in which employer flexibility is promoted and internal labour markets, which depended upon age and seniority-based remuneration and promotion systems, are being replaced by performance-based reviews that rely heavily on subjective judgments, contribute to the erosion of job protection.[9] Actuarial considerations that are inherent in pension and insurance schemes are antithetical to individual assessments. Thus, age discrimination in employment, especially when it comes to mandatory retirement and the related questions of pensions and benefits, is a 'wicked' problem – and one which courts have limited institutional capacity to resolve.[10]

What role do and should constitutional courts play when it comes to balancing dignity and distributional issues in age discrimination complaints brought by older workers? Mandatory retirement policies typically are the result of bargains between employers and employees and they involve a series of interconnected trade-offs, such as deferred or back-loaded compensation in exchange for a set termination date. These policies are inextricably linked to pensions, whether state or occupational, and under certain demographic and economic conditions (a growing elderly population and stagnant productivity growth) involve large intergenerational transfers.[11] Courts need principled reasons to interfere with voluntary agreements, whether bargained individually or by social partners, that are enmeshed in a complex range of employment and economic policies that involve political trade-offs between competing social values and interests. However, simply deferring to policies

---

8 Fudge and Zbyszewska (2015), above n 5; A Numhauser-Henning, 'The EU ban on age discrimination and older workers: Potentials and pitfalls' (2013) 29 Int J Comp Lab Law and Indus Relations 391.

9 Numhauser-Henning, Julén Votinius and Zbyszewska, Chapter 7 in this book; and Julie Suk, 'From antidiscrimination to equality: Stereotypes and the life cycle in the United States and Europe' (2012) 60 Am J Comp L 75.

10 Ann Numhauser-Henning and Mia Rönnmar, 'Concluding discussion' in Ann Numhauser-Henning and Mia Rönnmar (eds), *Age Discrimination and Labour Law: Comparative and Conceptual Perspectives in the EU and Beyond* (Kluwer Law International 2015) 252, quoting A Blackham, 'Addressing the ageing workforce: A critical examination of legal policy objectives and values in the United Kingdom' (2016) Ageing Soc, April 1–32.

11 Morely Gunderson, 'Age discrimination in employment in Canada' (2003) 21 Contemp Econ Policy 318.

designed to achieve intergenerational solidarity may be problematic for a number of reasons. The model of intergenerational solidarity underlying many of the national policies that allow for direct age discrimination may no longer reflect social and economic realities. Moreover, specific groups of workers, such as women, members of ethnic or racial minorities, and the disabled, never fit the normative model on which the particular notion of intergenerational solidarity in question was based in the first place. It is in this context, as O'Cinneide explains, that courts often turn to 'constitutional principles and domestic and international human rights law' for direction as to how to apply general legislative prohibitions on age discrimination.[12]

3. THE LEGAL ARCHITECTURE OF AGE EQUALITY IN CANADA AND THE EU

Age has not, historically, been expressly referred to in international or European human rights instruments.[13] However, there is a movement internationally within Europe and in the Americas to devise and adopt instruments that protect and promote the rights of older persons.[14] Moreover, certain national constitutions, such as the Canadian Charter of Rights and Freedoms, and supranational instruments, like the EU Charter of Fundamental Rights, provide open-ended guarantees of equality rights on the basis of age.

3.1 Canada: The Charter of Rights and Freedoms and Human Rights Codes

Canada is a federal state in which employment is a matter of provincial and territorial jurisdiction, except when it pertains to federally regulated undertakings. Thus, there are fourteen different human rights statutes, each covering discrimination on enumerated protected characteristics across a broad material scope, including employment, services, and accommodation. Some date to the early 1960s, so there is a long history of human rights adjudication by specialized tribunals in Canada. Although human rights statutes in Canada follow a common pattern – for

---

12 O'Cinneide (2015), above n 1, 55.

13 Ibid.

14 Ibid; Numhauser-Henning, Julén Votinius and Zbyszewska, Chapter 7 in this book.

example, all prohibit discrimination on account of age in a wide range of activities, and all have a direct horizontal effect – they differ in important detail.

Until recently, although age was a protected characteristic in every Canadian human rights statute, mandatory retirement was effectively permitted as were age-related distinctions relating to pension plans. These exemptions recognized that mandatory retirement policies and pension plans were seen as major social achievements for older workers and that they had become a central feature of many employment regimes. Some jurisdictions capped the protection against age discrimination at 65, whereas others exempted bona fide retirement and pension plans from the prohibition against age discrimination. One jurisdiction, Manitoba, has long had an open-ended prohibition of age discrimination with a general bona fide occupational qualification defence. Now almost all Canadian jurisdictions have adopted this approach of providing a general prohibition against age discrimination with a general bona fide occupational defence. However, even where there is a general ban on age discrimination, most jurisdictions continue specifically to exempt pension, disability and insurance plans that exclude individuals over the age of 65 from the prohibition against age discrimination.[15] Thus, while mandatory retirement policies are prima facie a form of direct age discrimination, it is open to employers to justify them under human rights legislation and, if there is an exemption pertaining to age caps in relation to certain types of benefits, there is no need for employers to provide a justification for excluding employees who are over the age of 65 from certain employment-related benefits.

Although Canada's human rights laws are not part of the Constitution, the SCC has found they are 'quasi-constitutional' such that other laws must be interpreted in ways that are consistent with them.[16] The SCC has developed a 'purposive' approach to anti-discrimination legislation that has resulted in a convergence across the different jurisdictions. Most significantly, in 1999 it unified earlier approaches to justifications that distinguished between direct and adverse effect discriminatory standards.[17] Once a complainant establishes a prima facie case of discrimination, the burden shifts to the employer to establish a bona fide

---

15 See for example, *Human Rights Code*, RSO 1990, c H.19, ss 24(1)(b), 25(2.1); *Charter of Human Rights and Freedoms*, RSQ, c C-12, ss 20, 20.1; *Human Rights Code*, RSBC 1996, c 210, ss 13(3), 13(4).

16 *Insurance Corp. of British Columbia v. Heerspink* [1982] 2 SCR 145.

17 *British Columbia (Public Service Employee Relations Commission) v. B.C.G.S.E.U.*1999, 3 SCR 3 ('*Meiorin*').

occupational qualification or requirement (BFOQR) defence. The employer must show on the balance of probabilities: (1) that the employer adopted the standard for a purpose rationally connected to the performance of the job; (2) that the employer adopted the particular standard in an honest and good faith belief that it was necessary to the fulfilment of that legitimate work-related purpose; and (3) that the standard is reasonably necessary to the accomplishment of that legitimate work-related purpose. To show that the standard is reasonably necessary, it must be demonstrated that it is impossible to accommodate individual employees sharing the characteristics of the claimant without imposing undue hardship upon the employer.[18] Although there is no standard definition of 'undue hardship', courts and human rights tribunals have set out a number of factors, which include: whether the employer would incur substantial costs in order to accommodate the individual; the effect of accommodation on the health and safety of the complainant, all employees, and the general public; and whether or not the accommodation would result in a substantial interference with the existing rights of other employees.[19]

In 1982, Canada entrenched a justiciable bill of rights, with a robust equality provision that included among its enumerated grounds age as a protected characteristic. The equality rights are open-ended in that they cover analogous grounds, and it is possible to bring equality claims that engage intersecting characteristics, such as sex and race or, more pertinently, age and sex.[20] Unlike the human rights statutes, which have horizontal effect, the Charter has only direct vertical effect. It has an unlimited material scope, and provides a general defence in section 1, which requires the State to demonstrate that any restriction or limitation on the Charter-protected right is demonstrably justified in a free and democratic society. The SCC has read this justification as a proportionality review, although it has also modified the rigour of the review depending upon the type of policy in question.[21]

---

18 Ibid para 54.

19 *Central Alberta Dairy Pool v. Alberta (Human Rights Commission)* [1990] 2 SCR 489; *Central Okanagan School District No. 23 v. Renaud* [1992] 2 SCR 970.

20 *Withler v. Canada (Attorney General)* [2011] 1 SCR 396.

21 *R v. Oakes* [1986] 1 SCR 103; *Irwin Toy Ltd v. Quebec (Attorney General)* [1989] 1 SCR 927.

3.2 The EU: The Employment Equality Directive and the Charter of Fundamental Rights and Freedoms

The Amsterdam Treaty provided new competences for EU institutions to 'take appropriate action to combat discrimination based on sex, racial or ethnic origin, religion or belief, disability, age or sexual orientation'.[22] This power was used as a legal basis for the subsequent adoption of the Employment Equality Directive 2000/78/EC, which expanded the scope of EU discrimination law beyond sex to age, as well as religion, disability, and sexual orientation. The resulting non-discrimination framework guarantees variable levels of protection to different grounds.[23]

The EU's recognition that age is different from other protected characteristics is made explicit in the Employment Equality Directive, which permits a wider range of justifications for differential treatment with respect to age than any other ground. Article 6.1 of the Directive provides for general justification of such discrimination in a broad range of circumstances related to legitimate employment policies and labour market objectives, as long as the measure at issue is both appropriate and necessary. As is the case in Canada, the Directive also allows Member States to fix ages for admission to occupational social security schemes or entitlement to retirement or invalidity benefits by exempting them from the prohibition on age-related discrimination. Differential treatment on grounds of age, as well as other protected characteristics, can also be justified on the basis of a public policy exclusion (Article 2.5), and Article 4 contains an exemption covering all grounds for genuine and determining occupational requirements. Member States can exclude the military sector from the protection against discrimination on age and disability grounds (Article 3.4).

Like Canada, the EU provides a constitutional guarantee of equal treatment on the basis of age. The EU Charter of Fundamental Rights contains a number of provisions that are relevant to age-related claims of discrimination. Article 21 contains a ban on discrimination on a range of grounds, including age, and Article 25 states that the Union 'recognises and respects the rights of the elderly to lead a life of dignity and independence and to participate in social and cultural life'. Article 34.1

---

22 Article 13 Treaty of the European Union (TEU) was inserted into the EC Treaty by the Treaty of Amsterdam in 1999 (now Article 19 Treaty on the Functioning of the European Union (TFEU)).

23 C Kilpatrick, 'The Court of Justice and labour law in 2010: A new EU discrimination law architecture' (2011) 40 Indus L J 280.

mentions social security and social assistance in the case of old age and Article 15 refers more generally to the right to work.

A comparison of the legal architecture of prohibitions against age discrimination suggests that the Canadian Charter and human rights statutes provide greater protection than the EU Employment Equality Directive and Charter of Fundamental Rights. The Employment Equality Directive's protection against age discrimination is limited to employment and occupation and thus has a narrower material scope than is the case in Canada under both the Charter and human rights legislation. Under Canadian human rights codes, policies or requirements that discriminate on the basis of age can only be justified as bona fide occupational requirements, which require the employer to demonstrate that any individual accommodation will result in undue hardship, whereas the Canadian Charter simply provides a general limitation clause. Under the Employment Equality Directive, the duty of individual accommodation is limited to disability, and there is no general requirement to show that individual accommodation would result in undue hardship as part of the defence that an age-related policy is reasonably necessary. Moreover, the EU Charter applies only to EU institutions and to EU law, whereas the Canadian Charter applies to all governmental action. Thus, there are limited opportunities for individuals to bring cases under the EU Charter to the CJEU.

4. CANADIAN AND EU JURISPRUDENCE COMPARED: HOW PEAK COURTS TREAT AGE DISCRIMINATION CLAIMS BROUGHT BY OLDER WORKERS

4.1 Canada: From Strict to Relaxed Scrutiny and Distinction to Discrimination

4.1.1 Overview

In Canada, the first complaints that mandatory retirement policies discriminated against older workers on the basis of age were brought under human right codes and the SCC initially subjected employers' justifications of these policies to a high level of scrutiny. These cases dealt with mandatory retirement policies for specific occupations – firefighting and police officers – that were lower than the generally accepted retirement age (which was 65) and which employers sought to justify on the ground that they were necessary to protect public health and safety. In 1990, when the SCC issued a trilogy of decisions relating to the constitutionality of mandatory retirement policies for university professors and medical doctors and general age-related cut-offs in human rights legislation, the justifications that the employers and governments offered had to do with the complex interaction of employment and social policies, such as state and occupational pensions, intergenerational solidarity, performance reviews and organizational planning. The Court has also had to address constitutional challenges to welfare policies and statutory superannuation benefits on the ground that these discriminated against older workers on the basis of their age.

4.1.2 Mandatory retirement challenges

The first two cases in which the SCC had to determine whether mandatory retirement policies contained in collective agreements were justifiable involved occupations in which the employers raised a public safety defence and the Court imposed a high standard of justification. The high-water mark of the SCC's scrutiny of mandatory retirement policies was *Ontario Human Rights Commission et al. v. Borough of Etobicoke*, which dealt with a bona fide occupational qualification or requirement (BFOQR) defence that was essentially a public safety justification.[24]

Etobicoke, which was decided in 1982, the same year that the Charter was entrenched, focused on the legality of a provision in a collective agreement that stipulated that firefighters should be mandatorily retired at age 60. Under the Ontario human rights legislation in effect at that time, workplace discrimination based on age was prohibited, although the protection had an upper limit of age 65 for the purposes of employment. The Code also provided a general BFOQR defence.

Writing on behalf of a unanimous Court, Justice McIntyre set out the elements of the BFOQR defence: first, that the requirement be imposed honestly, in good faith, and in the sincerely held belief that it furthers a legitimate end, and second, that the requirement 'be related in an objective sense to the performance of the employment concerned, in that it is reasonable and necessary to assure the efficient and economical performance of the job without endangering the employee, his fellow employees and the general public'.[25] Noting that the second element of the defence depended upon the evidence and nature of employment, Justice McIntyre went on to declare:

---

24 *Ontario Human Rights Commission v. Etobicoke* [1982] 1 SCR 202.
25 Ibid 208.

> We all age chronologically at the same rate, but aging in what has been termed the functional sense proceeds at widely varying rates and is largely unpredictable. In cases where concern for the employee's capacity is largely economic, that is where the employer's concern is one of productivity, and the circumstances of employment require no special skills that may diminish significantly with aging, or involve any unusual dangers to employees or the public that may be compounded by aging, it may be difficult, if not impossible, to demonstrate that a mandatory retirement at a fixed age without regard to individual capacity, may be validly imposed under the Code. In such employment, as capacity fails, and as such failure becomes evident, individuals may be discharged or retired for cause.[26]

The employer was required to adduce evidence about the duties to be performed, the relationship between the ageing process and the safe, efficient performance of these duties to warrant that the retirement age was in 'the interests of safety of the employee, his fellow employees and the public at large'.[27] Since the employer failed to provide any evidence of the relationship between ageing and the performance of the specific job duties, the SCC affirmed the decision of the Board of Inquiry, the first level of adjudication, that the employer had not established a BFOQR defence. The Court also dismissed the employer's argument that a mandatory retirement policy contained in a collective agreement should be considered bona fide in the absence of evidence that the provision was inserted for an ulterior reason. In McIntyre J's opinion, this approach effectively would allow the parties to contract out of the human rights code, and therefore was contrary to public policy.[28]

Although *Etobicoke* seemed to emphasize the need for an individualized approach to assessing whether or not an older employee is capable of safely performing job duties in order for employers to meet their statutory human rights obligations, the Court moved away from requiring individual assessment of older workers' ability to perform their jobs in order for employers to justify their policies. In 1989, in *Saskatoon (Human Rights Comm.) v. Saskatoon*, the SCC dealt with a mandatory retirement policy contained in a collective agreement that set the age of retirement for firefighters at 60.[29] On the basis of the evidence before it, the Board of Inquiry concluded that increasing age was related to a deterioration in a firefighter's ability to perform job-related tasks and that

---

[26] Ibid.

[27] Ibid 210.

[28] Ibid.

[29] *Saskatchewan (Human Rights Commission) v. Saskatoon (City)* [1989] 2 SCR 1297.

there was no reliable testing procedure that would accurately determine how an individual firefighter would be able to cope in an emergency situation. Justice Sopinka stated that the 'proper' approach to individualized testing was that the employer had to establish why it was impossible to deal with employees on an individual basis in order to establish the reasonableness of the requirement.[30]

Since these cases dealt with what was effectively a public safety defence, the SCC did not have to address justifications that raised issues of how mandatory retirement policies are woven into both the state's social policies and employers' employment practices. In 1985, in *Winnipeg School District v. Craton*, the Court considered a conflict between Manitoba's Human Rights Act, which prohibited age discrimination, and the Public Schools Act, which empowered school boards to establish a compulsory retirement age.[31] Unlike most other jurisdictions in Canada, the human rights legislation in Manitoba did not restrict protection against age discrimination in employment to individuals under 65. The Court characterized human rights legislation as quasi-constitutional in that it takes precedence over other legislation and affirmed its earlier position that the mere fact that the mandatory retirement policy was part of a collective agreement did not, per se, constitute a BFOQR. However, it was not called upon to determine whether the mandatory retirement policy constituted a BFOQR.

Etobicoke, *Saskatoon* and *Winnipeg School Board*, which were decided between 1982 and 1989, suggested that the SCC would subject mandatory retirement policies to rigorous scrutiny to see if they passed constitutional muster. However, in 1990, when it released three decisions that dealt with constitutional challenges to mandatory retirement policies and to statutory restrictions of the protection against age discrimination in employment to individuals who were less than 65 years of age, the Court was badly divided over how to interpret the Charter.[32]

Two of the mandatory retirement cases (*McKinney* and *Harrison*) involved challenges by university professors and librarians to mandatory retirement policies contained in collective agreements with their employers, whereas the third (*Stoffman*) dealt with a medical doctor who challenged the mandatory loss of hospital privileges at age 65. *McKinney* was the lead decision. The question of whether the Charter applied to a

---

30 Ibid 1313.

31 *Winnipeg School Division No. 1 v. Craton* [1985] 2 SCR 150.

32 *McKinney v. University of Guelph* [1990] 3 SCR 229; *Harrison v. University of British Columbia* [1990] 3 SCR 451; *Stoffman v. Vancouver General Hospital* [1990] 3 SCR 483.

mandatory retirement policy contained in a collective agreement depended upon whether or not universities could be considered to be government actors since the Court had already ruled that the Charter applied only to public action.[33] Writing for a four-member majority, Justice La Forest held that the Charter did not apply to the collective agreement between the professors' union and the university.

Despite finding that the Charter did not apply to the mandatory retirement policy in the collective agreement, La Forest considered whether the policy would, if it were a law, have violated section 15 of the Charter. Quoting Chief Justice Dickson's earlier observation that 'work is one of the most fundamental aspects in a person's life, providing an individual with a means of financial support and, as importantly, a contributory role in society', he stated that 'mandatory retirement takes this away, on the basis of a personal characteristic attributed to an individual solely on his association with a group'.[34]

In determining whether the infringement of the Charter's equality rights was a justified limitation, the Court had to assess whether the party seeking to uphold the limitation has demonstrated that it was animated by a significant and legitimate aim, and that the manner of achieving that goal was proportionate (rationally connected and minimally impairing). La Forest J accepted that the university's goals with respect to the mandatory retirement policies, which he described as '(1) to enhance and maintain their capacity to seek and maintain excellence by permitting flexibility in resource allocation and faculty renewal; and, (2) to preserve academic freedom and the collegial form of association by minimizing distinctive modes of performance evaluation', were legitimate.[35] He also concluded that there was a rational connection between mandatory retirement and the tenure system since alternatives to mandatory retirement such as competency hearings and just cause determinations 'would be difficult and costly and constitute a demeaning affront to individual dignity'.[36] He also accepted that mandatory retirement contributed to faculty renewal and facilitated long-term planning since a university is a closed system with limited resources.

The approach La Forest J adopted to the minimum impairment limb of the proportionality test was one of deference when the issues involved striking a balance between the claims of legitimate but competing social values. In the case of broadly based social measures like these, where

---

33 *RWDSU v. Dolphin Delivery Ltd* [1986] 2 SCR 573.
34 *McKinney*, above n 32, 278.
35 Ibid 281.
36 Ibid 284.

government seeks to mediate between competing groups, it is by no means easy to determine with precision where the balance is to be struck.[37]

Emphasizing that the policy was part of a negotiated agreement, provided opportunities for the young and was a method of redistributing important social resources, he held that mandatory retirement of tenured professors and librarians would constitute a justifiable limitation of the Charter's protection of equality rights.

Given that Justice La Forest's analysis of the proportionality of the mandatory retirement policy was so closely tied to the specific employment context of the university, what was remarkable was the ease with which he upheld the Ontario Human Rights Code's prohibition against discrimination in employment on grounds of age to persons between the ages of 18 and 65 as a justifiable limitation.[38] Although he readily found that the age-related restriction in the human rights code constituted discrimination, he deferred to the government's justification for it. He emphasized both how 'mandatory retirement has become part of the very fabric of the organization of the labour market in this country'[39] and the extent to which age is different from other protected characteristics.[40] Significantly, Justice La Forest characterized mandatory retirement and age discrimination as a 'complex socio-economic problem that involves the basic and interconnected rules of the workplace throughout the whole of our society' and he raised the Ontario legislature's concern that the effect of abolishing mandatory retirement on 'pension plans, youth employment, the desirability of those in the workplace to bargain for and organize their own terms of employment, the advantages flowing from expectations and on-going arrangements about terms of employment, including not only retirement, but seniority and tenure and, indeed, almost every aspect of the employer-employee relationship' was unknown.[41] Highlighting both the permissive nature of the human rights provision and the fact that the union movement and individual employees struggled to obtain it, he held that the impugned provision met the minimal impairment test.

The majority's easy acceptance of the provision excluding workers over the age of 65 from employment-related age discrimination when other much more limited techniques were available is troubling. Although

---

37 Ibid 285.
38 *Human Rights Code*, 1981, SO 1981, c 53, s 9(a).
39 *McKinney*, above n 32, 295.
40 Ibid 296.
41 Ibid 302.

La Forest J linked his justification of mandatory retirement policies to pensions, he did not require the Ontario government to revise its human rights provision so that mandatory retirement depended upon the existence of a bona fide pension plan, as was the case in other provinces. He simply ignored the problem that setting a maximum age of 65 beyond which human rights legislation does not apply to employment in order to accommodate mandatory retirement 'effectively denies protection to those who may need it the most – persons beyond the age of 65'.[42]

Similarly, in *Stoffman v. Vancouver General Hospital*, La Forest J's approach to the minimum impairment limb of the proportionality test was to ask whether the hospital had a reasonable basis for concluding than the withdrawal of hospital privileges for physicians over the age of 65 minimally impaired the doctors' rights to equal treatment on the basis of age. The majority readily accepted that in the 'current climate of budgetary restraint pervasive in the public sector' the governing Board of the hospital was justified in 'concluding that its ability to bring new doctors on staff depended on the timely retirement of some of those already there'.[43] While he accepted that the assumption of declining capabilities for those 65 and over would 'not always hold true' and that it operated 'with regard to the hospital's requirements rather than with regard to each individual doctor's health and capabilities', he concluded that the alternative, performance evaluation, would be demeaning for older workers.[44]

In their dissents, Justices L'Heureux-Dube and Wilson, the first two women on the SCC, used an intersectionality analysis to reveal how policies that may be beneficial for some workers, disadvantage other groups who have experienced a history of subordination and who have been subject to detrimental stereotypes. L'Heureux-Dube J noted that 'women often have either lower or no pension income since a greater proportion of them are in jobs where they are less likely to be offered pension plan coverage', are 'more susceptible to interrupted work histories, partly as a result of childcare responsibilities, and are prone to have lower lifetime earnings upon which pension benefits are based'.[45] Similarly, Wilson J pointed out that 'immigrant and female labour and the unskilled comprise a disproportionately high percentage of unorganized workers', and represent 'the most vulnerable employees' who would

---

42 Gunderson (2003), above n 11, 323.
43 [1990] 3 SCR 483 528–9.
44 Ibid 529, 530.
45 *McKinney*, above n 32, 433–4.

be hardest hit by mandatory retirement at age 65.[46] These judges held that the mandatory detriment policies and the restriction on protection against age discrimination in employment to individuals under the age of 65 failed the minimal impairment limb of the proportionality test.

This split over the reasonableness of mandatory retirement in the university context resurfaced two years later in *Dickason v. University of Alberta*, in which the complaint that the collective agreement provision requiring faculty members to retire at 65 was raised under the province's human rights statute and not the Charter. Despite recognizing that human rights applied to private actors who should not be given the same degree of deference as the government in developing policies that made trade-offs between different groups of workers, the majority of the SCC was guided by the analysis previously developed in *McKinney*.[47] The majority emphasized the distinctive employment context of universities, and took a very deferential stance to the collective agreement.[48] The majority also stressed the difference between age and other grounds of discrimination 'since everyone of no matter what religion, colour, social origin, nationality or gender becomes older with the passing of time'.[49] Given that the majority used the proportionality test developed under the Charter instead of the human rights' BFOQR test to determine whether the mandatory retirement policy was justified, it is not surprising the SCC dismissed the complaint.

In her dissent, Justice L'Heureux-Dube emphasized that the standard of scrutiny of a BFOQR should be strict since this case involved a human rights complaint and not a constitutional challenge. She interpreted McIntyre J's decision in *Etobicoke* as establishing a 'presumption that policies of mandatory retirement are illegitimate, save in the clearest of cases'.[50] She stated that the collective agreement 'must be scrutinized to ensure that it does not discriminate unfairly against a minority of the union membership'.[51] She also demurred with the majority's characterization of age discrimination as different from other grounds, stating that we fear old age since it is associated with infirmity and dependence and thus 'may be more likely to discriminate against elderly people, in a futile attempt to distance ourselves from what will inevitably occur to

---

46 Ibid 415.
47 *Dickason v. University of Alberta* [1992] 2 SCR 1103 1129.
48 Ibid.
49 Ibid 1132–3.
50 Ibid 1166.
51 Ibid 1173.

each one of us'.[52] Having made her case for strict scrutiny of the BFOQR she challenged the connection between mandatory retirement, tenure, faculty renewal and university planning, and ensuring performance while simultaneously protecting individual dignity. Again she emphasized the significant and detrimental impact that mandatory retirement could have on women.[53] Joined by Justice McLachlin, she held that the mandatory retirement policy was not saved by a BFOQR defence.

Dickason illustrates the extent to which the SCC's deferential approach under the Charter to mandatory retirement policies infiltrated their interpretation of human rights statutes in cases in which the BFOQR defence turned on employment policies. Although the SCC continued to require stricter scrutiny of BFOQR defences where the crux of the justification was public safety, it stopped short of imposing an obligation on employers to make accommodations for individuals who were detrimentally affected by a justifiable general policy. In *Large v. Stratford*, the SCC held that individual accommodation for older workers over the age of 60 was inconsistent with the concept of a BFOQR defence in cases in which the employer had discharged the obligation of showing that individual assessment was impractical, since it is not individual characteristics that are determinative but, rather, general characteristics reasonably applied.[54]

After the SCC developed the *Meiorin* 'unified approach' to the BFOQR, which imposed an obligation on employers to demonstrate that individual accommodation would be unduly harsh in order to meet the minimal impairment limb of the BFOQR, the approach in *Large*, which rejected the requirement for individual accommodation in cases where a general rule was justified, was questionable. The issue of individual accommodation was first raised in the context of a challenge to a mandatory retirement policy in 2009, when the SCC was called upon to consider the application of the *Meiorin* test in the context of a human rights statute in which the protection from age discrimination was expressly declared not to apply to a decision to terminate an employee if the decision was taken pursuant to a bona fide retirement or pension plan. The dispute in *NB (Human Rights Commission) v. Potash* was over how 'bona fide' should be interpreted in connection with a pension plan under the New Brunswick Human Rights Code.[55] The Human Rights Commission took the position that the mandatory retirement must meet all of the

52 Ibid.
53 Ibid 1191.
54 [1995] 3 SCR 733.
55 [2008] 2 SCR 604.

components of the *Meiorin* test, such that the employer must show that it would be impossible to accommodate individual employees without undue harshness.

Writing for the majority, Abella J adopted an interpretive approach that only required the employer to show that the pension plan was not a sham. Explicitly rejecting the invitation to reconsider its approach to mandatory retirement in general and in particular its decisions in *McKinney* and *Dickason*, she noted that most Canadian jurisdictions exempt pension plans from age discrimination claims and have different provisions for dealing with pension plans and BFOQR.[56] Reading the term 'bona fide' in light of legislation that referred to pension plans, she downplayed how the term was used in a human rights context. By contrast, although McLachlin J stopped short of requiring an individual assessment of the adequacy of the pension plan for each employee because it conflicted with the very premise of pension plans – which is to treat groups of people in a similar fashion – she imposed an obligation on the employer to 'demonstrate that the provision under which the employee is terminated is a reasonable measure in terms of the functionality and sustainability of the plan'.[57] The benefit of this approach is that it would have imposed an obligation on the employer to adduce evidence that mandatory retirement at a specified age was necessary for the integrity of the plan. Moreover, it is compatible with the intersectionality analysis adopted in dissenting judgments in *McKinney* and *Dickason*, under which the court would probe to see if groups sharing more than one protected characteristic were disadvantaged by the mandatory retirement policy.

When faced with exemptions to the statutory protection against discrimination on the basis of age in employment for those over 65, the SCC has adopted a reasonable basis approach to proportionality analysis. It has deferred to government decisions when it comes scrutinizing policies that have to balance the rights and entitlement of competing groups, and has simply ignored the minimal impairment limb of the proportionality analysis. Moreover, the Charter has contributed to the SCC applying a variable level of scrutiny to justifications of mandatory retirement policies raised in the context of human rights complaints. The rigour of the scrutiny depends upon the nature of the BFOQR, with public safety justifications attracting a higher level of scrutiny than those relying on employment policies. The SCC has deferred to collective agreements that balance the rights and entitlements of different groups of

---

56 Ibid 619.
57 Ibid 634.

employees and it has taken a hands-off approach to scrutinizing pension plans. The majority of the Court has failed to take up an intersectionality analysis to see if the mandatory retirement policy in question had a disproportionate impact on groups who shared two or more protected characteristics, and it has not imposed a requirement for individual assessment or individual accommodation as part of the minimum impairment test. As the SCC relaxed the standard of scrutiny it applied to some of the justifications for mandatory retirement policies, governments across Canada abolished age-related restrictions in human rights codes that permitted mandatory retirement policies without requiring employers to offer a justification, which meant that the justifications offered for mandatory retirement became even more significant.

4.1.3 Age-related restrictions on access to employment and social benefits

Despite relaxing the standard of scrutiny in the context of mandatory retirement, the SCC was unanimous that explicit age-based employment distinctions were a form of discrimination that needed to be justified. The SCC's early (and fleeting) willingness to subject government policies to scrutiny that discriminated against employees on the basis of their age was demonstrated in *Tetreault-Gadoury v. Canada (Employment and Immigration Commission)*, which was released the year after *McKinney*.[58] The applicant was terminated from her job just after she turned 65 and she was denied ordinary state unemployment insurance benefits on the basis of her age. For a unanimous SCC, Justice La Forest found that the section of the Unemployment Insurance Act terminating benefits at age 65 violated the Charter. He identified 'the most harmful and singular aspect' of the provision to be that:

> it permanently deprives the applicant, and any other person of her age, of the status of a socially insured person by making her a pensioner of the state, even if she is still looking for a new job. Regardless of her personal skills and situation, she is as it were stigmatized as belonging to the group of persons who are no longer part of the active population.[59]

Having found that the provision was discriminatory, La Forest J went on to determine whether it constituted a reasonable limit. The legislation was designed to achieve what the Court accepted as three legitimate

---

[58] *Tétreault-Gadoury v. Canada (Employment and Immigration Commission)* [1991] 2 SCR 22.

[59] Ibid 40.

goals: (1) preventing those over 65 from receiving a 'double' return of both pension and unemployment benefits; (2) preventing the abuse of unemployment insurance by those individuals who intended to retire; and (3) tailoring the benefits of the Unemployment Insurance Act to other social programmes that the government designed specifically for those over the age of 65. The Court skipped over the rational connection step and moved immediately to the minimum impairment limb, citing *McKinney* for the proposition that the government should be accorded considerable flexibility when evaluating measures that attempt to strike a balance between claims of legitimate but competing social values. La Forest J found that the problem of 'double compensation' could have been achieved simply by deducting pension receipts from unemployment benefits, and thus the exclusion of people over the age of 65 from unemployment benefits was too broad. He noted that the government had failed to adduce any evidence to show that individuals over the age of 65 abuse unemployment benefits more than other groups, that it could not afford to extend unemployment benefits to those over 65 or that it had any programme to address the problem of 65-year-olds who must continue working because their pension is insufficient. La Forest J emphasized the disproportionate impact of 'denying unemployment benefits precisely to those who need them most', and concluded that the government had not satisfied the requirement of minimal impairment.[60]

This case was the apogee of the SCC's rigorous scrutiny of policies that discriminated against older workers. Instead of simply relaxing the justification for age-related discrimination, in the face of a mounting number of age-related challenges to social policies, the SCC imposed an additional hurdle on applicants to prove that explicit age-based distinctions were discriminatory because it creates a disadvantage by perpetuating prejudice or stereotyping.[61] In *Withler v. Canada (Attorney-General)* the SCC dismissed a Charter challenge to the constitutionality of two statutes that reduced surviving spouses' federal supplementary death benefits by 10 per cent for each year by which their husbands were older than 60 and 65 respectively when they died. On behalf of a unanimous SCC, McLachlin CJC and Abella J reasoned that although the provisions in question drew a distinction on the basis of age, they were not discriminatory because they did not either perpetuate or result in any negative or invidious stereotyping. The Court looked at the supplementary death benefit plan in the context of the package of benefits, 'viewed

60 Ibid 46.

61 *R v. Kapp* [2008] 2 SCR 483.

as a whole and over time', to which the surviving spouses were entitled, and concluded that it corresponded to their needs.[62]

The problem with the SCC's decision in *Withler* is not the result, but rather the way that the Court arrived at it. Instead of dismissing the complaint for failing to establish that the age distinction was discriminatory, the onus should have shifted to the government to show that the package of benefits met the needs of surviving spouses, which was what the Court found. Should the Court also impose an obligation on the government to show that individual assessment was not feasible?[63] Since cut-off rules and eligibility rules will inevitably cause hardship in individual cases and a principled basis for diagnosing and resolving individual hardship that is attentive to broader fiscal concerns is not obvious, a better solution is to impose an obligation on the government to show that the age distinction did not have a disproportionate impact on groups that shared two or more protected characteristics.

4.2 The EU and Employment Discrimination Against Older Workers

4.2.1 Overview

Equal treatment has been characterized as a constitutional principle of the EU protecting individuals against discrimination within the scope of EU law.[64] In *Mangold*, the CJEU recognized non-discrimination on the grounds of age as a general principle of EU law and gave the Employment Equality Directive direct horizontal effect.[65] It also declared that this principle is set out in Articles 21 and 23 of the EU Charter of Fundamental Rights.[66] According to the Court, age protection in the Directive should be given an expansive and purposive interpretation in line with the equal protection.[67] In *Fuchs*, the Court stated that the prohibition of discrimination on grounds of age set out in the Directive 'must be read in the light of the right to engage in work recognized in

---

62 *Withler*, above n 20, 431.

63 Pnina Alon-Shenker, '"Age is different": Revisiting the contemporary understanding of age discrimination in the employment setting' (2013) 17 Can Lab L and Employment L J 13, 55.

64 O'Cinneide (2015), above n 1; H Meenam, 'Age discrimination and the future development of elder rights in the European Union: Walking side by side or hand in hand' in I Doron and A M Soden (eds), *Beyond Elder Law* (Springer 2012) 57.

65 *Mangold v. Helm* C-144/04 EU:C:2005:708.

66 *Kücükdeveci* C-555/07 EU:C:2010:21, para 21.

67 See *Mangold*, above n 65, and *Kücükdeveci*, above n 66.

Article 15(1) of the Charter',[68] whereas in *Hennigs* the Court took into account the right to engage in collective bargaining set out in Article 28 of the Charter.[69] As we will see, in the context of mandatory retirement policies these two provisions tend to cancel each other out.

The CJEU does not consistently invoke the general principle and Article 21(1) of the Charter in age discrimination cases, which may, in part, be explained by how the issue is framed by the referring court.[70] Moreover, unlike the SCC, which requires an applicant to show that an age-related distinction is discriminatory, the CJEU has taken a 'very pragmatic approach' to the identification of age discrimination that simply looks at comparing whether an individual is treated differently than another individual on the basis of age.[71] The likely reason for the more relaxed threshold for establishing age-related discrimination under the Employment Equality Directive as compared to under the Canadian Charter is that the former's material scope is more restricted and it is also more explicit about the kinds of justifications permitted. The Directive does not apply to social security and social protection schemes or to state payments providing access to employment or maintaining employment, and Member States can establish retirement ages. The Directive also specifically delineates three different types of justifications that are permitted – a general justification relating to legitimate employment and labour market policies; a public policy exclusion pertaining to public security, public order, and the protection of health and the rights and freedoms of others; and genuine and determining occupational requirements – unlike the case in Canada, which rolls the different kinds of justifications into one broad BFOQR. With respect to the first justification, the CJEU emphasized that Member States enjoy broad discretion in their choice, not only to pursue a particular aim in the field of social and employment policy, but also in the definition of measures capable of

---

68 Joined cases *Fuchs and Köhler v. Land Hessen*, C-159/10 and C-160/10 EU:C:2011:508.

69 Joined cases *Hennigs and Mai* C-297/10 and C-298-10 EU:C:2011:560.

70 Christa Tobler, 'EU age discrimination law and the older and younger workers: Court of Justice of the European case law development' in Ann Numhauser-Henning and Mia Rönnmar (eds), *Age Discrimination and Labour Law: Comparative and Conceptual Perspectives in the EU and Beyond* (Kluwer Law International 2015) 99.

71 Elaine Dewhurst, 'The development of EU case-law on age discrimination in employment: Will you still need me? Will you still feed me? When I'm sixty-four' (2013) 19 Eur L J 5 527.

achieving it.[72] Moreover, the CJEU is clear that it is up to the national court to ascertain, in the light of all the relevant evidence, whether national measures are an appropriate and necessary means of achieving a legitimate aim.[73]

The benefit of this approach to justifications is that the CJEU must identify the kind of category a specific justification falls into and it can tailor the strength of scrutiny it applies to the different types of justifications. For example, in *Mangold* a German rule excluded workers over the age of 52 from the normal protections available to employees in fixed-term employment in order to facilitate employment for older workers.[74] The CJEU imposed a standard of strict scrutiny on measures designed to assist older workers in finding employment by lowering employment protection, requiring the Member State to objectively justify the policy by showing that it had adopted the least restrictive means. However, the Court does not uniformly apply a strict proportionality test to all age-related distinctions that are detrimental to older workers. In cases involving mandatory retirement policies that are being justified on the ground that they are a means of achieving legitimate employment and labour market goals, the CJEU has adopted a light touch rationality approach. By contrast, the CJEU imposes a heavier burden on employers or states that seek to justify an occupationally specific mandatory retirement policy on the ground of public safety or as a genuine occupational requirement. A strict standard of scrutiny is also applied when older employees are denied employment-related social benefits.

4.2.2 Mandatory retirement

Although the Directive specifically acknowledges that a Member State can set a retirement age, the CJEU can scrutinize whether termination clauses that impose mandatory retirement can be justified.[75] It has dealt with two general types of mandatory retirement cases: general mandatory retirement provisions and occupationally specific provisions that are imposed for employment and labour market policy reasons, and occupationally specific mandatory retirement rules that are justified either on the

---

[72] *Fuchs and Köhler*, above n 68.

[73] E Dewhurst, 'Intergenerational balance, mandatory retirement and age discrimination in Europe: How can the ECJ better support national courts in finding a balance between the generations' (2013) 50 CML Rev 1333.

[74] *Mangold*, above n 65.

[75] *Palacios de la Villa v. Cortefiel Servicios SA*, C-411/05 EU:C:2007:604, *Age Concern England v. Secretary of State for Business, Enterprise and Regulatory Reform*, C-388/07 EU:C:2009:128.

ground of public safety or as genuine occupational requirements. The level of scrutiny the CJEU imposes on justifications relating to mandatory retirement requirements varies from a light touch scrutiny of justifications relating to employment and labour market goals to a rigorous level of scrutiny for public safety justifications and occupational requirements.[76] The variable level of scrutiny can be explained in light of the type of justification offered: the former, which requires deference to Member States' policy choices, and the latter, which depends upon objective criteria relating to the nature of the job and well-defined requirements, like public safety, security and health.

The Court has given Member States a wide margin of discretion in justifying retirement ages under Article 6(1) of the Directive, accepting intergenerational solidarity in terms of access to employment, preventing humiliating forms of employment termination, flexibility for employers, and a balance between social policy and budgetary concerns as legitimate aims for mandatory retirement policies.[77] Member States are required to adduce evidence that the policies are justified, and not simply rely on generalizations, although the CJEU has not been explicit about the type of evidence required.[78] Moreover, the CJEU has emphasized the role of social partners in negotiating mandatory retirement polices and the adequacy of pension income as elements to be considered in determining whether the policy is reasonably necessary. All of these considerations, except for the adequacy of pension income, also feature in the SCC's acceptance of general mandatory retirement policies.

The CJEU has not, however, been consistent in its treatment of the availability of a sufficient pension income in assessing whether a general

---

[76] Monika Schlachter, 'Mandatory retirement and age discrimination under EU Law' (2011) Int J Comp Lab Law and Indus Relations 27 290; Tobler (2015), above n 70; Dagmar Schiek, 'Proportionality in age discrimination cases: Towards a model suitable for socially embedded rights' in Ann Numhauser-Henning and Mia Rönnmar (eds), *Age Discrimination and Labour Law: Comparative and Conceptual Perspectives in the EU and Beyond* (Kluwer Law International 2015).

[77] In *Age Concern England*, above n 75, the CJEU made it clear that public policy objectives should be designed to advance the public interest rather than simply reducing costs for employers or enhancing their competitiveness. See *Palacios de la Villa*, *Rosenbladt v. Oellerking Gebaudereinigungsges mbH* C-45/09, joined cases *Georgiev v. Technicheski Universitet, Sofia* C-250/09 and C-268/09 EU:C:2010:699, *Fuchs and Köhler*, above n 68; *Torsten Hörnfeldt v. Posten Meddelande AB* C-141/11 EU:C:2012:421; *European Commission v. Hungary* C-341/08 EU:C:2012:687.

[78] *Age Concern England*, above n 75.

mandatory retirement policy is reasonably necessary. In *Palacios de la Villa* the national collective agreement fixed a retirement age of 65, subject to a condition that the employees affected had made sufficient contributions under the national social security scheme to become entitled to a full retirement pension. The Court noted that the measure took into account both the age of employees and their pension entitlements, as well as allowing collective agreements to modify the operation of the retirement age scheme. Yet, in *Age Concern* the CJEU did not require the UK law to take into account either the existence or adequacy of a pension in setting a mandatory retirement age of 65, nor did it require the policy to have been the result of an agreement between the social partners. The difference in the level of scrutiny imposed by the Court in the two cases may be the result of the nature of the case. In *Palacio*, the CJEU was asked to assess a specific mandatory retirement provision, whereas in *Age Concern* a civil society organization representing elders was challenging the provisions of the UK Employment Equality (Age Discrimination) Regulations 2006 on the ground that the UK government had failed properly to transpose the age provisions of Directive 2000/78/EC into UK law. Thus, *Age Concern* dealt with whether it was justifiable for a government to allow employers to impose mandatory retirement policies, and not whether a particular policy was justifiable. As such, it is analogous to the SCC's decision in *McKinney* upholding the exclusion of employees over the age of 65 from protection against age-related discrimination in employment.

Although the CJEU has referred to the availability of pension entitlements in determining whether compulsory retirement schemes are justified, it has stopped short of considering whether or not the pension is adequate in the case of the individual applicant.[79] The CJEU was concerned that there was a pension plan that had been agreed to by the social partners, and not with the adequacy of the pension in any particular case. Like the SCC, the CJEU has not required individual assessment of pension benefits in order for a mandatory retirement policy to meet the minimal impairment test. It is likely that the CJEU considers it to be too intrusive upon the employment and social policy competences of Member States, and thus a violation of the principle of subsidiarity, to require them to demonstrate that part-time, temporary, casual, or low-waged workers who are required to retire upon reaching a specified age are entitled to an adequate pension. A less intrusive position, and one which is more tightly aligned with an anti-discrimination and human

---

79 *Rosenbladt*, above n 77; *Hörnfeldt*, above n 77.

rights approach to age discrimination, would be to require Member States to adduce evidence that these schemes do not have a disproportionate impact upon groups of workers who *could* be identified by other grounds of prohibited discrimination, such as sex or disability.

The CJEU's treatment of employment and labour market justifications for occupationally specific mandatory retirement policies has been remarkably similar to the SCC's approach to justifications under the Charter. As was also the case in Canada, most of these challenges are lodged by self-employed professionals, such as dentists or doctors, or high-status and relatedly well-paid employees in standard employment contracts, for instance university professors and state prosecutors. Both the CJEU and SCC have accepted intergenerational solidarity, avoiding demeaning performance reviews, and workforce planning and budgetary reasons as legitimate goals of mandatory retirement policies.[80]

Although the CJEU has imposed a slightly higher level of scrutiny of justifications in these cases than it has in the general mandatory retirement policies, in each of these cases it held that the policy was justified. To date, the only case in which the CJEU has decided that a mandatory retirement policy for a specific occupational group did not pass the proportionality analysis was *Commission v. Hungary*, a case that had an important and well-known political subtext about judicial independence.[81] A law was introduced, abruptly reducing the retirement age for judges by eight years and detaching the retirement age for judges from eligibility for the social security pension. Although the Court considered the objectives – the standardization of the age limit for compulsory retirement in the public sector and the establishment of a more balanced age structure facilitating access for young lawyers to these professions – to be legitimate, applying what was in effect a strict proportionality test to the execution of the changes, it held that they were not necessary or appropriate.[82]

By contrast with the looser proportionality standard applied to justifications of mandatory retirement policies on the ground of employment and social policies, as was also the case in Canada, the CJEU has adopted a stricter proportionality standard to scrutinize public safety

---

[80] *Petersen v. Beerufungsausschuss fur Zahnärzte fur den Bezirk Westfalen-Lippe*, C-341/08 EU:C:2010:4; *Fuchs and Köhler*, above n 68; *Georgiev*, above n 77.

[81] *European Commission*, above n 77; Tamás Gyulavári and Nikolett Hös, 'Retirement of Hungarian judges, age discrimination and judicial independence: A tale of two courts' (2013) 42 Indus L J 289.

[82] Ibid 295.

justifications and genuine occupational requirements.[83] In *Petersen* the issue was an age limit of 68, after which dentists providing public care under the German health insurance system were no longer authorized to do so. The German government attempted to justify the age limit on two separate grounds. Firstly, it argued the age limit was justified in order to protect the health of patients obtaining dental care under the national statutory health insurance scheme, as 'general experience' indicated that dentists suffered a decline in performance after the relevant date. Secondly, it argued that the measure was justified under the provisions of Article 6(1) as necessary to give effect to the legitimate employment policy objective of opening up new places on the public care panel for younger dentists. Since the age limits did not apply to dentists in private practice, the Court again concluded that they could not be justified as being 'necessary' under the provisions of Article 2(5), although it did not question the generalization that skill deteriorates with age. Adopting an approach similar to that of the SCC in *Stoffman*, the CJEU accepted that the age restriction for dentists was justified on the basis of inter-generational solidarity in that specific occupational context.

In *Prigge* the CJEU was faced with whether the provisions of a collective agreement that required Lufthansa pilots to retire at the age of 60 could be justified under Article 2(5) or whether it constituted a genuine occupational requirement under Article 4(1).[84] The social partners identified the safety of airline passengers as the object of the provision, and the CJEU accepted it as an appropriate measure under Article 2(5). The CJEU also accepted that capabilities deteriorate with age. However, it concluded that the measure was not necessary since national and international legislation set an upper age limit of 65 for pilots and imposed some restrictions, and no evidence has been presented to justify why a lower age limit has been set in the collective agreement. The Court was also not prepared to accept that the mandatory retirement age of 60 for pilots constituted a 'genuine and determining' occupational requirement under Article 4(1), since no evidence had been presented to show that the lower age limit was necessary when it came to ensuring the safety of Lufthansa passengers in particular. While the CJEU rigorously scrutinizes age as a proxy for physical capacity, it has not gone as far as

---

[83] *Petersen*, above n 80; *Prigge v. Deutsche Lufthansa AB* C-447/09 EU:C:2011:573; Schiek (2011), above n 4, Schlachter (2011), above n 76.

[84] *Prigge*, above n 83.

the SCC to impose an obligation to show that individual assessment is not feasible in order to establish that the age requirement is necessary.[85]

4.2.3 Age-related restrictions on access to employment and social benefits

The final set of cases deals with individuals who have been denied social benefits linked to the termination of their employment because they had reached an age at which they are entitled to draw a pension at the time of their dismissal. Prior to the Employment Equality Directive, it was common for severance and redundancy payment schemes to exclude employees who were eligible for a retirement pension in order to ensure that these employees did not receive 'double' compensation. In these cases, the CJEU has applied a strict proportionality test in determining whether the employment policy was justified. In *Andersen*, the applicant, who was 63, was entitled to a reduced pension, which he wanted to postpone while he continued to work to the generally accepted retirement age (of 67).[86] The CJEU held that the legislation was not 'manifestly inappropriate' in light of the objective of preventing double compensation and assisting long-service employees while they found employment. However, since the legislation did not allow older workers who wished to remain in the labour market to temporarily waive their pension entitlement in favour of obtaining a severance allowance, the Court held that it was unnecessary. Similarly, in *Toftgaard*, the CJEU held that the refusal to grant availability pay to civil servants who reached the age of 65 and who were entitled to a pension was unnecessary since some individuals, such as the applicant, wanted to continue working until their retirement age (which in this case was 70).[87] The CJEU's approach to these cases is similar to that of the SCC of Canada in *Tetrault-Gadoury*, where the Court found there was a less restrictive manner of dealing with the problem of double compensation without causing hardship to the employee, even though in the Canadian case the employee who was terminated and denied state unemployment benefits had reached the general retirement age.

Andersen and *Toftgaard* can be distinguished from the subsequent case of *Tekniq*, which involved a challenge to the Danish legislation denying severance pay to employees who on termination would receive an old-age

---

85 See *Saskatchewan (Human Rights Commission) v. Saskatoon (City)*, above n 29.

86 *Ole Andersen v. Region Syddanmark* C-499/08 EU:C:2010:600.

87 *Toftgaard v. Indenrigs- og Sundhedsministeriet* C-546/11 EU:C:2013:603.

pension and had joined the pension plan before the age of 50.[88] In this case, the employee was informed that when he turned 67, which was the general retirement age, that he would be terminated. Since he was over the age of 65 and entitled to a state pension, the applicant was denied severance pay under the impugned legislation. Following *Andersen*, the CJEU held that the legislation was appropriate in light of its aim. However, the Court held that the legislation was necessary since the applicant would not be risking a reduced pension on account of early retirement and the loss of the severance payment 'does not appear capable of causing a significant loss of income to the departing employee in the long term'.[89]

The key to understanding *Tekniq* is the CJEU's statement that the denial of severance benefits was not unduly prejudicial to the 'legitimate interests of workers who have reached the normal retirement age'.[90] However, it is not clear that the normal retirement age is critical to finding that a scheme that reduces the benefits paid to older workers is reasonably necessary. *Odar* involved a challenge to an occupational social security scheme provided in a social plan on the ground that it discriminated by providing workers over the age of 54 – who had been made redundant and who were eligible for a pension – with less compensation than a younger comparator.[91] The Court dismissed this complaint on the ground that 'a national provision aimed at granting compensation for the future, protecting younger workers and facilitating their reintegration into employment, while taking into account the need to achieve a fair distribution of limited financial resources in a social plan' was legitimate under Article 6(1).[92] Noting that Member States and social partners have a broad discretion to choose the measures to implement this aim, the Court concluded that the 'reduction in compensation granted to workers who, on the date of termination of employment, are financially secure, does not seem unreasonable in light of the purpose of such social plans, which is to enhance protection for workers [for] whom the transition to new employment is challenging due to their limited financial means'.[93]

---

88 *Ingeniörforeningen i Danmark v. Tekniq* C-515/13 EU:C:2015:115.
89 Ibid para 41.
90 Ibid para 44.
91 *Johann Odar v. Baxter Deutschland GmbH* C-152/11 EU:C:2012:772.
92 Ibid para 42.
93 Ibid para 48.

5. CONCLUSION

Despite very different constitutional architecture and anti-discrimination instruments in Canada and the EU, the SCC's and CJEU's approach to resolving employment discrimination claims brought by older workers is virtually the same. Both defer to political authorities and social partners when it comes to justifying mandatory retirement policies in order to achieve employment and labour market goals, and they look to the same set of features – the age of retirement, the availability of pension income, the existence of a collective agreement – to determine whether the policy is reasonably necessary. Neither of the peak courts considers the adequacy of pension income in the individual case, nor do these courts require evidence that pension income does not disadvantage groups that share another protected characteristic along with age in order to justify mandatory retirement policies as reasonably necessary for achieving employment and labour market policies. Moreover, both the SCC and CJEU subject occupationally specific, mandatory retirement policies – which are adopted either to protect public safety or as a genuine occupational requirement – to a higher level of scrutiny, although neither court requires individual assessment or individual accommodation in order to establish that the age-related distinction is reasonably necessary. Policies or laws that deny older workers employment-related benefits and entitlements are also subjected to rigorous scrutiny by both courts, and both are concerned about the adequacy of income for older workers. Both the SCC and CJEU 'apply variable standards of review depending upon the nature of the age distinction in question and the employment or social policies which it is supposed to be advancing'.[94]

What appears to be more robust constitutional protection against age discrimination in Canada has not resulted in stricter scrutiny of employment-related distinctions that detrimentally affect older workers. In fact, the Canadian example shows that constitutional protection against age discrimination in employment can sometimes make it more difficult to establish age discrimination in the first place, especially if what is being challenged is a state social policy.

The similarity in the SCC's and CJEU's approach to age discrimination does not accord with a recent comparison of workplace discrimination laws in Canada, the US, and the EU. Comparing the legal treatment of workers with disabilities or with family responsibilities in the three jurisdictions, Banks, Nunin and Topo found that the way that courts

94 O'Cinneide (2015), above n 1, 69.

operationalize the idea of equal opportunity differs greatly despite the structural similarities in each jurisdiction's anti-discrimination law.[95] They argued that the originating context (whether the initial target was race or gender, for example) of each jurisdiction's anti-discrimination law influenced the doctrine of employer responsibility that animates each jurisdiction's test of what counts as a justification. However, my comparison of how the SCC and CJEU resolve age discrimination claims brought by older workers shows that the courts resolve the cases in a very similar manner despite significant differences in the legal structure of the protection against age discrimination in employment in Canada and the EU. When it comes to how courts deal with age discrimination in employment, it appears that the legal origins of anti-discrimination in Canada and the EU have had a negligible influence.

This chapter suggests that the distinctive nature of age as a protected characteristic has resulted in similar approaches by the SCC and CJEU to resolving age discrimination claims in employment brought by older workers. Like all protected characteristics, a core goal of the prohibition against age discrimination in employment is to promote individual dignity by combating negative stereotypes and prejudices.[96] However, age differs from other protected characteristics in several important respects. Unlike other protected characteristics, age-related distinctions apply 'horizontally to a large population with different needs at a given time, and vertically throughout the lives of the members of this population'.[97] Moreover, many age-related distinctions often serve beneficial social purposes, although these distinctions often involve a trade-off between individual choice and collective well-being.[98] Thus, it is likely that courts will continue to treat age differently than other grounds of discrimination. Their challenge is to develop a principled approach to justifying age-related distinctions in employment that make the trade-offs explicit and require evidence, both of the reason why a specific balance was selected and why it is still appropriate in light of profound changes in labour markets, employment practices and pension schemes for the elderly.

---

[95] Kevin Banks, Roberta Nunin and Adriana Topo, 'The lasting influence of legal origins: Workplace discrimination, social inclusion and the law in Canada, the United States and the European Union' in M Finkin and G Mundlak (eds), *Comparative Labor Law* (Edward Elgar Publishing 2015).

[96] O'Cinneide (2015), above n 1, 69.

[97] *Withler*, above n 20, para 76.

[98] Suk (2012), above n 9, 97; Numhauser-Henning, Chapter 4 in this book.

4. The elder law individual versus societal dichotomy – a European perspective

Ann Numhauser-Henning

1. INTRODUCTION[1]

1.1 Introductory Remarks

In elder law, two dichotomies of central importance have been singled out: – the autonomy vs. paternalism and the individual vs. societal dichotomy, respectively.[2] As will become clear in this chapter, these two dichotomies 'overlap' considerably and are thus not easy to separate completely – and perhaps this is not even necessary. It can be said that the autonomy vs. paternalism dichotomy is mainly about values, whereas the individual vs. societal dichotomy addresses the more organizational level. I have chosen the individual vs. societal dichotomy as the headline for this chapter, because in my opinion this dichotomy lends itself particularly well to illustrating the differences between the US and European/EU setting, respectively. However, one can also describe the contents of this chapter in terms of autonomy vs. paternalism. Moreover, I have chosen age discrimination law as an example where this dichotomy plays out in a particularly illustrative way, and I follow up with an overview of more general welfare developments in the European perspective. The main line of argument is that autonomy at the individual level – however attractive this may sound these days – may well lead to

[1] This work was carried out within the Norma Elder Law Research Environment (www.jur.lu.se/elderlaw) funded by Ragnar Söderberg's Foundation and The Marianne and Marcus Wallenberg Foundation.

[2] I Doron, 'A multi-dimensional model of elder law' in I Doron (ed.), *Theories of Law and Ageing: The Jurisprudence of Elder Law* (Springer 2009) 70.

more or less extreme vulnerability as the outcome; thus autonomy does not necessarily serve as the evident ideal. This perception is also an obvious key to the understanding of European developments as compared to those of the US.

In the rest of this section follows a somewhat more comprehensive introduction to the theoretical framework for this chapter. Thereafter the issues of concern will be discussed and analysed in relation to EU age discrimination law and in particular its acceptance of compulsory retirement (Section 2) as well as in relation to more general welfare developments in the European setting (Section 3), concluding with some final remarks in Section 4.

1.2 The Elder Law Individual vs. Societal Dichotomy ...

Traditional elder law has been described in terms of 'a positivist-professional approach' to law, meaning that the area of study is being defined by the client to be served by the legal professional or by the topics of special relevance to these elderly clients.[3] The needs of the ageing individual perceived through the lens of the legal professional have thus been the focus of attention, as have protective and supportive functions of legal intervention, forming a view of elder law as 'inherently' paternalistic. On the other hand, principles of autonomy and independence can also be said to inform elder law, forming the basis for the legal counselling so characteristic of traditional elder law. Against this backdrop, 'the paternalism vs. autonomy dichotomy' and 'the individual vs. societal dichotomy' have thus been described by Israel Doron as two dichotomies characterizing elder law.[4]

Doron himself in his multi-dimensional model of elder law proposes a more genuinely pluralistic approach to elder law.[5] Nevertheless the four concepts of paternalism, autonomy, individual and societal (community) are still crucial to his understanding of the elder law field. His model is otherwise described in five dimensions: the preventive, the protective, the supportive and the empowering dimensions forming a square, and, in the centre is the 'Legal Principles Dimension' (fundamental principles of universal coverage).[6] The preventive and the protective dimensions work

---

[3] I Doron, 'Jurisprudential gerontology: Theorizing the relationships between law and aging' in V L Bengtson, D Gans, N Putney and M Silverstein (eds), *Handbook of Theories of Aging* (Springer 2009) 644.

[4] Doron (2009), above n 2.

[5] Ibid 70.

[6] Ibid 60.

at the individual level, whereas the supportive and empowerment dimensions are situated at community level. A full picture of the rights of the elderly according to Doron requires 'an examination of the various legal dimensions in his model, at the same time not representing a closed list but rather an open framework of a variety of fundamental approaches'.[7]

The protective dimension typically implies paternalistic measures at work on the individual level, but through community/societal action. In a first 'statutory generation', according to Doron, we are looking at the granting of powers to public institutions to intervene in support of vulnerable individuals. A second statutory generation in this dimension implies criminalization and reporting/monitoring of elder abuse and the like, whereas the third statutory generation implies protection against domestic violence in terms of civil law. Here, we are always on the societal/community side of the individual vs. societal dichotomy, dealing with paternalism rather than autonomy. As Doron notes:

> This state of affairs makes this legal dimension a double-edged sword: by treating the elderly paternalistically and making it possible to detract from their autonomy based on the ethical claim that the state has the right and obligation to intervene in one's life in order to protect the individual either from others or from him- or herself, the law substantiates the negative stereotype of the elderly population.[8]

On the paternalistic and societal/community side we also find the supportive dimension, which provides more or less institutionalized support – in addition to externalized state interventions proper – to the social support networks of the elderly, family-friendly employment policies and the like.

With the preventive and empowering dimensions – whether at individual level or societal – we lean towards autonomy. Creating legal planning tools is one way of strengthening the individual in the process of growing old, as is focusing the abilities of the elderly themselves – eventually creating a proper legal setting – to preclude legal intervention. Still, these legal dimensions have been criticized, as their points of departure once again define the elderly as a more or less powerless group.

---

7 Ibid 71.
8 Ibid 64.

I have thus chosen to argue my points in this chapter in terms of the individual vs. societal dichotomy, focusing on basic institutional differences between the US and the EU and how these inform both age discrimination law and social developments more generally.

1.3 … and the Role of Vulnerability …

Elder law has thus been accused of being inherently paternalistic, 'internalizing ageist presumptions through the suggestion that older persons *per se* are, like children, especially in need of the protection of the law'.[9] In relation to this criticism, vulnerability is a crucial concept that aligns with the following method of argument: vulnerability equals weakness equals incapacity. This is not the only way to argue, though. A theory of reference for the Norma Elder Law Research Environment with regard to its emancipatory character is American law professor Martha Albertson Fineman's 'Vulnerability Theory'.[10] According to this theory, vulnerability is a *universal* human condition characterizing the relationship between the individual and the state. It is the state's duty to guarantee equality of opportunities and decent living conditions that follow from the notion of equal value of all persons. The theory leads to an emphasis on the duty of society to provide the resources and institutions necessary to overcome the dependency and shortcomings that characterize human life – and not only old age. At the foundation of Albertson Fineman's theory is thus the idea that 'the vulnerability of our embodied beings and the messy dependency that often comes in the wake of physical or psychological needs cannot be ignored throughout any individual life and must be central to theories about what constitutes a just and responsive state'.[11] However, vulnerability must not be equated with harm any more than age inevitably means loss of capacity – it also presents opportunities for innovation and growth, creativity and fulfilment. 'A responsive state must ensure that its institutions provide meaningful access and opportunity to accumulate resources across the life-course and be vigilant that some individuals or groups of individuals

---

[9] Cf for instance, M Hall, 'Equity theory: Responding to the material exploitation of the vulnerable but capable' in I Doron (ed.), *Theories of Law and Ageing: The Jurisprudence of Elder Law* (Springer 2009) 107.

[10] See Mattsson and Katzin, Chapter 5 in this book. See also, for instance, M Fineman, 'The vulnerable subject and the responsive state' (2010) 60(2) Emory L J 251.

[11] M Fineman, '"Elderly" as vulnerable: Rethinking the nature of individual and societal responsibility' (2012) 20(2) Elder L J 71–112, 71.

are not unduly privileged or disadvantaged.'[12] US reality, to a larger extent than the European reality, is based on the premise that individuals are responsible for their own welfare; it imposes expectations of self-sufficiency and independence on rich and poor, advantaged and disadvantaged alike – and the elderly. Vulnerability in this society is rather perceived as a result of 'poor life choices' and lack of control. Fineman, on the other hand, thus argues that vulnerability is a universal condition positioned as the polar opposite of the liberal subject, constructed 'as invulnerable, or at least differently vulnerable' and representing 'the desirable and achievable ideals of autonomy, independence and self-sufficiency'. She argues further that 'dependency' is also universal and merely a physical or developmental aspect of the human condition – not a failure on the part of the individual or the family. Dependency 'has been assumed to attach to the elderly as a group' and is also assigned to the private sphere in contrast to the liberal subject, 'who dominates the public sphere'.[13] According to Fineman, the political subject must be developed in a more inclusive manner 'to reflect aspects of the human condition that are currently ignored or vilified' because the liberal subject reflects only 'one of a range of developmental stages that an actual human individual passes through in the course of a "normal" lifespan'.[14] This, says Fineman, must be central to our theories about what constitutes a just and responsive state. 'While society cannot eradicate our vulnerability, it can and does mediate, compensate, and lessen our vulnerability through programmes, institutions and structures.'[15] The conclusion is that '[a] vulnerability approach is an integrated approach to society, not one of either separate spheres or competing generations'.[16]

Hall, too, relates inherent paternalism to the undeniable vulnerability of older people that characterizes the process of ageing (at least in modern Western societies) and divides this vulnerability into two major aspects: social vulnerability and personal vulnerability. To avoid a paternalistic – and even ageist – view that this vulnerability equals weakness equals incapacity, Hall promotes the idea of rethinking vulnerability within the conceptual framework of equitable fraud; she offers 'a sophisticated theoretical model for understanding vulnerability as both situational and relational as opposed to the capacity/autonomy duality'[17]

---

12 Ibid 72.
13 Ibid 87.
14 Ibid 88
15 Ibid 97.
16 Ibid 110.
17 Hall, above n 9, 109–10.

thus implying '"a third way" to respond to the material exploitation of the vulnerable but capable'.[18]

The idea of the universal character of vulnerability as the basis for state interventionism can be said to offer a means of confronting the accusation that elder law is 'inherently paternalistic'[19] and thus characterized by what has been called 'the paternalism vs. autonomy dichotomy'[20] of elder law.[21] It also offers a basic argument for the societal approach in the 'individual vs. societal dichotomy'.

1.4 ... in a European Setting

There is no doubt that there is a considerable difference between Europe and the US in the scope for societal/community and the paternalistic perspectives on the one hand, and on the other their relation to more individualized autonomy perspectives. Numerous studies have made it clear that the societal/collective approach is significantly more important in the European setting than in elder law as traditionally developed in the US and elsewhere, the explanation being that Europe and the EU more explicitly fall back on social welfare conceptions. The 'European social model' is thus most frequently contrasted with that of the US and in terms of issues such as wealth, poverty, inequality and unemployment. Measured in gross domestic product (GDP), the US is considerably richer than Europe, whereas Europe stands out as having a significantly smaller proportion of poor citizens and consequently a clearly greater degree of equality.[22] This higher level of equality is reflected in considerably higher European government expenditures in terms of social benefits and transfers and also in the universalistic character of European welfare states. Europe is far from having a common welfare state, though, and over the past two decades or so inequality has increased significantly in Europe in terms of lower social spending, privatization

---

18 Ibid 118.

19 Cf Doron (2009), above n 2, Preface.

20 Doron (2009), above n 2, 70.

21 Cf also Bichenbach and others on *universalism* as a model to conceptualize abilities in disability law and, possibly, also elder law, see D Surtees, 'What can elder law learn from disability law?' in I Doron (ed.), *Theories of Law and Ageing: The Jurisprudence of Elder Law* (Springer 2009) 93 with further references.

22 C Hermann, 'The European social models: Contours of the discussion' in M Frangakis, C Hermann, J Huffschmid and K Lorant (eds), *Privatization Against the European Social Model, A Critique of European Policies and Proposals for Alternatives* (Palgrave Macmillan 2009) 83.

and tax cuts.[23] Still, despite this neoliberal restructuring, the concept of the welfare state, 'which is not just obliged to the owners of capital but to all citizens, enjoys the widest support in most European countries'.[24] This 'presence' of community and welfare structures is thus reflected in various studies in the Norma Elder Law Research Environment.[25]

2. EU AGE DISCRIMINATION LAW

Comparing working-life regulations in Europe and the US in terms of their different views on liberalism and markets – and thus the role of the individual – is nothing new. According to Adnett and Hardy, convention has been 'to contrast the market-oriented, employment-at-will policies in the US with the more neo-corporatist European Social Model with its establishment of diverse, non-waivable worker rights'.[26] According to these authors, however, precisely 'equal opportunities legislation presents a real problem for the conventional interpretation … since such legislation restricts employers' behaviour yet is more extensive in the US'.[27] In my opinion this is not necessarily so. The explanation is to be found in the different starting points – the US employment-at-will doctrine as compared to European employment protection – and the differences in the function/interpretation of discrimination law as described later in this chapter.

The different trajectories of European and American anti-discrimination law were the subject of two workshops held in Florence and Harvard Law School in 2010 and 2011, respectively, and the results

---

23 Cf Blackham, Kullmann, Pettersson and Zbyszewska, Chapter 8 in this book; Pettersson and Katzin, Chapter 12 in this book; and Mattsson, Axmin and Holm, Chapter 13 in this book, respectively.

24 Hermann (2009), above n 22, 82 with further reference to Krätke.

25 Cf for instance, A Numhauser-Henning, 'Labour law, pension norms and the EU ban on age discrimination: Towards ultimate flexibilization?' in A Numhauser-Henning and M Rönnmar (eds), *Age Discrimination and Labour Law, Comparative and Conceptual Perspectives in the EU and Beyond* (Kluwer Law International 2015); M Rönnmar, 'Protection of established position, social protection and the legal situation of the elderly in the European Union' in M Rönnmar and A Numhauser-Henning (eds), *Normative Patterns and Legal Developments in the Social Dimension of the EU* (Hart Publishing 2013). See also Trolle Önnerfors, Chapter 14 in this book. See also further, Section 3 in this chapter.

26 N Adnett and S Hardy, 'The peculiar case of age discrimination: Americanising the European social model?' (2007) 23 Eur J L & Econ 29.

27 Ibid 30.

were reported in 2012 in a special issue of the *American Journal of Comparative Law*.[28] Here the view is that while non-discrimination laws within Europe are widening, strengthening and more actively litigated, in the US the corpus of anti-discrimination law that emerged from the civil rights movement has been significantly weakened because several of its key provisions and conceptions have been rejected or sharply limited by state and federal judiciaries.[29] The workshops nevertheless arrived at the conclusion that Europe faces equally daunting challenges. The different trajectories are ascribed cultural and ideological differences in relation to the role of the state in the provision of welfare; in the American political system the respective political and institutional systems are clearly polarized, whereas the EU system is more technocratic, elitist and consensual. A temporal explanation is also given for that fact that Europe lags behind with respect to US developments in anti-discrimination regulation.

The principle of equality is no doubt regarded as a principle of universal application.[30] However, in an international perspective the protection against discrimination of precisely older persons, or on the grounds of age more generally, is clearly underdeveloped compared to many other grounds of discrimination such as sex or ethnicity; thus this protection is uncertain.[31]

In such an international perspective the protection offered regarding age discrimination within EU law – and thus at a regional European level – relatively speaking is well developed. A ban against age discrimination is thus part of the EU Charter of Fundamental Rights (CFR) and its Article 21, containing an open list of non-discrimination grounds and now part of the EU Treaty. No doubt, the development of such a right was inspired by the early ban on discrimination against older persons in the US, as regulated in the Age Discrimination in Employment Act (ADEA) back in 1967. ADEA was modelled on Title VII of the 1964

---

28 (2012) 60(1) Am J Comp L.

29 G de Búrca, 'The trajectories of European and American antidiscrimination law' (2012) 60 Am J Comp L 1–22. She mentions the narrowing of the disability concept, restrictions in the 'disparate impact doctrine' and making affirmative action constitutionally suspect; ibid 4.

30 See Fudge, Chapter 3 in this book.

31 C O'Conneide, 'Constitutional and fundamental rights aspects of age discrimination' in A Numhauser-Henning and M Rönnmar (eds), *Age Discrimination and Labour Law, Comparative and Conceptual Perspectives in the EU and Beyond* (Kluwer Law International 2015).

Civil Rights Act and contains an asymmetric ban that protects only older persons.[32]

The EU ban – in stark contrast with that of the US – covers all ages; promotion of intergenerational solidarity is a mission at constitutional level for the EU (Article 3.3 para 2 TEU). Thus intergenerational tensions are part of the very ban and open up what I (with Hendrickx) have called the 'double bind' of EU non-discrimination law.[33] On the one hand there is the 'human rights rationale', reflected in the main design of discrimination bans as a complaints-led right to protection for the individual against stereotyping practices and dignity offences in the liberal tradition. On the other hand, there is scope for more instrumental interests at societal level, including active ageing policies/strategies but also – as we will see – in the defence of age as a traditional social stratifier. Thus it is precisely the ban on age discrimination – despite this ban being detailed at secondary law level in the 2000/78/EC Equal Employment Directive, which covers a number of different non-discrimination grounds in working life – that has been given a weaker template than other discrimination bans.[34] According to Article 6.1 in the Employment Equality Directive 'member states may provide that differences of treatment on grounds of age shall not constitute discrimination if … they are objectively and reasonably justified by a legitimate aim, including legitimate employment policy, labour market and vocational training objectives and if the means of achieving that aim are appropriate and necessary'.

According to preamble 14 of the Employment Equality Directive, the Directive is without prejudice to national provisions laying down retirement ages, or the continued setting of age limits for admission to occupational social security schemes for entitlement to retirement or invalidity benefits according to Article 6.2 of the Directive. In addition, according to preamble 25, despite the prohibition of age discrimination

---

[32] Amendments in 1978 increased the age of mandatory retirement to 70 and subsequent amendments have brought all workers over the age of 40 under the statutory umbrella and essentially prohibited mandatory retirement at any age. However, employers are free to offer financial incentives for voluntary 'mandatory retirement' according to the 1990 Older Workers Benefit Protection Act.

[33] Cf Numhauser-Henning (2015), above n 25, and F Hendrickx, 'Age and European employment discrimination law' in F Hendrickx (ed.), *Active Ageing and Labour Law, Contributions in Honour of Professor Roger Blanpain* (Intersentia 2012).

[34] Cf Numhauser-Henning, Julén Votinius and Zbyszewska, Chapter 7 in this book.

being an essential part of meeting the aims set out in employment guidelines and encouraging diversity in the workforce:

> differences in treatment in connection with age may be justified under certain circumstances and therefore require specific provisions which may vary in accordance with the situation in Member States. It is therefore essential to distinguish between differences in treatment which are justified, in particular by legitimate employment policy, labour market and vocational training objectives, and discrimination which must be prohibited.

These writings thus reflect a tension between active ageing strategies and age as a traditional social/labour-market stratifier, in terms of the individualistic approach on the one hand, and on the other the partly conflicting interests behind the societal approach.

The double bind is thus reflected in what must be called the ambiguity of the Employment Equality Directive as concerns age discrimination. The balance must be struck by the Court of Justice of the European Union (CJEU) in its interpretations of first and foremost the scope for justification of direct age discrimination according to Article 6.1. There is already a considerable amount of case law (see further Chapters 3 and 7 of this book) and the Court has been criticized for using a far from transparent mix of proportionality tests in these cases.

A particularly lenient test has been applied in cases concerning compulsory retirement.[35,36] In *Hörnfeldt*, the acceptability of compulsory retirement was stated in the following way:

> the automatic termination of employment contracts for employees who meet the conditions as regards age and pension rights has, for a long time been a

---

[35] See cases *Palacios de la Villa v. Cortefiel Servicios SA* C-411/05 EU:C:2007:604; *Age Concern England v. Secretary of State for Business, Enterprise and Regulatory Reform* C-388/07 EU:C:2009:128; *Rosenbladt v. Oellerking Gebaudereinigungsges mbH* C-45/09 EU:C:2010:601; *Georgiev v. Technicheski Universitet Sofia* C-250/09 and C-268/09 EU:C:2010:699; *Fuchs and Köhler v. Land Hessen* C-159/10 and C-160/10 EU:C:2011:508; *Torsten Hörnfeldt v. Posten Meddelande AB* C-141/11 EU:C:2012:421 and *European Commission v. Hungary* C-341/08 EU:C:2012:687.

[36] Cf M Schlachter, 'Mandatory retirement and age discrimination under EU Law' (2011) 27 Int J Comp Lab Law and Indus Relations 287–99; C Kilpatrick, 'The Court of Justice and labour law in 2010: A new EU discrimination law architecture' (2011) 40(3) Indus L J 280–301; and E Dewhurst, 'Intergenerational balance, mandatory retirement and age discrimination in Europe: How can the ECJ better support national courts in finding a balance between the generations?' (2013) 50 CML Rev 1333. Cf also Fudge, Chapter 3 in this book.

> feature of employment law in many member states and is widely used in employment relationships. It is a mechanism which is based on the balance to be struck between political, economic, social, demographic and/or budgetary considerations.[37]

Other accepted aims have been intergenerational fairness in terms of access to employment – in contradiction with the negation of the lump-of-labour fallacy theory of national economics[38] but quite in line with political requests in the wake of the recent economic crisis and high youth unemployment figures within the EU – and the prevention of humiliating forms of employment termination. Moreover, both Member States and the social partners are said to enjoy 'broad discretion' in relation to justifying aims/measures.[39]

The acceptance of compulsory retirement by means of justifying continued direct age discrimination can be understood as a move in defence of the standard employment contract as developed throughout the previous century.[40] The standard employment contract builds on certain trade-offs between younger and older workers. In his 'life-cycle theory of mandatory retirement', Lazear explains how wage-setting under the standard employment contract builds on an implicit contract model, according to which wage premiums (not responding to actual productivity) are paid towards the end of a career on the assumption that the employment relationship will come to an end at a fixed point in time.[41]

This trade-off contrasts significantly with the traditional notion of employment protection in Europe.[42] Despite great variety among Member States as regards the more detailed design of dismissal protection, employment protection is generally known to characterize the EU. This is

---

[37] *Hörnfeldt*, above n 35, 28.

[38] See, however, Dewhurst (2013), above n 36, with further references.

[39] Cf A Numhauser-Henning and M Rönnmar, 'Age discrimination law and social partners and collective bargaining' in B J Mulder, M Jenum Hotvedt, M Nesvik and T L Sundet (eds), *Sui generis – Festskrift til Stein Evju* (Universitetsforlaget 2016).

[40] Cf M Freedland, 'Burying Caesar: What was the standard employment contract?' in K Stone and H Arthurs (eds), *Rethinking Workplace Regulation: Beyond the Standard Contract of Employment* (Russell Sage Foundation 2013).

[41] E Lazear, 'Why is there mandatory retirement?' (1979) 87 J Polit Econ 1261.

[42] See further Rönnmar, Kullmann, Numhauser-Henning and Ulander-Wänman, Chapter 9 in this book as well as A Numhauser-Henning and M Rönnmar (eds), *Age Discrimination and Labour Law, Comparative and Conceptual Perspectives in the EU and Beyond* (Kluwer Law International 2015).

reflected in Article 30 of the CFR, which states that 'every worker has the right to protection against unjustified dismissal, in accordance with Union law and national laws and practices'. I have related both the acceptance of compulsory retirement and an eventual preservation of the ban to the process of flexibilization of work.[43] In an EU setting, non-discrimination regulation can generally be seen as an answer precisely to the individualization of work and a general weakening of standard employment protection.[44]

According to Alexander Somek, rights to non-discrimination generally should be perceived as a forerunner of work flexibilization and neoliberalism itself.[45] He thus elaborates on bans on discrimination as a substitute for employment protection. The 'neoliberal weakness' of non-discrimination law, according to Somek, is its elitist design, building on formal equality and meritocracy/capability as the common denominator for any treatment. We thus deal with a deep-seated normative deficiency as the true character of non-discrimination law. It has no distributive function in itself. Basically, according to Somek, 'anti-discrimination law is ... a strategy of calibrating and strengthening market rationality'.[46]

In the US, compulsory retirement is long since prohibited – arguably an aim of the ADEA.[47] From the very beginning, US non-discrimination law has been a measure to – albeit among other things – come to terms with the hegemonic employment-at-will doctrine that is a substitute for

---

43 Numhauser-Henning (2015), above n 25.

44 It is reflected in case law that once compulsory retirement sets in work beyond pensionable age typically/frequently is given the form of fixed-term employment. Cases such as *Georgiev* and *Fuchs and Köhler* show us that in certain professions, the compulsory retirement regime comes with an institutionalized order of (only) fixed-term work openings. On the other hand, should the ban be upheld, the complex process of terminating a permanent employment promotes fixed-term employment of (also) older employees in general. It is notable, however, that although compulsory retirement is legally accepted by the CJEU, compulsory retirement is far from a general practice in EU Member States. According to a 2011 report, based on the situation per 31 December 2009, 24 of 29 Member States did have a set age for automatic termination (compulsory retirement), concerning specific professions and/or public employees. However, 23 out of 29 Member States *did not* have a general rule on compulsory retirement that was also applicable to the private sector; D O'Dempsey and A Beale, *Age and Employment* (Report from the Network of Legal Experts in the Non-Discrimination Field to the European Commission 1 July 2011).

45 A Somek, *Engineering Equality* (Oxford University Press 2011).

46 Ibid, 151. Cf also Numhauser-Henning (2015), above n 25.

47 Cf Adnett and Hardy (2007), above n 26, 36.

employment protection.[48] No doubt, the flexibilization of both labour-market production and employment practices is also an important reality in the US, but it is not so obviously linked to the destruction of employment protection devices. The protective dimension of accepting compulsory retirement in the EU setting – and thus justifying direct age discrimination as part of the mandatory retirement theory – does not really fit the US perspective. (Upholding) a ban on age discrimination is 'a stand in' for employment protection both in the US and in the EU – but with opposing starting points. In an EU setting, not upholding the ban is a way to defend employment protection as it stands. Mandatory retirement is a *sine qua non* for traditional European employment protection.

Adnett and Hardy thus describe in their 2007 article the introduction of precisely EU age discrimination law in terms of 'Americanizing' the European social model.[49] They, too, see the establishment of equal treatment or non-discrimination regulation as first and foremost related to market function, or in the case of the EU to expanding economic integration. Nevertheless, their conclusion is that the EU ban on age discrimination in the Employment Equality Directive is 'a very peculiar attempt to Americanize the European Social Model'.[50] This seems even more so, given the way the ban on age discrimination has worked in the end, still accepting compulsory retirement.

Let's take a look at this from the perspective of the individual vs. societal dichotomy. The presence of a general equal treatment principle within the 'Legal Principles Dimension' in Doron's 'Multi-dimensional Model of Elder Law' sends, as Doron says, 'a positive message regarding the status of the elderly in society' – 'its implicit notion of normalization' makes the older population an integral and equal part of society.[51] Generally speaking, this universalism works to promote autonomy and individual approaches to elder law. However, the ambiguous design of the ban on age discrimination in the European setting, allowing for a relatively broad scope of justification of direct age discrimination, gives room for a continued paternalistic approach accompanied by collective institutionalist solutions. Accepting compulsory retirement can thus be

---

48 Adnett and Hardy (2007), above n 26, 39, with reference to Neumark and Stock, suggest that age discrimination laws in the US have led to a greater use of Lazear contracts – standard employment contracts with a certain amount of stability.

49 Adnett and Hardy (2007), above n 26.

50 Ibid 40.

51 Doron (2009), above n 2, 61.

seen as an action in defence of the standard employment contract and against the older employee's individual rights to non-discrimination. In that sense this justified practice works against individual rights and autonomy – compulsory retirement can be seen as a paternalistic intrusion in individual life. It defends the traditional order, upholding the relationship between the standard employment contract and associated employment protection rights, but also rules on mandatory retirement and the standard pension contract. Not upholding the ban can thus be seen as a paternalistic approach, protecting a traditional social order with paternalistic traits.

Regarding the collective approach, Suk has argued along much the same lines as I do here, in relation not only to age but also sex discrimination law, as mandatory maternity leave can be seen as a parallel to mandatory retirement in its paternalistic character – acceptable in the EU but not in the US.[52] She ascribes this to different understandings of the state's role in advancing equality.

> In the United States, employment equality is closely tied to preserving individuals' choice to work, whereas in Europe, employment equality requires collectively imposed norms about the role of work in a person's life cycle. The comparison highlights the tradeoffs between protecting individual autonomy and combating the social and economic forces that undermine equality.[53]

Suk identifies two distinctive theories of the relationship between equality and individual choice. 'In the United States employment equality requires individuals' choices to work to remain unconstrained by group-based stereotypes. In Europe, equality requires a set of shared norms about the role of work in a human being's life cycle, which are maintained by collective coordination and threatened by individual exercises of choice.'[54] It is about different theories of the liberal state. Mandatory maternity leave goes further than mandatory retirement practices – these rules are truly compulsory and even criminalized in some Member States if the employer violates them. In addition, the justification – the health and safety of pregnant workers/new mothers (but also stereotyped mothering) – is clearly paternalistic. Even collective action justifications are argued, a purpose being to remove the minimum standard from employer-employee negotiations.

---

[52] J C Suk, 'From antidiscrimination to equality: Stereotypes and the life cycle in the United States and Europe' (2012) 60 Am J Comp L 75.

[53] Ibid 75.

[54] Ibid 76.

Suk draws our attention to what she calls 'the legal double helix' of equal protection and substantive due process.[55] Liberty/equality norms amalgamate in a hybrid norm reflecting 'the understanding that the state should not impose a particular vision of the good life on individuals in a pluralistic society'.[56] This legal double helix of equal protection and substantive due process thus characterizes the view on mandatory maternity leave, simultaneously reflecting women's equality claims with anti-paternalistic liberty claims that aim to protect individuals' rights to choose employment options/family constitution, free of traditional gender stereotypes. This is reflected in the famous case *Cleveland Board of Education v. LaFleur*,[57] where a public school required pregnant school teachers to go on unpaid leave for seven months. This policy was rejected not only on equal treatment grounds but also on the Supreme Court's 'substantive due process theory' that invalidates mandatory maternity leave. There was thus a right 'to be free from unwarranted governmental intrusion into matters so fundamentally affecting a person as the decision whether to bear or beget a child'.[58] The Due Process Clause was violated when the state presumed the generalization that pregnant women are incapacitated, unduly penalizing a female teacher for deciding to bear a child.[59] In *LaFleur* it was about the fundamental right to bear a child; in other cases the right to choose to work has been the main concern.[60] With regard to the legal double helix metaphor this amounts much to the same. Thus, in his dissenting opinion in *LaFleur*, then-Justice Rehnquist made a connection precisely between mandatory maternity leave and mandatory retirement, in this case drawing our attention to 'the jeopardy in which the Court's opinion places longstanding statutes providing for mandatory retirement of government employees'[61] with reference to the parallel fundamental right to pursue one's occupation. Lately, courts have also invalidated compulsory retirement schemes with reference to the hybrid equality-liberty norm just described.[62]

Europe, on the other hand, is described as justifying mandatory laws 'as a means of promoting the availability of a balanced lifestyle (whether

---

55 Ibid 84 with reference to L H Tribe, 'Lawrence v. Texas: The "Fundamental Right" that dare not speak its name' (2004) Harv L Rev 1892, 1898.

56 Suk (2012), above n 52, 88.

57 *Cleaveland Board of Education v. LaFleur* 414 US.

58 Ibid at 640.

59 Ibid at 648.

60 See, for instance, *Bradwell v. Illinois*, 83 US 130 (1872).

61 These rules were later abolished by legislation!

62 See Suk (2012), above n 52, 89 with further references.

desired or not) for all'.[63] 'European-style mandatory maternity leave (with or without mandatory paternity leave) would disturb the American hybrid substantive due process-equal protection constitutional norm', concludes Suk, as 'the intertwining of liberty and equality has always infused US anti-discrimination law, particularly its challenges to labor regulations protecting women'.[64]

The legal double helix of equal protection and substantive due process in US non-discrimination law can be viewed as an interesting 'parallel' to the European double bind. However, this hybrid norm takes its two intertwined helices from the same pole/side of our dichotomy – the individual approach with its (neo-)liberal connotations. Therein it also confirms the basic difference between the US and Europe as argued here, and by no means the tension between an individual approach to equality and welfare state considerations at a more collective level.

The analysis so far in this chapter of the EU ban on age discrimination has been made mainly from a labour law point of view. Given that non-discrimination devices – as argued above and with Somek – are an important measure in relation to the process of flexibilization of work, from the individual older worker's point of view it may seem important also to be one of/included in the groups protected by such regulation in the European setting. On the other hand, it may well be for the best – at least in Europe, where employment protection devices still exist along with fairly high standards of statutory and occupational pension schemes – to be covered by an accommodated retirement scheme. The alternative, as I have discussed elsewhere, may well be an ultimate process of flexibilization of both work and pensions.[65] Suk poses the crucial question in relation to mandatory maternity leave: 'does it [, that is, not accepting such leave as mandatory,] reflect the importance of work to women's dignity and self-worth, or the tragic and undesirable consequence of a competitive labour market structured around male norms?'[66]

Older workers thus may be better off upholding decent, although collective, retirement orders than striving on their own to maintain a reasonable standard in their old age. Here also, the vulnerability approach presents itself as an alternative argument to support exceptions from the equality approach and the limited ability of equality theory to come to terms with structural and political inequalities in the real world. Formal equality within liberal law design is thus elitist in character and does not

---

63 De Búrca (2012), above n 29, 13.
64 Suk (2012), above n 52, 88.
65 Numhauser-Henning (2015), above n 25.
66 Suk (2012), above n 52, 79.

really challenge the existing allocation of resources and power, although bans on indirect discrimination that challenge existing 'reference norms' may do so to a somewhat greater extent than bans on direct discrimination.[67]

3. GENERAL WELFARE DEVELOPMENTS AND OLD AGE – EU AND THE WELFARE STATE IN FLUX

This chapter is intended to provide a better understanding of the European social model and recent developments in relation to the individual vs. societal dichotomy. Here, I will explore EU law developments as such and also more general welfare developments.

According to the Lisbon Treaty the EU is 'a highly competitive social market economy' (Article 3.3 TEU).[68] The social facet is reflected in additional aims listed in the Article itself, such as full employment, combating of social exclusion and discrimination, promotion of social justice and protection as well as equality between women and men and solidarity between generations. According to the EU 2020 Strategy, this is to be achieved through 'smart, sustainable and inclusive growth'.[69] The European Community – and later the EU – was long seen first and foremost as an economic project: it was designed to create an internal market. A social dimension has successively developed throughout the years. Nevertheless, a 'decoupling' of economic and social integration was long seen as a basic characteristic (and flaw) of the EU[70] and Fredman has developed the argument that its origin in an internal 'free market' has always threatened to prioritize economic freedom ahead of

---

67 Numhauser-Henning (2015), above n 25; and A Christensen, 'Structural aspects of anti-discriminatory legislation and processes of normative change' in A Numhauser-Henning (ed.), *Legal Perspectives on Equal Treatment and Non-Discrimination* (Kluwer Law International 2001).

68 Cf also the Lisbon Strategy 2000 – Presidency Conclusions, Lisbon European Council, 23 and 24 March 2000, 'Putting decisions into practice: A more coherent and systematic approach'. The claim of the EU was to be 'the world's most competitive knowledge-based economy while maintaining a European Social Model'.

69 COM(2010) 2020 final.

70 See F Scharpf, 'The European social model: Coping with the challenges of diversity' (2002) J Common Mark Stud 645.

social rights, a basically domestic domain.[71] Whereas economic integration at EU level has been constitutionalized through individual rights – such as the four basic freedoms regarding workers, services, establishment and capital – social integration has mainly focused on coordinating still-different national models of social law and policy. No doubt, the label 'social market economy' and giving treaty status to the Charter of Fundamental Rights have been taken to further the social policy concerns at EU level,[72] making social policy, social cohesion, consumer protection and public health 'shared competences' (Articles 4, 14 and 168(4) TFEU). Nevertheless, EU solutions to social imbalances resulting from European economic integration are still more than a highly topical endeavour.[73] The CJEU's continued judicial activism concerning EU market freedoms of services, establishment and capital, reflected inter alia in the *Laval* and *Viking* cases,[74] has prompted comprehensive debates on continued market hegemony; other initiatives by the Commission have been labelled 'as pushing neoliberalism with undue emphasis'.[75] In the wake of these developments, one could expect a less clear-cut divide between the US and the EU in relation to the individual vs. societal dichotomy.

In Section 2 I elaborated on how the social market ambition manifests itself in the area on non-discrimination law and precisely regarding the ban on age discrimination with its double bind and conflicting individual and collective approaches. In this section I will briefly address overall

---

[71] S Fredman, 'Transformation or dilution: Fundamental rights in the EU social space' (2006) 12 (1) Eur L J 41.

[72] Cf Fredman (2006), above n 71, and D Schiek, 'Transnational collective labour agreements in Europe' in M Rönnmar (ed.), *EU Industrial Relations v National Industrial Relations, Comparative and Interdisciplinary Perspectives* (Wolters Kluwer 2008) 85 with footnote 8. See also D Schiek, 'Re-embedding economic and social constitutionalism: Normative perspectives for the EU' in D Schiek, U Lambert and H Schneider (eds), *European Economic and Social Constitutionalism after the Treaty of Lisbon* (Cambridge Books Online 2015).

[73] See further, for instance, D Schiek, U Lambert and H Schneider (eds), *European Economic and Social Constitutionalism after the Treaty of Lisbon* (Cambridge Books Online 2015) as well as U Neergaard, R Nielsen and L Roseberry (eds), *Integrating Welfare Functions into EU Law: From Rome to Lisbon* (DJØF 2009).

[74] *Laval* C-341/05 EU:C:2007:809 and *ITWU, FSU v. Viking Line ABP, OU Viking Line Eesti* C-438/05 EU:C:2007:772.

[75] Schiek, Lambert and Schneider (2015), above n 73, 2. See also, for instance, N Countouris and M Freedland (eds), *Resocialising Europe in a Time of Crisis* (Cambridge University Press 2013).

developments in other areas of the social dimension and welfare society such as social security and elder care.

The welfare state as we know it, and in terms of institutionalized social security, developed from the late 1900s onward.[76] Social security has been described in terms of a complement to wage-work society, designed to address the risks typically implied by this way of organizing society. It was about covering the period after wage work, during pensioned years and including widowhood, but also for shorter breaks due to illness, unemployment and, eventually, childbirth and child-rearing.[77] In the period following the Second World War, therefore, complex welfare societies had developed throughout Europe, informing in intrinsic ways the function of both individuals and markets. Welfare society was thus a companion to industrialization, just like – at least in Europe – the standard employment contract. Despite this common basis, resulting welfare societies have been described in terms of different models or regimes, also within Europe. The most famous categorization is probably that of Esping-Andersen.[78] He identifies three main regimes: the 'liberal' welfare state of the Anglo-Saxon world with typically modest or means-tested support mechanisms, the 'corporatist' or conservative welfare state of Germany and other central-south European countries built on contributions and family derived rights, and the 'social-democratic' regime of Scandinavia, built on universalism as a standard that also permits the inclusion of middle-class people. Later on, Esping-Andersen revisited his categorization of welfare regimes in the post-industrial perspective, including demographic ageing and the malfunction of labour markets and family.[79] This malfunction, says Esping-Andersen, lies in the interaction between the composite parts 'forming' contemporary welfare regimes – that is, labour markets, family and the welfare state. The Anglo-Saxon regime is characterized as basically market-biased, whereas the Scandinavian model combines universalism with individualization. As for the corporatist or conservative regime, Esping-Andersen distinguishes between southern Europe (and Japan and the Antipodes!) as 'powerfully familialistic'. In this fourth 'Mediterranean welfare regime', the unit of

---

76 F Ewald, *L'Etat Providence* (B Grasset 1986).

77 Cf A Christensen, 'Normativa grundmönster i pensionssystemet' in C Henrichsen, A Storgaard and J Vedsted-Hansen (eds), *Lovens Liv, Festskrift till Jörgen Dalberg-Larsen* (DJØF 2000).

78 G Esping-Andersen, *The Three Worlds of Welfare Capitalism* (Polity Press 1990).

79 G Esping-Andersen, *Social Foundations of Postindustrial Economics* (Oxford University Press 1999).

social protections, social rights and redistributive attention is the family (via the male breadwinner) rather than an economic status group (corporation), and one characteristic is the extremely residual nature of social assistance programmes.[80] Nevertheless, Esping-Andersen concludes that the 'threefold' categorization will suffice for most purposes. Moreover, as a result of time, most of today's social security regimes in Europe involve a mix of all these models.

Typically speaking, European welfare societies have organized life at collective level in a three-phase model with precisely age as a social stratifier: phase one consists of childhood and education, phase two represents active life in a wage-work society, and phase three is the idle 'after life'.[81] However, social change in terms of post-industrial society – and also women's emancipation and ageing populations – has implied profound change in welfare society as well. As Schiek says: '[i]n short, rigid life-course patterns are no longer adequate, and related patterns of employment and social policy are increasingly dysfunctional'.[82] This transformation started in the 1980s to 1990s and has been characterized by economization, risk-transformation and individualization.[83] The challenge is about ensuring that 'old' social risk policies continue to function effectively, despite 'new' economic and demographic pressures, and efficiently meeting 'new' social risks with new policy developments.[84] New social risks management is often formulated in terms of supporting independence – and thus individualism and autonomy – whereas old social risks are more about managing dependence in terms of collective and even paternalistic solutions. The direction of change can be described as a development from social solutions to social problems to economic solutions, shifting finally to what is mainly regarded as economic problems with cost cuts as an important goal. In addition – although at different levels in different societies – it implies a 'risk shift' from the

---

80 Cf also M Ferrera, 'The "Southern Model" of welfare in social Europe' (1996) 6(1) J Eur Soc Policy 17–37.

81 Cf Christensen (2000), above n 77.

82 D Schiek, 'Age discrimination before the ECJ – Conceptual and theoretical issues' (2011) 48 CML Rev 777. See also D Anxo, G Bosh and J Rubery (eds), *The Welfare State and Life Transitions: A European Perspective* (Edward Elgar Publishing 2010).

83 Cf J Zinn, 'Risk, social inclusion and the life course – Review of developments in policy and research' (2013) 12 Soc Policy Soc 319 and Esping-Andersen (1999), above n 79, Ch 3.

84 P Taylor-Gooby, 'New social risks in postindustrial society: Some evidence on responses to active labour market policies from Eurobarometer' (2004) 57(3) Int Soc Sec Rev 45.

state to communities, families and individuals.[85] So far, generally speaking, post-industrial adaptation of the European welfare states can be said to draw them more towards the US situation. Solutions to new social risks are now harder to come by, not only due to the character of the risks themselves but also due to the fact that these typically concern marginalized or vulnerable groups in society that are less likely to engender a broad understanding/legitimacy.[86] This is especially true for the current transitional period of moving away from old social risk regimes. In fact, the acceptance of compulsory retirement just described in Section 2 above is an example of a prolonged compromise with old social risk schemes in the midst of a new social risk regime in terms of non-discrimination regulation. Broader attempts to bridge this shift have (nevertheless) been made at EU level, for instance in the 2020 Strategy and the additional Integrated Economic and Employment Guidelines in terms of activation, adaptability, lifelong learning, gender equality, integration of vulnerable groups and, more generally speaking, inclusive societies.

As can be expected there are considerable differences among the EU Member States in confronting new social risks – and the downsizing of the welfare state – due to historical characteristics such as those forming the basis for Esping-Andersen's different welfare regimes. There seems to be a policy of 'corporatist inclusion' through employment, with somewhat different standards of obligation in countries such as France and Germany; more generally inclusive strategies in Sweden providing good access to work and benefits; and weaker policies in the UK, with negative activation through obligation and only targeted activation policies.[87] Such differences – but also some similarities – among some Member States, especially in relation to older workers/retirees, are interestingly reflected in Chapter 8 of this book. A final conclusion, comparing elder reforms in the Netherlands, Sweden, Poland and the UK, is thus the identification of an increased acceptance of neoliberal ideologies across the Member States studied, resulting in 'a growing individualization of the risks of ageing, a focus on (bounded) individual

---

[85] Cf J Hacker, *The Great Risk Shift: The Assault on American Jobs, Families, Health Care, and Retirement* (Oxford University Press 2006) but also U Beck, *Risk Society: Towards a New Modernity* (Sage 1992) and A Giddens, *The Third Way: The Renewal of Social Democracy* (Polity Press 1998).

[86] This is the main hypothesis of Taylor-Gooby (2004), above n 84.

[87] Cf Taylor-Gooby (2004), above n 84.

choice, and a potential retreat from government or collective action and intervention'.[88]

Various studies in the Norma Elder Law Research Environment and related research have concerned other aspects of this restructuring of the welfare state. Per Norberg has described how the normative foundations of Swedish public security schemes concerning sickness and unemployment have always differed – sickness being compensated at a higher level than unemployment – and how this normative characteristic in relation to recent reforms creates difficulties in the current social setting of more flexible and competitive labour markets.[89] Stendahl, too, describes the amendments in the Swedish sickness insurance – away from long-term protection of the established position in terms of the income-replacement principle towards a more market-functional logic.[90]

The Swedish pension reform in the late 1990s is an example of 'successful' pension reform in the wake of both globalization and population ageing.[91] It was thus built on a broad understanding among all social actors, facilitated by a common awareness of shortcomings of the previous system, and despite its character of a shift away from a defined benefits scheme built on the best 15 years of pay to a more 'sustainable' defined contributions scheme related to lifelong earnings in actuarial terms.[92] Notwithstanding, there are still important protective traits at 'collective' level in this new scheme, such as very generous rules on pension benefits for child-rearing years (to counteract gender effects of the new scheme) and for periods when the individual has relied upon different types of social security benefits.

These are but examples of the downsizing of European welfare states considered 'typical' of our time. In the European setting, however, the

---

[88] See also A Blackham, 'Addressing the ageing workforce: A critical examination of legal policy objectives and values in the United Kingdom' (2016) Ageing Soc April 1; M Kullmann, 'Extending working life: The Dutch government's response' (2016) 1 Eur Lab L J 31; A Zbyszewska, 'Active aging policies in Poland: At the intersection of welfare state restructuring and labour market reregulation' (2016) Int J Comp Lab Law and Indus Relations (forthcoming); and H Pettersson, 'Managing the ageing population: Swedish legal approaches to older workers in the 1970s and the 2010s (unpublished manuscript).

[89] P Norberg, *Inkomstskyddet vid övergång från sjukskrivning till arbete eller arbetslöshet* (Iustus 2014).

[90] S Stendahl, 'Social otrygghet som värde – den nya incitamentsbaserade sjukförsäkringen, Om inkomstbortfall, skyddad position, normative grundmönster och rättens nivåer' (2015) 128(3–4) TfR 295.

[91] See also Inghammar, Norberg and Brokelind, Chapter 10 in this book.

[92] Cf Christensen (2000), above n 77.

European Convention of Human Rights (ECHR) and the European Court of Human Rights's interpretation of these rights in recent case law comprise an important obstacle to total degradation of the welfare state. The convention protects not only pension rights but also other social security rights as property rights, under Article 1 of Additional Protocol 1 to the ECHR, eventually in conjunction with the prohibition of discrimination provided in Article 14 ECHR.[93]

Elder care and nursing homes are other central aspects of elderly life. Doctoral student Mirjam Katzin is currently writing her thesis about 'Citizens as customers – social rights and the marketization of elder care' within the Norma Elder Law Research Environment. The reason is, of course, that this is a relevant approach to elder care, in the development of this care in Swedish society from mainly publicly organized care in the 1970s towards privatization and choice, accompanied by increased family responsibility, in the past two decades. Such developments clearly represent a shift/movement from collectively organized solutions 'equal to all' into more individualized solutions implying free choice, while also at the same time placing responsibility on the individual and family.[94] It is obvious that the 'responsibilizing' of family is but another way to organize welfare in terms of state abstention. This development thus represents a strengthening of the individual side of the dichotomy discussed here. Kapp has described the nursing-home industry in the US and its complex legal system of rules, regulations, and case law, as ever more elaborate supervision and control. Kapp himself argues instead for an 'autonomy model' based precisely on consumer choice within a competitive marketplace, very much like the one recently introduced in Sweden (without the detailed supervisory regulation!).[95] Given the different starting points of the US and Sweden/Europe's relation to the

---

[93] Cf, for instance, ECtHR 16 December 1974, *Müller v. Austria,* Decision 5849/72 53; ECtHR 20 July 1971, *X. v. the Netherlands*, Decision 4130/69 9; ECtHR 23 February 1995, *Gasus Dosier- und Fördertechnik GmbH v. the Netherlands,* 15375/89 para 53; and ECtHR 18 November 2004, *Pravednaya v. Russia,* 69529/01. See further, for instance, M De Pauw, 'Interpreting the European Convention on Human Rights in light of emerging human rights issues, an older person's perspective' (2014) Hum Rts & Intl Legal Discourse 2.

[94] See M Katzin, 'Valfrihet istället för jämlikhet – förändrade målsättningar för äldreomsorgspolitiken?'(2014) (3–4) Socialvetenskaplig Tidskrift 310–27. Cf also Pettersson and Katzin, Chapter 12 in this book.

[95] B M Kapp, *The Law and Older Persons: Is Geriatric Jurisprudence Therapeutic?* (Carolina Academic Press 2003) 102–3. Cf also I Wendt and A Gideon, 'Services of general interest provision through the third sector under EU competition law constraints: The example of organising healthcare in England,

respective poles of the individual vs. societal dichotomy, this situation appears a bit surprising: suddenly, Sweden is representing a 'model' as regards individual choice.

The decline of the welfare state has been ascribed to post-industrial societies' struggle to harmonize welfare claims with economic efficiency in a globalized world. The EU, with its still 'asymmetric' constitutionalization of economic and social rights, respectively, has been accused – also after the adoption of the Lisbon Treaty – of undermining the achievements of the continental and social-democratic welfare state, making the EU a 'testing ground for the turf battle between national welfare states and EU market making'.[96] Still, the EU is 'believed to be capable of responding to economic challenges in more or less socially solidaristic ways'.[97] Although the welfare society is thus being called into question in Europe in recent decades, and market logic is gaining ground, there is still no doubt that the concept of the welfare state is still 'alive and kicking' in Europe as compared to the US.[98]

4. CONCLUDING REMARKS

The individual vs. societal dichotomy is thus regarded as a characteristic of elder law, as is the autonomy vs. paternalism dichotomy. At the same time, elder law has been described as 'inherently' paternalistic. In my opinion, both dichotomies address the same issues to a large degree: the individual vs. societal dichotomy does so at an organizational/

Wales and the Netherlands' in Schiek, Lambert and Schneider (2015), above n 73, comparing the UK (mainly traditionally public providers) with the Netherlands (well-established private providers). U Neergaard, 'Services of general economic interest under EU law constraints' Schiek, Lambert and Schneider (2015), above n 73, sees the hitherto hegemony of EU competition law rules as a threat towards a proper functioning of services of general economic interest, though.

[96] U Liebert, 'Reconciling market with Social Europe? The EU under the Lisbon Treaty' in Schiek, Lambert and Schneider (2015), above n 73, 63 with further reference to Leibfried. See also Schiek (2015), above n 72, 41.

[97] Liebert (2015), above n 96, 65.

[98] Cf for instance, Countouris and Freedland (2013), above n 75; M Rigaux, J Buelens and A Latinne (eds), *From Labour Law to Social Competition Law?* (Intersentia 2014) and Schiek, Lambert and Schneider (2015), above n 73.

institutionalist level and the autonomy vs. paternalism dichotomy does so at a value level. Autonomy may well also be seen as the opposite of dependency in an independence vs. dependence dichotomy. Fineman's theory of all humans as basically 'vulnerable' is helping to bridge the apparent contradiction between a genuinely individualistic/autonomy approach and a more societal – and thus easily paternalistic – approach in regard to the efforts to overcome the challenges of growing old/old age.

The intrinsic relationship between individual rights and collective solutions is particularly well reflected in EU age discrimination regulation, with its weak design and 'double bind' resulting in continued acceptance of direct age discrimination and with the acceptance of compulsory or mandatory retirement as perhaps the most extreme example. These practices are in stark contrast to US non-discrimination law, whether in relation to old age and mandatory retirement or gender discrimination. What Suk has called the 'legal double helix' or the hybrid norm of liberty and equality thus reflects the understanding that the state should not impose a particular vision of the good life on individuals in a pluralistic society 'premised on normative, arguably paternalistic, judgments about the proper role of work in the lives of new mothers and old persons'.[99] European mandatory retirement, on the other hand, 'can itself be understood as promoting the equality of vulnerable labor market participants'.[100]

> Mandatory retirement is primarily a way in which a democratic state effectuates its citizens' shared substantive conception of what it means to age and exit from the labour market with dignity ... In Europe, the state pursues equality by promoting a normative vision of the ideal life cycle, one which involves balancing work with other worthwhile pursuits, such as parenting (and mothering in particular), vacations, and leisure in old age. Regulations aim to make this life cycle available to all, even if it requires restricting some individuals' choices.[101]

No doubt the European practices concerning non-discrimination and not least compulsory retirement represent a paternalistic stand on the role of work in everybody's life; thus they work against autonomy and free choice at the individual level. In fact, the continued acceptance of compulsory retirement in general terms is a reflection – and a defence – of the standard employment contract as developed during the former century in combination with the standard pension contract and as a

99 Suk (2012), above n 52, 97.
100 Ibid 89.
101 Suk (2012), above n 52, 96ff.

complement to social security. This goes hand in hand with employment protection devices developed in Europe (and to some extent in EU law) during the same period. No doubt, and again as Suk states, 'as societies become increasingly pluralistic, such normative visions are less shared and the state's promotion of them seems injurious to those who reject the traditional roles assigned to women and older people'.[102] This exclusion will also apply to all those who, due to globalization and flexibilization of labour markets, no longer fit the traditional trade-off in industrialized society and complementary pension and social security schemes.

On the other hand, de Búrca has pointed to how the US 'is criticized for its implicit insistence that all citizens are able-bodied, willing and active market participants at all stages of their lives, and for neglecting the welfare and dignity especially of those individuals who are not'.[103] Perhaps we can see the EU's 'weaker template' of precisely age discrimination bans (and the compulsory character of maternity rights) as 'difficult trade-offs between an equality law focused on combating stereotypes and an equality law that combats the totality of social, economic, and cultural forces that produce inequality'.[104] As I see it, this involves the age-old question of formal vs. substantive equality all over again. In addition, interventions at societal level may well be required, not only to protect but also to support and empower the older individual.

This chapter is thus about the individual vs. societal dichotomy. As it has turned out – in a US and European/EU setting – it is as much about the market (made up by individuals and free choice) and welfare state mechanisms. Whereas EU discrimination law thus accommodates both individual and societal approaches to equality, general welfare developments in both EU law and the Member States can be described as increasingly biased towards 'marketization', to the detriment of its social dimension. This is due to the continuing asymmetrical constitutionalization of market freedoms as compared to social rights, despite treaty amendments in line with the concept of a 'Social Market Economy'. This is also due to general developments in terms of technological evolution and globalization.

Despite a more or less clear trend towards increased marketization and decreasing welfare institutions everywhere, Europe has still not given up on its social ambitions – that is, if we are to believe legal scholarly discourse. In addition, within economic science, ideas have been put

102 Ibid 97.
103 De Búrca (2012), above n 29, 13.
104 Suk (2012), above n 52, 98.

forth about overcoming the dualist thinking of market vs. the social state.[105] 'Dichotomising the institutional world into "the market" as contrasted to "the state" has been proven "grossly inadequate" and misleading, if not a dangerous "oversimplification of our design options".'[106] However, it has also been said that the recent global financial and economic crisis has slowed the progress of the EU's search for a stable normative and institutional order[107] – not least as regards a social dimension in welfare terms and collective solutions. This is even more true in light of the current refugee/immigration crisis!

105 Cf E Ostrom, *Governing the Commons* (Cambridge University Press 1990) as well as *Understanding Institutional Diversity* (Princeton University Press 2005) and also Esping-Andersen (1999), above n 79, 178ff.

106 Ostrom (2005), above n 105, 256.

107 Schiek, Lambert and Schneider (2015), above n 73, 4.

5. Vulnerability and ageing

Titti Mattsson and Mirjam Katzin

1. INTRODUCTION[1]

This chapter aims to discuss and investigate the usefulness of Martha Albertson Fineman's vulnerability theory as a theoretical framework and analytical tool for elder law. An increasingly ageing population is a global demographic trend of our time that is threatening to cause severe economic and social challenges in the near future.[2] The growth of ageing populations worldwide has led to intensive discussions about the urgency of addressing the rights and roles of older persons; many observers argue that a rising number of older persons will greatly increase dependency on social welfare systems. For example, the EU 2015 Ageing Report analyses the economic and budgetary impact of an ageing population over the long term and presents a forecast for increasing expenditures to cover pensions, unemployment, healthcare, long-term care, and education transfers for the Member States.[3]

The elder-law discipline in Europe and the United States has developed in order to address legal considerations with regard to older people's situations, needs and difficulties and how these relate to organizational and structural circumstances in society.[4] Discussions are needed to determine approaches to the discipline on a theoretical level, theories and methods that should be used and the overarching research goals to be

---

[1] This work was carried out within the Norma Elder Law Research Environment (www.jur.lu.se/elderlaw) funded by Ragnar Söderberg's Foundation and the Marianne and Marcus Wallenberg Foundation.

[2] For a description and analysis of the demographic situation and its expected consequences for society, see for example Scott, Chapter 2 in this book.

[3] European Commission 2015.

[4] Cf Ann Numhauser-Henning, 'Äldrerätt – ett nytt forskningsfält inför stora utmaningar' in Kirsten Ketscher, Kåre Lilleholt, Eyvind Smith and Aslak Syse (eds), *Velferd och Rettferd. Festskrift till Asbjörn Kjönstad 70 år* (Gyldendal Juridisk 2013) 433, 435.

pursued. There is also a need to discuss whether elder law should focus on older people as a group based on biological age and its legal status, or if the discipline could extend to a more general, lifespan-oriented research field. Ageing is a basic human condition which by necessity influences the relationship between the state and the individual in different ways.

One way to approach research questions about the state and the judicial system in relation to ageing is to analyse society's obligation to provide the resources and institutions required to overcome vulnerability and shortcomings during citizens' lifespans; this calls for the use of the vulnerability theory developed by Martha Fineman. Fineman's concern is to approach social-responsibility issues by factoring in the individual's whole lifespan. The focus is not on an individual's claims in a particular case, but on a more general level, encompassing policy issues relevant for both today's elderly and the elderly of the future.[5] This theory is an integrated part of the Norma Elder Law Research Environment and has been applied by several of the researchers in the group.[6]

In short, Fineman argues that the core of being human is to be vulnerable, and not autonomous, free and independent, as is often

---

[5] Titti Mattsson, 'National ombudsman for the elderly: A solution for a more responsive welfare state?' (2013) 36 (3/142) Retfaerd 22.

[6] See for example, Helene Brodin and Titti Mattsson, 'Lägst ner på skalan? Hälso- och sjukvårdens bemötande av äldre kvinnor som migrerat till Sverige' (2014) 21 Socialvetenskaplig Tidskrift 372; Mirjam Katzin, 'Tillbaka till familjen: privat och offentligt ansvar i den svenska äldreomsorgen' (2014a) 37 (2/145) Retfaerd 37; Mirjam Katzin, 'Valfrihet istället för jämlikhet – förändrade målsättningar för äldreomsorgspolitiken?' (2014b) 21 Socialvetenskaplig Tidskrift 310; Titti Mattsson, 'Participation for all? Challenges and tools for realizing the goal with focus on health services' in Marlies Hesselman, Antenor Hallo de Wolf and Brigit Toebes (eds), *Socio-Economic Human Rights in Essential Public Services Provision* (Human Rights Law Series, Routledge Press 2016) 205–21; Titti Mattsson, 'E-government for the distribution of public services in Sweden: Privatization, vulnerability and social responsibility reshaped' in Martha Fineman, Ulrika Andersson and Titti Mattsson (eds), *Privatization, Vulnerability, and Social Responsibility: A Comparative Perspective* (Routledge 2017) 222–36; Titti Mattsson, 'A right to active ageing for all? On the status of the elderly in social services and health care' in Ann Numhauser-Henning (ed.), *Introduction to the Norma Elder Law Research Environment: Different Approaches to Elder Law* (Lund University 2013); Mattsson (2013), above n 5; Eva Ryrstedt, 'Dementa äldre personer; vem ska bestämma' (2016) 1 Tidskrift utgiven av Juridiska Föreningen i Finland 179; Eva Ryrstedt, 'Får jag inte bestämma något själv? En studie av kvarstående bestämmanderätt hos dementa äldre' (2015) 21 Socialvetenskaplig Tidskrift 329.

asserted in jurisprudence.[7] The theory focuses on how an integrated lifespan approach can guide political and institutional practices in taking societal responsibility for the individual's dependency and vulnerability throughout life. A vulnerability analysis emphasizes our interdependency within social institutions and the need for public responsibility for our shared vulnerability. Furthermore, it provides arguments against the privatization of social need, and for a more responsive state. It also proclaims that equal opportunities can be achieved only by offering different ways that institutional frameworks can overcome vulnerable situations.

When writing about elder law, several of the researchers in the Norma Elder Law group have found it useful to argue along the lines of vulnerability, using Fineman's theory in different contexts. The theory has been applied in several fields of elder law focused upon in the Norma Elder Law Research Environment, such as social welfare law, health law, public law and family law. The authors of this chapter have written extensively using the theory. They are also part of Fineman's research group at Emory Law School in Atlanta, USA, and are founder and member respectively of the Law and Vulnerabilities research group at the Faculty of Law at Lund University, Sweden.[8]

This chapter's main focus is a presentation of Fineman's theory and how it conceptualizes vulnerability. The presentation is integrated with a discussion of the applicability of the theory for elder law research. The chapter concludes with some remarks on the challenges facing policy-makers, such as mainstream, entrenched conceptions of older people and the need to add new perspectives in research and politics.

---

[7] The following presentation of the vulnerability theory is a compilation of the central parts of Fineman's theory as described in her academic publications. The articles and books that have been used include *The Vulnerable Subject: Anchoring Equality in the Human Condition* (Princeton University Press 2013); '"Elderly" as vulnerable: Rethinking the nature of individual and societal responsibility' (2012) 20 Eur L J 71; 'Grappling with equality: One feminist journey' in Martha Fineman (ed.), *Transcending the Boundaries of Law: Generations of Feminism and Legal Theory* (Routledge Press 2011); 'The vulnerable subject and the responsive state' (2010) 60 Emory L J 251; 'The vulnerable subject: Anchoring equality in the human condition' (2008) 20(1) Yale J L and Feminism 1; and *The Autonomy Myth: A Theory of Dependency* (The New Press 2004).

[8] See further www.law.lu.se/#!lawandvulnerabilities.

2. THE VULNERABILITY THEORY AND ELDER LAW

2.1 A Theoretical Project

Elder law and societal response to older people's needs and situations can be explained by applying the theoretical lens of Fineman's vulnerability theory. Martha Albertson Fineman is the Robert W. Woodruff Professor of Law at Emory University, and one of today's leading figures of feminist legal theory. She is committed to creating and maintaining a platform for feminist and critical legal theory and has carried out groundbreaking work on the regulation of the family as an institution. Her theories reveal the discursive structures of the law and open up for new ideas how society's institutions can be constructed to include a larger public responsibility for equality and a good life for everyone.

Fineman's theoretical project during the last decade can be described as an attempt to create a new, critical narrative for the law that has its starting point in our shared vulnerability rather than a liberal conception of the autonomous and self-preserving individual. Through a feminist critique of liberal ideals, Fineman demonstrates how a societal discourse starting from individualism and autonomy works to sustain an unjust distribution of power, influence and resources.[9] Even if Fineman takes her starting point in the North American context, the framework can also be applied to a Nordic welfare state; the regulation and extent of the elder care system is entirely different, but Nordic and North American contexts manifest the same kind of tendencies, for example concerning privatization of responsibilities for older people.

Fineman's thinking can be placed in the borderland between critical theory and normative ethics of care,[10] and her theoretical project strives to transform the fundamental ideals of the law. The ethics of care is

---

[9] Mirjam Katzin, 'Det mänskliga villkoret: intervju med Martha Fineman' (2015) 50–51 Fronesis 119.

[10] See for example, Nel Noddings, an American philosopher who provides a feminist theory of care, arguing that caring is the foundation of morality. Her standpoint in *Caring: A Feminine Approach to Ethics and Moral Education* (University of California Press 1984) is that a caring relation is ethically basic to humans. Compare the care-focused feminist Carol Gilligan in *In a Different Voice* (Harvard University Press 1993), who also argues that caring is socially engendered to woman and therefore consequently devalued. In law, see for example Jonathan J Herring who has written on the law's treatment of caring and how adopting an ethic of care could transform the law in *Caring and the Law* (Hart Publishing 2013).

based on the self as deeply vulnerable, profoundly relational and interdependent. The role of the law is to promote relationships of care. Care is a universal, inevitable experience, and should therefore be recognized and valued. We are not born independent, but into caring relationships. Therefore we should focus on how the law can enable people to care, and not on individual rights and abstract general principles. This perspective problematizes the liberal ontological understanding of the autonomous individual as natural and pre-societal, with a free will and independent, as a fiction upon which the legal system is built and that ignores the societal provisions that can meet our most basic needs.

Two theoretical questions are central in Fineman's work. First, what does it mean to be human? And secondly, what does this say about how we should organize our society? This means that the theory is not concerned with specific instances of harm or injury, but with resilience against risk and harm during the life course. The theory strives to describe systems of thought in the law, with a critique of liberal ideology and autonomy as a starting point.

Vulnerability should not be understood in Fineman's work as shorthand for deservingness or as social disadvantage, but as something shared and universal.[11] As a result comparisons should not be made between individuals based on how vulnerable they are, but between states and institutions based on how good they are at providing us with resilience to our shared vulnerability. Identities are relevant to the extent that they are constructed in legal systems and used to confer privileges and power, but not in and of themselves. The theory is applicable to both elder law and other areas of law. It can be used to show how subjects are created and how autonomy and vulnerability are key concepts that can be used in the relevant discourse. Vulnerability theory analysis shifts critical attention towards the examination of privilege and the mechanisms of neoliberalism that supposedly undermine the role of the state – while in

---

11 The idea that vulnerability is a structuring feature of existence and not a condition of life that should be associated with helplessness, disempowerment and lacking capability is also a fundamental standpoint in the decade-long interdisciplinary research programme *Engaging Vulnerability* at Uppsala University (financed with the support of the Swedish Research Council and headed by Professor Don Kulick; see www.engagingvulnerability.se). There are several theorists who have used vulnerability as a central concept in their theories. See for example, Judith Butler, who argues in *Precarious Life: The Powers of Mourning and Violence* (Verso 2004) for a theory of vulnerability that is focused on the human capacity for loss, death and tragedy. For elder law, see also Jonathan J Herring, *Vulnerable Adults and the Law* (Oxford University Press 2016).

actuality the state is merely narrowing its reach to confer privilege on limited segments of the population. In this way, Fineman explains, only certain subsidies are understood as such and equated with dependency, while subsidies serving the status quo come to be viewed as 'investments' or somehow 'earned'.[12]

Fineman criticizes the idea of the autonomous subject in law. The autonomous-individual standpoint leaves out the fact that at many times in our lives, we are totally dependent on other people – as children, elderly, sick or with lesser functions – and that we therefore need society to survive. The idea of autonomy presupposes a healthy adult with capacities and resources to live independently, without relying on others or on subsidies from society. In reality, our ability to handle the risks of life depends on our context, our position and our resources, but the ever-present risks of sickness, accidents, natural disasters and death are common and universal. This approach goes against a stigmatizing tendency to talk about 'vulnerable groups' as a point of departure for redistribution and politics of equality. It also poses opposition to a limited welfare state, which reaches out only to those in need. Fineman is arguing for a legal and societal narrative originating in the shared human condition of vulnerability in a life-cycle perspective. This narrative is the basis for a legal and social order that institutionalizes a common responsibility for everyone's vulnerability, instead of conferring this obligation on the family. It implies a strong, generous and universal welfare state and a public responsibility for need, dependence and a good life.

Another criticism concerns the use of the concept 'equality' in law. Fineman argues that Western understanding of 'equality' is influenced by the philosophy of liberal individualism and the creation of the liberal subject.[13] The liberal notion of equality includes the idea that all human beings are by nature free and endowed with the same rights. Thus the understanding of equality is focused on formal equal treatment and the prohibition of discrimination; and is therefore inattentive to underlying social inequalities. Legal systems' formal notion of equality does not take into account the differences that exist between individuals, regardless of whether these differences are contextual or embodied. Close at hand is a critique of the system of rights and anti-discrimination as a starting point for equality politics, as these strategies begin with the individual as a

---

[12] Fineman (2008), above n 7, 16.

[13] For centuries the concept of 'equality' has been associated by John Locke's philosophy in *Two Treaties of Government* (first published in 1689, Ian Shapiro (ed.), Yale University Press 2003).

receiver and carrier of resources and rights and therefore miss unjust structural and institutional distribution of power. Thereby, Fineman challenges the formal notion of equality, as it leaves undisturbed or even validates existing arrangements that privilege some and disadvantage others, and does not challenge existing allocation of resources and power. Instead, she proposes a different view of equality, in which a substantial level of material and economic resources should be granted.[14]

Fineman identifies the narrative of the liberal society as the story of the social contract, using social contract theory[15] to explain that the existence of society makes individual autonomy significant and primary – as if being part of society should be based on an autonomous choice.[16] She finds the social contract to be a theoretical fiction, a metaphor used to protect the status quo, because it is portrayed to be legitimated through consent:

> Social contract theory engages the concept of individual autonomy at two fundamental levels. Paradoxically, individual autonomy is viewed in the first instance as ceded to the state in order to confer upon it the authority to preserve order. Order is preserved so that the individuals initially giving up their autonomy may enjoy future full autonomy in their interactions with each other.[17]

The metaphor of the contract imagines autonomous adults, capable and equal individuals engaged in a process employing wit, knowledge, and skill, choosing to step into society as into a contractual relationship with agreed-to conditions. The metaphor is used to justify the fact that individuals are bound by societal norms; it legitimates sanctions and sets expectations for individuals and institutions. It is thus a cornerstone of liberal thought.

---

14 Fineman (2012), above n 7, 132–4.

15 The social contract theory, in short, is the view that persons' moral and political obligations depend on a contract or agreement among those who form the society in which these persons live. A recent social-contract theorist is John Rawls; see in particular *A Theory of Justice* (Clarendon 1972).

16 The social contract theory has been criticized by several other feminists such as Carole Pateman (see *The Sexual Contract* (Stanford University Press 1988) and Susan Moller Okin (see *Justice, Gender and the Family* (Basic Books 1989)) among others.

17 Fineman (2004), above n 7, 211.

3. THE CONCEPTION OF OLDER PEOPLE IN AGEING LAW

3.1 Conflicting Norms According to the Vulnerability Theory

Studying the area of ageing law reveals the conflicting norms in the legal system and its reforms. Fineman points out how Western legislation is primarily informed by a liberal and autonomous, self-preserving subject, which is the ideal, and by stigmatizing those who appear not to live up to this ideal. When it comes to older people, they are in many ways caught between these conflicting ideas, which result in different problematic policy choices. This becomes obvious in times of demographic changes and the need for policy-making attention to these changes. Unfortunately, the debate tends to reflect certain stereotyped portraits of who older people are and what they need. Fineman highlights difficulties in the political discussions of the older population in the United States[18] that are similar to those we can see in the Swedish discussions.[19] The elderly often seem to be portrayed as either constantly dependent – in need of state protection because of illness, weakness, loneliness and sometimes lack of money – or not dependent at all, being in good health and with a financial and private situation that enables them to handle their daily lives by themselves. The norms of the autonomous subject represent various ideologies and interests, stemming from different legislative times and policy-making approaches. One task for elder law is to analyse the premises on which regulations are built and rebuilt. One way to understand these intersecting norms is to analyse the presumed legal subject of a certain context. The legal subject is a presupposed or implicit (but also sometimes explicit) abstraction, which serves as a framework for the legal system. The way we envision the legal subject informs what is reasonable in designing law. It is a figure that we use to determine what we are going to prioritize and it defines the position of the state vis-à-vis the individual.

3.2 Dependent and Stigmatized or Independent and Autonomous

The society's response to older people is often based on negative descriptions concerning their capacities and possibilities to live independently, with images of the elderly as 'needy' owing to physical and mental

---

18 Fineman (2012), above n 7, 101.

19 Mattsson (2013), above n 5, 16.

incapacity that renders them worthless for the labour market. In this situation, society is not demanding self-sufficiency and independence of older people; the older people are perceived as needing protection, and society's response is instead guided by paternalism and deprives the elderly of their agency. Capacity is something that is assigned to some people and disregarded in others. Older people are thus positioned as needing intervention to enable independence. When a group is thus constructed as a 'vulnerable group', a stigma is created as well as a border between different groups of people. The pathology of the 'welfare recipient' works to mask an existing order of inequality and the structures behind it.

Fineman points out that the older person's or the ill person's claim is based on the past, while the child's claim is based on the future. Society would rather focus on the investment in the future than on the coming death of the older person whose contributions are already made. Fineman states that societies which cut back on care are going to have a crisis with their ageing population. Part of the support for children stems from pro-natalist policies; society makes it easier for people to have children, which is why it is easier for people to see that investing in children is investing in the future. This makes the claims of the elderly more difficult to advance, because their contributions have been consumed and may thus be ignored.[20]

The liberal discourse, on the other hand, has a definition of citizenship which is autonomous and independent but also rational, self-sufficient and responsible, in which the individual pursues his or her own interest and attempts to secure property and liberty. This ideal is transferred to an increasing degree to older people, as they are portrayed as active, responsible, self-sufficient and autonomous. This tendency is a reaction to stigmas and paternalism related to old age. However, the reaction leads the discourse in a problematic direction. According to Fineman, this view of the human being as autonomous and self-sufficient is out of context and of body. In the book *The Autonomy Myth: A Theory of Dependency*, Fineman identifies the autonomous subject as the starting point for liberal democracies' legal systems, social orders and institutions. She works with analyses of how the Western legal tradition presumes a human subject that is free, independent and self-preserving and at the same time healthy, adult (but not old) and with a stable job on the regular labour market. This image does not take into account family relationships, human needs and the fragility and vulnerability of life. The autonomous role is easier

20 Katzin (2015), above n 9, 126.

to fill for the privileged individual with resources, whose risks and vulnerability are carried and balanced by others.

As we are in fact not autonomous but vulnerable and in need of support, especially in certain phases in life (such as when we are older), and if the law presupposes autonomy, this vulnerability must be carried by institutions other than the state. The primary institution for this vulnerability is the family, which becomes a repository for our inherent living conditions. According to Fineman's work, the family is therefore more than an institution used to organize reproductive duties; it is also the sphere in which our fundamental vulnerability is recognized and, at best, handled. Through Fineman's analytical framework it can be shown how the regulation of the family and of the welfare state becomes a way of marking the boundary between a public, politicized sphere and the private, depoliticized sphere, and how subjects and problems are differently constructed in relation to this boundary.[21] The idea of autonomy also works to put a restraint on the state at the same time that it professes to confer 'agency' by recognizing the individual as the primary and autonomous actor, the 'liberal subject'.[22]

Fineman identifies several fundamental flaws in the liberal idea of society and the subject. First of all, we are born into different circumstances that are unequal, and not, as the liberal idea suggests, equipped with the same possibilities to choose our life paths. The relationships into which we enter on a family, economic or societal level cannot be compared to a free-market contract situation in which we are supposed to have the same bargaining abilities. Instead, these relationships are often built on inequalities, and the idealization of contract and individual autonomous choice masks society's role in perpetuating these inequalities.[23]

4. THE STATE'S RESPONSE TO OLDER PEOPLE'S NEEDS

4.1 The Problematic Non-Interventionist Policy

Allowing the liberal ideal of the autonomous subject to inform the state's response to older people's needs will lead, according to Fineman, to a range of problematic legal and policy choices, including undervaluation

21 Fineman (2012), above n 7, 130.
22 Ibid 114.
23 Fineman (2011), above n 7, 51–2.

of care-taking, overvaluation of freedom of choice and stigmatization of groups that are seen as vulnerable and which will in turn be prone to monitoring, discipline and supervision. This effect can be shown through the way social welfare programmes differentiate between autonomy and security for older people. Fineman concludes: 'Not only is autonomy inappropriately prioritized in this comparison, safety and security are not conceptualized as necessary for its exercise.'[24]

Looking at the response of the state through a vulnerability perspective instead means highlighting how choice is made in an embedded situation and how the private/public distinction as a social construction generates our understanding of political issues. This could give insight into conflicts surrounding welfare states which are both similar to and different from the Scandinavian countries. By steadily degrading the public realm and the political influence on people's social conditions, welfare state withdrawal, privatization and marketization change the basis of citizenship from social and universal to contractual and conditional. Fineman defines privatization as an active withdrawal of the state from many areas of social life.[25] She points out that a legal system that assumes such a non-interventionist policy will ignore the unequal patterns that characterize the private sphere, and view human needs and dependencies as something that should be handled privately.[26]

4.2 Privatization of Care and Derivative Dependency

In many societies, older people's care needs are not seen as a political matter but as a private one – something that should be handled within the family or paid for privately. Even in the Scandinavian welfare states, with their relatively generous public elder care, a majority of the elder care work is performed informally by family members and unpaid.[27] An increase in the percentage of elder care being performed by relatives can also be seen in recent decades, as public elder care has been downsized.[28] This could be understood through Fineman's analysis of the construction of the dividing line between the public, political sphere and the private,

---

24 Fineman (2012), above n 7, 122.

25 Martha Fineman, Ulrika Andersson and Titti Mattsson (eds), *Privatization, Vulnerability, and Social Responsibility: A Comparative Perspective* (Routledge 2017).

26 Fineman (2008), above n 7, 5.

27 Trustee or so-called 'good-man' duties are often performed by family members; see further Ryrstedt, Chapter 15 in this book.

28 Katzin (2014a), above n 6, 37–8.

supposedly apolitical sphere. The division between public and private spheres means that problems facing individuals will be regarded not as a responsibility to society but as belonging to a different domain.[29] The notion of the division between public and private is based on the ideals of independence, self-sufficiency and agency, explaining individual failures as weaknesses or inabilities – the division between the public and private means that these failures are not regarded as the responsibility of society.[30]

The family, which is the private sphere, works in this way as a mediation institution between the state and the individual. The family operates to mediate the state's responsibility with respect to the individual, so that individual needs for social support are referred first to the family. Fineman uses the concept 'derivative dependency' to describe a dependency that is derived from the need for care that 'inevitable dependents' have. Older people who are ill need to be cared for; the fact that most of us get old and will need care is inevitable and biological. Derivative dependents are those who care for others, and they must rely on economic, emotional, physical and other kinds of resources in order to undertake that care. Derivative dependency has economic and structural dimensions. The economic dimension concerns the work situation for the unpaid care worker, for example the younger relative caring for an older person. The structural dimensions are the social factors that affect and are affected by the care work, for example who is doing the care work, for what reasons, and how it relates to the regular labour market and the prevailing social security system. Fineman shows that by turning questions about informal care work and derivative needs into a private matter, the public escapes responsibility for care for older people, at the same time that the costs for derivative dependents are made invisible. Care work, according to Fineman, should be seen as a social responsibility, and the costs should therefore be handled by the public.[31] Derivative dependency is socially constructed and connected to historical gender roles; because the family is the mechanism through which it is assigned, this inevitably leads to gendered roles within the family itself. As women take most of the care responsibilities in the family, the costs connected to this derivative dependency will also be unevenly divided between the sexes.

---

[29] Fineman (2008), above n 7, 20.
[30] Fineman (2012), above n 7, 130.
[31] Fineman (2004), above n 7, 35–45.

The resources needed to undertake unpaid informal care work are not fully recognized and are therefore provided for only to a limited extent by the public. Fineman makes a parallel to soldiering, which could also be seen as work done for the benefit of society as a whole but which is structured in a completely different way. In contrast with the case of soldiers, society does not pay taxes, create institutions, and have mechanisms to compensate for care-taking when caretakers leave their service. This comparison could reveal a way to support care work and recognize that care work has costs. In privatizing dependency within the family, the private sector and the state are let off the hook. Market institutions benefit from this organization of the family because they get workers and consumers through society's reproduction, and the state gets taxpayers and citizens. However, these institutional actors do not pay for or give support to this reproduction of society.[32]

4.3 Marketization and Freedom of Choice

Another response to older people's life situation has been to marketize care for older people, a strategy that is pursued in different ways and to different degrees in welfare states around the globe, but which can generally be spotted as a tendency of the neoliberal age. This can entail deregulation of elder care or incentives for the development of a market of privately provided elder care. In Sweden, this is done through a freedom-of-choice system in elder care, which is a quasi-market where older people could choose from a number of assigned care providers, and the care is paid for by the public. Another tendency in the same vein is tax reform, which subsidizes the purchase of elder care services on an entirely private elder care market.[33] In a marketized care system, the quality of care is assumed to be partly an individual responsibility – the care recipient is responsible for making the individual choice to leave a bad provider for a better one. This notion of the citizen as an active, rational consumer distorts the reality of the care situation and helps shift the problem to a private sphere. Potential inequalities in relation to choice are rendered invisible and possible problems are defined as private matters.[34] According to this logic, individual differences in access to and quality of elder care become natural because the outcome relates to individual preferences as well as to personal responsibility. This is

---

32 Katzin (2015), above n 9, 122–3.

33 Katzin (2014b), above n 6, 314.

34 Alexandru Panican and Torbjörn Hjort, 'Valfrihet – en utmaning för det sociala medborgarskapet' (2011) Arbetsmarknad & Arbetsliv 3, 32–3.

rationalized by a discourse justifying and normalizing market entry in all aspects of social life, based on a description of reality bound by certain economic laws of nature.[35]

The freedom-of-choice reforms in elder care presume a citizenship with a so-called 'active' dimension, which means that citizens have responsibility for their own well-being and that individuals should protect themselves against risks by exercising choice in relation to the market. The market is central to this idea and represents a place where individuals can act independently, freely and according to their own interests; this will lead – indirectly – to the outcome that is best for everyone.[36] As citizens in liberal democracies, such individuals lack strong social rights that respond to their inherent vulnerability or temporary dependency.

> Instead of social rights, we have liberty and autonomy: the right to make choices, the right to contract. This principle informs our economic, legal, and political theories and is indispensable to the rhetoric of personal responsibility that pervades current discussions about entitlement reform. The image of the autonomous liberal subject has also profoundly shaped society's responses to revelations of dependency or need.[37]

Furthermore, as Fineman argues, the general description of the autonomous subject fits better with certain privileged positions than with others. The relationships we are in, or create – social, economic or on a family level – do not operate according to the ideal of the free market and the contract situation in which we are all assumed to have the same bargaining power. Rather, the idealization of the contract and of individual choices hides the structural inequalities that exist on a societal level and thus assists in consolidating them.[38]

Fineman points out several flaws in the general description of individual choice or personal responsibility. She points out that we are born into certain social conditions that, at least partly, form our life path and the choices that we make. Furthermore, as embedded creatures, we always make choices within social contexts. Choices of welfare services can therefore be determined not only by market forces or rational choice;

---

[35] Margaret M Somers, *Genealogies of Citizenship: Markets, Statelessness and the Right to Have Rights* (Cambridge University Press 2008) 3.

[36] Björn Hvinden and Håkan Johansson (eds), *Citizenship in Nordic Welfare States: Dynamics of Choice, Duties and Participation in a Changing Europe* (Routledge Press 2007) 35–42.

[37] Fineman (2012), above n 7, 114.

[38] Fineman (2011), above n 7, 51–2.

they are always formed by institutional and other social conditions.[39] Fineman describes the differences in abilities to make choices as being a question of resilience: the assets that we have at hand when choosing and pursuing our life paths or in dealing with the downfalls of life. People generally make active attempts to manage the risks of life. However, those with greater assets will more effectively find ways to meet their needs, due to the advantages they possess. The promotion of values such as freedom of choice therefore risks enhancing the benefits for the already resourceful citizens who can use their economic, institutional, social, cultural, bodily and other assets to ensure that they get the most out of the welfare state.[40]

Privatization of welfare rests on ideas of individual autonomy and self-sufficiency – this is especially so for marketization, which presumes the market to be a place for free interaction between equals rather than a social sphere where societal structures are in action. In this way, marketization of elder care can be understood as an expression of privatization discourse that reformulates the problems of care from public to private. According to Fineman, this individualization discourse will, in turn, decontextualize care and conceal conditions and effects that are linked to structural inequalities.

5. THE VULNERABILITY APPROACH OF THE WELFARE STATE

5.1 Our Shared Vulnerability as a Starting Point

Applying vulnerability theory to welfare state policies regarding older people's care needs indicates that using autonomy as a starting point leads to unequal burden-sharing and other structural inequalities. The myth of equality of social conditions advanced by the liberal legal subject obstructs our view and our ability to see the ways in which the human condition is susceptible to harm or vulnerable. The human condition is one of inherent dependency on other people and social institutions. By taking shared vulnerability – the universal and inevitable aspect of the human condition – as a starting point for legislation, the need for a more responsive and encompassing state becomes apparent. The vulnerability approach recognizes that we are embodied, and therefore vulnerable

---

[39] Fineman (2004), above n 7, 226.

[40] Fineman (2008), above n 7, 13–15.

through our human frailty, as well as embedded in contexts, relationships and institutions that can make us both vulnerable and resilient. Furthermore, the shared-vulnerability perspective demonstrates that autonomy is unattainable. There are already bonds, subsidies and institutions in place to handle our dependencies. Society is already involved in our lives; however, because this is hidden, the inequalities of these interventions and the way that society distributes privilege are not fully seen. Fineman concludes: 'Vulnerability places the individual entirely within societal contexts by developing the relationships between vulnerability and resilience and societal institutions and resources.'[41]

The vulnerability approach reveals that safety is a prerequisite for the autonomy for older people, and not in conflict with it: safety is necessary for the full use of one's abilities and capacities. Fineman points out that vulnerability should also be seen as generative, as it makes us reach out to others, form relationships, and build institutions. Our vulnerability cultivates the virtues of compassion and cooperation. Full autonomy and self-sufficiency are neither attainable nor desirable. Instead, Fineman argues that 'we want and need the webs of economic and social relationships that sustain us'.[42]

5.2 Resilience and the Life-Course Perspective

Social institutions arise in response to our vulnerability to provide us with resilience. State institutions are given content through law and directly or indirectly allocate resilience and privilege. Resilience is defined as the resources that we have built up over our lifetimes through participation in society and its institutions, and this accumulation provides us with different degrees of security and agency. This resilience can be seen as the toolkit we have to manage our embodied and embedded dependencies. It can be understood as the resources and assets that allow us to take risks.[43] Social welfare services should therefore be seen as a resource for resilience and a response to our vulnerability. However, it is important that these reforms are not guided by paternalism but by participation and respect for differences and diversity. The resources that we gain through societal institutions should be understood as ways to build our resilience and give us resources, which can come in material, social, or economic forms, as well as relational forms.[44]

---

41 Fineman (2012), above n 7, 139.
42 Fineman (2004), above n 7, 28.
43 Fineman (2012), above n 7, 139.
44 Ibid 128.

According to Fineman, resilience should be understood in a life-course perspective, rather than being considered individual and instant.[45] It is not a characteristic that one is born with; it is generated over time and in response to the challenges of living as a vulnerable being. Having a life-course perspective on social welfare for older people would mean not positioning old age as a separate category of human existence, and instead recognizing it as one end of a continuum of the life of a human being. It also highlights that older people are embedded and embodied in the same way as everyone else, which means that their needs will differ and develop as their circumstances change. Older people have had their chances to accumulate resources, so their situations will also differ to a great extent, and therefore the responses to their needs will also have to differ. A perspective based on the life course will also direct focus to the differences people have in the possibility to accumulate resources before old age.

> When society considers how to confront the problems associated with the end of life, we cannot focus only on the situation of individuals who are already among the elderly, but must also take into account those younger individuals who will age into the category eventually, as well as those who may experience dependency and need care even though they are young.[46]

One way to put focus on the lifespan and the complexity of human needs is to highlight universal concerns for every human being, such as participation, influence and dignity. These principles are central to all persons, especially at a time when the emphasis on influence and self-determination creates demands on participation and activity from each individual. Public means for upholding these principles therefore seem central to state resilience. Many older people are in need of help at some point, to be listened to and assisted by someone else. Thus, there is a constant need for both individual and collective actions to uphold national social welfare and health systems for everyone who is and will be in need of them.[47]

---

[45] Cf the field of life-course research, which originated in the 1960s, analysing people's lives with social or cultural contexts, and for example seeing ageing as a continuous process that is experienced throughout life.

[46] Fineman (2012), above n 7, 140.

[47] Mattsson (2013), above n 5, 22.

6. CONCLUSION

The aim of this chapter has been to discuss and investigate the usefulness of Martha Albertson Fineman's vulnerability theory as a theoretical framework and analytical tool for elder law. The overall conclusion is that there is an increasing need for theoretical approaches to studies of the ageing population in Europe, and the vulnerability theory has broad applicability for studies that focus on the significance of the institutional and organizational conditions in society that can create reasonable living conditions for older people.

Vulnerability theory can be useful for different kinds of analyses of the legal position of older persons as well as structural implications for the elderly due to demographic, technical, social and economic changes in European society. At the same time, the theory problematizes the conceptualization of the elderly as a group – yet another important task for elder law. Fineman makes the point that this group approach ignores the universal vulnerability we all experience throughout life and creates the risk of unnecessary competition among different groups in society. This risk increases because today most societies already have problems in prioritizing distribution of their scarce economic, social and other resources.

A starting point that must be accepted by users of the theory is that ageing is more a part of life than a distinct group of (older) persons. The elderly, like everyone else, are persons who live with present and future changing needs and circumstances on a daily basis. This makes their needs as complex and varying as the individuals themselves. In addition, application of the theory gives insight into the importance of institutional and organizational conditions in society for the creation of individuals' resilience.

Moreover, the theory shows that many approaches in policy-making for older people risk being stigmatizing or paternalistic. The designation of the elderly as a 'vulnerable' population reinforces the inferior position of older people in relation to the ideal, autonomous, independent and self-sufficient liberal subject. It thus also creates the risk of unnecessary competition among different groups in society. Taking a more general approach to vulnerability, as a state of being for the whole population and its effects on society, avoids conflicts that arise on the grounds of belonging – or not belonging – to a prioritized group.

Applying the vulnerability theory makes it clear that some societal and policy responses to older people's needs rest on perceptions of older people that are at odds with the human condition of our shared vulnerability. In some cases this will lead to a political reaction to the elderly, based on stigmatizing them as a 'vulnerable group' and therefore using paternalistic measures without giving these individuals strong social rights and the right to participation in their own welfare. In addition, this type of response is not connected to a life-course perspective, in which the resilience and assets belonging to older people are understood against the background of the context of their former lives and the institutions that have surrounded their life circumstances.

Another common and problematic response is to make the vulnerabilities, needs and dependencies of older people invisible by placing the responsibility for them on the family. This will in turn lead to costs for the derivative dependents, who will need to adjust their lives in order privately to bear the burden of care for the older relative. As informal caretakers to a large degree are women, the social costs of unpaid care work will be unevenly shared between the sexes. In addition, families with sufficient economic resources to buy elder care on a private market will be better off financially.

A third and final response from policy-makers, and one which is becoming increasingly evident, is to expect older people to be autonomous and able to act fully as citizens. This attitude ignores the fact that we all live embodied and embedded lives, in which our possibilities to act autonomously differ from person to person and over a life course. This response therefore risks enhancing existing structural inequalities between different groups of older people.

The alternative approach, according to Martha Fineman, would be to start from our shared and inherent vulnerability, in which we all need or risk needing the care and support of others and of societal institutions. Applying this perspective would demand a public, universal and generous responsibility for older people's care needs – a responsibility that is neither stigmatizing nor paternalistic. By providing the means to accept the standpoint that vulnerability is a lifelong state of the human being, the vulnerability theory provides a fruitful theoretical framework for the study of ageing in the context of law.

6. Intergenerational aspects of elder law: conflict, solidarity – or ambivalence

Jenny Julén Votinius and Mia Rönnmar

1. INTRODUCTION[1]

Theories on intergenerational relations have been developed extensively in political and moral philosophy on equity and justice, the field of sociology focusing on family relations, and in scholarship on attitudes and values in a larger (welfare) societal context. The focus of attention in this chapter is not on morals and ethics, or on relations and attitudes. Instead, the analysis in this chapter concerns the structural level that accommodates the organizing mechanisms for society; the mechanism in question here is law. In order to increase understanding of how intergenerational relations play out and are met in elder law, this chapter suggests the introduction of intergenerational *ambivalence* into the binary solidarity-conflict approach.

As with the rest of the world, the demographic development of Europe is characterized by a growing population, longer lifespans, and decreased birth rates.[2] In many respects, longer lives represent important societal progress. However, when declining mortality rates are not matched by a corresponding increase in births, the composition of the population in

[1] This work was carried out within the Norma Elder Law Research Environment (www.jur.lu.se/elderlaw) funded by Ragnar Söderberg's Foundation and the Marianne and Marcus Wallenberg Foundation.

[2] On the demographic change, see for example *The 2015 Ageing Report: Underlying Assumptions and Projection Methodologies: European Economy 8* (Publications of the European Union 2014). The most aged populations are in the developed countries. In developing countries, population ageing has begun rather recently; W Thompson, 'Population' (1929) 34 Am J Sociol 959; J C Caldwell, *Demographic Transition Theory* (Springer 2006) 307ff. *World Population Ageing 2013* (United Nations 2013).

terms of age fundamentally changes. The current development – implying proportionally fewer young people in the population – is often referred to as a demographic shift.[3] From a societal perspective, this demographic shift is not unproblematic. The demands associated with an ageing population must be dealt with in a wide range of policy areas, including the fields of medical care, senior housing, elder care, public transport and urban planning.[4] Above all, this shift involves a changing economic situation that must be handled. These new economic developments are resulting not only from the increasing demands on the social systems; they are even more the result of the fact that an increasingly smaller share of the population is becoming responsible for supporting more and more people. In terms of national economics, society faces an increasing *dependency ratio*.[5] The intensified influx of people into the senior community and the fact that more and more people are becoming very old are putting more pressure on social income support systems, notably the pension system.[6] The demographic trend presents major challenges to society, particularly regarding the securing of (health) care mechanisms, and regarding the economic situation and the social inclusion of older people. Ultimately, all these challenges must be handled by taking into account intergenerational relations, the outcome of which is put into practice in policies and legal rules governing different areas of society.

This development brings to the fore questions about the relationship between the old and the young in the legal context. This is also something that is reflected in this book, although none of the other chapters make intergenerational aspects as such subject to legal analysis. Nonetheless, several chapters address legal challenges that stem from or involve the relationship between generations, in areas such as welfare systems, elder care, and transfers of property among generations within the family. Thus, Chapter 10, by Andreas Inghammar, Cécile Brokelind and Per Norberg, on

---

[3] Cf Wolfgang Lutz, Warren Sanderson and Sergei Scherbov, 'The coming acceleration of global population ageing' (2008) 451 Nature 716.

[4] For a broader picture of the challenges associated with the ageing population, see S Harper, 'The challenges of twenty-first-century demography' in C Torp (ed.), *Challenges of Ageing: Pensions, Retirement and Generational Justice* (Palgrave Macmillan 2015).

[5] Within the EU today, there are 29 persons aged 65 and over per 100 persons of working age (15–64 years). In 2030 this number is expected to be 39, and in 2050 it is expected to be 49 (Eurostat 2015).

[6] In 2014, more than 18 per cent of the population in the EU was aged 65 or over, and 5 per cent of the population was over 80. The same numbers for 2080 are expected to be 30 per cent and 12 per cent, respectively.

flexible retirement, is presented within the discourse of sustainable pensions, which is highly relevant from an intergenerational perspective. Chapter 12, by Hanna Pettersson and Mirjam Katzin, addresses challenges posed by a development where an increasing responsibility for elderly care is placed on – predominantly younger – family members as welfare systems are levelled down. Chapter 14, by Elsa Trolle Önnerfors, discusses how the descendants' reserved share in inheritance law forms a legal historical point of view, whereas Chapter 15, by Eva Ryrstedt, deals with problems that can arise when a younger relative – who also is a future inheritor – is appointed 'good man' (trustee) or administrator for an elderly person with a mental disablement. Chapter 13, by Titti Mattsson, Martina Axmin and Emma Holm, also contains intergenerational aspects, although outside the area of law, in the discussion on intergenerational solidarity as a possible motive for participants in medical research. In the present chapter, the intergenerational perspective is the very focal point of the analysis, which suggests that legal response to intergenerational conundrums can be explored beyond the dichotomy of solidarity and conflict that is often applied in the policy discourse in the explored areas of law. The chapter is structured as follows. Section 2 lays out the theoretical and conceptual framework, and introduces the notion of *intergenerational ambivalence* as an additional tool in the legal analysis. Section 3 situates the discourse on intergenerational relations in a broader legal and policy context. Section 4 highlights some intergenerational aspects and challenges in the area of labour law and industrial relations, using examples from European Union (EU) law and Swedish national law. Drawing on the previous sections, in an integrated analysis based on the 'solidarity, conflict and ambivalence model', Section 5 acknowledges and discusses the complexity of intergenerational relations in the field of elder law. Section 6 concludes the discussion.

2. THEORETICAL FRAMEWORK

Much of the legal scholarly debate on intergenerational aspects has revolved around the idea of intergenerational justice as a principle for just distribution of resources, organization of the society, and legislation.[7]

---

7 J Rawls, *A Theory of Justice* (Harvard University Press 1971) and *Justice as Fairness: A Restatement* (Harvard University Press 2001). See further, J Chet Tremmel (ed.), *Handbook of Intergenerational Justice* (Edward Elgar Publishing 2006); A Gosseries, 'Intergenerational justice' in Hugh LaFollette (ed.), *The Oxford Handbook of Practical Ethics* (Oxford University Press 2003) 459; A

In legal science, intergenerational aspects have mostly been researched within the area of environmental law dealing with climate change, and mostly with a focus on responsibilities towards future generations as regards the preservation of natural resources.[8] There is strong potential in developing the intergenerational perspective in relation to other areas of legal science, and there are indeed important examples of how this can be done. Thus constitutional lawyers have emphasized the need to discuss clauses that exclude changes in the constitution – so-called entrenchment clauses or eternity clauses – from the perspective of their implications for the political sovereignty of future generations.[9] In the area of public law, and also in law and economics, focus has been on the intergenerational considerations in regulations fostering sustainability in welfare systems and other sectors of public finances.[10]

Claims for intergenerational justice can be made both with reference to forthcoming generations, and with reference to different generations that are living simultaneously together; both diachronic and synchronic or, as Rawls defines it, both intertemporal and intratemporal existence.[11] This

Gosseries and L H Meyer (eds), *Intergenerational Justice* (Oxford University Press 2009); J Thompson, *Intergenerational Justice: Rights and Responsibilities in an Intergenerational Polity* (Routledge 2009).

[8] See P Lawrence, *Justice for Future Generations: Climate Change and International Law* (Edward Elgar Publishing 2014). See also (2010) 10 IGJR 1 (Special Issue: Ways to Legally Implement Intergenerational Justice).

[9] See for instance, A Gosseries, 'The intergenerational case for constitutional rigidity' (2014) 27(4) Ratio Juris 528–39; A D'Aloia and F Roccisano, 'Intergenerational justice: An economic and juridical analysis' in I Barković Bojanić and M Lulić, *Contemporary Legal and Economic Issues III* (Faculty of Law, Josip Juraj Strossmayer University of Osijek 2011); P Häberle, 'A constitutional law for future generations – The "other" form of the social contract: The generation contract' in J Chet Tremmel (ed.), *Handbook of Intergenerational Justice* (Edward Elgar Publishing 2006) 215; Bruce Auerbach and Michelle Reinhart, 'Antonin Scalia's constitutional textualism: The problem of justice to posterity' (2012) 1 IGJR 17.

[10] See for instance, U Davy, '"Social Europe" in old-age security? EU policies of public and private pensions' in L Leisering, *The New Regulatory State* (Palgrave Macmillan 2011), 153.

[11] The idea about rights of future generations is not uncontroversial; cf R De George, 'The environment, rights, and future generations' in E Partridge (ed.), *Responsibilities to Future Generations: Environmental Ethics* (Prometheus Books 1981) 157; O Herstein, 'The identity and (legal) rights of future generations' (2009) 777 Geo Wash L Rev 1173; B H Weston, 'The theoretical foundations of intergenerational ecological justice: An overview' (2012) 34 Hum Rts Q 251.

division is of significance in relation to the topic of this chapter and its scope. Although the development of legal structures and the legal acknowledgement of a particular understanding of justice may always have far-reaching consequences in the long-term perspective, the main focus for the discussion in this chapter is the immediate intergenerational aspects of the relation between coexisting generations.

Key to the understanding of intergenerational justice are the notions of *solidarity* and *conflict*; the exercise of intergenerational justice generates intergenerational solidarity, which is achieved through the balancing of conflicting interests between generations. The pairing of solidarity and conflict has also been used to frame intergenerational matters in legal science, notably within the areas of environmental law and constitutional law. However, in the field of elder law – understood here as the field of law dealing with older persons' legal position in everyday life, including components such as the labour market, social insurance, elder care and family relations – it is more difficult, and sometimes even impossible, to apply reasoning based strictly on intergenerational solidarity and intergenerational conflict. In these areas of society, which harbour social institutions at the very core of people's lives, contradicting approaches and outcomes seems to emerge simultaneously in the intergenerational context. The intergenerational experience is thus not characterized only by conflict or solidarity, but rather by a complex coexistence of these two positions. Although the notions of conflict and solidarity are central in analysing intergenerational relations, an additional concept seems to have an equally important function: the concept of intergenerational *ambivalence*.

The notion of intergenerational ambivalence has developed in theories on intergenerationality within the areas of sociology and social psychology. The conceptual framework for this idea rests on an acknowledgement that people are involved in intergenerational relationships in three different capacities: as individuals, as part of families and personal relationships, and as members of society.[12] These different capacities interact in shaping different and sometimes incompatible attitudes and actions in intergenerational matters. Involvement in intergenerational

---

[12] V Bengtson, R Giarrusso, J B Mabry, and M Silverstein, 'Solidarity, conflict, and ambivalence: Complementary or competing perspectives on intergenerational relationships?' (2002) 64 J Marriage Fam 568; K Lüscher, 'Advancing the field: Ambivalence: A "Sensitizing Construct" for the study and practice of intergenerational relationships' (2011) 9 J Intergener Relatsh 191; K Prinzen, 'Intergenerational ambivalence: New perspectives on intergenerational relationships in the German welfare state' (2014) 34 Ageing Soc 428.

relations in one's capacity as an individual implies a position in which age-based views are based on *individual* self-interest, expressed as a narrow focus on direct gains for the generation to which one belongs. By shifting to one's capacity as a member of a family or a close relationship, attention turns to other governing perceptions, which are of a *relational* nature. Here, age-based considerations involve feelings such as empathy, dependence and emotional engagement in relation to the needs of people in other age groups. Finally, in the perspective of a member of society, *societal* interest is to the fore; thus, age-related attitudes and actions are based on their perceived effects, for example on social cohesion and sustainability of welfare systems. Although developed within social science to understand the minds and actions of individual persons, this conceptual framework also has an explanatory potential within legal science – and notably within elder law. The intergenerational ambivalence experienced on the individual level is collectively projected into the law, in its capacity as an organizing mechanism for society.

In law, this profound ambivalence can materialize in three seemingly different ways. First, it can result in legal vagueness, to the detriment of the power and proper functioning of the law.[13] Second, this can play out in the form of contradicting legal norms. Both these outcomes represent a failure of the legal order to confront and deal with this ambivalence. The third alternative represents a way out; the ambivalence is acknowledged and, to the greatest possible extent, dealt with.

In the following, these three manifestations of intergenerational ambivalence in elder law will be discussed with examples from the area of labour law and industrial relations, against the background of the legal and policy framework in the area of intergenerational relations.

3. LEGAL AND POLICY FRAMEWORK – AIMING FOR INTERGENERATIONAL SOLIDARITY

3.1 International Initiatives

The importance of promoting intergenerational relations has been emphasized in the international policy agenda since the mid-1990s. In 1995, the UN proclaimed 1999 as the International Year of Older People with the

[13] Cf J Julén Votinius, 'Parenthood meets market-functionalism: Parental rights in the labour market and the importance of the gender dimension', in A Numhauser-Henning and M Rönnmar (eds), *Normative Patterns and Legal Developments in the Social Dimension of the EU* (Hart Publishing 2013) 186.

specific theme 'Towards a Society for All Ages', defined as a society that enables different generations to 'invest in one another and share in the fruits of that investment, guided by the twin principles of reciprocity and equity'.[14] In the conceptual framework accompanying this arrangement, 'Multigenerational relationships' was one of four key facets.[15] Further steps were taken in 2002, with the adoption of the International Plan of Action on Ageing, and in 2012 the Economic and Social Council requested the Commission for Social Development to adopt advancement of social integration and intergenerational solidarity as one of three guiding themes for the preparations for the twentieth anniversary of the International Year of the Family in 2014.[16]

3.2 Legal and Policy Framework of the EU

Since 2008, intergenerational solidarity has had a prominent place in EU law: Article 3.3 of the Lisbon Treaty makes it one of the core objectives of the Union. However, already in 1997, a first step towards a more explicit intergenerational perspective was taken in the treaty context, in the Amsterdam Treaty through the principle of sustainable development. The EU Charter of 2000, which applies to the EU and to the Member States when implementing EU law, became legally binding through the adoption of the Lisbon Treaty and has a more developed intergenerational approach. The preamble of the Charter states that the rights therein entail responsibilities and duties with regard to other persons, the human community and future generations. A number of articles are relevant from the intergenerational perspective, such as Article 21, according to which any discrimination on the grounds of age shall be forbidden;

[14] United Nations, Resolution adopted by the General Assembly [on the report of the Third Committee (A/50/628)] 50/141 International Year of Older Persons: towards a society for all ages, December 1995. This resolution followed the Proclamation on Ageing of 16 October 1992 (A/RES/47/5).

[15] United Nations, Conceptual framework of the programme for the preparation and observance of the International Year of Older Persons in 1999. A/50/114 22 March 1999.

[16] United Nations, Madrid International Plan of Action on Ageing, 2002, adopted at the tenth plenary meeting of the Second World Assembly on Ageing 12 April 2002 (part 3 of 5 of the Report of the Second World Assembly on Ageing (A/CONF.197/9); United Nations, Economic and Social Council, Resolution adopted by the Economic and Social Council, Preparations for and observance of the twentieth anniversary of the International Year of the Family (E/RES/2012/10); cf United Nations, 2013 Report of the Secretary-General on intergenerational solidarity and the needs of future generations (A/68/322).

Article 24 on the rights of the child; and Article 25 on the rights of the elderly to lead a life of dignity and independence and participate in social and cultural life.

Since the early 1990s, European Commission policy documents have emphasized the importance of intergenerational solidarity for meeting the challenges of population ageing.[17] A Council Declaration in 1993, following the European Year of Older People and Solidarity between Generations, confirmed the principle of intergenerational solidarity as the essential basis for policy development by Member States.[18] The Green Paper *Confronting Demographic Change: A New Solidarity between the Generations* called for new forms of solidarity between the generations, based on mutual support and the transfer of skills and experience.[19]

With regard to intergenerational aspects of labour law and industrial relations, which will be discussed later in this chapter, it is important to emphasize that the development of EU strategies for intergenerational solidarity has been parallel, and subsequently integrated, with the development of strategies for active ageing. Active ageing refers to a range of areas, but in effect it has been most developed in policies regarding active ageing in employment; the overall emphasis is very much on promoting labour market opportunities and enhancing the employment conditions and employability of older employees.[20] In 2001 and 2002, two general EU targets were adopted to increase labour market participation of older workers and promote sustainable pensions: the Stockholm target, to ensure that half of those aged 55–64 were in employment by 2010, and the Barcelona target, to increase actual retirement age by five years by

---

17 Council Decision on Community action for older people (91/49/EEC; OJ L 28 of 2 February 1991 29); Council Decision on the organization of the European Year of the Elderly and of Solidarity between Generations (1993) (92/440/EEC: OJ L 245 of 26 August1992 43); cf Proposal for a Council Decision on Community support for actions in favour of older people (95/C115/06) COM(95) 53 final.

18 Declaration of Principles of the Council of the European Union and the Ministers for Social Affairs, meeting within the Council of 6 December 1993 to mark the end of the European Year of Older People and Solidarity between Generations (93/C 343/01; OJ C 343 of 21 December 1993 1).

19 Commission – Green Paper, 'Confronting demographic change: A new solidarity between the generations' COM/2005/0094 final, 6.

20 A Walker and T Maltby, 'Active ageing: A strategic policy solution to demographic ageing in the European Union' (2012) 21 Int J Soc Welfare 117; cf Commission, Commission Staff Working Document ex-ante evaluation accompanying document to the decision of the European Parliament and the Council on the European Year for Active Ageing (2012) SEC(2010) 1002 final.

2010. The active ageing policy of raising employment rates for older workers is part of the EU's growth and job strategy Europe 2020, where this aspect is addressed in the flagship initiative towards full employment – the 'Agenda for new skills and jobs'. The 2012 European Year of Active Ageing and Intergenerational Solidarity intensified integration of policies to promote intergenerational solidarity with policies for active ageing.

Active ageing in the form of longer working lives is a central area for policy measures to promote intergenerational solidarity within the EU. Labour law and industrial relations therefore comprise an important area for regulating intergenerational matters. The following section highlights how intergenerational aspects and challenges have been identified and dealt with in labour law and industrial relations, and discusses collective bargaining developments in the EU and Sweden aimed at overcoming intergenerational conflict and promoting intergenerational solidarity.

4. INTERGENERATIONAL ASPECTS OF LABOUR LAW AND INDUSTRIAL RELATIONS[21]

4.1 Intergenerational Aspects of EU Labour Law

The labour market situation differs for older and younger workers, and an ageing population, economic crisis, and youth unemployment increase the risk of intergenerational conflict – especially when it comes to the perceived competition for jobs, at both micro- and macro-level. Such intergenerational conflict relates, for example, to entry into the labour market and access to permanent (instead of flexible or precarious) employment, and to the access to and strength of employment protection in restructuring and redundancy situations. The picture is complex, however. Employment protection and seniority rules are seen by some as affording necessary protection for older workers, while others view them as barriers for the entry of younger workers into the labour market.

---

21 This section draws upon earlier research in the fields of age discrimination law and intergenerational collective bargaining; see especially B ter Haar and M Rönnmar, 'Intergenerational bargaining, EU age discrimination law and EU policies – An integrated analysis', Report for the project iNGenBar 2014; M Rönnmar, 'Intergenerational bargaining in Sweden', Report for the project iNGenBar 2014; and A Numhauser-Henning and M Rönnmar (eds), *Age Discrimination and Labour Law: Comparative and Conceptual Perspectives in the EU and Beyond* (Kluwer Law International 2015).

Age has traditionally served as an important and legitimate social and economic stratifier, and has greatly influenced organization of labour markets and the design and content of labour law and collective bargaining. The (2000/78/EC) Employment Equality Directive introduced the ban on age discrimination in EU law.[22] The protection against age discrimination covers all chronological ages; both older and younger workers are protected. According to the preamble to the Directive, the prohibition of age discrimination is an essential part of meeting the aims set out in the European Employment Strategy and the Employment Guidelines. The prohibition of old-age discrimination helps to reduce ageism, and is also an important aspect of the EU Active Ageing Policy. However, according to Article 6(1) of the Employment Equality Directive, differences of treatment on grounds of age do not constitute discrimination if they are objectively and reasonably justified by a legitimate aim, including legitimate employment policy, labour market, and vocational training objectives, and if the means of achieving that aim are appropriate and necessary.[23] In principle, EU age discrimination law – through a large scope for justification of age-related differential treatment, specific exemptions and a broad margin of appreciation for Member States and social partners – enables direct and indirect age-related regulation as well as intergenerational bargaining and collective bargaining on age-related measures for older and younger workers.[24] A comparative analysis of some EU Member States reveals that a large number of directly and indirectly age-related labour law rules and practices still exist in the areas of recruitment, working conditions, flexible employment, employment protection and compulsory retirement.[25]

The Court of Justice of the European Union's age discrimination case law reflects an acceptance of rules on compulsory retirement, among other things in terms of justification on grounds of intergenerational

---

[22] In addition, Article 21 of the EU Charter of Fundamental Rights contains an open list of discrimination grounds, including age.

[23] See further, Numhauser-Henning, Julén Votinius and Zbyszewska, Chapter 7 in this book and C Tobler, 'EU age discrimination law and older and younger workers: Court of Justice of the European Union case law developments' in A Numhauser-Henning and M Rönnmar (eds), *Age Discrimination and Labour Law: Comparative and Conceptual Perspectives in the EU and Beyond* (Kluwer Law International 2015).

[24] See ter Haar and Rönnmar (2014), above n 21.

[25] See M Rönnmar, 'Age discrimination and labour law: A comparative perspective' in A Numhauser-Henning and M Rönnmar (eds), *Age Discrimination and Labour Law: Comparative and Conceptual Perspectives in the EU and Beyond* (Kluwer Law International 2015).

fairness in relation to younger workers and their access to employment, both at a general labour market level and in a more specific organizational context. This reasoning contrasts with economic research, which emphasizes the 'lump of labour fallacy' and opposes assertions of intergenerational competition for jobs, as well as claims that compulsory (or premature) retirement schemes will help combat youth unemployment or that older workers crowd younger workers out of the labour market.[26]

4.2 Intergenerational Bargaining

In some EU Member States, intergenerational strategies, schemes or measures have been developed to promote inclusion of older and younger workers in the labour market, active ageing and longer working lives for older workers, and to combat youth unemployment. For example, France has traditionally emphasized early retirement and intergenerational redistribution. In 2013 a new and different attempt at intergenerational solidarity was made through the *contrat de génération*, based on the complementarity of younger and older workers. Under this scheme, companies may recruit a younger worker with a permanent employment contract, while simultaneously retaining (or hiring) an older worker. Intergenerational supervision and education is part of the scheme, and the state provides economic subsidies. It is still too early to evaluate the scheme, and account must be taken not only of the (relatively low) numbers of employees hired but also of any resultant change in attitudes and prejudices.[27]

The iNGenBar research project aimed to provide a comparative and interdisciplinary analysis of intergenerational bargaining in EU law and in specific EU Member States (France, Germany, Italy, the Netherlands, Sweden and the UK).[28] Here, intergenerational bargaining referred to the

---

[26] See for example, E Dewhurst, 'Intergenerational balance, mandatory retirement and age discrimination in Europe: How can the ECJ better support national courts in finding a balance between the generations?' (2013) 50 CML Rev 1333 with further references.

[27] See for example, S Robin-Olivier, 'Age discrimination and labour law in France' in A Numhauser-Henning and M Rönnmar (eds), *Age Discrimination and Labour Law: Comparative and Conceptual Perspectives in the EU and Beyond* (Kluwer Law International 2015) and the French report in the iNGenBar research project.

[28] The iNGenBar research project was coordinated by AIAS at Amsterdam University and funded by the European Commission. See further ter Haar and Rönnmar (2014), above n 21, and Rönnmar (2014), above n 21.

integration of policies and strategies for older and younger workers through collective bargaining and social dialogue.

For Sweden, the project focused on three case studies on *introduction agreements for younger workers*, *collective agreements on partial retirement for older workers* and *transition agreements*.[29] It became clear that Swedish labour law, industrial relations and collective bargaining lack a clear intergenerational dimension, as well as an articulated debate on intergenerational solidarity or conflict. To a large degree, the interests of younger and older workers and the labour market inclusion of these groups are dealt with separately and in parallel. The strategies to combat youth unemployment and to promote active ageing and a prolonged working life for older workers, respectively, are largely seen as separate, equally important and non-conflicting strategies. However, the emphasis on collective bargaining and social partner autonomy creates favourable basic conditions for intergenerational bargaining.

In recent years a number of national sectoral collective agreements called *introduction agreements* for younger workers have been concluded, and have attracted a lot of attention. Youth unemployment, labour market inclusion of younger workers and competence provision form a background, and the introduction agreements regulate fixed-term employments for younger workers, combining work with education, training and supervision.[30]

Several collective agreements – for both blue-collar and white-collar employees – offer possibilities for employees to apply for *partial retirement* from the age of 60 or 62.[31] The aim of this partial retirement is to provide an opportunity for a longer working life and create fruitful conditions for generational renewal.

Transition agreements cover all sectors and large parts of the labour market. They comprise an important complement to the statutory employment protection regulation on redundancy dismissals – but also to active labour market policies and unemployment insurance.[32] The transition

---

[29] An analysis of specific collective agreements was complemented by interviews with leading representatives of social partners.

[30] A government scheme to support and subsidize introduction employments for younger workers has also been put into place. See Government Regulation (2013:1157) and Government Report Ds 2013:20.

[31] See National Mediation Office, *Avtalsrörelsen och lönebildningen 2013. Medlingsinstitutets årsrapport* (National Mediation Office 2014) 137.

[32] Cf G Sebardt, *Redundancy and the Swedish Model. Swedish Collective Agreements on Employment Security in a National and International Context* (Iustus förlag 2005). A recent study by the Organisation for Economic

agreements provide employees facing dismissal owing to reasons of redundancy with different rights to severance pay, economic compensation and active transition support measures, by way of activities such as coaching, job-searching services, training and re-education. The agreements also provide support for employers in reorganizations and redundancy situations.

Swedish collective bargaining developments display a lack of direct and explicit intergenerational bargaining. However, several indirect and implicit intergenerational elements can be found in the collective agreements studied. These indirect intergenerational elements relate, for example, to generational renewal in terms of future competence provision, competence development and transfer of knowledge and experience between older and younger workers, and older workers' participation in education and supervision of younger workers, as ways to adapt the working environment to enable a longer working life. Still, intergenerational redistribution of employment between older and younger workers is alien to Swedish public policy and collective bargaining. The case studies suggest that there is limited integration or synergy among the three different types of collective agreements. This seems to be the case even though some collective agreements, such as introduction agreements and collective agreements on partial retirement for older workers, are concluded by the same collective bargaining partners. However, fruitful linkages can be found and developed, not least in the practical application of these agreements – for example when it comes to the educational element and the supervision of younger workers.

5. LEGAL MANIFESTATIONS OF INTERGENERATIONAL AMBIVALENCE

Intergenerational solidarity is an objective for the EU. It is also a policy-level conceptualization of the reconciliation between the needs and interests of different generations, and the efforts to counteract intergenerational challenges. At the same time, in both the legislative documents and on the policy level, little is said about how this solidarity should be realized. Intergenerational solidarity implies that the interests of different generations should be considered. However, because it is impossible to establish what actually is in the interest of a certain

Co-operation and Development (OECD) highlights the successful results of Swedish transition agreements; see OECD, *Back to Work: Sweden: Improving the Re-employment Prospects of Displaced Workers* (OECD 2015).

generation, the notion of intergenerational solidarity can be interpreted as supporting different normative solutions that are in fact mutually incompatible. Provisions requiring intergenerational solidarity are perhaps the most prominent examples of how intergenerational ambivalence plays out in law in the form of legal *vagueness*.

In the labour market context, for instance, conflicting interests can be attributed to the same generation – such as the interest in upholding an irrefutable right to retire at a certain age and the interest in inculcating a right to remain in employment without age-related restrictions. This intra-generational difference adds to the complexity discussed above in Section 2 on the ambivalence generated by the fact that different generations relate to each other in more than one way; they relate as individuals belonging to a certain age group, as family members or parties in other close relationships and as members of society. Consider the following example: employment policy measures to promote youth employment, such as a wage subsidy scheme, may conflict with the interest of older persons in their capacity as employees, but at the same time such measures can be in line with older persons' own interest as members of a community where youth unemployment constitutes a societal problem. It may also be in line with their own interest as a parent or a grandparent for whom the unemployment of young family members and relatives is negatively affecting everyday life. In the same way, the policy scheme may also have different implications for young persons, depending on whether they are regarded as individuals, as members of a small community such as a family, or as members of society. Thus the question of how such a policy scheme would meet the demand for intergenerational justice does have more than one answer.

Vagueness in law can lead not only to indeterminacies in legal rights and obligations. This lack of clarity allows for more interpretation and discretion, while it also opens up to the influence of age-related stereotypes and associated misconceptions about labour market mechanisms. An example of the latter has been described in Section 4 in this chapter – the so-called 'lump of labour fallacy'. An equally relevant example is labour market reform that aims at combating youth unemployment by dismantling employment security for young people, although there is simply no scientific evidence that this method actually works.[33] As regards stereotyping based on age, scholarship on ageism provides very concrete findings on how perceptions about people of different ages can

[33] J Gautiér, *Le chômage* (La Découverte 2009); L Eldring and K Alsos, 'European minimum wage: A Nordic outlook', Fafo Report 2012:16 49.

justify less favourable treatment of the age group in question. Examples of perceptions about young people are that they do not have the same needs as older people because they are not yet living an adult life, and that disadvantages for young people are legitimate, because in due time young people will become older and acquire the same rights as the rest of the adult population.[34] In the labour market, these perceptions – which ultimately conceive younger persons as less needy or less deserving – typically materialize in an understanding that it can be fair to impose lower demands on employment conditions for young employees. Common perceptions of elderly workers are that they are unwilling to continue developing their skills and that they do not possess up-to-date technical knowledge.[35] From a labour law perspective, these findings are of interest in relation to legal rules whereby work-related decisions are made upon the employer's assessment of the employee's qualifications, but also in relation to professional development and lifelong learning.[36] Another widespread – but incorrect – perception is that elderly persons are more likely than young people to leave their employments.[37] Intergenerational ambivalence that plays out as legal vagueness, which in turn allows for stereotyping, increases the risk of practices that disfavour certain age groups.

Vagueness is one way in which intergenerational ambivalence can play out in the legal order. Another way is through *contradictions* in the law.

---

[34] Cf W Loretto, D Colin and P J White 'Ageism and employment: Controversies, ambiguities and younger people's perceptions' (2000) 20 Ageing Soc 302; E Snape and T Redman, 'Too old or too young? The impact of perceived age discrimination' (2003) 13 Hum Resour Manage J 78.

[35] H P Van Dalen, K Henkens and J Schippers, 'Dealing with older workers in Europe: A comparative survey of employers' attitudes and actions' (2009) 19 J Eur Soc Policy 47; H P Van Dalen, K Henkens and J Schippers, 'Productivity of older workers: Perceptions of employers and employees' (2012) 36(2) Pop Dev Rev 309. For a more general discussion on expressions of age-related perceptions see C Krekula, 'Age coding – On age-based practices of distinction' (2009) 4(2) IJAL 7.

[36] Cf W Loretto, C Duncan and P J White, 'Ageism and employment. Controversies, ambiguities and younger people's perceptions' (2000) 20 Ageing and Society 279, 285 and 296; and J McMullin, 'Theorizing age and gender relations' in S Arber and J Ginn (eds), *Connecting Gender and Ageing: A Sociological Approach* (Open University Press 1995); C Itzin and C Phillipson, 'Gendered ageism: A double jeopardy for women in organizations' in C Itzin and J Newman (eds), *Gender, Culture and Organizational Change: Putting Theory into Practice* (Routledge 1995).

[37] C Krekula, *Åldersdiskriminering i svenskt arbetsliv: om ålderskodningar och myter som skapar ojämlikhet* (The Equality Ombudsman 2011).

In labour law, age works as an important organizing principle. Rules on seniority, mandatory retirement and also specific provisions on holidays and working time for young and old workers all openly relate to age. Illegitimate differentiation on the ground of age can potentially be counteracted by non-discrimination law. The Court of Justice of the European Union has been firm in expressing that the principle of non-discrimination on grounds of age, as specified in Directive 2000/78 and as protected in the EU Charter of Fundamental Rights, must be regarded as a general principle of EU law.[38] Simultaneously, the ban on age discrimination in EU law is subject to specific exemptions and gives a fairly broad margin of appreciation for Member States and social partners. The contradictory character of the area of age discrimination has been highlighted in another chapter in this book.[39] This broad scope for exceptions is inconsistent with the very idea of a fundamental right as a safeguard of the values that form the basis of the legal order itself. Thus, with regard to the ban on age discrimination in labour law, the ambivalence that stems from profoundly contradictory values in the intergenerational relations of the labour market has resulted in a legal contradiction – one that undermines the very idea of a fundamental right.

Labour law also provides many examples of *acknowledgement* of the impact of intergenerational ambivalence, in the sense that the complexity of intergenerational relations is more or less explicitly addressed. Some examples of such acknowledgement are described in the previous section of this chapter. This is the case for the French *contrat de génération*, legislation specifically designed to promote the relation between different generations in the labour market through the conclusion of collective agreements on simultaneous arrangements for younger and older employees. Collective agreements are also a solution used to acknowledge intergenerational relations in Sweden, although here different agreements have been designed to address particular intergenerational elements;

---

38 *Mangold v. Helm* C-144/04 EU:C:2005:709 para 75 and *Kücükdeveci v. Swedex GmbH & Co KG* C-555/07 EU:C:2010:21 para 21. Cf C O'Cinneide, 'Constitutional and fundamental rights aspects of age discrimination' in A Numhauser-Henning and M Rönnmar (eds), *Age Discrimination and Labour Law: Comparative and Conceptual Perspectives in the EU and Beyond* (Kluwer Law International 2015).

39 Numhauser-Henning, Julén Votinius and Zbyszewska, Chapter 7 in this book. See also F Hendrickx, 'Age and European employment discrimination law' in F Hendrickx (ed.), *Active Ageing and Labour Law, Contributions in Honour of Roger Blanpain* (Intersentia 2012); A Numhauser-Henning, 'The EU ban on age-discrimination and older workers: Potentials and pitfalls' (2013) 29 Int J Comp Lab Law and Indus Relations 391.

examples include introduction agreements, agreements of partial retirement, and transition agreements. In the area of working life, solidarity and tension between generations is often described as particularly relating to the distribution of employment opportunities. In the analysis of collective bargaining development, another aspect that should not be underestimated is the intergenerational transfer of knowledge. The fact that intergenerational ambivalence is acknowledged in labour law does not always mean that the challenges related to intergenerational aspects are regularly addressed and successfully defused, but it does mean that the ambivalence can be channelled into the determinative discourses that shape the legal area.

6. CONCLUDING REMARKS

The conceptual dichotomy of conflict and solidarity does not seem to provide a sufficiently sharp analytical tool to elaborate on the normative complexity of intergenerational relations in the area of elder law.

This is partly because elder law research does not deal primarily with matters related to future generations, but with synchronic relations – relations between different and coexisting generations. These two perspectives differ; while the former primarily raises an important moral call for decisions that take into account the interest of both the living and those yet to be born, the latter has to deal with concurring interests of groups that actually exist, and whose claims are very real and may in the end constitute a threat to social peace. Whereas attempts to create justice in a diachronic perspective make it difficult to assess the interests of future generations who cannot speak for themselves, the synchronic perspective poses a quite different challenge: to clarify the actual interest at stake and identify conflicting interests that must be reconciled.

Legal science has the possibility to develop intergenerational analysis that extends beyond the limiting dichotomy of conflict and solidarity. One alternative is to embrace the complexities of intergenerational relations in elder law, while investigating the ambivalence permeating intergenerational issues and the implications of this ambivalence for this field of law.

PART III

Elements of elder law

7. Equal treatment and age discrimination – inside and outside working life

Ann Numhauser-Henning, Jenny Julén Votinius and Ania Zbyszewska

1. INTRODUCTION[1]

An important characteristic of EU age discrimination law – and a central theme of this chapter – is its weaker template as compared to other grounds of non-discrimination regulation; this is reflected in the fact that direct age discrimination, to a considerable extent, can be justified.[2] One reason for this is greater uncertainty about its 'wrongness' when compared to other grounds. Of significance also is the fact that age hitherto has been used as an important social stratifier, and that an ageing population and the challenges it implies for post-modern societies, in more or less instrumental terms, is one of the driving forces behind the EU age discrimination law and elder policies developed in the last 20 years. All these factors are crucial to the discussion in this chapter, which explores the reasoning behind the significantly less comprehensive ban against discrimination that applies in age cases, and the potential of this ban to serve as an effective instrument for achieving equal treatment.

Ageing populations are a demographic trend generating difficult economic and social challenges around the globe. In Europe, low fertility rates contribute to this picture. The EU's overall ambitions are expressed in the Europe 2020 Strategy,[3] promoting a healthy and active ageing

---

1 This work was carried out within the Norma Elder Law Research Environment (www.jur.lu.se/elderlaw) funded by Ragnar Söderberg's Foundation and the Marianne and Marcus Wallenberg Foundation.

2 Cf also Fudge, Chapter 3 in this book.

3 Commission Communication, *Europe 2020, A Strategy for Smart, Sustainable and Inclusive Growth*, COM(2010) 2020 final. See also the Commission's

population to achieve social cohesion and higher productivity. High youth unemployment and the difficult situation of younger workers are also important issues in the Europe 2020 Strategy, potentially making the development of active ageing strategies even more challenging. A general goal has been set to have an employment rate of 75 per cent of all 20- to 64-year-olds in 2020 – and this is also reflected in the so-called Employment Guidelines.[4] Supporting active ageing across all aspects of life is a key measure for meeting these challenges. The EU declared 2012 'The Year of Active Ageing and Solidarity between Generations'.[5] This declaration was accompanied by a number of 'Guiding Principles for Active Ageing and Solidarity between Generations' in terms of employment, participation in society, and independent living.

These strategies find support in the EU Treaty provisions. The Lisbon Treaty now cites solidarity between generations as one of the Union's objectives (Article 3.3 Treaty of the European Union (TEU)) and the EU Charter of Fundamental Rights (CFR) apostrophizes (in Article 25) the rights of the elderly to lead a life of dignity and independence and to participate in social and cultural life. Article 34.1 mentions social security and social assistance in the case of old age and Article 15 refers more generally to the right to work. Younger workers and young people are also specifically targeted by Treaty provisions (Articles 47 and 165 Treaty of the Functioning of the European Union (TFEU)). Both the functioning of labour markets and the dependency ratio between active and inactive persons are crucial from this perspective, as are the interrelations between work and pensions and other parts of social security/social welfare institutions.[6]

Social dialogue is also one of the main pillars of the EU social model in relation to active ageing.[7] 'The 2015–2017 Work Programme of the

---

Communication *Taking Stock of the Europe 2020 Strategy for Smart, Sustainable and Inclusive Growth*, COM(2014) 130 final.

[4] Council Decision 2010/707/EU of 21 October 2010. See especially guidelines 7, 8 and 10.

[5] Decision No. 940/2011/EU, 14 September 2011, OJ 23.09.2011 No. 246/5.

[6] Cf for instance, *An Agenda for Adequate, Safe and Sustainable Pensions*, COM(2012) 55 final. See also the report *Implementation of the EU White Paper on Pensions, Status as of 20/03/2014*.

[7] Cf A Numhauser-Henning, 'La prohibición de la UE contra la discriminación por edad y el papel de los agentes sociales' in J Gorelli Hernández (ed.), *El derecho a la negociación colectiva, Liber amicorum Profesor Atonio Ojeda Avilés* (Junta de Andalucía 2014) and A Numhauser-Henning and M Rönnmar, 'Age discrimination law and social partners and collective bargaining' in B J

European Social Partners. Partnership for Inclusive Growth and Employment' entered into by BUSINESSEUROPE, CEEP, UEAPME and ETUC in 2015 is the fifth bipartite work programme to improve the functioning of labour markets 'achieving solutions that are fair, responsible and effective, contributing to economic recovery, building up social cohesion'. Increasing the active workforce to deal with demographic change is identified as one of the most important policy challenges for Europe 'to fully seize its growth and job potential …', and the social partners have declared their intention to negotiate an autonomous framework agreement concerning these issues.

In a labour market context older persons generally are understood as those who are perceived as approaching their post-employment years[8] and – from an EU policy point of view – 'the critical period with regard to old age and employment begins in the early end of a person's working life … which mainly concerns employees from the age of just above fifty years of age and older. It is also reflected in research on age discrimination, and on perceptions and attitudes regarding employee age.'[9] Age discrimination bans are an important way to counteract 'ageism' or 'false stereotyping based on social constructs'.[10] In 1975 Butler defined ageism as 'a process of systematic stereotyping and discrimination against people because they are old, just as racism and sexism accomplish this for color and gender'.[11] Ageism has later been defined as 'negative or positive stereotypes, prejudice and/or discrimination against (or to the advantage of) elderly people on the basis of their chronological age or on the basis of a perception of them being "old" or "elderly". Ageism can be implicit or explicit and can be expressed on a micro-, meso- or macro-level.'[12] This definition thus refers to the behavioural component

Mulder, M Jenum Hotvedt, M Nesvik and T L Sundet (eds), *Sui generis – Festskrift til Stein Evju* (Universitetsforlaget 2016).

8 Cf K Boudiny, '"Active Ageing": from empty rhetoric to effective policy tool' (2013) 33 Ageing Soc 1077.

9 J Julén Votinius, 'Intersectionality as a tool for analysing age and gender in labour law' in S Manfredi and L Vickers (eds), *Challenges of Active Ageing* (Palgrave Macmillan 2016).

10 D Schiek, 'Age discrimination before the ECJ – Conceptual and theoretical issues' (2011) 48 CML Rev 777, 781. See also J Shaw and H Shaw, 'Recent advancements in European employment law: Towards a transformative legal formula for preventing workplace ageism' (2010) 26 Int J Comp Lab Law and Indus Relations 273.

11 R N Butler, *Why Survive? Being Old in America* (Harper & Row 1975).

12 T N Iversen, L Larsen and P E Solem, 'A conceptual analysis of ageism' (2009) 61(3) Nordic Psych 4.

of discrimination as a key component, while it also indicates that differential treatment on the grounds of age may work to both the detriment and advantage of old people. As we shall see in Section 3, it is not always easy to tell when a measure is to the detriment or advantage of elderly workers; indeed, given that the EU ban on age discrimination is 'neutral' in that it covers all ages, any measure can be discussed in an intergenerational perspective.

Non-discrimination is then an important tool within active ageing strategies. It is, of course, also an expression of the growing importance of the right to non-discrimination and/or equal treatment as a fundamental legal principle that is gaining ground worldwide, including in the EU, over the last two decades – not least with important inspiration from the US.

According to Schiek, a genuine aim, and the main common rationale for non-discrimination law, is 'the aim of overcoming disadvantages related to *ascribed otherness*'.[13] From this, two other rationales can be derived: the right to individuation (or to enable persons to choose beyond stereotypes imposed on them) and the aim to preserve diversity (also requiring accommodation). Against this background – and as in the case of the US – non-discrimination regulation is traditionally designed as complaints-led individual claims in the liberal tradition.

Characteristic of age discrimination, however, is thus a wider uncertainty about its 'wrongness' when compared to other grounds, according to O'Cinneide.[14] Age-based distinctions are not linked to historically embedded patterns of group subordination and thus do not have a negative impact upon human dignity to the same degree as do distinctions based on archetypical non-discrimination grounds such as gender and race.[15] This has led to – again as noted by O'Cinneide – courts worldwide typically applying a light-touch 'rationality' test in relation to

---

13 D Schiek, 'Proportionality in age discrimination cases: Towards a model suitable for socially embedded rights' in A Numhauser-Henning and M Rönnmar (eds), *Age Discrimination and Labour Law: Comparative and Conceptual Perspectives in the EU and Beyond* (Kluwer Law International 2015) 83. See also Schiek (2011), above n 10.

14 C O'Cinneide, 'Constitutional and fundamental rights aspects of age discrimination' in A Numhauser-Henning and M Rönnmar (eds), *Age Discrimination and Labour Law: Comparative and Conceptual Perspectives in the EU and Beyond* (Kluwer Law International 2015) 54. Cf also ibid, the discussion on 'suspect' and 'less suspect' categories of discrimination. See also A G Poiares Maduro in *Coleman v. Attridge Law* C-303/06 EU:C:2008:61.

15 O'Cinneide (2015), above n 14, 54.

age discrimination. Similarly, in relation to the EU ban on age discrimination, we deal with what was described in Chapter 4 of this book as a 'double bind' – apart from the individual approach relating to the ban on age discrimination as a human right, we have a collective approach, encompassing active ageing concerns but also prolonged attention to age as a traditional social stratifier. In respect of the latter, Schiek has identified two different social policy concerns specifically related to age discrimination: the difficulties of complying with expected pension claims due to an ageing population, and the dysfunctional nature of certain traits of hitherto established labour law in relation to the more flexible life-course perspective required 'for the service-oriented economy or the knowledge and information society'.[16]

This double bind has resulted in the 'weaker format' of the age discrimination ban as compared to other non-discrimination bans, which is reflected in the fact that in some cases, direct age discrimination can be justified under the Employment Equality Directive. This distinctive approach seeks to balance the both dignitarian and distributional aspects and has been a central concern – as it has turned out – for the Court of Justice of the European Union's (CJEU) interpretation of the Employment Equality Directive in the Court's case law. This balancing of distributional and dignitarian concerns is also known to lead to particularly problematic or unfair results in cases of multiple or intersectional discrimination – that is, in cases where age interacts with other characteristics, such as disability, gender, or race, which are also prohibited grounds of discrimination intended to produce distinct forms of disadvantage.

The question is why age discrimination is still accepted to such a great extent in the context of the current EU age discrimination regulation within working life. Furthermore, can we also draw upon these explanations when explaining the differential treatment as regards age compared to other grounds in areas outside working life – this time not only due to instrumental social interests but also in terms of external and internal comparisons? The aim of this chapter is to highlight these characteristics/concerns of EU age discrimination law with emphasis on the situation of older employees. In the following, Section 2 introduces age discrimination law in general and provides an overview of this law at the EU level. In Section 3 we shift to a more detailed discussion of EU age discrimination law in the area of working life, drawing heavily upon studies

---

16 Schiek (2015), above n 13, 85.

carried out in the Norma Elder Law Research Environment.[17] Next, Section 4 addresses age discrimination bans outside working life through the example of the Swedish ban on age discrimination in medical care/elder care. This area has received far less study, on the part of the authors[18] as well as others.[19]

2. AGE DISCRIMINATION REGULATION – INTRODUCTORY REMARKS

2.1 International/Constitutional Level

EU developments are, of course, closely related to those at international level. The use of age-based distinctions in different social contexts has also become increasingly controversial from a global perspective. Already in 1967, age joined sex and race as a ground of prohibited discrimination in the US, in the form of the Age Discrimination in

---

[17] See A Numhauser-Henning and M Rönnmar (eds), *Age Discrimination and Labour Law: Comparative and Conceptual Perspectives in the EU and Beyond* (Kluwer Law International 2015); A Numhauser-Henning, 'Labour law in a greying labour market – in need of a reconceptualisation of work and pension norms: The position of older workers in labour law' (2013a) 4 Eur Lab L J 84; A Numhauser-Henning, 'The EU ban on age-discrimination and older workers: Potentials and pitfalls' (2013b) 29 Int J Comp Lab Law and Indus Relations 391; and A Numhauser-Henning and M Rönnmar, 'Compulsory retirement and age discrimination – The Swedish Hörnfeldt case put in perspective', in P Lindskoug, U Maunsbach, G Millqvist, P Samuelsson and H-H Vogel (eds), *Essays in Honour of Michael Bogdan* (Juristförlaget i Lund 2013) 401. See also A Numhauser-Henning and M Rönnmar, 'Age discrimination and labour law in a comparative perspective' in L Carlson, Ö Edström and B Nyström (eds), *Globalisation, Fragmentation, Labour and Employment Law – A Swedish Perspective* (Iustus 2016) and Julén Votinius (2016), above n 9.

[18] See, however, T Mattsson and H Jönson (eds), 'Likvärdighet och äldreomsorg – en introduktion', T Harnett and H Jönson, 'Sill och potatis till den ena och entrecote till den andra?' and S Erlandsson, '"Gammal" eller "funktionshindrad"?' all in (2014) Socialvetenskaplig Tidskrift No. 3–4 Special Issue; and H Jönson and T Harnett, *Socialt arbete med äldre* (Natur & Kultur 2015).

[19] Cf however, A Kydd and A Fleming, 'Ageism and age discrimination in health care: Fact or fiction? A narrative review of the literature' (2015) 81 Maturitas 432. Cited literature tends to concentrate on ageist attitudes/practices in health care, studied empirically, or on health rights proper (see also A Hendriks, 'The right to health in national and international jurisprudence' (1998) 5 Eur J Health L 289 and also A Hendriks, 'Patients' rights and access to health care' (2001) 20 Med Law 371).

Employment Act (ADEA). At domestic level, age as a prohibited ground has subsequently appeared in the constitutions of countries such as Canada,[20] South Africa and Finland. However, age is not expressly referred to in international instruments such as the Universal Declaration of Human Rights, the UN International Covenant on Civil and Political Rights,[21] the ILO Convention No. 111 Concerning Discrimination in Respect of Employment and Occupation, the European Convention on Human Rights (ECHR)[22] or the European Social Charter; in addition, there is still no international covenant proper on the prohibition of age discrimination.[23]

Despite this uncertain status of age discrimination as such in constitutional and international human rights law, national apex courts have been willing to a certain extent to review the compatibility of age-based distinctions with constitutional guarantees of equal treatment and non-discrimination; however, these courts have often accepted age-based distinctions 'if they can be shown to be rationally linked to the achievement of a legitimate aim'.[24] Moreover, in 2014 the Committee of Ministers of the Council of Europe adopted a new recommendation on the promotion of human rights of older persons, and in June 2015 the Members of the Organization of American States adopted a binding regional treaty protecting the rights of the elderly.[25]

---

[20] Cf Fudge, Chapter 3 in this book.

[21] This lack of reference notwithstanding, various UN declarations regarding the rights of younger and older persons have been endorsed by the UN General Assembly, for instance, the Vienna International Plan of Action on Ageing, the United Nations Principles for Older Persons (1991), and the Madrid International Plan of Action of Ageing; in addition, an Open-Ended Working Group on Ageing (UNGA) was established in December 2010 by General Assembly Resolution 65/182 to explore the need for a UN treaty on the human rights of older persons in particular.

[22] The European Court of Human Rights has recognized in its case law, however, that discrimination on the grounds of age can constitute a violation of Article 14 of the Convention in combination with Article 8.

[23] See further, for instance, B Mikolajczyk, 'International law and ageism' (2016) XXXV PYIL 83–107.

[24] Cf O'Cinneide (2015), above n 14, 59.

[25] The Inter-American Convention on Protecting the Human Rights of Older persons, adopted on 6 June 2015.

2.2 EU Level

In the EU, the Amsterdam Treaty (now Article 19 TFEU) provided new competences for EU institutions to take measures against discrimination inter alia on the grounds of age.[26] The CFR (after the Lisbon Treaty, legally binding and part of primary law) in its Article 21 contains a ban on discrimination concerning, among other grounds, age. Against this background, the European Council's Directive 2000/78/EC (the Employment Equality Directive) was adopted in December 2000.[27] It covers age as a ground – among others – for discrimination in the working-life context. Later an initiative was taken to broaden the scope of protection against discrimination, including on the grounds of age, to areas beyond working life, in parallel with that of the 2000/43/EC Directive dealing with discrimination on grounds of ethnicity.[28] We shall return to this issue in Section 4.1. Finally, the Commission's proposal for a European Accessibility Act regarding products and services on the internal market is the most recent development in this area.[29]

The status of equal treatment or non-discrimination on the grounds of age as a fundamental principle of EU law – and indirectly also Article 21 of the CFR – was first put to the test in the *Mangold* case.[30] Despite the fact that the Employment Equality Directive had not been implemented at the time, the CJEU considered a German rule on free access to fixed-term employment when the employee was 52+ years old in relation to Community law and Article 5(1) of the Fixed-Term Work Directive

---

26 Bob Hepple has referred to the following period as one of 'comprehensive and transformative equality', whereas Mark Bell has described it as a time hallmarked by 'widening and deepening' of equality law; see B Hepple, 'Equality at work' in B Hepple and B Veneziani (eds), *The Transformation of Labour Law in Europe: A Comparative Study of 15 Countries 1945–2004* (Hart Publishing 2009) 129–30; and M Bell, 'The principle of equal treatment: Widening and deepening' in P Craig and G de Búrca (eds), *The Evolution of EU Law* (2011). The terms 'comprehensive' and 'widening' refer to the broadened scope of non-discrimination regulation post-Amsterdam; 'transformative' and 'deepening' imply both the constitutionalization of non-discrimination and equal treatment as a fundamental right, but also a more 'substantive' approach to systemic inequalities.

27 Council Directive 2000/78/EC of 27 November 2000 establishing a general framework for equal treatment in employment and occupation, OJ 2000 L 303/16.

28 OJ L 180, 19.7.2000 COM(2008) 426 final.

29 COM(2015) 615 final.

30 *Mangold v. Helm* C-144/04 EU:C:2005:708.

1999/70/EC, and found that the rule was contrary because 'the principle of non-discrimination on grounds of age must ... be regarded as a general principle of Community law' and that 'consequently, observance of the general principle of equal treatment, in particular in respect of age, cannot as such be conditional upon the expiry of the period allowed for the Member States for the transposition of a directive'. Later, in *Kücükdevici*,[31] the Court elaborated further on the relation between this fundamental principle and the Employment Equality Directive. Here the Court reiterated the character of equal treatment on the grounds of age as a general principle of EU law – this time with an express reference to Article 21(1) of the CFR – and stated that 'the [Employment Equality] directive does not in itself lay down the principle of equal treatment ... but has the sole purpose of laying down, in that field, a general framework for combating discrimination on various grounds including age'. This time, the rule at stake was also found to be contrary to the specific regulation in Article 6.1 of the Employment Equality Directive. At the moment a Finnish case is pending that is once again testing the scope of the equal-treatment principle within EU law and Article 21(1) CFR.[32] The case relates to a Finnish supplementary tax on pensions and whether such a tax is precluded by the Employment Equality Directive and/or Article 21(1). In her opinion delivered on 28 January 2016 Advocate General Kokott concludes that the Employment Equality Directive does not apply to taxation of pension income; nor can this be assessed under Article 21(1) CFR, as EU law is not implemented in this case.[33]

A few words about multiple or intersectional discrimination are appropriate here. As indicated in Section 1, the balancing of distributional and dignitarian concerns that is involved in age discrimination cases immediately creates a number of tensions – as a result of competing policy interests in encouraging and supporting longer work lives on the one hand, and on the other the distribution of labour market opportunities in accordance with the principle of intergenerational solidarity. The CJEU's tendency to defer to national governments' employment policies, especially in relation to compulsory retirement and pension eligibility (see further Section 3 in this chapter), has proven to be particularly problematic – and revealing – in cases where age interacts with other grounds on which discrimination is prohibited, such as gender,

---

31 *Kücükdevici v. Swedex GmbH Co KG* C-555/07 EU:C:2010:21.

32 *Korkein hallinto-oikeus* C-122/15 EU:C:2016:65.

33 This conclusion was later confirmed by the CJEU in its judgment of 2 June 2016, EU:C:2016:391. Cf also the pending case *de Lange* C-548/15.

ethnicity, or disability.[34] Many workers belonging to these groups have not historically followed the normative employment pattern inherent in the standard employment contract and life course on which the prevalent notion of intergenerational solidarity is based; therefore, policy rules that seek to uphold that solidarity tend to disadvantage these workers in ways that are not only unfair but also inherently systematic.[35] For example, age or service-related requirements or cut-offs typically fail to account for the fact that disabled workers or women will likely have work histories that do not reflect the norm, as they are more prone to have career interruptions or atypical jobs – by reason of either their disability in the first case or their engagement in provision of unpaid care work within the home. Such workers may be unable to accrue pension entitlements that are equal to those of other workers, or even sufficient to live on, or may not be entitled to wage increments or other employment-related benefits that are tied to seniority and years of service.

Yet, while the aggravated consequences of discrimination operating on multiple grounds have been recognized by the European Commission[36] and the Parliament,[37] a prohibition on this basis has not yet been enacted at the EU level or in most EU Member States. Instead, as it currently stands, the variegated structure of the Employment Equality Directive tends to promote an approach that treats various grounds of discrimination as parallel but separate harms.[38] Similarly, the CJEU's approach to cases where multiple discrimination grounds interact – whether expressly or not – confirms not only the Court's unwillingness to question Member State policies, or require national courts to more deeply probe evidence

---

[34] Schiek (2011), above n 10; P Chaney, 'Mainstreaming intersectional equality for older people? Exploring the impact of quasi-federalism in the UK' (2013) 28 Public Pol and Admin 21; L Roseberry, 'Multiple discrimination' in M Sergeant (ed.), *Age Discrimination and Diversity: Multiple Discrimination from an Age Perspective* (Cambridge University Press 2011) 16.

[35] J Fudge and A Zbyszewska, 'An intersectional approach to age discrimination in the European Union: Bridging dignity and distribution?' in Numhauser-Henning and Rönnmar (2015), above n 17.

[36] European Commission, *Strategy for Equality between Women and Men 2010–2015* document drawn on the basis of COM(2010) 49 final, SEC 92010 1080, 11.

[37] European Parliament, Legislative resolution of 2 April 2009 on the proposal for a Council directive on implementing the principle of equal treatment between persons irrespective of religion or belief, disability, age or sexual orientation, COM(2008) 426 P6 TA (2009) 211.

[38] Cf case *Odar* C-152/11 EU:C:2012:772.

presented by national states to justify their policies, but also the Court's 'blindness' to the systemic nature of the disadvantage that such policies create.[39]

3. EQUAL TREATMENT AND AGE DISCRIMINATION – INSIDE WORKING LIFE

3.1 The EU Employment Equality Directive

The Employment Equality Directive applies to conditions for access to employment, self-employment or occupation; vocational guidance and training; employment and working conditions, including dismissals and pay; and membership of and involvement in a trade union or an employer's organization (Article 3). The Directive applies to Member States when legislating, social partners when concluding collective agreements, and employers. The Employment Equality Directive is aligned with the other non-discrimination directives and encompasses prohibitions of direct and indirect discrimination, harassment, and instruction to discriminate, provisions on positive action and active measures and a rule on a reversed burden of proof.

However, the ban on age discrimination differs from bans for most other discrimination grounds in that direct differential treatment can be justified if it concerns a legitimate aim, and the measure at issue is both appropriate and necessary (Article 6.1). Legitimate aims shall be related to employment policy, labour market and vocational training objectives, and the Member States – as well as the social partners – enjoy broad discretion in defining these aims as well as measures for achieving them. Article 6.2 of the Directive also stipulates that Member States may provide that setting age limits in occupational social security schemes for admission or entitlement to retirement or invalidity benefits (including the use of age criteria in actuarial calculations in the context of such schemes) does not constitute discrimination on the grounds of age. Moreover, Article 4 contains an exemption covering all grounds under the Directive for so-called GOR (genuine and determining occupational) requirements. There is also Article 2.5 and the exemption for legislative measures necessary for public security and public order as well as for the protection of health and the rights and freedoms of others. Finally, we

[39] Cf the cases of *Rosenbladt v. Oellerking Gebaudereinigungsges mbH* C-45/09 EU:C:2010:601 and *Kücükdevici*, above n 31, which both illustrate this particularly well.

have Article 3.4 and the exception for the armed forces in relation to age and disability.

3.2 The EU Age Discrimination Ban at Work

3.2.1 Introduction

The subject of the EU ban on age discrimination and its implications for both older workers and labour law has been developed in numerous publications within the Norma Elder Law Research Environment[40] as well as by other authors.[41] The relevant case law is fairly generous now and has caused significant discussion – and also criticism – especially in relation to the different standards of the proportionality test applied by the CJEU.[42] Moreover, given the ambiguity of the age discrimination ban set out in the Directive, these interpretations work to the detriment, as well as the protection, support and empowerment, of older people, in the intrinsic ways described here.

3.2.2 Compulsory retirement and pension-related working conditions

Quite a few cases brought before the CJEU have concerned compulsory retirement, which is still an acceptable practice in EU law despite the ban on age discrimination and in stark contrast to policies in the US.[43] Whereas retirement age as such is outside the scope of the Employment Equality Directive, the termination of employment in terms of retirement

40 Cf n 17 above.

41 Cf for instance, C Tobler, 'EU age discrimination law and older and younger workers: Court of Justice of the European Union case law developments' in Numhauser-Henning and Rönnmar (2015), above n 17, and, for example, Schiek (2011), above n 10; M Schlachter, 'Mandatory retirement and age discrimination under EU law' (2011) 27 Int J Comp Lab Law and Indus Relations; C Kilpatrick, 'The Court of Justice and labour law in 2010: A new EU discrimination law architecture' (2011) 40(3) Indus L J 280–301; and E Dewhurst, 'Intergenerational balance, mandatory retirement and age discrimination in Europe: How can the ECJ better support national courts in finding a balance between the generations?' (2013) 50 CML Rev 1333.

42 Cf n 17 above and n 41 above.

43 See *Palacios de la Villa v. Cortefiel Servicios SA* C-411/05 EU:C:2007:604; *Age Concern England v. Secretary of State for Business, Enterprise and Regulatory Reform* C-388/07 EU:C:2009:128; *Rosenbladt, Georgiev v. Technicheski Universitet, Sofia* C-250/09 and C-268/09 EU:C:2010:699; *Fuchs and Köhler v. Land Hessen* C-159/10 and C-160/10 EU:C:2011:508; *Torsten Hörnfeldt v. Posten Meddelande AB* C-141/11 EU:C:2012:421; and the *European Commission v. Hungary* C-341/08 EU:C:2012:687.

is not. Despite the fact that compulsory retirement in principle amounts to direct age discrimination it may be acceptable under the exception rule in Article 6.1 of the Employment Equality Directive. Significant for cases of compulsory retirement is the lenient proportionality test applied by the CJEU. Schlachter, for instance, has distinguished two separate standards when it comes to the justification of differential treatment in this area; one 'control standard' as regards general systems of compulsory retirement such as in the cases *Rosenbladt* and *Hörnfeldt*, and another, considerably stricter standard when it comes to special professional groups such as in the cases *Petersen*,[44] *Rosenbladt, Georgiev, Fuchs and Köhler* and, later, *European Commission v. Hungary*.[45]

Inducing people to work beyond pensionable age is a core concern in active ageing policies. To make people work longer, they must have both the practical and the legal possibility to do so, and in this respect, of course, the acceptance of compulsory retirement is a key issue. Legitimate aims accepted so far by the CJEU include intergenerational fairness in terms of access to employment, prevention of humiliating forms of employment termination, and a reasonable balance between labour market and budgetary concerns. In these cases, the CJEU has given much consideration to Member States' traditions because 'the automatic termination of the employment contracts for employees who meet the conditions as regards age and contributions paid for the liquidation of their pension rights has, for a long time, been a feature of employment law in many Member States and is widely used in employment relationships'.[46] Not only the Member States but also the social partners, when applying Article 6.1 in the Employment Equality Directive, are said to have a broad margin of discretion 'in choosing not only to pursue a

---

[44] *Petersen v. Beerufungsausschuss fur Zahnärzte fur den Bezirk Westfalen-Lippe* C-341/08 EU:C:2010:4.

[45] Schlachter (2011), above n 41. Cf also Schiek (2011), above n 10, and Fudge, Chapter 3 in this book.

[46] *Hörnfeldt*, above n 43, judgment, 28. According to a 2011 report, based on the situation as at 31 December 2009, 24 of 29 Member States did have a set age for automatic termination (compulsory retirement), concerning specific professions and/or public employees. However, 23 out of 29 Member States *did not* have a general rule on compulsory retirement that was also applicable to the private sector: D O'Dempsey and A Beale, *Age and Employment*, Report from the Network of Legal Experts in the non-discrimination field to the European Commission 1 July 2011 (2011).

particular aim in the field of social and employment policy, but also in defining measures to implement it'.[47]

In situations concerning pension reform and/or pension-related age differentials in redundancy/dismissal situations, the CJEU has been known to apply a stricter standard.[48] The case *European Commission v. Hungary* concerned pension reform for judges, prosecutors and notaries, lowering the age of compulsory dismissal from 70 to 62 years of age. The 'standardization' of compulsory retirement age was a relevant aim in relation to Article 6.1, according to the CJEU, but the regulation did not meet the requirements for being appropriate and necessary. An individual assessment proved 'the provisions at issue abruptly and significantly lowered the age-limit for compulsory retirement, without introducing transitional measures of such a kind as to protect the legitimate expectations of the persons concerned'.[49]

The *Andersen* case concerned reduced redundancy payments in a situation of collective dismissals for employees already entitled to employer-paid retirement benefits at the age of 63.[50] Whereas the CJEU found 'the aim of preventing compensation on termination from being claimed by persons who are not seeking new employment but will receive a replacement income in the form of an occupational old-age pension to be legitimate',[51] upon closer scrutiny the measure was found to be neither appropriate nor necessary as it neglected the individual employee's wish not to opt for the pension but to continue working.[52] In *Odar*, however, reduced redundancy payments related to the date of a right to early retirement was deemed appropriate since 'it made sense to reduce the severance pay of employees who are financially secure, and to facilitate the transition to new employment for employees with more

---

47 The quote is from *Palacios de la Villa*, above n 43 – the first to accept compulsory retirement (judgment, 68). Cf also the later cases *Rosenbladt*, *Georgiev*, above n 43, 67, *Hörnfeldt*, above n 43, 32 and *Odar*, above n 38, 47 and further Numhauser-Henning and Rönnmar (2016), above n 7.

48 See cases *Petersen*, above n 44; *Ole Andersen v. Region Syddanmark* C-499/08 EU:C:2010:600; *Prigge v. Deutsche Lufthansa AB* C-447/09 EU:C:2011:573; *Johann Odar v. Baxter Deutschland GmbH* C-152/11 EU:C:2012:772; *HK Danmark v. Experian A/S* C-476/11 EU:C:2013:590; *Toftgaard v. Indenrigs- og Sundhedsministeriet* C-546/11 EU:C:2013:603; and *Ingeniörforeningen i Danmark v. Tekniq* C-515/13 EU:C:2015:115.

49 *European Commission v. Hungary*, above n 43, judgment, 67–8.

50 See also *Dansk Industri (DI), acting on behalf of Ajos A/S v. Estate of Karsten Eigil Rasmussen* C-441/14 EU:C:2015:776.

51 *Andersen*, above n 48, judgment, 44.

52 Cf also *Prigge*, above n 48.

limited financial resources'[53] and also necessary as it provided only for a reduction in the amount of compensation granted to older workers.[54] In *Toftgaard*, however, the refusal to grant availability pay to civil servants who had reached the age of 65 – the default retirement age for the civil servants was in fact 70 years of age – and who were entitled to a pension, was indeed (and in parallel to that in *Andersen*) regarded as going beyond what was necessary.

A conclusion following *Toftgaard* was that whenever we deal with age-related working conditions and situations that are 'pre'-default retirement age, a stricter standard applies; this may also be the case when there is no default age for retirement.[55] Recent case law, however, may call for a revision of this conclusion. In *Tekniq*, severance allowance – a few months of extra pay to the long-time employed (12, 15 or 18 years) – was not paid to workers entitled to a state retirement pension. The aim – to help older (but not 65+) workers find new employment – was found a legitimate aim under Article 6.1, whereas restricting the allowance to those not entitled to a state pension did not appear unreasonable and thus not 'manifestly inappropriate'. Nor was the fact that the rule treated those who would actually receive a state pension in the same way as those who are eligible for such a pension enough to make it inappropriate/ unnecessary. Here, the consequences for the employees at issue were carefully scrutinized – in parallel with both *Andersen* and *Toftgaard* – but were found to be proportionate; the amount of compensation was 'a limited lump sum which does not appear capable of causing a significant loss of income to the departing employee in the long term'. The solution at stake 'does not appear unduly to prejudice the legitimate interests of workers who have reached the ordinary age of retirement'.[56] Now, we have to conclude that in regard to working conditions such as redundancy and availability pay the CJEU also applies a stricter proportionality test in relation to workers 65 years or older – or beyond the applicable default retirement age – and scrutinizes the effects for the individual employee (despite, as in *Tekniq*, accepting differential treatment of workers in terms of the right to a state pension, when these effects were limited).

---

[53] *Odar*, above n 38, judgment, 48.

[54] Ibid 51–2.

[55] Cf A Numhauser-Henning, 'Labour law, pension norms and the EU ban on age discrimination: Towards ultimate flexibilization?' in Numhauser-Henning and Rönnmar (2015), above n 17.

[56] *Tekniq*, above n 48, judgment, 44.

3.2.3 To uphold – or not to uphold – the ban on age discrimination

Whereas upholding the ban on age discrimination would have meant an attack on (or at least a partial replacement of) the standard employment contract as developed during the twentieth century,[57] the continued acceptance of compulsory retirement is rather an integral part of the standard employment contract.[58] Accepting compulsory retirement thus implies support for the standard employment contract and the continued use of age as a social stratifier. This challenges the flexibilization functions of non-discrimination law. Anti-discrimination law has thus generally been seen as an expression of the general trend towards individualization going hand in hand with the flexibilization of labour markets experienced in recent decades. The ban on (age) discrimination is thus, generally speaking, stepping in as a *replacement* for employment protection in these times of flexibilization of work.[59]

At first glance, of course, eliminating compulsory retirement – which in itself implies immediate cessation of employment – would promote not only active ageing in terms of work beyond retirement age, but also employment protection. In addition, at individual level, older workers typically push for legislation to make compulsory retirement illegal. This mainly seems to be to the detriment of the younger generations in the sense that older workers thus do not abstain from their developed employment protection, or from 'senior' working conditions, irrespective of whether these comprise wages or vacation. However, a frequent argument in favour of compulsory retirement, now also accepted by the

---

[57] See further M Freedland, 'Burying Caesar: What was the standard employment contract?' in K Stone and H Arthurs (eds), *Rethinking Workplace Regulation: Beyond the Standard Contract of Employment* (Russell Sage Foundation 2013) and K Strauss, 'Equality, fair mutualisation and the socialisation of risk and reward in European pensions' in N Countouris and M Freedland (eds), *Resocialising Europe in a Time of Crisis* (Cambridge University Press 2013).

[58] Cf E Lazear and his mandatory retirement theory: E Lazear, 'Why is there mandatory retirement?' (1979) 87(6) J Polit Econ 1261. Compulsory retirement thus builds on an implicit contract model, stating that employers pay employees a wage premium towards the end of their careers on the assumption that the employment relationship will come to an end at a predictable, fixed point in time.

[59] Cf the US, where bans on discrimination were always regarded as having a key (replacement) function in relation to the dismissal-at-will doctrine; cf J Fineman, 'The vulnerable subject at work: A new perspective on the employment at-will debate' (2013) 43 Swedish L Rev 278. On this line of argument see further Rönnmar, Kullmann, Numhauser-Henning and Ulander-Wänman, Chapter 9 in this book.

CJEU, is that should there be no formalized 'end' to the employment relationship; as the employee grows old we cannot avoid situations in which employment contracts are terminated in forms which are humiliating for older workers.[60]

The ban on age discrimination is first and foremost in place to tackle dismissals related to the individual. The extent to which sickness and reduced working capacity amount to just cause for dismissal on personal grounds differs among the Member States. There are, however, good reasons to believe that upholding the ban on age discrimination – and thus, as a general rule, requiring just cause for dismissal at any age – would lead to an increased emphasis on 'capability' as an employment requirement, and the undermining not only of active ageing strategies but also employment protection well before retirement age. In the UK, one result of the abolishment of statutory compulsory retirement is assumed to be an increased use of performance management; regular reviews, consultation and documentation designed to monitor employee performance and build a case for either voluntary retirement or a dismissal that will hold up against the UK unfair dismissal legislation.[61]

A weakening of employment protection in such terms, generally speaking, will make way for an increase in flexible employment (if any) for workers who are approaching pension age. No one – and certainly not the former employer – will be willing to go through a dismissal for personal reasons again. Ironically, this is also why acceptance of compulsory retirement in itself seems to support an increase in flexible employment beyond retirement.[62] In both *Rosenbladt* and *Hörnfeldt* the Court – in accepting compulsory retirement at a certain age – pointed to the fact that the possibility of other employment (under the auspices of the ban on age discrimination) still existed, should the individual prefer not to retire. Often enough, such employment would take the form of a fixed-term contract, whether with the old or a new employer.[63] In the

---

60 *Hörnfeldt*, above n 43. Cf also *Rosenbladt*, *Georgiev*, above n 43, and *Fuchs and Köhler*, above n 43. Cf J C Suk, 'From antidiscrimination to equality: Stereotypes and the life cycle in the United States and Europe' (2012) 60 Am J Comp L 75–98.

61 Cf C Barnard and S Deakin, 'Age discrimination and labour law in the UK: Managing ageing' in Numhauser-Henning and Rönnmar (2015), above n 17.

62 Numhauser-Henning (2013a).

63 Cases such as *Rosenbladt*, *Georgiev*, above n 43, and *Fuchs and Köhler*, above n 43, show us that in certain professions, the compulsory retirement regime comes with an institutionalized order of (only) fixed-term work openings.

same way, otherwise restricted use of fixed-term employment is frequently more generous beyond 'normal' pension age. This is the case in Sweden, where there are no restrictions whatsoever concerning individuals of 67+. Whether an unlimited scope for fixed-term work beyond retirement age really is acceptable has been discussed in relation to the Fixed-Term Work Directive, in principle requiring some kind of restriction.[64] In *Mangold* the CJEU made it clear that a German rule on fixed-term employment at the age of 52, which was put in place to facilitate access to the labour market, was disproportionate in respect of the Fixed-Term Work Directive and the general principle of non-discrimination. However, in a reasoned opinion the Commission has now accepted old age (67 years of age) as an objective criterion under Article 5.1a of the Directive.[65] As yet there is no case arguing that an employer's preference for a fixed-term contract over a permanent one with regard to older workers in itself amounts to age discrimination.

What we have not discussed so far is the inherent weaknesses of the discrimination ban itself – the substitute, as it were, for employment security in times of flexibilization – due to the 'elitist' design of non-discrimination regulation in general. Age discrimination may well turn out to be a weak friend in need![66] Indeed, the design, generally speaking, works to the detriment of older workers, because the reference norms representing the foundation of comparison in cases of alleged discrimination are basically meritocratic. Therefore, the non-hiring of an older applicant may well be defended by arguments about the more 'up-to-date' education of a younger candidate, while a dismissal may be defended by arguments about the older worker's ability to work and availability in terms of working time. Some of these problems could

64 Cf the infringement case between the Commission and Sweden concerning whether Sweden has rightfully implemented the Fixed-Term Work Directive, among other things pointing to the fact that Sweden is accepting unlimited fixed-term work, post-67 years of age. Cf MEMO/08/69 31 January 2008 of the European Commission and the European Commission's reasoned opinion 21 February 2013 C(2013) 822 final with a complementary reasoned opinion 22 April 2014 C(2014) 2380 final.

65 See n 64 above.

66 Cf C O'Cinneide, 'Completing the picture: The complex relationship between EU anti-discrimination law and "Social Europe"' in Countouris and Freedland (2013), above n 57, with further references to A Somek, *Engineering Equality: An Essay on European Anti-Discrimination Law* (Oxford University Press 2012).

possibly be avoided by requiring 'proactive' measures (compare reasonable accommodation) in relation to age as well, but such a development has yet to be seen.

3.2.4 Age-related wage-setting

We conclude this section with just a few words about age-related wage-setting. This is seen as a constituent of the standard employment contract, whereas seniority wage-setting practices tend to work to the detriment of active ageing: they become very expensive when employees grow older. Still, these practices are common and the question is to what extent they – as compulsory retirement – are still found to be compatible with a ban on age discrimination. It is already evident from the CJEU's case law in sex-discrimination cases that experience in terms of length of service – and thus with an indirect connection to age – is a justified criterion as far as wage-setting is concerned, without the employer having to establish the bearing this experience has on the performance of specific tasks entrusted to the employee at stake.[67] This does not mean that a more 'automatic' age-related wage-setting system is acceptable as demonstrated by the *Hennigs* case.[68] A collective agreement, providing that the basic pay determined on appointment of the employee was based directly on the employee's age, was found impermissible under Article 6.1 of the Employment Equality Directive, whereas there was a broad scope for the social partners providing a transitional way out of these practices also in somewhat discriminatory terms.[69]

The experience of countries that have already eliminated compulsory retirement is that there is a continued need of age distinctions in employee benefits (also indicated by the very exception in Article 6.2 of the Employment Equality Directive). For instance, Canadian legislation and case law recognize 'the principle that even in the absence of

---

67 See for instance, *Danfoss* C-109/88 EU:C:1989:383 and *Cadman* C-17/05 EU:C:2006:633. See also *Tyrolean Airways Tiroler Luftfahrt Gesellschaft mbH v. Betriebsrat Bord der Tyrolean Airways Tiroler Luftfahrt* C-132/11 EU:C:2012:329.

68 *Hennigs v. Eisenban-Bundesamt* and *Land Berlin v. Alexander Mai* C-297/10 and 298/10 EU:C:2011:560.

69 See further, A Numhauser-Henning and M Rönnmar (2016) and cases *Specht et al. v. Land Berlin* C-501/12 EU:C:2015:2005 and *Unland v. Land Berlin* C-20/13 EU:C:2015:561. Cf also *HK Danmark*, above n 48, where age-related retirement contributions – increasing with age – were considered legitimate under Article 6.1 of the Directive.

compulsory retirement employers, employees and government policy-makers cannot simply disregard the inevitable consequences of ageing when establishing employment benefits' such as long-term disability plans, and 'the need to balance the competing interests that bargaining unit members have at different times in their lives is an inherent part of the collective bargaining process. Moreover, younger employees generally want higher wages, while older employees may prefer such benefits as life insurance, pensions or retirement allowances.'[70]

4. EQUAL TREATMENT AND AGE DISCRIMINATION – OUTSIDE WORKING LIFE

4.1 Introduction

At the EU level a proposal is currently pending for a directive extending the prohibition against discrimination on the grounds of (among others) age beyond working life – the so-called Horizontal Directive.[71] The proposal covers an area such as social protection, including social security and health care. Despite encountering serious difficulties[72] over the years – the adoption of the Horizontal Directive requires unanimity – the proposal was 'resuscitated' by the Juncker Commission[73] and, following a progress report, the Council of the EU concluded in June 2015 that there was 'a strong political will in favour of continuing this work'.[74] Still, there is considerable resistance towards adopting the

---

[70] R Charney and M Horner, 'Defending age distinctions in employee benefits after the elimination of mandatory retirement' (2013) 17 Can Lab L and Employment L J 255.

[71] OJ L 180, 19.7.2000, COM(2008) 426 final.

[72] See further L Waddington, 'Future prospects for EU equality law: Lessons to be learnt from the proposed Equal Treatment Directive' (2011) 36 Eur L Rev 163.

[73] The Juncker Commission has made it a priority to maintain the proposal and convince national governments to give up their current resistance in the Council. See Juncker's opening statement in the European Parliament Plenary Session, *A New Start for Europe: New Agenda for Jobs, Growth, Fairness and Democratic Change, Political Guidelines for the next European Commission*, available at http://ec.europa.eu/priorities/docs/pg_en.pdf.

[74] Outcome of the Council Meeting 3398, 18–19 June 2015 8. See also the Progress Report 9011/15, Brussels, 4 June 2015. Cf also the footnoted consolidated text of the proposal presented to the Council of the European Union on 11 December 2014, 15705/14 ADD 1 _REV 1, Brussels, 4 December 2014.

Horizontal Directive. Major concerns include the proposal infringing on national competences as well as the inclusion of social protection and education. There are also Member States that would have preferred more ambitious provisions for certain aspects, especially in regard to disability.[75] The Commission still clings to its original proposal containing a scope for the justification of direct age discrimination *whenever* there was a legitimate aim and the means were appropriate and necessary – a scope even broader than that of the Employment Equality Directive. The double bind thus prevails in this context as well. Moreover, in 2015 the Latvian presidency added a new exemption for preferential charges, fees or rates in respect of persons in a specific age group (Article 2(6)(c)), the aim being to allow commercial entities to charge different rates based on the age of the customer; the amendment was opposed by certain Member States as being too broad. Whereas the future of the Horizontal Directive is still uncertain (to say the least), several EU Member States – including Germany, Poland and Sweden – have already expanded the scope of the ban on age discrimination beyond working life. Here we will discuss the example of Sweden.[76]

In Swedish law, gender, age and other discursively and institutionally constructed categories such as ethnicity and sexual orientation are not identified as intersecting. In the preparatory works of the Swedish Discrimination Act (2008:567), the covariance of several grounds of discrimination is only briefly touched upon, and solely from the point of view of how the supervision of the various bans on discrimination should be organized.[77] The case law on discrimination involving more than one ground is very limited, and the few cases where age has been treated as part of the same legal matter as other grounds for discrimination all relate to working life.[78] The common thread for court cases hitherto is that they

---

[75] Cf further also Waddington (2011), above n 72.

[76] Concerning Poland, see for instance L Mitrus, 'Age discrimination and labour law in Poland' and, concerning Germany, M Schlachter, 'Age discrimination and labour law in Germany', both in Numhauser-Henning and Rönnmar (2015), above n 17.

[77] Government Inquiry Report SOU 2006:22 217.

[78] Since the adoption of the Discrimination Act in 2008, the Equality Ombudsman has brought action in fewer than ten cases involving more than one ground of discrimination relating to working life, the provision of goods and services and the area of education. Three cases involve discrimination on the ground of age: Swedish Labour Court judgments AD 2009 No. 11, 2010 No. 91 and AD 2013 No. 64.

have been framed as cases of multiple discrimination.[79] It is thus only in parallel to each other that age and other categories have been recognized as important in the legal context; intersectional effects of age and other categories are not addressed in a more general and comprehensive way, as questions of legal significance in their own right.

4.2 The Swedish Ban on Age Discrimination in Medical Care/Elder Care

The Swedish Discrimination Act (2008:567) implements existing EU law regulations on age discrimination, but also does more. It has the character of a 'single non-discrimination Act' covering all regulated grounds – sex, transgender identity or expression, ethnicity, religion or other belief, disability, sexual orientation and age – as well as various areas of society. It has been an express aim of the Swedish legislator to create a discrimination regulation treating all covered grounds equally. The Act is monitored (all grounds and areas) by the Equality Ombudsman (*Diskrimineringsombudsmannen*, DO). Thus, all grounds – including age – are now in principle covered by the existing bans in different areas of society.[80] This does not mean that the protection is necessarily equal. As we shall see, in particular the ban on age discrimination is limited by a broad scope for justified differential treatment – as is the case in EU law and the Employment Equality Directive. The areas covered, however, are thus considerably broader in the Swedish Discrimination Act than EU law up to this point. These areas include working life, education, goods, services and housing, health/medical care and social services, the social insurance system, unemployment insurance and financial aid for studies, national military service and civilian service as well as public employment when assisting the public. Age is still excluded as a protected ground concerning national military service and civilian service. Here, we look deeper into the implications of an age-related ban on discrimination in the area of health and medical care and social services.

According to Chapter 2 Section 13 in the 2008 Discrimination Act, discrimination on any ground, including age, is thus prohibited with regard to (1) health and medical care and other medical services, (2) social services activities and (3) support in the form of special transport services, national special transport services and housing adaptation

[79] E Schömer, 'Multiple discrimination: A smokescreen over differences' (2012) 36 Retfaerd 138.

[80] Age outside working life included since 1 January 2013, see further Government Bill Prop 2011/12:159.

allowances. Chapter 2 Section 13b contains a rule on the scope for continued differential treatment on the grounds of age. The ban thus does not apply to (1) application of a certain age requirement prescribed in law, and (2) other differential treatment on the grounds of age with a legitimate goal and where the means to achieve that goal are appropriate and necessary to attain the aim – thus articulating a fairly broad scope for direct age discrimination.

Generally speaking, in relation to health services and medical care, 'need/necessity' is the decisive criterion – a criterion that should not need to yield for age.[81] However, the regulation thus contains an exemption concerning age – an exemption parallel to that of the Employment Equality Directive, but with no specification whatsoever. According to the preparatory works, the ban covers both administrative/procedural acts and factual acts and can regard access to care, coverage and contents of care and the cost implied.[82] Care priorities are set by national guidelines.[83] Priority is thus decided by need/necessity and in accordance with three ethical principles: the human dignity principle (*människovärdesprincipen*), the need and solidarity principle (*behovs- och solidaritetsprincipen*), and, the cost-effectiveness principle (*kostnadseffektivitetsprincipen*). This last principle implies that there shall be a reasonable relation between costs and effects – in terms of health and quality of life – when making a choice between certain activities or measures. The cost-effectiveness principle is second to the other two principles. Severe conditions precede less severe ones despite costs and age, and other personal characteristics are of no concern in relation to need, but in the individual case attention may be given to circumstances limiting the 'utility' (*nyttan*) of care measures. Here (old) age may well be relevant.

Legally established age limits usually aim first and foremost at ensuring the protection of young persons. Otherwise, fixed ages may concern payment (for instance free care for certain age groups, such as the young or retired) and/or preventive measures offered to certain groups (such as influenza vaccinations for persons of 65+ years). Here, regional and local authorities have a certain scope for discretion.[84]

---

[81] Government Bill Prop 2011/12:159 46 (Government Inquiry Report SOU 2010:60 13).

[82] Additionally, a discriminatory treatment/reception/attitude by public employees attending the public is as such generally banned by the Discrimination Act, ch 2 sec 17. This may be of special importance precisely in care activities.

[83] Government Bill Prop 1996/97:60, bet. 1996/97: SoU14 and Rskr 1996/97:186.

[84] Government Bill Prop 2011/12:159, 46ff.

The extended ban on age discrimination in Sweden in relation to health care and medical services has thus been given the same ambiguous or weak template as the EU ban in working life according to the Employment Equality Directive, and – possibly – the Horizontal Directive. At a more practical level there also seems to be a parallel to the double bind disguised in the cost-efficiency principle, which thus opens up for the justification of direct age discrimination in terms of cost versus effectiveness in what has to be regarded as a collective interest approach.

So far, there is little case law involving the bans on discrimination and their application in health care and medical services in Sweden.[85] According to a report by the Swedish Equality Ombudsman, a typical feature of experienced discrimination in – among others – the health/medical care sector is a combination of 'stereotyped' attitudinal treatment and the actual treatment.[86] According to another DO report, care is typically construed to meet the needs of 'normal' human beings; individuals tend to be categorized into groups and also reduced to these categories – for example, the psychologically ill person gets less somatic care, and fewer painkillers are given for the oldest old persons because it is 'normal' for them to be in pain.[87] It is also well known that care is far from equally distributed in Swedish society.[88] First, women make up two-thirds of all people 80 years or older, which makes equal care a gender issue. Moreover, men can rely to a larger extent on their spouses, whereas women – who live longer – are likely to live alone. Women are prescribed more psychopharmacological drugs that cause side effects such as confusion and, generally, the elderly are less often treated with alternative methods (such as cognitive behavioural therapy). The better educated are given more expensive and more modern psychopharmacological drugs and better access to specialized medical care.

---

[85] In case T 5507-12, judgment 26 June 2014, the Supreme Court found discrimination on grounds of sexual orientation to be at hand. A lesbian woman was not provided care (a fertility investigation) at her regular care unit (*vårdcentral*) but was referred to a special clinic for homosexual women.

[86] DO, Delar av mönster (Parts of Patterns), Report 2014:1 60. See also Kydd and Fleming (2015), above n 19, concluding that negative attitudes are usually reported in acute health care settings, where targets and quick turnover are encouraged.

[87] DO, Rätten till sjukvård på lika villkor (The right to care on equal terms), Report 2012:4 46.

[88] Cf the report 'Ojämna villkor för hälsa och vård. Jämställdhetsperspektiv på hälso- och sjukvården' (Unequal conditions for care. An equal treatment perspective on health care and medical care), December 2011 110ff.

An interesting conclusion in social work research related to the Norma Elder Law Research Programme is that equality in elder care seems to be discussed rather in relation to internal comparisons (with other patients, sometimes with the same disease) than in relation to external comparisons, which is the tradition in relation to the disabled (generally compared to other non-disabled groups in society).[89] Another study concludes that there are considerable differences in relation to how support for elderly and younger persons, respectively, is construed – in two different categories, not really comparable, and with the result that differential treatment is not perceived as age discrimination.[90] According to Harnett and Jönson, a potential external reference in elder care is that the older person will be able to live just as he or she did before. This is a weak reference, however, frequently rejected by reference to the disability as the reason for the elderly person's transfer to an elder care facility in the first place. The resulting limitations were viewed not as related to lack of support for older persons, but as related to weakening abilities as such. For elderly people, when it comes to being compared to other groups, it is more about what one can (not!) do than about the support one needs. In a disability context, external comparisons are considered legitimate.[91] Disabilities are seen as caused by a lack of accommodation and are discussed in terms of accommodation and inclusion/integration, whereas elder care is contextualized precisely in a discourse of care. The question is this: should a person in elder care be compared with persons his/her age in general, or, with younger disabled persons?[92] Erlandsson shows us how – despite the fact that the development of social services is being guided by the principles of justice, universalism and equal treatment – adults in need of care are still divided into two categories; persons 65 years or older and disabled persons (mainly less than 65 years of age). These categories have different rights to support depending on their current age and also the age at which the 'disability' occurs. Persons 65 years or older were thus found to be united by care needs stemming from their ageing bodies. Persons with disabilities were construed as citizens with a joint experience of discrimination and difficulties caused by an inaccessible society. 'In accordance with this, elderly policy documents focus mainly on issues related to elder

89 Cf Harnett and Jönson (2014), above n 18.
90 Erlandsson (2014) Socialvetenskaplig Tidsskrift No. 3–4.
91 Government Inquiry Report SOU 2008:77, *Möjlighet att leva om andra.*
92 Harnett and Jönson (2014), above n 18, 263.

care, while disability policy documents emphasize issues of participation, equality and accessibility.'[93]

In the design of EU discrimination law (basically reflecting the civil rights approach, age discrimination included) we do not see this difference – it is generally argued precisely in terms of participation, equality and accessibility. Non-discrimination regulation, as well as ageing policies, is thus often discussed in terms of inclusion, and the ageing individual is compared to other individuals of different ages in a similar situation. This is the perspective that lies at the heart of non-discrimination law and the one that truly fosters an intergenerational approach. However, the application of 'another' context can be disguised in the interpretation of a situation perceived as similar/comparable or not, as well as within the accepted scope for justification of direct age discrimination! The double bind permits a collective approach to age differentials when those are compatible with the European social model. In a context like the Swedish one, where the ban on age discrimination also applies to the areas of health care, medical care and social services, practices such as those described here may well be decisive for the potential impact of non-discrimination regulation. A principle of need may be decisive as the distribution of health/medical care is concerned, but a continued focus on the (differentiated) need for 'care' contextualized in certain ways tends to leave out issues of the accessibility/quality of support. At the same time, it is said that 'health must lie at the core of society's response to population aging' and prohibitions of age discrimination are regarded as a crucial tool in making rights and dignity in ageing 'the norm'.[94] All of this could be typical for age discrimination bans in the area of social services/elder care – not only in Sweden, but in general. Only time will tell. These aspects give us reason to revisit the capability issue as the core concern. There is no doubt that reduced capability is a real concern in regard to many elderly. A real ambition of inclusion as the goal for equal treatment/a ban on age discrimination must therefore be accompanied by requirements of reasonable accommodation – requirements that are not yet introduced in relation to age.

93 Ibid 284. Cf also H Gautun and A S Grødem, 'Prioritising care services: Do the oldest users lose out?' (2015) 24 Int J Soc Welfare 73.

94 L O Gostin and A Garsi, 'Governing for health as the world grows older: Healthy lifespans in aging societies' (2014) 22 Elder L J 111, 114, 121.

5. CONCLUDING REMARKS

The principle of equality is a principle of universal application, and as Doron says, it sends 'a positive message regarding the status of the elderly in society'; 'its implicit notion of normalization' makes the older population an integral and equal part of society.[95] In EU law up to this point, restricting the ban on age discrimination to the area of working life, the weaker template of precisely this discrimination ban as compared to those for other grounds does reflect, however, that older workers still may be treated differently to a considerable extent. According to the Employment Equality Directive and its Article 6.1, direct age discrimination may be justified, and the ban is characterized by its 'double bind' that paves the way for the ban to work in intrinsic ways – to the detriment as well as protection and support of older workers. The double bind implies that the ban balances often conflicting distributional and dignitarian concerns.

The current state of EU age discrimination law reflects its underlying, partly conflicting human rights and economic rationales, respectively. The CFR, and the right to equality, the right to non-discrimination and the rights of the elderly emphasize the human rights rationale. At the same time, the traditional role age plays in the organization of labour markets and the design of labour laws is partly maintained and reflected in the broad scope for justification of age-related differential treatment, including compulsory retirement. This practice honours traditional use of age as a social stratifier and may well be favourable to older workers, protecting them in relation to the precarization of both work and pensions. At the individual level it is easy to see that this continued acceptance of compulsory retirement works to 'stereotype' the old-age individual in terms of ageism and dignity harm.

In EU law we have not yet seen a ban on age discrimination beyond working life. The Swedish example – having adopted a ban on age discrimination in areas such as health/medical services and social services/elder care – shows that there is a significant likelihood that a broad scope for justification of continued differential treatment on the grounds of age will prevail, thus also applying a double bind here, and creating a scope for the collective interest approach within a cost-effectiveness logic. Added to this is the tradition within social services/

---

[95] I Doron, 'A multi-dimensional model of elder law' in I Doron (ed.), *Theories of Law and Ageing: The Jurisprudence of Elder Law* (Springer 2009) 61.

elder care of dealing with people 65+ years of age in terms of care and internal comparisons rather than using concepts of other types of discrimination law in the liberal tradition: inclusion and equality in comparison with more externalized categories. Such practices undermine the potential effects of a ban on age discrimination and perpetuate attitudes of paternalism and dependency. Moreover, these practices also disregard the value of real quality in health and medical care from the point of view of an ageing society. It is true that the quality or level of health care is not an issue as such for non-discrimination law; nor are distributional concerns – but they may well be an effect of the comparisons that we allow ourselves to make!

8. The rationales of government action on ageing and the extension of working lives

Alysia Blackham, Miriam Kullmann, Hanna Pettersson and Ania Zbyszewska

1. INTRODUCTION[1]

EU Member State governments have introduced a range of measures to extend working lives and thereby address population ageing. This chapter evaluates the rationales driving government action as enacted through law and policy, drawing on work conducted within the Norma programme and integrating methods ranging from analysis of discourse to content analysis. We focus on measures in four EU Member States: the UK, Netherlands, Poland and Sweden.[2] The four countries vary significantly in their industrial and labour contexts, including in the involvement of the social partners, and have different exposure to the risks of demographic ageing. For example, in the Active Ageing Index[3] employment indices (which are largely based on labour force participation), Sweden ranks first, the UK ranks third, the Netherlands is in eighth place and Poland is ranked 24th. This is consistent with Organisation for Economic

[1] This work was carried out within the Norma Elder Law Research Environment (www.jur.lu.se/elderlaw) funded by Ragnar Söderberg's Foundation and the Marianne and Marcus Wallenberg Foundation.

[2] In this project, we exclude consideration of collective bargaining and rationales of the social partners.

[3] A measure developed in 2012 by the European Centre for Social Welfare Policy and Research in Vienna (ECV) in collaboration with the European Commission's Directorate General for Employment Social Affairs and Inclusion and the United Nations Economic Commission for Europe. See Active Ageing Index 2012: Concept, Methodology and Final Results Methodology Report Submitted to European Commission's DG Employment, Social Affairs and Inclusion, and to Population Unit, UNECE (European Centre 2013).

Co-operation and Development (OECD) data: of the four countries, Sweden has the highest labour force participation rate for older people (78 per cent), and Poland the lowest (46 per cent). The average age at which individuals receive an old-age pension is also the highest in Sweden (63.6) and lowest in Poland (57), with the Netherlands and the UK positioned in between (at 62.7 and 58.3, respectively).[4] Thus, the countries differ significantly in the level of workforce engagement of older people and the measures required to address demographic ageing. Despite these variations, all four countries are seeking to increase participation rates for older workers. Thus, recognizing the substantial differences between the Member States, it is still informative to consider broader lessons from the diversity of employment-related approaches to population ageing.

In looking at the logic through which governments justify their interventions in this field, we consider the different policy rationales in each Member State. We study the types of government action that are perceived as possible and desirable, and how change is achieved in the particular national contexts. Drawing on the different experiences, we reflect on broader trends in the way ageing is being managed across the EU. Specifically, we identify a neoliberal reform tendency, with an associated individualization of the risks of ageing. By 'neoliberalism', we mean a theory of political and economic practice, which seeks to maximize wellbeing via market mechanisms. This often manifests in liberalization, deregulation, and privatization of public and state services, and through the withdrawal and reconfiguration of collective responsibility.[5] However, neoliberalism does not necessarily entail deregulation (only):[6] rather, the core aim of neoliberalism is to extend market mechanisms to every social domain. Not surprisingly, we see neoliberal tendencies manifesting in different ways, and to different degrees, in the four countries that we are studying. While neoliberal ideologies have been prevalent in the UK for many years, and were crucial in shaping Poland's transition from a state-socialist command economy to a free-market liberal democracy, it is perhaps more surprising to see similar trends in Sweden, with its traditionally Nordic/social democratic welfare

---

[4] Eurostat.

[5] See Leah Vosko, *Managing the Margins: Gender, Citizenship, and the International Regulation of Precarious Employment* (Oxford University Press 2010) and David Harvey, *Spaces of Global Capitalism: Towards a Theory of Uneven Global Development* (Oxford University Press 2006).

[6] Michel Foucault, *The Birth of Biopolitics: Lectures at the Collège de France, 1978–1979* (Picador 2010) 132.

system. This chapter argues that despite significant diversity across EU Member States, the rationale for managing ageing has largely relied on neoliberal ideas and conceptions of work and individual responsibility. This has a significant practical impact on the types of reforms that are being implemented to extend working lives. In the sections that follow we consider EU trends, then address each of the four Member States in turn. Finally, we conclude by raising some broader related themes and discussions.

2. EU TRENDS

Before considering the situation in individual Member States, it is informative to consider EU-level trends in ageing policy, as these likely influence trends at the national level. First, interventions at the EU level have focused on addressing age discrimination in employment. Following Council Directive 2000/78/EC of 27 November 2000 establishing a general framework for equal treatment in employment and occupation ('the Employment Equality Directive'), which gives specific expression to the general principle of non-discrimination on the grounds of age,[7] Member States have been required to adopt age discrimination legislation in national law, potentially improving labour-market prospects of older workers.[8]

Second, EU measures have focused on promoting 'active ageing' (that is, 'helping people stay in charge of their own lives for as long as possible as they age and, where possible, to contribute to the economy and society'),[9] including designation of the year 2012 as the European Year for Active Ageing and Solidarity between Generations, with associated activities and interventions.

Third, while not specifically directed towards older workers, EU programmes have sought to promote 'flexicurity', or the integration of employment flexibility with security, and the notion of 'employability'.[10]

---

[7] *Kücükdevici v. Swedex GmbH* C-555/07 EU:C:2010:21 and *Mangold v. Helm* C-144/04 EU:C:2005:708.

[8] Cf Numhauser-Henning, Julén Votinius and Zbyszewska, Chapter 7 in this book.

[9] European Commission, 'Active Ageing' (*Employment, Social Affairs & Inclusion*, no date) http://ec.europa.eu/social/main.jsp?catId=1062, accessed 11 March 2016.

[10] Cf Rönnmar, Kullmann, Numhauser-Henning and Ulander-Wänman, Chapter 9 in this book.

These programmes have significant potential to affect the employment conditions of older workers in specific Member States.

3. THE UNITED KINGDOM

3.1 Overview of Legal and Policy Developments[11]

3.1.1 Supply-side interventions – influencing older workers' actions

Pension reforms have been introduced in the UK to alleviate the perceived burden of ageing on pension systems, deter early exit from the labour market, and promote extended workforce participation.[12] In particular, the coming years will see a number of increases to the UK state pension age (SPA). For women, the SPA will increase from 60 to 65 by 2018.[13] For both women and men, the SPA will increase to 66 by 2020 and to 67 by 2028.[14] The age at which a company or personal pension can be claimed was also increased in 2010 from 50 to 55 years old. Therefore, individuals will need to work for longer before they can draw on pension entitlements.

At the same time, reforms have been introduced to extend private pension coverage to more employees. With the progressive roll-out of pension 'automatic enrolment' under the Pensions Act 2008 (UK) c 30 s 3, from October 2012 employers are increasingly being required to enrol workers into a workplace pension scheme if these workers are aged between 22 and the SPA, earn more than £9,440 a year and work in the UK. However, the level of saving required under the scheme (which is eventually increasing to 8 per cent of an employee's income) is unlikely to address chronic issues of 'under-saving' for retirement.[15]

To support older workers in employment, a right to request flexible working has been introduced for all employees (including older workers)

---

[11] This material is drawn from Alysia Blackham, 'Addressing the ageing workforce: A critical examination of legal policy objectives and values in the United Kingdom' (2016) Ageing Soc (forthcoming).

[12] Chris Phillipson, 'Work and retirement transitions: Changing sociological and social policy contexts' (2004) 3 Soc Policy Soc 155, 156.

[13] Pensions Act 2011 (UK) c 19.

[14] HM Treasury and HM Parliament, *Autumn Statement 2011* (Stationery Office 2011) 23.

[15] Select Committee on Public Service and Demographic Change, 'Ready for ageing?' (Report of Session 2012–13, 14 March 2013) 10. Individuals may also 'opt-out' from the scheme, which may reduce its effectiveness.

with 26 weeks' service from 30 June 2014.[16] Employers must deal with these requests in a 'reasonable manner', but can refuse an application if they have a 'good business reason' for doing so.[17] While the right to request is a 'weak' piece of legislation,[18] it may help to change employers' attitudes towards flexible working. The UK government has also introduced programmes to build the employability of older workers, including through the Train to Gain programme (which ran from 2006–10, and supported workers to improve their skills and employment prospects),[19] and the New Deal 50 Plus and Flexible New Deal programmes, which provided targeted back-to-work help for people over 50.

3.1.2 Demand-side interventions – changing employer practices

Since 2000, legislative interventions relating to age and employment in the UK have focused primarily on preventing age discrimination in the workforce. UK legislation in this area was driven by the Employment Equality Directive, which was implemented in the UK by the Employment Equality (Age) Regulations 2006 (UK) SI 2006/1031 ('the Regulations'), and later consolidated into the Equality Act 2010 (UK) c 15 ('the Equality Act'). Protection from age discrimination is limited in three key ways. First, direct discrimination because of age can be objectively justified if the treatment is shown to be 'a proportionate means of achieving a legitimate aim' (s 13(2)). This does not apply to any other protected characteristic. Second, indirect discrimination may also be justified as a proportionate means of achieving a legitimate aim (s 19(2)). Third, Schedule 9 of the Equality Act includes a number of specific exceptions to the prohibition of age discrimination in employment, including for occupational requirements that are a proportionate means of achieving a legitimate aim (sch 9, s 1(1)).

Compulsory retirement has been a key focus of age discrimination policy in the UK. Indeed, mandatory retirement is a major area in which employers might seek to justify direct age discrimination. Since its

---

16 Employment Rights Act 1996 (UK) c 18 s 80F; Children and Families Act 2014 (UK) c 6 s 131. This right previously applied only to workers with caring responsibilities.

17 Employment Rights Act 1996 (UK) c 18 s 80G; Children and Families Act 2014 (UK) c 6 s 132.

18 Richard Croucher and Clare Kelliher, 'The right to request flexible working in Britain: The law and organisational realities' (2005) 21 Int J Comp Lab Law and Indus Relations 503, 507.

19 Department for Work and Pensions (DWP), 'Building a society for all ages' (2009) 32.

introduction in 2006, UK age discrimination legislation has always provided scope for employers to adopt a retirement age for their workforce. However, the national default retirement age (DRA) of 65 created by the Regulations was abolished by the Employment Equality (Repeal of Retirement Age Provisions) Regulations 2011 (UK) SI 2011/1069 ('2011 Regulations'). Employers may still implement an employer-justified retirement age (EJRA) so long as it can be objectively justified as a proportionate means of achieving a legitimate aim. However, there is significant legal uncertainty regarding precisely when an EJRA will be 'justified'.[20]

Finally, the UK government has introduced a number of programmes to address attitudes towards older workers, including: the Age Positive campaign (launched in 2000) to 'tackle ageism in the workplace' by raising awareness of the 'business benefits of recruiting and retaining workers aged over 50' and promoting good employer practice;[21] the Everyday Ageism Project, which aims to raise awareness of ageism by encouraging people to share their experiences of ageism online;[22] support for the Age Action Alliance, an independent partnership of public, private and voluntary organizations 'working together [to] combine our thinking, experience and diverse skills to improve the lives of older people';[23] and the appointment of a Business Champion for Older Workers, responsible for 'making the case for older workers within the business community and challenging outdated perceptions'.[24]

3.2 Rationales of Government Action

While there has been a fair amount of legislative and policy activity in the area of ageing and employment, and substantial academic discussion of these developments, there has been only limited consideration of what

---

20 See *Seldon v. Clarkson Wright & Jakes (A partnership)* [2012] UKSC 16 (25 April 2012).

21 Ibid 31.

22 See www.everydayageism.co.uk/.

23 Age Action Alliance, 'Age Action Alliance – Improving older people's lives … together' (no date), http://ageactionalliance.org/, accessed 11 July 2014.

24 DWP, 'A powerful new voice for older workers' (GOV.UK, 14 July 2014), www.gov.uk/government/news/a-powerful-new-voice-for-older-workers, accessed 25 August 2014.

these measures are trying to achieve, and if these objectives or rationales are appropriate.[25]

Thus, as part of research conducted within the Norma programme, a two-stage research design was employed to identify, clarify and evaluate the values underlying government policy in the area of ageing and employment,[26] as a proxy for identifying government rationales in this area. In the first phase, the study used qualitative content analysis to examine the values evident in 19 government policy documents. Phase 2 tested the relative importance of the identified values, as measured by frequency of use, via quantitative content analysis of the same documents.[27]

Using qualitative data analysis, six key objectives or values underlying UK laws relating to ageing and employment were identified:

1. *sustainability* of the economy, pension system and workforce;
2. *adequacy* of income for the elderly;
3. *equality* for all workers;
4. *social inclusion*;
5. *intergenerational solidarity*; and
6. *efficiency*.

However, the values remained indeterminate and had multiple (often contradictory) meanings in the sample of documents, and government documents showed limited consensus regarding how the values should be prioritized in the event they conflicted. This reveals the challenges of

---

[25] See for example, Sandra Fredman, *Discrimination Law* (Clarendon Law Series, 2nd edn, Oxford University Press 2011); Sandra Fredman and Sarah Spencer (eds), *Age as an Equality Issue* (Hart 2003); Malcolm Sargeant (ed.), *The Law on Age Discrimination in the EU* (Kluwer Law International 2008); Malcolm Sargeant, 'The Employment Equality (Age) Regulations 2006: A legitimisation of age discrimination in employment' (2006) 35 Indus L J 209; Malcolm Sargeant, 'Mandatory retirement age and age discrimination' (2004) 26 Employee Relations 151; Susan Bisom-Rapp and Malcolm Sargeant, 'Increasing the employment rate of older workers' (2011) 27 Int J Comp Lab Law and Indus Relations 301; Wendy Loretto, Sarah Vickerstaff and Philip White (eds), *The Future for Older Workers: New Perspectives* (Policy Press 2009); Lucy Vickers and Simonetta Manfredi, 'Age equality and retirement: Squaring the circle' (2013) 42 Indus L J 61; Sarah Vickerstaff, Jenny Cox and Linda Keen, 'Employers and the management of retirement' (2003) 37 Social Policy Admin 271.

[26] This research is published as Blackham (2016), above n 11.

[27] For a full description of these methods, see ibid.

identifying and normatively assessing values in government policy, and the very real disagreement that remains regarding values in the area of ageing.

That said, while the values underlying UK government policy might be interpreted in a collectivist light, they were all actually geared towards an individualistic focus, with individual choice mentioned frequently in the sampled documents. Choice was seen as something which should be 'achievable at all stages of life, and should underpin all public policies'.[28] Removing a national retirement age was seen as an exercise in promoting individual choice and freedom,[29] and a way of reducing government intervention in the activities of employers and employees. This is entirely consistent with an Anglo-Saxon and neoliberal model of individual rights and freedoms:[30] while employees may still retire, this is ultimately an individual decision, which must be negotiated at an individual (and not governmental) level. Government policy was focused on providing older workers with choices that were 'real',[31] 'informed',[32] 'better'[33] and 'genuine'.[34] Thus, individual choice and freedom resided at the core of government policies.[35] This is consistent with the core values evident in UK policy-making more generally, and closely aligned with the central ideas of neoliberalism.

---

28 HM Government, 'Opportunity age: Meeting the challenges of ageing in the 21st century' (March 2005) 3.

29 DWP, (2009), above n 19, 31; HM Government, 'The equality strategy – Building a fairer Britain' (December 2010) 16; Department for Business Innovation and Skills (BIS), 'Phasing out the default retirement age: Consultation document' (July 2010) 4; BIS, 'Phasing out the default retirement age: Government response to consultation' (13 January 2011) 2; HM Government, 'The equality strategy – Building a fairer Britain: Progress report' (22 May 2012) 7.

30 See Neal M Ashkanasy, Edwin Trevor-Roberts and Louise Earnshaw, 'The Anglo cluster: Legacy of the British Empire' (2002) 37 J World Bus 28.

31 Performance and Innovation Unit, 'Winning the generation game: Improving opportunities for people aged 50–65 in work and community activity' (April 2000) 6, 46.

32 HM Government, (2005), above n 28, 17, 21.

33 HM Government, 'Preparing for our ageing society: A discussion paper' (2008) 5, 6.

34 Performance and Innovation Unit (2000), above n 31, 47.

35 See BIS, (2011), above n 29, 2; DWP, 'Fuller working lives: A framework for action' (June 2014) 3, 5.

4. THE NETHERLANDS

4.1 Overview of Legal and Policy Developments[36]

Even though the Netherlands is facing an ever-ageing workforce, there is no holistic strategy to address demographic ageing. However, policies and regulations directed towards the broader labour market often affect older workers, and are generally aimed at increasing employability and participation rates.

4.1.1 Supply-side interventions

The Dutch government has sought to discourage early retirement and extend working life by raising the statutory pensionable age. Reforming the General Old Age Pensions Act (AOW) will raise the statutory pension age to 67 years by 2021, after which it will be linked to life expectancy.[37]

In addition, the government has introduced provisions allowing all employees to ask their employer for permission to attend job-related training (Article 7:611a Civil Code). A reasonable request must be granted if the training is needed for the performance of the job and to continue the employment contract, in a case where the employee's job will disappear or the employee is no longer capable of performing the job.

With the introduction of new dismissal laws from 1 July 2015, employers dismissing their employees must pay them a 'transitional allowance' of up to 75,000 EUR, to facilitate work-to-work transitions.[38] However, an employee is not obliged to use the allowance for that purpose. Payment of this allowance is conditional upon having worked for at least two years for the employer. Employees who at the time of the dismissal have reached the age of 50 benefit – transitionally – from a more generous allowance. If the employer can prove that he or she has invested in the more general 'employability' of the employee, instead of providing job-related training specifically, the total allowance amount can be reduced.[39] Because this allowance applies to all employees with at least two years' service, it is claimed to narrow the inequality gap between permanent and flexible employees, as in the past permanent employees benefited from quite generous severance payments.

---

[36] This section draws upon Miriam Kullmann, 'Extending working life: The Dutch government's response' (2016) 7(1) Eur Lab L J 31.

[37] Article 7 AOW.

[38] *Kamerstukken* II 2013/14, 33 818, no. 3, 40.

[39] Article 7:673 Civil Code.

The transitional allowance is part of the government's strategy to rebalance flexibility and security, limiting the use of successive fixed-term employment contracts and their total duration in order to facilitate and speed conversion into a permanent employment contract. Consequently, from 1 July 2014, the number of successive fixed-term employment contracts has been limited to three contracts within two years, with interim periods not exceeding six months. Collective agreements, however, may provide for a more flexible application of fixed-term employment contracts (for example in the temporary-agency work sector) or if required by the intrinsic nature of the work, due to aspects such as the production process or for project-financed work (for instance in media, cultural and academic sectors).

In relation to 'activation', the government and social partners (in the Labour Foundation, a national consultative body consisting of employers' and employees' representatives) concluded a Social Agreement on 11 April 2013 which aims to prevent unemployment and provide job security. For this, the government has provided a budget of almost 600 million EUR of co-financing to contribute to improved functioning of the labour market by funding vocational education, apprenticeship placements and health measures. The private sector will contribute at least an equal amount to these sectoral plans. This money should facilitate transitions from work-to-work and from unemployment-to-work. A bridging unemployment insurance (*Brug-WW*) offers the unemployed additional support to enable transitions with substantial retraining while receiving unemployment benefits. The government has also introduced a '50-plus workers action plan', administered by the Employee Insurance Agency (UWV), with a budget of 101 million EUR to support the labour-market position of older workers.[40] This plan aims at empowering job-seekers and stimulating employers to invite the older unemployed for a job interview.

At the enterprise level, employers have developed 'age-conscious' human resources (HR) policies.[41] However, it remains up to the employer's discretion to adopt such a policy. It is therefore doubtful how much employers will actually be willing to invest in job-related or broader employability of their employees, particularly for flexible staff.

---

40 See www.uwv.nl/overuwv/pers/dossiers/50-plus.aspx.

41 Ecorys, Langer doorwerken met beleid. Parels: goede praktijken van duurzame inzetbaarheid van werknemers, 12 October 2009.

4.1.2 Demand-side interventions

Prejudices continue to exist among Dutch employers and young(er) employees about older workers. According to the Policy Agenda 2020 (agreed upon by the Labour Foundation in 2011), employers are reluctant to hire older workers, perceiving them as being sicker more often, more expensive in terms of wages and additional days off and less productive.[42] In addressing these prejudices, the legislator has introduced a mobility bonus, enabling employers to benefit from a reduction in social insurance contributions for older workers.[43] The maximum amount an employer can save is 7,000 EUR per year per employee for a full-time job for a maximum of three years. From 1 January 2015, the age for being eligible for such a bonus was raised from 50 to 56 years. This bonus should encourage employers to employ older unemployed workers and facilitate sustainable participation of these workers in the labour market. The government has also restricted unemployment benefits, which may particularly affect the older unemployed: from 1 July 2015, the Unemployment Insurance Act determines that after six months of unemployment, any job will be considered 'suitable', regardless of the individual's skills or experience, or if the position offers lower pay. The maximum duration to receive unemployment benefits has also been reduced from 36 to 24 months.[44]

Age discrimination is prohibited by the Equal Treatment in Employment (Age Discrimination) Act (*Wet gelijke behandeling op grond van leeftijd bij de arbeid*), which implements the Employment Equality Directive. However, age differentiations in relation to employment conditions and dismissal, particularly because the pension age is or has been reached, can often be justified. While issues of age discrimination are generally part of discussions about retirement, it is only cursorily touched upon, if at all, in the context of the active ageing strategies mentioned above.

---

[42] Stichting van de Arbeid, *Beleidsagenda 2020: investeren in participatie en inzetbaarheid* (9 June 2011).

[43] Wet van 12 juli 2012 tot wijziging van de Wet financiering sociale verzekeringen in verband met bonussen voor werkgevers voor het in dienst nemen van oudere uitkeringsgerechtigden en arbeidsgehandicapte werknemers, Stb. 2012, 323, Article 47.

[44] For workers who have become unemployed between 1 October 2006 and 1 January 2020 and who have reached at least the age of 60 in that period, a special transitional unemployment scheme has been established (Act on Income Provisions for Older Unemployed (*Wet inkomensvoorziening voor oudere werklozen*)).

4.2 Rationales of Government Action

A general neoliberal trend can be detected in the government's actions. Several general – though implicit – rationales can be seen. Raising the pensionable age is generally aimed at making social security and pension systems more sustainable (read: affordable), in line with EU policy. An implicit additional goal is to not overburden younger generations with the costs of the greying working population, although this is more explicitly discussed in relation to reforming the pension system. It seems the government's approach is geared towards 'activation' of as many people as possible, thus increasing labour-market participation rates. Measures promoting this activation strategy consist of tax incentives in relation to the (long-term) unemployed, such as the mobility bonus. Even though not explicitly meant to do so, the mobility bonus might contribute to the social inclusion of workers who are distanced from the labour market. However, whether the bonus provides not just activation on behalf of workers but also encourages employers to employ older workers depends largely on the employer's preferences and perceptions. It remains to be seen whether that strategy will succeed, particularly given the reluctance of employers to hire older workers aged over 45, and the gap between age 45 and the age for being eligible for the bonus (56+). The transitional allowance and individual choice regarding how to spend that allowance hint at an individualization trend, given individuals themselves are responsible for making 'wise' choices – as in choosing to use the amount for work-to-work transitions. Individualization can also be detected behind the government's decision to reduce unemployment benefits, highlighting the responsibility of individuals to find work as quickly as possible or suffer the consequence of reduced benefits. An additional likely effect of this allowance is that employers will increasingly use short-term flexible workers (that is, on contracts of up to two years in length), because then the allowance need not be paid and no conversion towards a permanent employment contract applies. Consequently, this is likely to increase labour-market segmentation, endangering the government's strategy for making social security and pension systems sustainable.

5. POLAND

5.1 Overview of Legal and Policy Developments[45]

Poland has very low labour force participation rates for those aged over 50. Poles retire earlier than other European workers, and often before the statutory retirement age. The prevailing trend towards early exit is a legacy of post-transition polices adopted in the early 1990s to tackle high unemployment. The policy mix adopted to reverse this trend has included pension reforms and, more recently, a range of supply- and demand-side active labour-market policies. These measures have targeted unemployed people over 50, with some policies also directed at the 45+ cohort.

5.1.1 Supply-side interventions

The earliest interventions designed to extend working lives were implicit in pension reform, which concentrated on measures to limit early-exit options, create incentives to work longer, and increase the statutory pension entitlement age. The 'old' defined-benefit state-funded pension scheme has been replaced with one combining the state pension with individual savings accounts, operating on a defined-contribution principle.[46] A subsequent 2009 'bridge pension' reform streamlined possibilities for early retirement, eliminating many early-exit pathways previously available for a range of occupations.[47] In 2013, the statutory retirement age was increased to 67 for women and men,[48] although this increase is subject to phase-in periods (by 2020 for men and 2040 for women).[49]

---

45 This section draws upon Ania Zbyszewska, 'Active aging through employment: a critical feminist perspective on Polish policy' (2016) Int J Comp Lab Law and Indus Relations (forthcoming).

46 This change was introduced in 1999. However, since February 2014, the mandatory individual account 'pillar' has been transformed into a voluntary element of the old-age pension scheme: now consolidated in Journal of Laws 2015, item 748, with further amendments.

47 Law of 19 December 2008 on Bridge Pensions, now consolidated in Journal of Laws 2015, item 965.

48 Law of 11 May 2012 on changes to the statute on retirement and benefits from the Social Insurance Fund and other statutes, Journal of Laws 2012, item 637.

49 Highly unpopular, this latter change may be repealed in the future if the currently governing Law and Justice administration keeps its campaign promise to reinstate the previous 60/65 age rules.

To support older workers with job retention and activate older job-seekers, the previous Civic Platform-led government undertook a range of active labour-market measures under its 2008 Government Programme for Social Activation of Older People (renewed in 2012) and the 2013 programme Solidarity between Generations: Actions for Increasing Employment Activation of Persons 50+. Amendments to statutory instruments, primarily the Statute on the Promotion of Employment and Institutions of the Labour Market,[50] introduced a number of subsidies, including loans for entrepreneurial activities for unemployed persons over the age of 50. To address concerns about skills mismatches and improve employability of older job-seekers (50+) or persons 45+ registered in a job centre or at risk of job loss due to prospective collective redundancy, subsidies were introduced for paid internships, and education, skills development, and vocational training activities, with the vocational training supported by the National Training Fund established in 2014. Older unemployed people can also apply for a refund of job-search costs or travel to a job centre, a training facility, or to meet a prospective employer. Job centres are obligated to prioritize older job-seekers by presenting them with a job offer, training placement, or an alternative assignment (in public works) within a six-month period. Finally, some limited work-family reconciliation measures were enacted to assist older workers. For example, the Labour Code now entitles all workers to 14 days of paid leave to care for a dependent person who is not a child,[51] which could facilitate care for grandchildren or an elderly spouse.

5.1.2 Demand-side interventions

Statutory and policy instruments have been introduced to stimulate employer demand for older people, primarily through introduction of various cost savings for firms hiring or already employing older workers. The Promotion of Employment and Institutions of the Labour Market statute entitles employers to subsidies for up to half the salary costs associated with hiring unemployed 50+ persons; they can also claim training costs for workers who are above 45 and the costs of adapting the workplace to older job entrants' needs. Salary subsidies can be drawn for 12 to 24 months, or even as long as four years, with the duration of the

---

[50] Law of 20 April 2004, now Journal of Laws 2015, item 149, with further amendments.

[51] Act of 25 June 1999 on pecuniary benefits from social security in case of sickness, and maternity, Article 32(1)(3), Article 33(1)(2); now consolidated in Journal of Laws 2014, item 159, with further amendments.

subsidy depending on the worker's age. Moreover, employers hiring an unemployed person who is older than 50 are exempt from payments into the Labour Fund for a period of 12 months; this waiver is available to all employers with staff above the ages of 55 (women) and 60 (men). Since 2008, another cost-saving incentive is a change to sick-leave rules, which reduced the number of annual paid sick-leave days older workers can claim, and which employers fund at an 80 per cent replacement rate, from 33 to 14.[52] This shifts responsibility for income replacement from employers to the Social Security institution after a shorter period of illness.

Despite various labour cost and tax incentives for employers, and employability measures aimed at improving older people's labour-market standing, negative attitudes towards older people prevail in many Polish workplaces and it is not uncommon that subsidized jobs are eliminated when the subsidy 'dries up'. Substantively, the Polish Labour Code mandates equal treatment and prohibits all direct and indirect discrimination on the grounds of age (Article 11^2, Article 11^3).[53] Moreover, retirement is not mandatory and the Polish Supreme Court has confirmed that attaining pensionable age does not constitute a lawful ground for an employer's unilateral termination of an employment contract,[54] apart from cases of collective redundancies. In practice, however, studies confirm prevalent discriminatory attitudes and practices, especially at the stage of hiring, but also in training opportunities and termination.[55] Age discrimination is by and large a 'silent' problem, as very few complaints are actually filed with the Workplace Inspection Agency or the Labour Courts. While the 'active ageing' policy documents enacted by the Civic Platform government paid significant attention to challenging stereotypes and biases, the emphasis was primarily on information campaigns, promotion of age management techniques in workplaces, and the dissemination of best practices. At the same time, it was suggested that protective provisions, such as the Labour Code's four-year pre-retirement period during which an employee cannot be unilaterally dismissed

---

52 Provision of Labour Code, amended by Act of 19 December 2008 amending the Law on promotion of employment and labour market institutions and other legislative acts, Journal of Laws 2009, no. 6 item 33.

53 Introduced by the 2003 Labour Code amendment bringing Polish law into compliance with the EU law. Equal treatment is further specified in Articles 18^{3a}–18^{3e} of the Labour Code.

54 Sąd Najwyższy, SN 21 January 2009 (II PZP 13/08).

55 Bożena Kłos, 'Dyskryminacja ze względu na wiek osób starszych na polskim rynku pracy', Studia BAS (2011) 2(26) 183–210.

(Article 39)[56] or have their work terms and conditions unilaterally changed by the employer (Article 42),[57] should be reviewed and potentially repealed, as they may contribute to age discrimination and impede the objectives of extending working lives. However, given recent political changes and the Law and Justice Administration's distinct take on labour-market policy, it is not known whether this sort of amendment will be introduced.

5.2 Rationales of Government Action

Analysing Poland's recent 'active ageing' and extension of working-life measures, we can see some attempt to balance the individualization of risk – which is particularly evident in pension reform and the objective of moving from a 'welfare state' to a 'workfare' state[58] – with some emphasis on the sharing of risks and responsibilities between employees, employers and the state. As in broader EU policy, long-term sustainability of the economy, the pension system, and workforce is invoked as the key rationale for action, with income adequacy for older people also driving policy change – particularly the increase and equalization of the retirement age. Interestingly, the notion of intergenerational solidarity is invoked to mobilize older people to *remain* in the labour market. Policy documents tend to characterize the barriers faced by older people and their premature deactivation as the result of faulty policy choices, and negative attitudes on the part of employers and older unemployed people themselves. Similarly, in proposing ways forward, emphasis is placed on the one hand on fostering active engagement, employability, and skills development to prepare older people for the challenges of the labour market, and on the other the combating of negative employer attitudes, raising awareness about the benefits of an older workforce, and encouraging adaptation of jobs and organizational practices to fit the needs of older people. The state is assigned some responsibility for change in this

---

[56] Introduced by Act on Pre-retirement Benefits of 30 April 2004, Journal of Laws 2004, no. 120 item 1252. However, a similar protective period has existed in Polish law since 1975.

[57] These principles do not apply when the dismissal of the protected employee results from the employer's bankruptcy or liquidation or when the changes to work terms and conditions result from a broader change in a workplace, that is a new collective agreement.

[58] *Poland 2030 – Development Challenges*. Board of Strategic Advisers to the Prime Minister of Poland; see www.polska2030.pl.

policy discourse, serving as a facilitator of these changes (and relationships), organizer of education and institutional (care) infrastructure, and enabler of the third sector, to support the development of a 'welfare society'. However, this notion of shared responsibility and risk is not yet borne out by concrete measures. So far, the task of adapting and responding to the needs of the labour market has been placed primarily on older job-seekers, with state-supported education and skills development measures deployed to assist them. Apart from the recent focus on the promotion of age management, no or very few measures have been adopted to require firms and employers to assume their own share of responsibility through adaptation of work and jobs to welcome and support older people. The only concrete actions taken with labour demand in mind have been focused on cost-cutting incentives for employers.

In autumn 2015, the Law and Justice party unseated the ruling Civic Platform and formed a majority government. One of its popular campaign promises was to reverse the 2013 pension reform and return the age at which a retirement pension can be drawn by women and men from 67 to 60 and 65, respectively. Whether this promise will be kept, and whether it is accompanied by other policies reversing or changing the course taken on the issue of 'active ageing' by the previous administration, remains to be seen.

6. SWEDEN

6.1 Overview of Legal and Policy Developments[59]

Sweden undertook a major pension reform process in the 1990s, significantly earlier than many other countries that are now facing an ageing population.[60] In the old pension system, pension benefits were based on earnings from the 15 years when the income of the individual was the

---

[59] This section draws upon Hanna Pettersson, 'Managing the ageing population: Swedish legal approaches to older workers in the 1970s and the 2010s' (manuscript).

[60] Tobias Laun and Johanna Wallenius, *A Life Cycle Model of Health and Retirement: The Case of Swedish Pension Reform* (SSE/EFI Working Paper Series in Economics and Finance No. 741, 2012) 2; Luis Ferruz Agudo and Mercedes Alda García, 'The reform of some European public pension systems: Spain, Italy and Sweden: A breakthrough?' (2010) 15 Pensions: An International Journal 297, 304. See also Inghammar, Brokelind and Norberg, Chapter 10 in this book.

highest; this did not provide incentives for older people to work longer, because the wages of individuals tend to level off in their 40s or 50s. The present system, on the other hand, provides a rather steep increase in the value of lifetime pension benefits for those who keep working after the age of 65.[61] Pension benefits are calculated on the basis of predicted economic growth and cohort-specific life expectancy,[62] meaning benefits are sensitive to demographic change. Thus, major changes to the pension system have already been made that encourage 'active ageing' and prevent excessive burdening of the pension system. Still, in 2013 around 80 per cent of the Swedish working population drew their pension at the age of 65 or earlier.[63]

The need to prolong working life was established as a larger-scale priority in Swedish political discourse during the 2006–14 centre-right government. In 2011, an official inquiry was initiated; the purpose of the Retirement Age Inquiry (*Pensionsåldersutredningen*) was to find ways to extend working life. The Retirement Age Inquiry was completed in 2013, but has not yet resulted in new legislation. However, the current social democratic/green government has declared an ambition to pass new legislation on increased age limits for pensions and prolonged employment protection for older workers before the 2018 election.[64]

This section will focus on the proposals and the reasoning found in the reports of the Retirement Age Inquiry, since they constitute a recent and important example of policy discussions on how to extend working life in the Swedish context. Also, as was just mentioned, the current government seems to share the major ideas and goals put forward by the Inquiry. However, the Minister currently responsible has emphasized the necessity of simultaneously addressing questions on work environment for older workers, if the age limits for retirement are to be changed.[65] This could suggest somewhat different government rationales emerging, with greater emphasis than before on working-life power relations.

---

61 Laun and Wallenius (2012), above n 60, 3–4.

62 Gabriella Sjögren Lindquist and Eskil Wadensjö, 'Sweden: A viable public-private pension system' in Bernhard Ebbinghaus (ed.), *The Varieties of Pension Governance* (Oxford University Press 2011) 241.

63 Government Inquiry Report SOU 2013:25 *Åtgärder för ett längre arbetsliv* 41.

64 See for example, Joel Dahlberg, 'Höjd pensionsålder före nästa val', Svenska Dagbladet (Stockholm 19 October 2015).

65 Ibid.

6.1.1 Supply-side interventions

The Swedish pension system has already been reformed to encourage working longer, although this measure has not actually increased retirement ages. Therefore, several additional measures have been suggested.

First, it is suggested that the government increase the age limit at which a pension can be drawn, from 61 to 62. Although the Commission of Inquiry concluded that 'theoretically' there should be no reason to change the age limit – retiring at 61 already incurs a financial penalty – an initial rise to 62 years was recommended. Not only would a raised age limit generate greater tax revenues, it would also help prevent the 'short-sightedness' that currently makes some people retire early, only to discover later that they are not able to achieve a reasonable standard of living.[66]

Second, the Retirement Age Inquiry suggested creating a 'recommended retirement age', to be annually adjusted to reflect average life expectancy at the age of 65. The idea was that the new recommended retirement age would replace the current 'norm' of retirement at 65.[67]

Third, it was suggested that the Swedish Pensions Agency provide citizens with enhanced and comprehensive information about the economic advantages of retiring later, so that they can make active decisions regarding retirement. Otherwise, individual retirement decisions will continue to be made through 'passive reactions' based on information provided by employers, unions, and authorities,[68] and on expectations among colleagues and friends.[69] The Retirement Age Inquiry also suggested enhanced (re-)education opportunities for older workers. Sweden has a comparatively generous public system for financial support for students. However, since the system presupposes repayment of student loans, there are age limits for financial support. The Retirement Age Inquiry recommended the introduction of higher age limits and more generous terms. More specifically, the age limit for financial support should be raised from 54 to 57, and students aged 45 years or more should be able to receive additional financial support. Furthermore, shorter training programmes should be developed for older people who need to upgrade their skills or change occupations.[70]

---

[66] Government Inquiry Report SOU 2013:25 288.
[67] Ibid 48, 274.
[68] Ibid 269.
[69] Ibid 265.
[70] Ibid 231.

6.1.2 Demand-side interventions

Swedish employment protection legislation applies to permanent employees until they reach the age of 67. Until then, age is not an acceptable ground for dismissal. When an employee turns 67, however, a 'window' of suspended employment protection enables dismissals to be made without referring to any ground apart from age. This regulation was put to the test before the Court of Justice of the European Union (CJEU) in the *Hörnfeldt* case, where it was found acceptable by the CJEU, since the 67-year limit was regarded as appropriate and necessary in order to achieve a balance between a number of political, economic, social and demographic aims, including the establishment of a right to work until the age of 67 and the need to adapt to demographic developments.[71]

The Retirement Age Inquiry proposed that this age limit be increased from 67 to 69 years. The current regulation in the Act on Employment Protection aims to protect older employees from unpleasant legal disputes regarding their personal ability to work.[72] Although this risk was acknowledged by the Retirement Age Inquiry, an age limit of 69 was thought to avoid the risk of employers dismissing employees on a routine basis when they turn 67. Furthermore, the suspension of employment protection should no longer be of a temporary nature. The question of extending employment protection was framed primarily in terms of discrimination. According to expert advice submitted to the inquiry, biological age is no indicator of physical, mental or social capability, at least until the age of 70. Further, as a result of increased life expectancy, it was noted that it will become difficult to achieve a reasonable pension if working only until the age of 67.[73]

A fairly strong belief in the potential of discrimination law seems to have become established in Sweden. The Commission of Inquiry concluded that age discrimination might be a bigger working-life problem than discrimination on other grounds – the example of ethnicity was mentioned – but that knowledge about it is inadequate. Therefore, a

---

71 *Torsten Hörnfeldt v. Posten Meddelande AB* C-141/11 EU:C:2012:421. Cf Numhauser-Henning, Julén Votinius and Zbyszewska, Chapter 7 in this book, as well as A Numhauser-Henning and M Rönnmar, 'Compulsory retirement and age discrimination – The Swedish Hörnfeldt case put in perspective' in Patrik Lindskoug, Per Samuelsson, Ulf Maunsbach, Göran Millqvist and Hans-Heinrich Vogel (eds), *Essays in Honour of Michael Bogdan* (Juristförlaget i Lund 2013) 401.

72 Government Bill Prop 1981/82:71 105; Government Inquiry Report cf SOU 2013:25 185.

73 Government Inquiry Report SOU 2013:25 186–7.

special research venture on age discrimination was proposed, along with strengthened legislation on age discrimination, and efforts to review the results of the legislation after a few years.[74]

It was also concluded that employees in general were affected by several types of work environment problems – not only related to physical, but also, increasingly, to psychosocial work issues – which were seen as contributing to premature exits from working life. The Swedish Work Environment Agency should receive increased resources to strengthen their development efforts, including the supervision of so-called systematic work environment initiatives. There should also be programmes to disseminate knowledge about how workplaces can be adapted to an older workforce.[75] As previously mentioned, the government currently in power has declared work environment a crucial issue when it comes to prolonging working life.

6.2 Rationales of Government Action

The proposals of the Retirement Age Inquiry described here place responsibilities on both employers and employees, as well as on the state. Employers should be under greater pressure to enhance the work environment and avoid age discrimination; employees should work longer and be prepared to undergo training in order to stay employable; and public authorities should provide better financial support for training, and monitor and lead efforts to improve the work environment.

A welfare state logic is clearly present in the Swedish approach to prolonging working life, as evidenced by the emphasis on public responsibilities for work environment and (re-)education opportunities, as well as the aim to put pressure on employers not to routinely dismiss older employees. Particularly interesting for our purposes, however, is the emphasis placed on the behaviour of the working population cited throughout the main report and the sub-reports. The reports convey concern about the failures of individuals to act in a manner that would serve their own interests, and thereby also the interests of society, by retiring later. A sub-report states that economic research has had trouble explaining the fact that most people in Sweden choose to retire at the age of 65.[76] The practice of retiring 'early' is considered puzzling not only for economic reasons. It is pointed out that work brings a lot more than

---

[74] Ibid 217–30.

[75] Ibid 199–216.

[76] Government Inquiry Report SOU 2012:28 *Längre liv, längre arbetsliv. Förutsättningar och åtgärder för äldre att arbeta längre* 275.

an income: it also brings with it individual autonomy, as well as improved quality of life and social participation.[77]

A central reason for introducing a recommended retirement age is the failure of some people to make economically rational decisions. The same applies for the information efforts that the Pensions Agency is required to undertake. In the context of employment protection, individual gains – such as being able to work as long as one wants without being subject to discrimination, and achieving an acceptable pension – are tied to the needs of society, such as serving the economy and increasing labour supply. This makes Sweden an interesting example of a combined approach often associated with contemporary neoliberalism: the encouragement of entrepreneurial individual behaviour as part of a larger, macroeconomic scheme with similar, interest-maximizing aims, but at the level of society. Calling into question the conception of a 'good life', either individually or at the level of society, is largely absent from the discourse, except in assuming the benefits of waged work at an individual level, and the societal benefits of growth and good public finances.

7. ANALYSIS AND DISCUSSION

In sum, then, legal and policy interventions relating to older workers in the four Member States largely fall into two categories: those affecting supply- or worker-side factors, which are designed to incentivize individuals to remain in the workforce for a longer period, and which include increasing pension ages, moving to private pension provision, limiting early exit, facilitating flexible working and improving employability; and interventions aimed at demand- or employer-side factors, to boost demand for older workers, such as the introduction of age discrimination legislation, reforms of mandatory retirement regulations, conducting attitudinal programmes and reducing employment costs for older workers.

From the foregoing discussion, a number of themes emerge. First, all four Member States appear to be shifting the risks of ageing to individuals, rather than ensuring risks are collectivized via social security or other forms of government protection. For example, in Sweden, which has traditionally been governed via a Nordic social democratic welfare state model, many of the measures proposed to manage the risks of ageing are directed to managing employee behaviour. While some

77 Government Inquiry Report SOU 2013:25 24.

measures are directed to employers and public authorities, and the state is assumed to have responsibilities for providing training opportunities and managing the work environment, this has become less of a focus than individual work capacity. Similarly, the Dutch government relies substantially on providing tax incentives to employers and tightening eligibility for social protection to promote longer working. While Polish policy documents suggest a focus on shared responsibility between government, employers and employees, this has not yet been borne out in practice. A focus on individual responsibility is particularly evident in Polish pension reform, although how this reform will develop under the current Law and Justice administration remains to be seen. Thus, we are witnessing a move towards a government focus on individual employability and responsibility, rather than organizational or governmental reform, to address demographic change. This is reminiscent of Brown's argument that contemporary neoliberalism relies on the production through governance of responsible citizens, who appropriately self-invest in a context of macroeconomic vicissitudes and needs, which make all of these investments practices of speculation.[78] It is also consistent with trends at the EU level, which have seen a strong focus on individual employability[79] and individual 'activation'.[80] Thus, our case studies suggest that we are witnessing a trend towards a fundamental reallocation of risk in Member States,[81] away from state and collective structures, and towards individuals.

Second, and similarly, the national case studies demonstrate a renewed focus on individual choice in all four jurisdictions. Government policy is often justified on the basis that it will enhance and facilitate greater individual choice in relation to employment. This may serve to enhance

---

78 Wendy Brown, *Undoing the Demos: Neoliberalism's Stealth Revolution* (Zone Books 2015) 84.

79 Roland Kadefors, 'Employability of older people: A scientific review, conclusions and recommendations' (1 November 2010) available at socav.gu.se/digitalAssets/1347/1347760_employability-report-111026.pdf; Eurofound, 'Health and employability of older workers' (European Observatory of Working Life, 25 April 2005) www.eurofound.europa.eu/observatories/eurwork/articles/health-and-employability-of-older-workers, accessed 24 February 2016.

80 David Foden and Maria Jepsen, 'Active strategies for older workers in the European Union: A comparative analysis of recent experiences' in M. Jepsen, D. Foden, and M. Hutsebaut (eds), *Active Strategies for Older Workers* (ETUI 2002), 437–60.

81 Ulrich Beck, *Risk Society: Towards a New Modernity* (Sage 1992).

individual autonomy and freedom. However, it is also clear from government discourses that these choices can and should be bounded by economic considerations – there is a sharp distinction between 'good' and 'bad' choices, and government action is designed to facilitate 'good' choices, such as a decision to remain in employment into old age. This is particularly evident in Sweden, where there is obvious governmental confusion as to the economically 'irrational' behaviour of the population, as people retire too early for their own good. Thus, government action continues to be aimed at facilitating 'good', economic utility-maximizing choices; including through education and economic pressure to continue working. Again, this is entirely consistent with trends at the EU level.[82]

Third, then, these case studies seem to indicate that, at least in these four Member States, government actions and rationales for action have been tending to converge rather than diverge. While all four Member States have significantly different histories and traditions, their approach to ageing is strikingly similar. This may well be attributable to EU encouragement and soft law brought about by actions such as the European Semester process. However, the success of EU interventions varies significantly across the Member States. While all four countries have anti-discrimination laws in line with EU standards, in Poland the 'culture' of human rights is not well developed: few discrimination complaints are received, and government policy generally focuses on combating stereotypes and bias through awareness-raising and age management techniques, rather than a focus on improving the enforcement of discrimination laws.

Thus, the growing uniformity in the countries' approaches to ageing might instead be attributable to the increasing dominance of neoliberal ideologies across the EU. In Poland, we can witness these neoliberal tendencies in the context of pension reform and the governmental focus on activation and employability: indeed, policy documents adopted prior to 2015 expressly identified a shift from a 'welfare state' to a 'workfare state' as a desirable direction of change. Similarly, in Sweden, trends towards neoliberalism emerge in the expectation that people should behave like the neoliberal, interest-maximizing subject.

Fourth, the rationales of government action in these Member States are interesting, as much for what they *leave out* as for what they explicitly say. In the UK, for example, government interventions appear to be driven by a policy myth of the idealized older worker: someone who is probably educated, male and working in a white-collar job, and capable

82 David Stratton 'Promoting choices for older workers' (SSRR 2006).

and willing to continue in work into old age. Older workers in the Netherlands are also assumed to work until they reach pensionable age, irrespective of whether they are actually capable of doing so. Polish policy documents more openly acknowledge the impact of caring needs and gender differences on older workers' workforce participation. Indeed, the increase and equalization of pension ages under the former Civic Platform administration were partially rationalized as being necessary to mitigate the consequences of different work histories and unequal sharing of care work on pensions. Despite this more gender-aware framing of Polish policy, however, few concrete or sufficient measures have been adopted to support older workers of either gender in employment. In Sweden, the situation of workers with low wages has been taken into account by the Retirement Age Inquiry, and rules were suggested that would increase the economic gains of working longer for people with low wages and low pensions. Similarly, the risk of physical and/or mental exhaustion for certain older workers is part of the reason for the planned measures to enhance the work environment for older workers. Differences in working conditions for female-dominated and male-dominated jobs have also been addressed in this context. Even though the myth of the idealized older worker is not dominant or uniform in all the countries, it could be part of the explanation as to why governments are so perplexed at 'irrational' individual behaviour in relation to retirement.

In this chapter we have considered the rationales for government action in relation to measures to extend working lives in the Netherlands, Poland, Sweden, and the UK. While recognizing the significant differences between these countries, we have also identified a growing acceptance of and trend towards neoliberal ideologies across the Member States studied. This has resulted in growing individualization of the risks of ageing, a focus on (bounded) individual choice, and a potential retreat from government or collective action and intervention.

At the same time, despite extensive legal and political change to address the challenges of demographic ageing, we can see that many of these reforms are having limited success in practice. Ageing – and improving workforce participation rates for older workers – are complex and multi-faceted problems with no clear or easy solutions. Further, government approaches to the issue are highly fragmented and sometimes contradictory. Thus, it is unsurprising that existing approaches are having only limited success in practice. This, then, calls into question the appropriateness of a neoliberal partial retreat from government regulation, and the individualization of the risks of ageing, as a means of effectively addressing demographic change.

9. Employment protection and older workers

Mia Rönnmar, Miriam Kullmann, Ann Numhauser-Henning and Carin Ulander-Wänman

1. INTRODUCTION[1]

Employment protection is at the heart of labour law. The understanding and legal content of employment protection changes over time, and may also differ between jurisdictions.[2] The aim of this chapter is to add to the field of elder law through an analysis of the function, content and future challenges of employment protection from the perspective of older workers and a prolonged working life. EU law and comparative European law are in focus, and statutory, collective bargaining and case law developments are analysed.

Several concepts are relevant when discussing employment protection and older workers. The concept of age is central to age discrimination law; in EU age discrimination law it refers not only to old age, but to any chronological age. The concept of older workers must be defined in a contextual way. EU statistics often cover the 55–64 age group, and in discussions related to working life older workers are often workers who are 55 years or older.[3] The concept of ageism refers to beliefs, attitudes, norms and values to justify age-based prejudice, discrimination and

[1] This work was carried out within the Norma Elder Law Research Environment (www.jur.lu.se/elderlaw) funded by Ragnar Söderberg's Foundation and the Marianne and Marcus Wallenberg Foundation.

[2] See for example, B Hepple, 'European dismissal law?' (1997) 18(2) Comp Lab L J 204 and M Weiss, 'Job security: A challenge for European social policy' in N Countouris and M Freedland (eds), *Resocialising Europe in a Time of Crisis* (Cambridge University Press 2013).

[3] Cf Article 2 of the Commission's proposal regarding a European Year of Active Ageing (2012), COM(2012) 462 final.

subordination,[4] while the concept of pensionable age generally refers to the age for pension benefits within the public pension scheme.[5]

An ageing population is a troubling European trend that is equally relevant for developed countries in other parts of the world, such as Australia, Japan and the US.[6] 2012 was the European Year of Active Ageing and Solidarity between Generations, and the EU Active Ageing Policy, which is integrated into the Europe 2020 Strategy and the European Employment Policy, aims to promote a healthy and active ageing population, increase the labour market participation of older workers (55+) and prolong working life.[7]

The flexibilization of work relates to labour market segmentation, externalization and the legal tension between standard employment contracts, associated with employment protection and precarious and flexible employment. Atkinson's early model of the flexible firm, with core, peripheral and external groups of workers and employer deployment of strategies for numerical and functional flexibility is often referred to in this context.[8] Numerical flexibility relates to the form and duration of the employment contract and working-time arrangements, whereas functional flexibility is a matter of adaptability and versatility within permanent employment relationships, aimed at varying the content of work.

Today flexicurity is central to European employment policies and EU labour law. The EU law flexicurity discourse was inspired by national

---

[4] Cf further, T N Iversen, L Larsen and P E Solem, 'A conceptual analysis of ageism' (2009) 61(3) Nordic Psych 4.

[5] See further D O'Dempsey and A Beale (supervised by M Freedland), *Age and Employment*. European Network of Legal Experts in the Non-Discrimination Field (European Commission 2011).

[6] See A Numhauser-Henning, 'Labour law in a greying labour market – in need of a reconceptualisation of work and pension norms. The position of older workers in labour law' (2013) 4(2) Eur Lab L J 84–100, as well as A Numhauser-Henning and M Rönnmar (eds), *Age Discrimination and Labour Law: Comparative and Conceptual Perspectives in the EU and Beyond* (Kluwer Law International 2015).

[7] See for example, Decision No. 940/211/EU of the European Parliament and of the Council of 14 September 2011 on the European Year for Active Ageing and Solidarity between Generations (2012) (OJ [2011] L246/5). Article 25 of the CFR establishes the rights of the elderly. See further C O'Conneide, 'Article 25 – The rights of the elderly' in S Peers, T Hervey, J Kenner and A Ward (eds), *The EU Charter of Fundamental Rights. A Commentary* (Hart Publishing 2014) 693.

[8] See J Atkinson, 'Manpower strategies for flexible organisations' (1984) 28 Personnel Mgmt 28–31.

developments in Denmark and the Netherlands and by Wilthagen's flexicurity research, which developed the model of the flexible firm into a flexibility-security nexus.[9] Common principles of flexicurity have been adopted and integrated into the European Employment Strategy and the Europe 2020 Strategy. Flexicurity is an integrated strategy for simultaneous enhancement of both flexibility and security in the labour market. This strategy contains the components of flexible and reliable contractual arrangements; comprehensive life-long learning; effective active labour market policies; and modern social security systems. The EU law flexicurity discourse relates to reduced labour market segmentation, equal treatment of permanent employees and flexible workers, a new balance between numerical and functional flexibility, deregulation of employment protection, progressive employment protection, and employability. The focus on employability and labour market transitions creates crucial ties between security for employees and the flexicurity components of comprehensive life-long learning, active labour market policies, and modern social security systems. The emphasis is not on employment security in the current job, but on being employable in relation to the labour market as a whole.[10] The EU law flexicurity discourse is often criticized, most often for emphasizing flexibility.

At EU level, employment protection is only partly regulated. Article 30 of the EU Charter of Fundamental Rights (CFR) states that '[e]very worker has the right to protection against unjustified dismissal, in accordance with Union law and national laws and practices'.[11] In addition, the Fixed-Term Work Directive,[12] the 'restructuring' Directives

---

9 See T Wilthagen, *The Flexibility-Security Nexus: New Approaches to Regulating Employment and Labour Markets*, Flexicurity research paper FXP 2003-2, OSA/Institute for Labour Studies (Tilburg University 2002) and J Visser, 'Flexibility and security in post-standard employment relations: The Netherlands' in K V W Stone and H Arthurs (eds), *Rethinking Workplace Regulation: Beyond the Standard Contract of Employment* (Russell Sage Foundation 2013).

10 See C Ulander-Wäman, *Flexicurity och utvecklingsavtalet* (IFAU 2010:19).

11 The Explanations relating to the CFR clarify that Article 30 draws on Article 24 of the European Social Charter. See further J Kenner, 'Article 30 – Protection in the event of unjustified dismissal' in S Peers, T Hervey, J Kenner and A Ward (eds), *The EU Charter of Fundamental Rights. A Commentary* (Hart Publishing 2014), 805. Note should also be taken of ILO Convention No. 158 Termination of Employment Convention 1982.

12 Council Directive 1999/70/EC of 28 June 1999 concerning the framework agreement on fixed-term work concluded by ETUC, UNICE and CEEP, OJ 1999 L 175/43.

on Transfers of Undertakings[13] and Collective Dismissals[14] and various directives on non-discrimination regulate different aspects of employment protection. Employment protection regulation can, and does, differ in the Member States. Furthermore, following the economic crisis, austerity measures and deregulatory labour law reforms have been introduced in many Member States, including Greece, Portugal, Spain, and Italy. These measures have targeted employment protection regulation, as well as collective bargaining and industrial relations processes.[15]

The outline of the chapter is as follows. Section 2 provides a discussion of the relationship between employment protection and the ban on age discrimination, while Section 3 presents a discussion of the links between employment protection and flexible work – especially fixed-term work. Section 4 focuses on dismissal for personal reasons and reasons of redundancy. Section 5 explores the connection between employment protection and compulsory retirement and measures aimed at prolonging working life. Finally, Section 6 provides some concluding remarks.

2. EMPLOYMENT PROTECTION AND AGE DISCRIMINATION[16]

Non-discrimination law can be seen as one expression of the trends towards individualization and flexibilization of work. Non-discrimination law has grown in importance as the standard employment contract has given way to more flexible and individualized work arrangements.

[13] Council Directive 2001/23/EC of 12 March 2001 on the approximation of the laws of the Member States relating to the safeguarding of employees' rights in the event of transfers of undertakings, businesses or parts of undertakings or businesses, OJ 2001 L 82/16.

[14] Council Directive 98/59/EC of 20 July 1998 on the approximation of the laws of the Member States relating to collective redundancies, OJ 1998 L 225/16.

[15] See for example, C Barnard, 'The financial crisis and the Euro Plus Pact: A labour lawyer's perspective' (2012) 41 Indus L J 98; S Laulom, 'Dismissal law under challenge: New risks for workers' (2014) 4(3–4) Eur Lab L J 231–54; and C Barnard, 'The Charter in time of crisis: A case study of dismissal' in N Countouris and M Freedland (eds), *Resocialising Europe in a Time of Crisis* (Cambridge University Press 2013).

[16] Cf also Fudge, Chapter 3 in this book; Numhauser-Henning, Chapter 4 in this book; and Numhauser-Henning, Julén Votinius and Zbyszewska, Chapter 7 in this book.

Furthermore, the ban on age discrimination works to promote further flexibilization of working life.[17] However, another important relation exists between employment protection and non-discrimination law. In situations where employment protection is weak or less developed – as in the US with its employment-at-will doctrine – non-discrimination law and age discrimination law are particularly important as a means of protection for employees. Non-discrimination law developed early in the US.[18] In Europe, on the other hand, with its more developed regulation of employment protection, non-discrimination can be seen as a replacement mechanism in times of weakening employment protection – or, as Somek explains, even as a forerunner of flexibilization.[19] Moreover, non-discrimination regulation does not imply a certain quality of treatment and, generally speaking, has no distributional functions. On the contrary, the 'elitist' design of non-discrimination law in general results instead in a weakness of the ban on age discrimination.[20] This 'elitist' design works to the detriment of older workers, because the reference norms representing the foundation of comparison in cases of alleged discrimination are basically meritocratic. Therefore, the non-hiring of an older applicant may well be defended by arguments about the more 'up-to-date' education of a younger candidate, while a dismissal may be defended by arguments about the older worker's lack of capability.

The (2000/78/EC) Employment Equality Directive introduced the ban on age discrimination in EU law, and Article 21 of the CFR on non-discrimination contains an open list of non-discrimination grounds, including age. The protection against age discrimination in EU law covers all chronological ages, but due inter alia to the problem of an ageing population, there is a clear emphasis on old age in the design and development of age discrimination law. The prohibition of old-age discrimination helps reduce ageism, and is also an important aspect of the EU Active Ageing Policy. However, according to Article 6(1) of the

---

17 See A Numhauser-Henning, 'Labour law, pension norms and the EU ban on age discrimination: Towards ultimate flexibilisation?' in Numhauser-Henning and Rönnmar (2015), above n 6.

18 See G Lester, 'Age discrimination and labor law in the United States' in Numhauser-Henning and Rönnmar (2015), above n 6.

19 See A Somek, *Engineering Equality* (Oxford University Press 2011). See also further Numhauser-Henning, Chapter 4 in this book.

20 Cf C O'Cinneide, 'Completing the picture: The complex relationship between EU anti-discrimination law and "Social Europe"' in N Countouris and M Freedland (eds), *Resocialising Europe in a Time of Crisis* (Cambridge University Press 2013).

Employment Equality Directive, differences of treatment on grounds of age do not constitute discrimination if they are objectively and reasonably justified by a legitimate aim, including legitimate employment policy, labour market, and vocational training objectives, and if the means of achieving that aim are appropriate and necessary.[21]

The Employment Equality Directive was imperative for the introduction of a ban on age discrimination in many EU Member States, and the ban was implemented into national law by way of legal regulation, often closely modelled on the provisions of the Directive.[22] In principle, EU age discrimination law – through a large scope for justification of age-related differential treatment, specific exemptions and a broad margin of appreciation for Member States and social partners – enables direct and indirect age-related regulation. A comparative analysis of a number of EU Member States also reveals that there are still many directly and indirectly age-related labour law rules and practices as well as collective bargaining schemes in the areas of recruitment, working conditions, flexible employment, employment protection and compulsory retirement. Furthermore, as is always the case regarding non-discrimination regulation, there is a strong emphasis on the individual-complaints-led model and the bans against direct and indirect age discrimination. Few examples exist of the regulation – and successful use – of a duty of reasonable accommodation, active measures or an adaptation of working time or work environment, as ways to combat age discrimination and promote active ageing and a prolonged working life in light of a rapidly ageing population (Section 5).[23]

Age has traditionally been influential in the organization of labour markets and labour law regulation. The ban on age discrimination and employment protection intersect, for example in fixed-term employment contracts for older workers, seniority rules in redundancy situations and compulsory retirement.

Seniority principles and age and length of service have traditionally been influential and remain so in many EU Member States when it comes to wage-setting and working conditions, such as periods of notice, length of annual leave, severance pay and specific bonuses. A reference

---

[21] Regarding this 'weaker design' of the ban on age discrimination see further Fudge, Chapter 3 in this book and Numhauser-Henning, Julén Votinius and Zbyszewska, Chapter 7 in this book.

[22] See further, M Rönnmar, 'Comparative analysis' in Numhauser-Henning and Rönnmar (2015), above n 6, for a comparative analysis of the relation between age discrimination and labour law.

[23] See Numhauser-Henning and Rönnmar (2015), above n 6.

to age and length of service in this context gives rise to directly or indirectly age-related differential treatment and thus needs to be justified. Legitimate aims put forward in this context include the value of experience on the job and rewarding loyalty as well as the need for extra protection of older workers.

Despite the ban on age discrimination, examples of directly age-related dismissals related to ageism and age stereotypes exist and surface in case law. Case law developments in the UK reflect that age-discriminatory dismissals can relate both to young and old age. In one case an 18-year-old woman was dismissed on grounds of (in)capability, and the employer made a number of inaccurate and stereotypical assumptions based on her age. In another case a well-known 53-year-old television presenter was dismissed when the employer 'wanted to refresh the programme and make it more attractive to a younger audience by bringing in new (younger) faces'.[24] The dismissals were found to be age-discriminatory and unjustified.

3. EMPLOYMENT PROTECTION AND FLEXIBLE WORK

There is a close relationship between fixed-term work and employment protection. Regulation of fixed-term employment contracts serves to prevent circumvention of the employment protection linked to permanent employment contracts. The more developed the employment protection regulation is, the more important a restricted use of fixed-term employment becomes.

EU law regulates aspects of flexible employment through the (97/81/EC) Part-Time Work Directive,[25] the (99/70/EC) Fixed-Term Work Directive,[26] and the (2008/104/EC) Temporary Agency Work Directive,[27] which form part of the EU law flexicurity strategy. The purpose of the

---

24 See further, C Barnard and S Deakin, 'Age discrimination and labour law in the UK: Managing ageing' in Numhauser-Henning and Rönnmar (2015), above n 6.

25 Council Directive 97/81/EC of 15 December 1997 concerning the Framework Agreement on part-time work concluded by UNICE, CEEP and the ETUC, OJ 1998 L 14/9.

26 Council Directive 1999/70/EC of 28 June 1999 concerning the framework agreement on fixed-term work concluded by ETUC, UNICE and CEEP, OJ 1999 L 175/43.

27 Directive 2008/104/EC of the European Parliament and of the Council of 19 November 2008 on temporary agency work, OJ 2008 L 327/9.

Fixed-Term Work Directive is to improve the quality of fixed-term work by ensuring the application of the principle of non-discrimination, and to establish a framework to prevent abuse arising from the use of successive fixed-term employment contracts or relationships. The purpose of the Temporary Agency Work Directive is to ensure the protection of temporary agency workers and improve the quality of temporary agency work, while taking into account the need to establish a suitable framework for the use of temporary agency work – with a view to contributing effectively to the creation of jobs and the development of flexible forms for working.

In many EU Member States (and other countries) specific fixed-term employment contracts for older and younger workers are used to promote the prolonging of working life for older workers and promote the entry of younger workers into the labour market.[28] The *Mangold* case[29] concerned a German regulation that provided a broader scope for successive fixed-term employment contracts for older workers and its relation to the Fixed-Term Work Directive and the Employment Equality Directive and the ban on age discrimination. The German regulation was found to be contrary to EU law.

Swedish law provides for an unlimited access to fixed-term employment for employees above the age of 67 years (the compulsory retirement age), as a way of promoting work after compulsory retirement and a prolonged working life.[30] Fixed-term work is regulated in the (1982:80)

---

[28] In many countries in and beyond the EU, rates of youth unemployment are high and younger workers are over-represented when it comes to flexible and precarious employment. There is specific regulation on fixed-term employment contracts for younger workers in many EU Member States, such as Finland, France, Poland, Spain and Sweden. These fixed-term employment contracts sometimes have an emphasis on training. Following the economic crisis, some countries like Spain, Greece, Italy and Portugal have also seen the emergence of fixed-term employment contracts specifically aimed at younger workers; these contracts are less focused on training and skills development and more directed at deregulation, cost-cutting and a 'levelling-down' of employment rights, in order to promote younger workers' entry into the labour market. Likewise, in the Netherlands a more generous use of fixed-term employment contracts has been introduced for younger workers up to the age of 27 years. See further, for example, J Julén Votinius, 'Young employees – Securities, risk distribution and fundamental social rights' (2014) 5(3–4) Eur Lab L J 387.

[29] *Mangold v. Helm* C-144/04 EU:C:2005:708.

[30] Cf *Torsten Hörnfeldt v. Posten Meddelande AB* C-141/11 EU:C:2012:421, paras 40–41 in the judgment, where the CJEU referred precisely to this possibility.

Employment Protection Act. Permanent employment is the main rule and fixed-term employment contracts are permitted only when agreed upon, and when specifically provided for by law or collective agreements. The regulation on fixed-term work was amended in 2007, and in part this reform represents a new standpoint on fixed-term employment contracts. A long list of fixed-term employment contracts has been replaced by a new form of fixed-term employment contracts – the general fixed-term employment,[31] supplemented only by temporary substitute employment, seasonal employment, probationary employment and precisely fixed-term contracts for employees above the age of 67 years. Thus, the scope for fixed-term employment contracts has broadened, and, as regards employees above the age of 67, it is in fact unlimited.[32]

4. EMPLOYMENT PROTECTION AND DISMISSAL FOR PERSONAL REASONS AND FOR REDUNDANCY[33]

4.1 Dismissal for Personal Reasons

In many EU Member States there are partly separate sets of rules related to dismissal for personal reasons and for redundancy, respectively. This is the case in Sweden. Whereas all dismissals require just cause, dismissal for personal reasons involves a close scrutiny of the employer's actions in the individual situation in order to avoid arbitrariness, whereas the employee protection in dismissal for redundancy relies mainly upon

[31] Section 5 of the (1982:80) Employment Protection Act.

[32] The European Commission has issued two reasoned opinions in relation to the Swedish implementation of the (1999/70/EC) Fixed-Term Work Directive. The Commission claims that Sweden has failed to correctly implement Clause 5.1 of the Framework Agreement of fixed-term work. In its last reasoned opinion (22 April 2014, C(2014) 2380 final) the Commission has seemingly accepted old age (67 years) to be an objective criterion under Article 5.1a of the Directive. See further S Englblom, 'Fixed-term-at-will: The new regulation of fixed-term work in Sweden' (2008) 24(1) Int J Comp Lab Law and Indus Relations 133–49, and www.tco.se/vara-fragor/Arbetsratt/Visstid/. Recently a Governmental Bill (Prop 2015/16:62) was accepted by Parliament in order to bring the existing regulation in line with EU law. A new legislative provision is introduced by which general fixed-term employments will be converted into indefinite employment contracts in more cases than at present; see also Government Inquiry Report, Ds 2015:29.

[33] See M Rönnmar, 'Comparative analysis', in Numhauser-Henning and Rönnmar (2015), above n 6.

seniority rules (Section 4.2). The vulnerability of older workers – due for example to ageism and possibly antiquated training and competence, but also to weakened performance – has influenced the content of employment protection in many EU Member States, and special protection for older workers has been afforded.[34]

In some EU Member States, such as Sweden, there is a general and important rule that sickness or old age does not constitute just cause for dismissal. In Sweden a concern for older and sick employees has characterized the statutory employment protection regulation from the very beginning.[35] Swedish employment protection is often viewed as strong, and the employer must have just cause for dismissal. Coupled with this basic just cause requirement are different rules obliging the employer (depending on whether the dismissal relates to personal reasons or reasons of redundancy) inter alia to negotiate with trade unions, give notice, provide the employee with alternative work, warn the employee, retrain the employee, apply seniority rules, and if necessary conditions are met, re-employ dismissed employees. Thus, in line with an *ultima ratio* principle, the employer must make an effort to avoid dismissing employees by first taking less radical measures.

The employer is obliged to conduct a thorough investigation into the possibilities for adaptation and rehabilitation and for finding alternative work for the employee.[36] In this context the employer's obligations are extensive; they relate, for example, to the adjustment of the work environment, work organization, working time and work tasks. These obligations follow not only from regulation in the (1982:80) Employment Protection Act, but also from related regulation on individual work environment adaptation in the (1977:160) Work Environment Act and regulation on rehabilitation in the (2010:110) Social Insurance Code.[37] An employee can be dismissed only after such measures have been taken, the possibility of finding alternative work has been tried and ruled out,

---

[34] Cf Fineman's theory on vulnerability, and Mattsson and Katzin, Chapter 5 in this book.

[35] Cf Government Bill Prop 1973:129, 18.

[36] Cf for example, Labour Court judgments AD 2013:78 and AD 2014:26.

[37] The Labour Court has clarified that the requirement for reasonable accommodation in the (2008:567) Non-Discrimination Act and the requirement for rehabilitation and work adaptation in cases of sickness in the (1982:80) Employment Protection Act are basically the same.

and the employee can no longer perform work of any importance for the employer.[38]

However, the extent to which sickness or reduced working capacity constitutes just cause for dismissal differs in the Member States. In Poland – despite a requirement for employers to justify dismissal – the scope for managerial prerogative is broad and older workers are specifically vulnerable. Poor or inaccurate work performance may be a ground for dismissal, and a dismissal is justified if the employer has a reasonable ground to believe that hiring another person would lead to better work results. In France it is feared that the procedure for consensual termination, introduced in 2008, will be used to encourage older workers to leave their jobs prematurely.[39]

4.2 Dismissal for Reasons of Redundancy

Redundancy dismissals are increasingly frequent in times of globalization, restructuring and economic crisis. Seniority rules (such as the last-in-first-out principle) and different forms of directly or indirectly age-related differential treatment still influence redundancy regulation in many countries in the EU and beyond.

In Sweden, the last-in-first-out principle is the main rule when it comes to redundancy selection. The employer has a unilateral right to decide when and if a redundancy situation exists, and in principle redundancy amounts to just cause.[40] The statutory seniority rules imply that the priority and selection of employees is to be made according to the last-in-first-out principle, that is according to each employee's total period of employment with the employer (and in the event of equal periods of employment, giving priority to senior age). The employee has to have sufficient qualifications for the tasks which remain after the redundancy (see further below). In principle, the order of dismissals

---

[38] Cf for example, Labour Court judgments AD 2013:78 and AD 2014:26. In individual dismissal disputes, both as regards dismissal for redundancy and personal reasons, the (1982:80) Employment Protection Act and the (2008:567) Non-Discrimination Act, and the bans on age discrimination and disability discrimination, may be invoked at the same time. Case law from the Labour Court reflects this 'regulatory overlap' of two parallel sets of rules; see for example, Labour Court judgments AD 2005:32, AD 2012:51, AD 2013:78 and AD 2014:26.

[39] See L Mitrus, 'Age discrimination and labour law in Poland' and S Robin Olivier, 'Age discrimination and labour law in France' in Numhauser-Henning and Rönnmar (2015) above n 6.

[40] See for example, Labour Court judgments AD 1993:61 and AD 1993:101.

encompasses all employees who work in the same production unit and who are covered by the same collective agreement (redundancy unit). These rules are thus potentially, indirectly age-discriminatory (with a directly age-discriminatory element, in the way in which the employee's age is decisive in situations when the period of employment of two or more employees is the same). However, the seniority rules are semi-compelling, and by concluding a local collective agreement the employer and the trade union may deviate from the statutory rules when determining the order of dismissals.[41]

In the Netherlands the age bracket or mirror principle applies. In a redundancy situation the employees within each category of interchangeable positions are divided into five age groups (15 to 25; 25 to 35; 35 to 45; 45 to 55 and 55+). Since 2015, the rule stipulates that three categories of employees are first selected for dismissal: (1) employees who are entitled to state pensions; (2) on-call workers; and (3) fixed-term employees whose contracts last less than 26 weeks. Thereafter the selection within each age group is done on the basis of the last-in-first-out principle. This process aims at spreading the dismissals evenly over different age groups in the company.[42]

Traditionally in the UK, age and length of service have been important, and the application of the last-in-first-out principle may be justified if used as one of a number of criteria. In Germany the rules on social selection apply with the aim of selecting those employees who are least in need of social protection for dismissal. Four decisive criteria must be taken into account: seniority within the company; age; number of dependents; and disability. The Federal Labour Court has held that this directly and indirectly age-related differential treatment is justified with reference to the aim of furthering the integration of older workers who find it particularly difficult to obtain a new job. Similarly, in France the

---

[41] See further, for instance, M Rönnmar and A Numhauser-Henning, 'Swedish employment protection in times of flexicurity policies and economic crisis' (2012) 28(4) Int J Comp Lab Law and Indus Relations 443.

[42] Particular rules on the selection of employees can also be agreed upon in a collective agreement or in a regulation adopted by an administrative body. See further M Kullmann, 'Unused potential? The risks of unemployed "older" workers' (2016) 7(3) Eur Lab L J 442–60; and E Verhulp and E Herdé, 'Age discrimination and labour law in the Netherlands' in Numhauser-Henning and Rönnmar (2015), above n 6. Cf also the similar Belgian age-pyramid principle and P Foubert, E Langhendries, N Marocchi and J Peeters, 'An EU perspective on age as a distinguishing criterion for collective dismissal: The case of Belgium and the Netherlands' (2013) 29(4) Int J Comp Lab Law and Indus Relations 416.

employer is obliged by statute to take the employees' ages, seniority and vulnerability into account in the selection process.

Seniority rules are thus potentially directly or indirectly age-discriminatory. These rules have not yet been explicitly tried by the Court of Justice of the European Union (CJEU) against the ban on age discrimination. However, such rules may be found acceptable according to EU law.[43]

In several EU Member States (such as France, Germany, the Netherlands, Poland, Sweden and the UK), severance pay and other forms of compensation in redundancy situations, set by legislation or collective bargaining or negotiation with works councils (such as transition agreements in Sweden (see further below) or social plans in Germany and France), are seniority-based and linked to length of service. At the same time older workers, having reached pre-retirement or retirement age, sometimes receive less or no compensation in such situations, with reference to their access to pensions and social security benefits.[44]

Global competition, technological development, and new ideas about how businesses should be organized and managed imply new and increasing demands on employees' ability to perform their work; this

---

43 Cf the Opinion of Advocate-General Bot in *Seda Kücükdeveci v. Swedex GmBH& Co. KG* C-555/07 EU:C:2010:21 para 43. O'Cinneide argues that 'it is also worth noting that many other relevant factors in redundancy decision making may have an indirectly discriminatory effect … granting older workers greater protection during redundancies can be seen as a positive action strategy, especially in particular member states where specific historical and economic factors may cause older workers may [sic] be in a much more vulnerable position than younger workers. Therefore, provided it is proportional, such preferential treatment might be treated as reasonably justified'; see C O'Conneide, *Age Discrimination and European Law* (European Commission 2005) 40. For a further discussion on length of service and professional experience as justification for age-related differential treatment, see joined cases *Hennigs and Mai* C-297/10 and C-298/10 EU:C:2011:560 and *Specht and others v. Land Berlin* C-501/12 to C-506/12, C-540/12 and C-541/12 EU:C:2014:2005.

44 However, in *Ole Andersen* the CJEU found the Danish rule and practice of not paying severance to an employee in case of redundancy dismissal, when the employee was eligible for old-age pension, to be disproportionate, unjustifiable and age discriminatory – because the rule did not take into consideration whether or not the employee in question actually received old-age pension or continued to work; see *Ole Andersen v. Region Syddanmark* C-499/08 EU:C:2010:600. Cf also *Toftgaard v. Indenrigs- og Sundhedsministeriet* C-546/11 EU:C:2013:603. In *Odar v. Baxter Deutschland GmbH* C-152/11 EU:C:2012:772 reduced redundancy payments related to a right to early retirement were indeed deemed appropriate.

development is relevant both in relation to dismissal for personal reasons and for redundancy. With today's emphasis on flexicurity, employees' security relates to a large extent to life-long learning and employability in relation to the labour market as a whole. Employees must have a broad competence awareness, and be able to follow the development of competence requirements in their sector of the labour market and continuously acquire new knowledge during their working lives.

The design and application of labour law and collective bargaining regulation is of major importance for older workers' employability. We have seen that according to Swedish law the employer must have just cause for dismissal. In a redundancy situation the employer must investigate the possibilities to provide the employee with alternative work,[45] make a selection of employees in accordance with the last-in-first-out principle,[46] and (under certain conditions) re-employ dismissed employees.[47] For all these rules of protection to apply, a prerequisite is that the employee has sufficient qualifications for the job.[48]

The way in which the requirement for sufficient qualifications is interpreted means that qualifications which at one time were considered adequate can be assessed as insufficient at a later point in time, in the same company and in relation to the same tasks. This has particular significance for employees with a long length of service and who are thus older. To become competitive in the long run, an employee whose education dates far back in time or who has been working for a long time with the same or similar work for the same employer is particularly dependent on the distribution of tasks and the skills development offered by the employer. If employees do not keep pace with the development of qualification requirements in their sector, they run a risk both of losing their jobs due to insufficient qualifications and not being employable in relation to the sector as a whole.[49]

---

45 Section 7 subsection 2 of the (1982:80) Employment Protection Act.

46 Section 22 of the (1982:80) Employment Protection Act.

47 Section 25 of the (1982:80) Employment Protection Act.

48 A study of Swedish case law focusing on the requirement for sufficient qualifications relating to redundancy dismissals in the (1982:80) Employment Protection Act shows that the requirement for sufficient qualifications was more commonly met among both white- and blue-collar workers during the first 20 years of application (from 1974) of the Act than during the last 20 years of application, see C Ulander-Wänman, 'Anställningsskydd och kvalifikationskrav i förändring' (2016) 22(3/4) Arbetsmarknad & Arbetsliv.

49 The (1974:981) Study Leave Act provides Swedish employees with a right to educational leave. The Act is, in principle, compulsory to the employee's

In Sweden, regulation in collective agreements can supplement or adapt the labour law legislation, and increase (or limit) the protection of employees in light of the conditions in different sectors. In a qualitative study (based on a number of interviews) of private employers' experiences of regulation in collective agreements in different sectors, none of the employers stated that they had identified a provision in a collective agreement that stimulated their willingness to employ and retain older workers. However, the employers could provide examples of different provisions that facilitated the phasing out of older workers and factors that limited employers' willingness to hire older workers.[50]

The managerial prerogative and the employer's right to direct and allocate work plays an important role in Swedish law. Employers have a right to decide how to organize their activities and how to distribute different tasks between separate positions.[51] Employers also have a right to decide how work should be carried out within the framework of existing employment contracts and collective agreements. We have seen that redundancy constitutes just cause for dismissal, and that employers have a unilateral right to decide on changes in their activities.[52] As a starting point, the employer determines the qualifications needed for a certain position. To meet the requirement for sufficient qualifications, the employee must possess the general and basic qualifications normally required for the position. A range of factors is included in the concept of qualifications, such as formal qualifications, experience, practical training

advantage. The employee independently determines the orientation of the education to undertake. There is no limit to the duration of the study leave. See Government Bill Prop 1974:148 24–5.

50 See C Ulander-Wänman, 'Swedish collective agreements and employers' willingness to hire and retain older workers in employment' (2016) 6(2) Nordic J Working Life Studies 61–79; and C Ulander-Wänman, *The Swedish Occupational Pension Scheme ITP2 – A Limiting Factor for Employees' Employability?* (manuscript). Cf with a Swedish study on intergenerational bargaining presenting a partly different picture. This study focused not on the local level and interviews with individual employers, but on the national sectoral level, using studies of collective agreements and interviews with leading representatives of trade unions and employers' organizations; see M Rönnmar, *Intergenerational Bargaining in Sweden.* Report for the project iNGenBar, Intergenerational Bargaining: towards integrated bargaining for younger and older workers in EU countries 2014.

51 Labour Court judgment AD 1987:42.

52 See Labour Court judgments AD 1997:121, AD 1993:101 and AD 1977:151. See also Government Bill Prop 1973:129, 123 and Government Bill Prop 1981/82:71, 65

and personal qualities.[53] An employee must not receive a position or a job that he or she cannot handle.[54] An express parallel is made to the employer hiring a new employee: the employee must meet a minimum standard in terms of education, experience and personal characteristics in relation to the work.[55] Thus, the employer cannot choose the employee that he or she thinks is best suited for the position.[56] The employee does not need to master the new tasks from the first day, but is instead entitled to a reasonable period of training.[57]

In a labour market in transition employers can invest in new technology and introduce new working methods and organizational practices that require new basic skills of employees. The introduction of new positions and demands for higher qualifications may result in the redundancy of 'old' positions, and subsequent dismissal of employees who do not fulfil the requirement for sufficient qualifications. Thus, the employer's right to direct and allocate work, and decisions as to which employees will receive company-specific training or other skills development affect the employee's employability, and this is especially true for older workers with a long length of service.[58] Although employers have a duty in principle to provide training for their employees, the individual employee has no legal right to be trained to acquire skills of a certain kind or to acquire basic and general qualifications for employment.[59]

Furthermore, the Swedish so-called transition agreements emphasize the importance of employability. These agreements cover large parts of the labour market, and constitute an important complement of statutory employment protection regulation on redundancy dismissals as well as active labour market policies and unemployment insurance. The transition agreements provide employees facing dismissal for reasons of redundancy with different rights to severance pay and economic compensation, along with active transition support measures such as coaching, job-searching services, training and re-education. They also provide

---

53 See Government Bill Prop 1973:129, 159 and Government Bill Prop 1981/82:71, 56ff.

54 See Labour Court judgments AD 1978:84, AD 1984:144, AD 1986:46, AD 1986:58, AD 1994:88, AD 1996:59, AD 2005:75 and AD 2009:92. See also Government Bill Prop 1973:129, 158–165 and 260.

55 See Labour Court judgment AD 1996:140.

56 See Labour Court judgment AD 2012:86.

57 See Government Bill Prop 1981/82:71, 57 and Labour Court judgment AD 1999:30. See also Government Bill Prop 1973:129, 159.

58 See Labour Court judgment AD 1993:197.

59 See Labour Court judgment AD 2005:75.

support for employers in re-organizations and redundancy situations. The transition agreements are administrated by transition foundations, set up by the social partners and collective bargaining, and the severance pay and transition support are financed by the employers, often through an insurance and premium-based scheme. Sebardt concludes that most of the transition agreements have shifted focus towards the realization of the individual's employability on the open labour market.[60]

5. EMPLOYMENT PROTECTION, COMPULSORY RETIREMENT AND WORKING BEYOND PENSIONABLE AGE

Against the backdrop of an ageing population, pension systems in many countries are being reformed with the aim of achieving better sustainability.[61] European and global trends observed in pension reform include an increase in the pensionable age or the introduction of a flexible pensionable age, a lowering of benefits, longer earnings periods (or life-long average earnings) and an adaptation to life expectancy. However, effecting changes in existing pension norms is a challenge.[62]

Rules on compulsory retirement reflect important links between labour law, employment protection and pension systems,[63] and the substantial

---

[60] See G Sebardt, *Redundancy and the Swedish Model. Swedish Collective Agreements on Employment Security in a National and International Context* (Iustus förlag 2005). See also a recent study on transition agreements from an intergenerational perspective, M Rönnmar (2014), above n 50, and OECD, *Back to Work: Sweden. Improving the Re-employment Prospects of Displaced Workers* (OECD 2015).

[61] Cf Fudge, Chapter 3 in this book; Numhauser-Henning, Chapter 4 in this book; and Numhauser-Henning, Julén Votinius and Zbyszewska, Chapter 7 in this book. Cf also Numhauser-Henning (2015), above n 17; A Numhauser-Henning, 'The EU ban on age-discrimination and older workers: Potentials and pitfalls' (2013) 29(4) Int J Comp Lab Law and Indus Relations 391; and A Numhauser-Henning and M Rönnmar, 'Compulsory retirement and age discrimination – The Swedish Hörnfeldt case put in perspective' in P Lindskoug, P Samulesson, U Maunsbach, G Millqvist and H-H Vogel, *Essays in Honour of Michael Bogdan* (Juristförlaget i Lund 2013).

[62] Cf Inghammar, Brokelind and Norberg, Chapter 10 in this book. See also A Numhauser-Henning, 'Labour law in a greying labour market – In need of a reconceptualisation of work and pension norms. The position of older workers in labour law' (2013) 4(2) Eur Lab L J 84–100.

[63] See in particular Numhauser-Henning (2015), above n 17. So, compulsory retirement is seen as a reflection of the standard employment/pension contracts

amount of case law from the CJEU in this area reveals that such schemes prevail in a number of EU Member States. However, compulsory retirement is not a general norm, and many different compulsory retirement rules can be found in the EU Member States.[64] Rules on compulsory retirement have been abolished in some EU countries as a result of the introduction of a ban on age discrimination. In Lithuania, Poland and the UK, for example, there is no general or statutory compulsory retirement. A compulsory retirement age can be set by legislation, collective agreements or personal employment contracts. Compulsory retirement rules may provide for the automatic termination of the employment relationship when the employee reaches a certain age (for example the pensionable age) or imply a possibility for the employer to terminate the employment relationship at a specific age.

In Sweden, compulsory retirement is regulated through the '67-year rule' in the (1982:80) Employment Protection Act,[65] tried and upheld by the CJEU in the *Hörnfeldt* case.[66] An employee has a right to stay in employment until the age of 67, when the employer may terminate the employment relationship after one month's notice and without having to provide objective grounds for dismissal. If the employer does not make use of this possibility, the permanent employment relationship continues; however, it does so with limited employment protection.[67] A Government Inquiry has proposed an increase of this age from 67 to 69 years.[68]

Much of the CJEU case law on old-age discrimination has dealt with compulsory retirement rules, and whether these rules are compatible with the ban on age discrimination. In many cases the CJEU has accepted compulsory retirement rules and found them justifiable. The Member States and the social partners have been given a broad margin of

---

and a trade-off between younger and older workers according to an implicit contract according to which wage premiums are paid towards the end of a career on the assumption that the employment relationship will come to an end at a fixed point in time – see further also E Lazear, 'Why is there mandatory retirement?' (1979) 87(6) J Polit Econ 1261.

64 Cf O'Dempsey and Beale (2011), above n 5.

65 Sections 32a and 33 of the (1982:80) Employment Protection Act.

66 *Hörnfeldt*, above n 30.

67 For example, the employee has only one month's notice, and is given no right of priority in accordance with seniority rules or rules on re-employment in redundancy situations. This part of the rule was not confirmed by the CJEU in the *Hörnfeldt* case, though. Cf also Labour Court judgment AD 2015:15 concerning a company age policy prohibiting fixed-term work after the age of 70.

68 See Government Inquiry Report SOU 2013:25.

appreciation, and when applying Article 6(1) the CJEU has found the differences of treatment on grounds of age to be objectively and reasonably justified by the legitimate aims, such as intergenerational fairness in terms of access to employment, prevention of humiliating forms of termination of employment, and a reasonable balance between labour market and budgetary concerns. The CJEU's case law so far indicates that compulsory retirement at a set (65+) age is seen as a fulfilment of the Employment Equality Directive's requirements, provided there is a reasonable system of pensions in place.[69] In its case law the CJEU has also referred to the fact that from the perspective of the individual, a rule on compulsory retirement does not necessarily mean definite withdrawal from the labour market. Working life can continue, often in fixed-term employment (Section 3). The CJEU has also decided some cases on compulsory retirement of specific professional groups or premature retirement, and here the Court has applied a stricter standard for justification.[70]

The CJEU's acceptance of rules on compulsory retirement harmonizes poorly with the promotion of active ageing and efforts to prolong working lives for older workers.[71] However, abolishment of compulsory retirement requires alternative ways of ending the employment relationship, such as voluntary retirement (encouraged with financial incentives) or performance management (followed by a possible dismissal on grounds of lack of performance). This entails a risk of weakening employment protection before actual retirement age.[72]

Recently, legislative reforms related to older workers, active ageing and employment protection have been introduced in the Netherlands. An increasingly ageing population has necessitated the gradual increase of the statutory pensionable age to secure the sustainability of the state's

---

[69] See further Numhauser-Henning and Rönnmar (2013), above n 61.

[70] See for example, *Prigge and Others v. Deutsche Lufthansa AG* C-447/09 EU:C:2011:573 and *European Commission v. Hungary* C-286/12 EU:C:2012:687. See further Fudge, Chapter 3 in this book and Numhauser-Henning, Chapter 4 in this book.

[71] It also contrasts with economic research on the 'lump of labour fallacy'; see for example, Elaine Dewhurst, 'Intergenerational balance, mandatory retirement and age discrimination in Europe: How can the ECJ better support national courts in finding a balance between the generations?' (2013) 50 CML Rev 1333.

[72] Cf further Numhauser-Henning (2013), above n 61, 391 and Numhauser-Henning (2015), above n 17.

finances, and in particular the pension system,[73] as well as to prevent labour shortages.[74] The statutory pensionable age will be raised to 66 years in 2018 and 67 in 2021, after which the pensionable age will be linked to life expectancy.[75] The government's policy not only aims at increasing the labour market participation of those between 55 years and pensionable age,[76] but also of those beyond pensionable age. However, despite this and the ban on age discrimination, a system of compulsory retirement applies.[77]

The Act on Working Beyond Pensionable Age was introduced in 2015 and aims at promoting active ageing and prolonging working life beyond pensionable age. It puts in place a 'labour law light' regime for employees beyond pensionable age. The Dutch government relies on CJEU age discrimination case law and its broad acceptance of compulsory retirement. As for the matter of justification, the government argues that the group of pensionable employees is not comparable in all respects to other employees; that the aim (facilitating working beyond pensionable age) is legitimate; and the measures (removing barriers) are appropriate (inter alia in light of the possibility of receiving a supplementary income by way of pension) and necessary.[78]

Creating a 'labour law light' regime for the group of pensionable employees entails changes such as reducing employment protection, in particular in relation to the dismissal of a pensionable employee, a further flexibilization of employment by allowing an increased use of successive fixed-term employment contracts, and reducing the entitlement to continued wage payment during sickness. While this regime makes employing pensionable employees more attractive for employers (for example, no pension and social security premiums are due so the hourly labour costs are less), it does not provide clear incentives for pensionable persons to

---

[73] Kamerstukken II 2014/15, 34 073, no. 5, 1. In particular the financial crisis has forced the state to reconsider labour market issues, such as the statutory pensionable age.

[74] Kamerstukken II 2014/15, 34 073, no. 3, 11.

[75] Article 7, Act of Working Beyond Pensionable Age.

[76] Kamerstukken II 2014/15, 34 073, no. 4, 2.

[77] See E Lutjens and M Heemskerk, 'Is pensioenontslag bij 65 jaar nog steeds geldig?' (2010) ArbeidsRecht 12.

[78] Kamerstukken II 2014/15, 34 073, no. 3, 22.

remain active as employees. Pensionable employees cannot accrue additional pension rights. However, they may supplement their pension by continuing to work.[79]

Furthermore, a general reform of Dutch dismissal law was introduced in 2015.[80] The main aim of this reform is to change the legal position of flexible workers and to amend the unemployment regulation.[81] This 'modernization' process, as the Dutch government calls it,[82] is needed to address the problematic growth of flexible forms of work, such as self-employment and fixed-term, temporary agency and part-time work. This development resulted, in particular, from the 1999 Flexibility and Security Act. With this reform of dismissal law the government is attempting to rebalance flexibility and security.[83] Consequently, fixed-term employment contracts are converted into permanent employment contracts more quickly.

Furthermore, a new provision has been introduced in the Civil Code, according to which employees, while in employment, may ask their employer for permission to attend job-related training.[84] That request, if it is 'reasonable', must be granted if needed for the performance of the job and if the employee's job will disappear or the employee is no longer capable of performing the job. Training and education is also a main philosophy behind the newly introduced 'transitional allowances', which employers must pay to dismissed employees. This allowance replaces the traditional severance pay.[85] A transitional allowance is not to be paid if

---

[79] The Commission proposed a system of receiving pensions while simultaneously receiving remuneration if work is continued. Commission, 'Supporting national strategies for safe and sustainable pensions through an integrated approach' (Communication) COM(2001) 362 final, 5.

[80] Dutch dismissal law has some specific characteristics. According to a two-way approach an employer, before being able to dismiss a permanent employee, needs to have either (1) the permission of the Employee Insurance Agency (*Uitvoeringsinstituut Werknemersverzekeringen*) or the sector committee, or (2) the permission of the court to rescind the contract (unless the employee consents to termination of the employment relationship). A permission from the agency is needed in two situations: if the dismissal is based on economic reasons and if the dismissal proceeds after two years of unfitness of the employee.

[81] See on the situation of long-term unemployment of those over 45 years and their difficulties in accessing the labour market, Kullmann (2016), above n 43.

[82] Kamerstukken II 2013/14, 33 818, no. 3, 2.

[83] Kamerstukken II 2013/14, 33 818, no. 3, 4–5.

[84] Article 7:611a of the Civil Code.

[85] The transitional allowance is capped at 75,000 EUR.

the employee has reached the statutory pensionable age or if the dismissal is related to a culpable act or omission of the employee.[86]

Some EU Member States, for example Poland and Lithuania, provide specific protection for older workers during a 'pre-retirement' period. In Poland the employer may not dismiss an employee who will reach retirement age in less than four years, if the employee's employment period would enable him or her to receive an old-age pension upon reaching this age. However, this rule is sometimes 'circumvented' by the employer through dismissal of the employee before he or she reaches the pre-retirement age. As a result, the protection is undermined and working life is shortened. Similarly, in Lithuania employees who will become eligible for old-age pension in less than three years are given priority in the selection process in a redundancy situation.[87]

Flexible working time is not only a way of balancing work-family responsibilities; it can also be a way of adapting the working situation to the needs of older workers and thereby prolonging working life. Rights to request (or genuine rights) to flexible working hours (for caregivers, parents or employees and so on) are found, for example, in the Dutch, Swedish and UK settings and also in EU law.[88] Similarly, in some EU Member States such as Sweden, statutory or collectively bargained schemes provide for partial retirement or part-time work for older workers. These schemes differ from traditional schemes on early retirement, as their purpose is to enable the older workers to prolong their working life.[89] Issues on working environment adaptation and flexible working hours are closely related to the issue of proactive measures and reasonable accommodation within the age discrimination law framework proper.

---

86 Article 7:673 para 7 under b and c Civil Code. For employees who at the time of the dismissal have reached the age of 50, a transitional rule determines that they benefit from a more generous allowance.

87 See L Mitrus, 'Age discrimination and labour law in Poland' in Numhauser-Henning and Rönnmar (2015), above n 6; and T Davulis, 'Age discrimination and labour law in Lithuania' in Numhauser-Henning and Rönnmar (2015), above n 6.

88 See Council Directive 2010/18/EU of 8 March 2010 implementing the revised Framework Agreement on parental leave concluded by BUSINESSEUROPE, UEAPME, CEEP and ETUC and repealing Directive 96/34/EC, OJ 1996 L 145/4.

89 See further Rönnmar (2014), above n 50.

6. CONCLUDING REMARKS

The function, content and future challenges of employment protection from the perspective of older workers and a prolonged working life are in focus in this chapter. Legal developments in EU law and policy and in national law in the Member States partly reflect a shift from the protection of older workers within the framework of traditional employment protection to an emphasis on flexicurity, employability, active ageing and a prolonged working life. Thus, the key challenge is not to regulate and secure employment protection in the current job, but to extend working life to and beyond pensionable age and invest in training and employability in relation to the labour market as a whole.

Older workers in today's labour markets are both vulnerable (in light of ageism, antiquated education, training and qualifications, physical capability and so on) and empowered (in light of experience, loyalty, motivation, mental capability and so on). Their need for special protection has influenced the content of employment protection in many EU Member States, and is reflected, for example, in the principle that old age or sickness does not constitute just cause for dismissal and in seniority rules in redundancy situations. Despite a partly harmonized EU law framework and a 'constitutionalization' of employment protection through Article 30 of the CFR, employment protection regulation in the Member States – and the strength of the protection it offers not only to older workers, but to employees generally – differs. Following the economic crisis and deregulation of employment protection in many Member States, older workers run a special risk. At the same time, in light of the current youth unemployment problem in the EU and from an intergenerational perspective, employment protection is seen both as providing necessary protection for older workers and hindering the entry of younger workers into the labour market.

There are important and often complex links between non-discrimination law and the flexibilization of work, and between non-discrimination law (including the ban on age discrimination) and employment protection. These links are influential in shaping statutory, collective bargaining and case law developments. In principle, EU age discrimination law, despite its human rights basis, enables continued age-related regulation through its large scope for justification of age-related differential treatment. There are many directly and indirectly age-related statutory and collectively bargained rules and practices in the area of employment protection in the EU Member States, such as regulations on flexible employment, seniority rules, seniority-based severance pay and compulsory retirement.

In many EU Member States, specific fixed-term employment contracts for older workers are used to prolong working life.

The Swedish example – that is, the key role that the notion of sufficient qualifications plays in dismissals for reasons of redundancy – highlights the crucial link between managerial prerogative, the right to organize the business and the right to direct and allocate work on the one hand, and on the other hand the employee's – and especially the older worker's – possibility of receiving adequate training and competence development while in employment, as a way to remain both sufficiently qualified in relation to the current position and employable in relation to the labour market as a whole.

Against this background, the transition agreements that provide employees facing redundancy with both economic compensation and active transition support measures function as an important complement. Similarly, in the Netherlands, recent reforms in the area of employment protection have emphasized employability, and have introduced rules on transitional allowance and a right for employees to request permission to attend job-related training.

An important question is this: Where should the responsibility lie for older workers' employability – with the individual employee, the individual employer, the social partners or society at large? In addition, are enough investments being made in education, life-long learning and active labour market policies, and are the investments adequate when it comes to content and regulation? It is not only a question of costs and budgetary means, but also of the difficulty in analysing current and future needs as regards qualifications and competence development, and of the ever-important 'matching' of supply and demand in the labour market. Furthermore, life-long learning must be viewed from a life-cycle perspective.

Rules on compulsory retirement reflect important links between labour law, employment protection and pension systems. Compulsory retirement is not a general norm in the EU, and the ban on age discrimination has resulted in the abolishment of compulsory retirement in some Member States. While the CJEU's acceptance of rules on compulsory retirement contravenes active ageing and efforts to prolong working lives for older workers, an abolishment of compulsory retirement risks weakening employment protection even before retirement age is reached.

In recent years a number of legislative reforms related to older workers, active ageing and employment protection have been introduced in the Netherlands. The Act on Working Beyond Pensionable Age aims to promote active ageing and prolong working life beyond pensionable age, and introduces a 'labour law light' regime for employees beyond pensionable age. The Act can be criticized for focusing too much on creating (predominantly economic) incentives for employers to hire or to continue to employ older workers and workers beyond pensionable age. Less focus is put on creating incentives and fruitful conditions for employees to stay in employment beyond pensionable age. In this context, adjustments of the pension system, flexible working time and working environment adaptation would be interesting measures.

To be able to promote active ageing, prolong working life and afford adequate protection for older workers, a diversified approach is needed, including not only traditional employment protection elements but also investments in training and competence development aimed at enabling transitions and employability, along with reasonable adjustments in work organization, working time and working environment.

10. Prolonged working life and flexible retirement in public and occupational pension schemes

Andreas Inghammar, Cécile Brokelind and Per Norberg

1. BACKGROUND AND CHALLENGES[1]

Public retirement schemes have been under significant scrutiny worldwide since the beginning of the financial crisis in 2008. Numerous governmental reports and academic presentations have documented the need to strengthen national retirement schemes by different means, not least by implementing – and enforcing – a prolonged working life.[2] Because recent generations are more likely than previous ones to obtain a

[1] This work was carried out within the Norma Elder Law Research Environment (www.jur.lu.se/elderlaw) funded by Ragnar Söderberg's Foundation and the Marianne and Marcus Wallenberg Foundation.

[2] See further, Stefan Domonkos, 'Promoting a higher retirement age: A prospect-theoretical approach' (2015) 24 Int J Soc Welfare 133; Bernard H Casey and Jörg Michael Dostal, 'Voluntary pension saving for old age: Are the objectives of self-responsibility and security compatible?' (2013) 47(3) Social Policy and Admin 287; Konstantina Kalogeropoulou, 'Addressing the pension challenge: Can the EU respond? Towards facilitating the portability of supplementary (occupational) pension rights' (2014) 16 Eur J Law Reform 747, primarily 752ff; but also the Swedish preparatory works, Government Inquiry Report SOU 2012:28 *Längre liv, längre arbetsliv. Förutsättningar och hinder för äldre att arbeta längre* and Government Inquiry Report SOU 2013:25 *Åtgärder för ett längre arbetsliv*; and with a labour and anti-discrimination law perspective, Ann Numhauser-Henning, 'Labour law, pension norms and the EU ban on age discrimination: Towards ultimate flexibilisation?' in Ann Numhauser-Henning and Mia Rönnmar (eds), *Age Discrimination and Labour Law. Comparative and Conceptual Perspectives in the EU and Beyond* (Kluwer Law International 2015) 115.

higher education,[3] and life expectancy has increased significantly over the past 50 years, the most relevant path to increase the number of years at work would be to extend working life to a higher retirement age. Many countries with public retirement schemes have followed this path and the development has gained speed along the financial crisis. However, attitudes and perceptions of retirement are not altered as easily as legal provisions, so retirement ages are still stranded around or below 65 years of age in most EU Member States.[4] While some public retirement schemes – like the Swedish system – have opened for a flexible retirement age or 'period during which the insured employee can chose to retire', other jurisdictions have been more explicitly normative in setting a fixed retirement age; some of these statutory retirement ages have been raised in the past few years.[5]

A somewhat alternative route to prolonged work life, instead of increased retirement age, is to accept flexible retirement in relation to part-time work, at least when the employee reaches a certain age or has been employed in the workplace for a certain amount of time. It could be argued that such part-time retirement opportunities could facilitate or promote a prolonged working life, especially for older blue-collar workers in physically challenging employments where the opportunity to continue working at the same pace might be considered less realistic.

As we will discuss in this chapter, these different approaches can very well be applied in parallel to an overarching aim of prolonged working life, but there are hurdles and objections that must be taken into account; these hindrances are at least partly related to the legal structure of different provisions. Such provisions in labour and social law collective agreements and tax law could be made to fit the overarching aim, but in some situations, they can also contradict each other and even be misleading in relation to the promotion of prolonged working life for sustainable retirement schemes.

---

[3] Since the late 1990s, however, development has been less dramatic. The years of financial crisis and increased youth unemployment, especially among the less educated, have added still other factors that delay full work-life participation.

[4] See further from the Eurostat, at http://ec.europa.eu/eurostat/statistics-explained/index.php/Labour_force_survey_statistics_-_transition_from_work_to_retirement#Further_Eurostat_information, accessed 13 December 2015.

[5] In Denmark and Germany from 65 to 67, in the UK from 65 to 68 in relation to the state pension (but indeed in general an open-ended upper limit) and in France from 60 to 62; see further Axel H Börsch-Supan, 'Challenges for European welfare states' (2015) 22 Int Tax Public Finance 534, primarily 540.

In this chapter we investigate more concretely the modern, three-pillar Swedish pension system. When Sweden underwent a dramatic financial crisis in the early 1990s, it became clear that the pension scheme implemented in the 1950s and 1960s urgently needed dramatic and far-reaching changes. The new public pension scheme came into force in 1998 and was implemented during the following 15 years; this system has drawn significant international attention, especially as it combines an earnings-based, defined-contribution system in a primarily pay-as-you-go system with a prefunded pension and balances against the financial development of the overall economy. A very important contributing factor to the public pension scheme is the existence of broadly applicable occupational schemes available to the vast majority of employees through the collective agreements. Even though the collective impact is more significant in Sweden than in other corresponding countries, the general picture of a workable but stable occupational retirement system could serve as an interesting example for lawmakers and academics in many parts of the world.

The public retirement schemes in the modern welfare states are generally constructed as pay-as-you-go systems, either wholly or partially.[6] While these public schemes provide a basic living for the retired person, and are usually related to previous income or contributions to the system, many welfare states adopt or require additional occupational schemes to be organized and financed by employers. These systems are based on individual contractual arrangements or are a result of collective agreements. In Sweden almost 90 per cent of employees are entitled to occupational pension schemes as a result of collective agreements.[7] From an EU perspective, interest in such schemes has recently been increased due to the coming into force of Directive 2014/50/EU of the European Parliament and of the Council of 16 April 2014 on minimum requirements for enhancing worker mobility between Member States by improving the acquisition and preservation of supplementary pension rights.[8] This Directive does not have great significance for this particular chapter, however, even though the Directive clearly indicates at least a partial

---

[6] With some exemptions, different forms of pay-as-you-go systems are applied all across the EU; see Karel Lannoo, Mikkel Barslund, Ales Chmelar and Marten von Werder, 'Pension schemes: Study August 2014' (2014) Directorate General for Internal Policies, Policy Department A: Economic and Scientific Policy, European Union 66–7.

[7] Government Inquiry Report SOU 2013:25 239.

[8] OJ 2014 L 128/1. Implementation of the Directive is due 21 May 2018.

Europeanization in terms of old-age pensions, at least when it comes to transnational workers' mobility.

For the vast majority of employees, the most interesting outcome would be to maximize the individual net pension benefit, regardless of the extent to which these benefits come from public schemes or occupational ones. However, for an in-depth understanding and analysis of the incentives for individuals and employers and the robustness of the system, our multilayer investigation of the pension system can be beneficial as we undertake a broader analysis of coherence within and between the different pillars of the overarching system. In the following we research and elaborate the legal opportunities available for achieving the overarching aim of a prolonged working life. We also connect this aim of public retirement policy to the entitlements established in occupational pension schemes. The first task is to study the features of the Swedish pension system, covering the main components of public and occupational schemes – including some major collective agreements – but also to some extent the private pension scheme. Secondly, we relate these provisions to the more recent development in Swedish tax law – and discuss the overarching political goal to promote work over pensions. The final discussion focuses on conflicts and incoherencies between these different parts of the retirement system and discusses the opportunities, under collective agreements, to have a flexible pension age, and placing the burden of such flexibilization with the employee or the employer.

A recent governmental inquiry – reported in SOU 2012:28 and SOU 2013:25 – undertook a significant project to compile and analyse data from the Swedish Pensions Agency (*Pensionsmyndigheten)* and Statistics Sweden (SCB). The projections clearly show that the percentage of paid work – of vital importance for the contribution to the pension schemes – is in continuous decline and has dropped dramatically in only a few decades; this decline will likely contrast sharply with the general opinion of a continuously longer working life.[9] Indeed, the report states that the percentage of life we dedicate to paid work has dropped dramatically for men, from almost 15 per cent in 1970 to slightly above 9 per cent in 2010, while women's increasing emancipation during the last 35 years has not resulted in any real increase in work-life percentage for females; in fact, this percentage has decreased by 0.5 per cent from around 8 per cent in 1980 to around 7.5 per cent in 2010.[10] In general, people are now

---

9 Government Inquiry Report SOU 2012:28 72–4.

10 See Table 5.8 in Government Inquiry Report SOU 2012:28 73.

spending a significantly lower portion of their lives in paid work than only a generation ago.[11]

Combining all these factors leads to the rather obvious but still challenging conclusion that in order to maintain current levels of retirement benefits, the retirement age must be raised from 65 years for those born in 1930 to almost 69 years for those born in 1995. In addition, life expectancy has increased dramatically over recent generations – so the number of years in retirement will also increase, even if people retire at 69 years of age.[12] So, while the overall picture clearly shows that the decrease in working years has to be addressed, primarily by raising the general pension age but also by providing for early entry into working life, the portion of work during a lifespan has decreased. Many might question whether there is a desire among the population to increase the working percentage. A related, or perhaps contributing, problem in this area is that several different normative influences in working life are contradictory to or provide for an incoherent body of norms that are unlikely to encourage prolonged working life – and would instead work to keep working time at its current level or even decrease it. This incoherence or conflict of interests – within the legal system – is the vital nerve of this chapter.

2. RETIREMENT SYSTEMS – AN OUTLINE OF THE SWEDISH CASE

2.1 Basic Features

The Swedish three-pillar pension system is often visualized as a 'cone' or triangle in which the different horizontal layers of contributions and benefits are described.[13] The base section, the foundation, of the cone represents the public pension scheme, which is in turn divided in two parts: the large, pay-as-you-go part, which is organized as a main

---

11 We believe this development to be very much unknown to the public and, on the contrary, to be in conflict with the overall impression of how working life has developed during the past one or two generations.

12 Government Inquiry Report SOU 2012:28 67, see the table and further references there.

13 In our opinion the 'cone' is actually more adequate in describing the variations in importance between the three layers of pension than the internationally more common three-pillar metaphor.

defined-contribution system,[14] and the smaller portion comprising prepaid pension funds. The centre of the 'cone' represents the important occupational pension schemes and the top of the cone constitutes any privately paid pension funds. The metaphor of a cone is excellent: not only does it visualize the different parts of the pension system, it also provides a picture of the relative importance of the different pension types.[15] It also extends the importance of interrelated schemes throughout the overall system. In countries with limited or no public pension schemes, the foundation of the cone will be less dominant, as will the middle section of the cone in labour markets with very limited occupational schemes. In relation to the definitions used in the EU,[16] the base of the cone constitutes the first-pillar pensions, the mid-section is second-pillar pensions and the top of the cone equals third-pillar pensions. Apparently, most EU countries do acknowledge this three-pillar pension system, but with more or less emphasis on the different pillars. The many flavours of this pension concept in different Member States create major difficulties in categorizing the parts of the scheme coherently. For instance, the EU Report referred to earlier categorized the prefunded part of the Swedish public pension scheme as a third-pillar mandatory private scheme, despite its obvious connection to the first pillar.[17] In 2013 the Swedish pensions system – with all parts of the 'cone' accounted for – distributed, or paid, a total of 362 billion SEK (38 billion EUR), had a total capital worth of 4.087 billion SEK (430 billion EUR) and contributions totalling 429 billion SEK (45 billion EUR).[18]

The public pension scheme is thus of most significant importance in an overall perspective, but the role of occupational schemes – mainly in relation to aggregated capital and contributions but also in relation to the

---

14 The notion of a defined-contribution system has recently been adopted, not only in Sweden but also in Norway and Poland; see for further international discussion Fabian Kindermann, 'Earnings related pension schemes and human capital formation' (2015) 14(1) J Pensions Econ and Finance 19, primarily 20.

15 Indeed, the Swedish Pensions Agency (*Pensionsmyndigheten*) coordinates online input from most banks and insurance companies, thereby allowing most employees to have a pretty good picture of their future pension based on public as well as occupational and private pension schemes; see www.pensionsmyndigheten.se and www.minpension.se.

16 For instance, in 'Pension systems in the EU – contingent liabilities and assets in the public and private sector', Directorate-General for Internal Policies, Policy Department 26.

17 Ibid 28.

18 Pensionsmyndigheten, Orange Rapport (Swedish Pensions Agency Annual Report 2014) ii.

benefits paid – cannot be overestimated. The 'top of the pension cone', representing private pension funds, contributes only a small part to the overall picture. Recent (2015) decreases in tax deductions for private pension funds are likely to marginalize the impact of private pension saving even further.[19]

2.2 A Modern, Sustainable, Public Pension Scheme

As mentioned in the previous section, public old-age pension schemes are commonly structured as pay-as-you-go, partly or wholly.[20] Such twentieth-century schemes have been repeatedly criticized during the past 20 years for being under-financed and unable to accommodate increasing numbers of pensioners in mature economies with modest productivity growth and low birth rates.[21]

The Swedish public pensions scheme was introduced in 1998 as a result of collaboration between almost all political parties in the Swedish Parliament (only the ex-communist Left Party and the Green Party, at the time representing altogether around 10 per cent of the parliamentary seats, remained outside the collaboration).[22] From an overall perspective the public pension scheme in Sweden is *income-related*, because the contributions – and subsequent benefits – are calculated in relation to income earned from employment by the employee during the span of their working life, even though there is also a basic income pension scheme (*garantipension*) financed by taxes. The latter provides basic financial support to retired individuals who did not hold employment or

[19] See further discussions and references in Section 2.5 in this chapter.

[20] Apart from Sweden, the pay-as-you-go principle is maintained in a number of countries, such as Germany, France, Belgium, Finland and Hungary. See further Kindermann (2015), above n 14, 19.

[21] There are numerous comments in the literature; see for instance Horst Siebert, 'Pay-as-you-go pensions face a bleak future', Financial Times (London 23 August 2000) as well as Thomas Lindh, Bo Malmberg and Joakim Palme, 'Generations at war or sustainable social policy in ageing societies?' (2005) 13 J Polit Philos 470, primarily 483–7; and Carlos Vidal-Melia, Maria del Carmen Boada-Penas and Ole Settergren, 'Automatic balance mechanisms in pay-as-you-go pension systems' (2009) 34 Geneva Pap R I-Iss P 287.

[22] The preparatory works for the development of the modern public pension scheme can be found in Government Bill Prop 1993/94:25 *Inriktningen av den ekonomiska politiken,* Government Inquiry Report SOU 1990:76 *Allmän pension*, Government Inquiry Report SOU 1994:20 *Reformerat pensionssystem* and Government Report Ds 2009:53 *Detta är pensionsöverenskommelsen.*

were part-time employed in low-income employment for significant parts of their working lives.[23]

The general features of the first-pillar public pension scheme are a mandatory, major pay-as-you-go pension combined with a smaller prefunded part. The pay-as-you-go section of the scheme is contribution-based and funded by contributions of 16 per cent of the annual pensionable income, for most people equal to salaried income, while the funding of the prefunded part covers only 2.5 per cent.[24] The contributions to the public pension system are income-based, but not progressive; they remain at 18.5 (16+2.5) per cent, and are primarily paid through employer contributions, which is explained in Table 10.1.[25] Notably, a redistributional effect of the system is maintained by the upper-earnings limit embedded in the scheme, even though corresponding contributions (from employers) are continued without limit in relation to the approximately 10.5 per cent contributions paid by the employers.[26]

The prefunded part of the public pension scheme, which aggregates the contribution of 2.5 per cent of employment income, is 'individualized'. For this small portion, employees may make decisions about investment. Numerous pension funds are available for the allocation of the pension scheme and the accrued funds of employees who do not make their own investment decisions are subject to financial placement, with the aim of securing a return on investment for the benefit of higher future pensions.

---

[23] The Basic Income Pension with a maximum corresponding to approximately 800 EUR per month is in many cases combined with needs-based social support such as housing benefit and the like; see further https://secure.pensionsmyndigheten.se/GarantipensionensStorlek.html, accessed 10 December 2015.

[24] The pension contribution is regulated in the (1994:1744) Act on general payroll tax.

[25] The individual pension fee of approximately 8 per cent is collected through the preliminary tax payment and deducted from the income tax 'automatically'. Contributions of approximately 10.5 per cent are paid monthly by the employer.

[26] The ceiling or highest income which generates benefits under the scheme is 7.5 income base amounts (*inkomstbasbelopp*), currently (2016) 444,750 SEK, approximately 46,800 EUR per annum.

Table 10.1 The Swedish public pension scheme

	Basic (low-income) pension scheme	**Earnings-related public pension scheme (since 1998)**	
		Earnings-related pay-as-you-go pension	Prefunded, *premium pension*
Qualification	Residence in Sweden. Maximum pension upon 40 years of residence (often combined with other social benefits).	Employment. In general, equivalent to 16% of the annual pensionable income is contributed to the pension system.	Employment. In general, equivalent to 2.5% of the annual pensionable income is contributed to individualized, prefunded pension funds (premiepension).
Financing of programme	Financed by taxes.	Employer's contributions in combination with compulsory (and automatically administered) employee contributions, but organized as pay-as-you-go.	Employer's contributions in combination with compulsory (and automatically administered) employee contributions are set aside in individualized pension funds.
Pension age	From 65	From 61	From 61
Calculation of pension	Provides only for the most basic financial support and is mainly applicable only to employees who have worked part-time or only short periods of life. The maximum income level is roughly 800 EUR per month.	The pension is dependent on the portion of employers' and individuals' contributions over the years of employment, but also related to general financial developments in society and the life expectancy in the year of retirement.	The contributions to the pension funds and the return of investment in those individualized funds, as well as the year of retirement, determine the level of pension.

Notes:
1. See further Andreas Inghammar, 'Der Übergang in der gesetzlich geregelten Ruhestand im schwedischen Renten- und Arbeitsrecht' (2010) 4 Neue Zeitschrift für Arbeitsrecht (zu Heft 20/2010) 145, 145.
2. All Swedish state pensions (including basic pension) can be postponed; each month of delayed retirement results in an increased benefit level calculated on actuarial principles. Around the age of 65 the increase is around 0.6 per cent per month. There is no upper limit for postponement.

2.3 Occupational Pension Schemes

Swedish occupational pension schemes vary significantly between different sectors of the labour market, such as private or public, but they also differentiate between blue- and white-collar employees. As a common feature they are all gender-neutral in relation to pension age and benefits, and they all form an important supplement to the mandatory public pension scheme, increasing the income of most pensioners to a level estimated at 60–75 per cent of the previous salary.[27] Collective agreements, either directly or indirectly, cover the vast majority of employees in the labour market; therefore the occupational pension schemes and their benefit or consequence of the collective agreement are very important.[28]

Historically, since the mid-1950s, occupational pension schemes were generally structured as *defined-benefit* schemes that emphasized a number of the last (highest paid) years of employment, but in the past 15 years the trend has shifted towards more *defined-contribution* schemes.[29] The shift from defined benefits to defined contributions is a result of increased awareness in many parts of the world and in many parts of the labour market that the unpredictability of a defined-benefit system, accumulated over years and generations of employees, represents a serious threat to the balance sheet of corporations and public employers.[30] Because the pension arrangements are generated over decades and

---

27 Press release from State Pension Agency 1 July 2013, https://secure.pensionsmyndigheten.se/kompensationsgrad13.html, accessed 13 December 2015.

28 Regardless of a decrease over the past 20 years, union membership is still comparatively high – at approximately 70 per cent. Even more importantly, the percentages of employers who are bound by collective agreements are even higher, approximately 90 per cent, leaving primarily small businesses outside the scope of collective agreements; see further Swedish National Mediation Office, '*Siffror och diagram om medlemsantal, organisationsgrad och kollektivavtalstäckning*' (2014) available at: www.mi.se/files/PDF-er/ar_diagram_och_tabeller/ar__2014_diatab/yrkesverksamma.pdf, accessed 11 November 2015.

29 Most recently the collective agreement for the municipal and public healthcare sector changed from *defined-benefit* to *defined-contribution* based occupational pensions. However, employees above 26 years of age who were already (permanently) employed were not obliged to switch, but could stay with their 'old' defined-benefit programme, while new recruited staff will be subject to the new, defined-contribution system. See the agreement AKAP-KL, 'Avgiftsbaserad Kollektiv Avtalad Pension', which entered into force 1 January 2014. The agreement is available at: http://skl.se/download/18.430f8b0b145ac911ed64e1ce/1399536098473/Overenskommelse-om-avgiftsbestamd-kollektivavtalad-pension-AKAP-KL.pdf, accessed 10 November 2015.

30 The problems have been monitored from a more general (and slightly more UK-centric) perspective in Ebony de Thierry, Helen Lam, Mark Harcourt and Geoff Wood, 'Defined benefit pension decline: The consequences for organizations and employees' (2014) 36 Employee Relat 654, 654.

built upon years of earnings and contributions, most Swedish occupational pension schemes still entail larger or smaller portions of defined benefits.

Swedish occupational pension schemes, as is further developed in Table 10.2, are related to the different sectors of the labour market and the distinction between blue-collar and white-collar employees. These systems hold extraordinary significance for white-collar pensioners; if they were mid-level or high earners, a large portion of their previous income was not accounted for in the public pension scheme.[31]

The state sector occupational scheme is regulated in the PA 03 collective agreement and for (mainly future) employees born 1988 or later, by the very recent PA 16.[32] The occupational scheme is organized as *defined benefits* and *defined contributions*.[33] The PA 03 takes into account all years of employment under the collective agreement, from 28 years of age to 65,[34] and covers salaries up to approximately 148,000 SEK (15,600 EUR) per month, which is significantly more favourable for high-level, state-employed income earners than the ordinary public pension scheme.[35]

The retirement age is flexible and allows for partial or full retirement from 61 years of age. The benefits paid from the defined-contribution part of the scheme will be correspondingly lower upon voluntary early retirement, due to the limited years of contribution and the increased number of years as a retiree.

---

31 Only annual income below 444,750 SEK was accounted for in 2016; see above for a discussion on the public pension scheme.

32 The PA 03 agreement can be found at: www.arbetsgivarverket.se/globalassets/avtal-skrifter/centralaavtal/pa-03/36265_pa-03-tot.pdf, accessed 11 November 2015. The PA 16 scheme, which covers only employees born 1988 or later, entered into force 1 January 2016. The new scheme provides for a defined-contribution scheme, wherein (public) employers make monthly payments of at least 6 per cent of the salary. See further '*Pensionsavtal för arbetstagare inom det statliga avtalsområdet 2016*', available at www.arbetsgivarverket.se/globalassets/avtal-skrifter/centralaavtal/pa-16/pensionsavtalpa16.pdf, accessed 29 March 2016.

33 PA 03 Chapter 3 (Defined Contributions) and Chapters 4–7 (Defined Benefits).

34 PA 03 Chapter 16. The age limit of 65 years of age (actually the month prior) for the calculation of pensionable income appears to be inherited from the previous compulsory pension age of 65, and is not necessarily up to date in terms of prolonged working-life efforts and the current 67-year pension age.

35 The ceiling is 30 x 59,600 SEK (30 x the indexed '*Inkomstbasbelopp*'). *Förordning* (2015:537) *om inkomstbasbelopp för år 2016.*

The part of the scheme that accounts for *defined benefits* stipulates a requirement of 30 years of work (under the collective agreement) for an employee's full participation.[36] However, only the last five years before turning 65 (if not retiring earlier) and not the 30 years of contributing employment are represented when the level of defined benefits is determined.[37] Because state employees are likely to maximize their employment position and income just before retirement, mainly as a result of experience and seniority, the structure of the *defined-benefit* part of the scheme increases the pension income for almost all employees. Meanwhile, the increase in pension does not correspond to an increased contribution to the scheme, but is instead a one-way extra injection from the employer to the individual retiring employee.[38]

Employees who choose to retire early can call upon payment of pensions under the collective agreement from age 61 (early retirement) and the employer contribution to the scheme will remain unaltered until the retiree is 65 years old and reaches the 'ordinary' retirement age under the scheme.[39]

The new agreement concerning employees born 1988 or later contains only a defined-contribution scheme and no defined benefits.[40] The employer contributions – and the eventual payments to the individuals – have been made more flexible and still reflect the decreased income protection for high-end income under the public pension scheme. Contributions are 6 per cent until the income ceiling is reached (see above) but increase to 31.5 per cent on income above this ceiling.[41] Currently, the proportion of (young) employees, born 1988 or later, is rather low in the state sector, but this will naturally increase over time. In the municipal sector, another collective agreement provides for a similar occupational pension scheme – the current KAP-KL and the future AKAP-KL.[42] The

[36] PA 03 Chapter 17; furthermore, only employment (*tjänstetidsfaktor)* after 28 years of age is recognized for the *defined-benefit* scheme, PA 03 Chapter 16.

[37] PA 03 Chapter 16.

[38] We shall come back to the impact that this structure is likely to have on mobility and flexibility during the final years of work.

[39] PA 03 Chapter 12 primarily refers to the defined-benefit programme, but PA 03 Chapter 8 is also of great interest because it provides for continued employer contributions until 65 years of age, even if the employee chooses early retirement (from 61 years) – and contribution levels remain unaltered, as if the employee were continuously working.

[40] PA 16 Section 1.

[41] PA 16 Chapter 4.

[42] The KAP-KL covers employees born before 1985 and the AKAP-KL covers those born 1986 or later. There are some options to enlist in the

KAP-KL is a combined defined-contributions and defined-benefits scheme that provides for supplementary earnings-related pensions for municipality employees. The scheme accounts for contributions based on income when the employees are already 21 years old (if employed under the collective agreement at that time).[43] The employer contributions to the scheme are 4.5 per cent on income below 30 income base amounts.[44] The defined-benefit part of the scheme does not include a prefunding of pension funds. Instead it refers to a percentage of the final salary, generally 55 per cent of a salary greater than 7.5 but below 20 income base amounts.[45] Income between 20 and 30 income base amounts (approximately 125,000–188,000 EUR per year) is only compensated at 27.50 per cent.[46]

The AKAP-KL, which is generally applicable to employees born 1986 or later, is a defined-contribution system, with no defined-benefit provisions included.[47] As with most modern Swedish occupational systems, the earnings-related contributions (and benefits) are accounted for only up to an income of 30 income base amounts,[48] and the employer's contributions are 4.5 per cent of the salary below 7.5 income base amounts and 30 per cent between 7.5 and 30 income base amounts.[49] The retirement age under the scheme is currently 67 years, which refers to the corresponding provision on compulsory retirement in the (1982:80) Employment Protection Act.[50]

AKAP-KL even if one was born before 1986 but, as we shall see, the structure of the new scheme is likely to be less favourable and only a few individuals would benefit from such a change of schemes.

[43] The pensionable income is calculated yearly between 21 and 65 years of age, KAP-KL Chapter 11.

[44] KAP-KL Chapter 9 and KAP-KL Chapter 11; 30 income base amounts is approximately 187,000 EUR per year – a highly unlikely income level for municipal employees (or anyone else in Sweden for that matter).

[45] There is a slight decrease in this benefit during a number of years, from 62.5 per cent for those born 1946 to 55 per cent for those born 1967 or later; see KAP-KL Chapter 21.

[46] Even in this regard there is a decrease from 31.25 per cent for those born 1946 to only 27.5 per cent if born 1967 or later, KAP-KL Chapter 21.

[47] AKAP-KL Chapter 1.

[48] AKAP-KL Chapter 2.

[49] AKAP-KL Chapter 3.

[50] AKAP-KL Chapter 1. Concerning compulsory retirement in Sweden see further *Torsten Hörnfeldt v. Posten Meddelande AB* C-141/11 EU:C:2012:421.

As an example of a private-sector occupational scheme, we have focused on the major blue-collar scheme, Avtalspension SAF-LO 1997, and the private-sector, white-collar ITP1 scheme.

The occupational pension scheme Avtalspension SAF-LO 1997 was concluded collectively by the major private parties of the Swedish labour market and covers the vast majority of Swedish blue-collar workers. The scheme offers a defined-contribution programme which, in parallel with other schemes, includes employers' contributions of 4.5 per cent of the employee's income that are to be individualized and invested in pension funds. Income above the ceiling in the public pension scheme (7.5 income base amounts) generates a contribution of 30 per cent.[51] The scheme does not include any defined benefits. The standard pension age is 65 years of age.[52] In contrast to the previous occupational schemes (and the public employment occupational schemes), the blue-collar workers' scheme is purely contribution-based and structured in payments into pension funds. The pension contributions to the occupational scheme are accounted for only until the month before the employee turns 65.[53] If the employee remains in employment or is re-employed after 65 years of age, contributions are paid (by the employer) only if this is explicitly agreed upon in the employment contract.[54]

The ITP1 occupational pension scheme, which in the future will enlist a vast majority of the private-sector white-collar employees, is similar in most aspects to the blue-collar workers' arrangement. The ITP1 covers employees born 1979 or later while another scheme, ITP2, is related to those born 1978 or earlier.[55] As for ITP1, the contributions are paid once the white-collar employee turns 25 years old and, similarly to the blue-collar scheme, are paid at 4.5 per cent on income below 7.5 base income amounts and 30 per cent on higher income.[56] Pension age under the programme is 65 years and employees who stay longer in service will have to make contractual arrangements with their employers in order to continue the contributions to the scheme after 65.[57]

The ITP2 is based on a previous agreement and covers employees currently aged 37 or older (born 1978 or earlier). The scheme also has a

---

51 'Försäkringar på arbetsmarknaden enligt lag och kollektivavtal 2015' (2015) Svenskt Näringsliv 29.

52 Ibid 29.

53 Ibid 29.

54 See further discussions in ibid 29.

55 Ibid 37.

56 Ibid 37.

57 Ibid 37.

Table 10.2 Overview of occupational pension schemes in Sweden

Occupational pension scheme	Category of employees	Contributions and benefits	Standard retirement age in the scheme
Avtalspension SAF-LO 2007	Blue-collar workers in private sector	Depends on employers' defined contributions, paid into the pension schemes, but individualized for the employee. Return on investment in pension funds will also be decisive. Contributions are generally 4.5% of the salary, but 30% for income above the public-scheme ceiling.	Normally 65
ITP1	White-collar employees in private sector, born 1979 or later	Earnings-related, based on employers' defined contributions of 4.5% or 30% respectively, paid into the pension schemes, but individualized for the employee. Return on investment in pension funds will also be decisive.	Normally 65 (pension can be paid already at 55 years of age)
ITP2	White-collar employees in private sector, born 1978 or earlier	Earnings-related defined-benefit scheme combined with a defined-contributions scheme (2%) which is paid into pension funds.	65 years of age
PA 03	Public employment in public authorities (state sector)	Earnings-related, partly based on employers' defined contributions paid into pension schemes. Contributions of 2+2.5 = 4.5% are paid by the employers. Also partly a defined-benefit scheme based on the last five years before retirement.	Normally 65 (but flexible from 61 years)
PA 16	State sector, born 1988 or later	Earnings-related, defined contributions = 2.5+2+1.5%.	Flexible from 61 years
KAP-KL (employees born 1985 and earlier)	Public employment in the municipal sector (local and regional municipalities, including public healthcare sector)	KAP-KL covers a combination of an earnings-related defined-contribution scheme and a defined-benefit scheme. The defined contributions are 4.5% and the defined-benefit scheme generates compensation for income above the public pension ceiling, with a maximum of 55% of previous salary.	KAP-KL 65 years, but some flexibility from 61
AKAP-KL (employees born 1986 and later)		AKAP-KL, the most recent agreement, regulates an earnings-related defined-contribution scheme only. The defined contributions are 4.5% for low and middle incomes, and 30% of high incomes.	AKAP-KL sets the age at 67

fixed pension age (normally 65 years) and contrary to ITP1, it cannot include contributions after the age of 65.[58] The programme is a defined-benefit scheme, which allows the retiring employee to have an occupational pension of 10 per cent until reaching the level of 7.5 income base amounts (while the public pension scheme is fully payable), 65 per cent in relation to previous income in the range of 7.5–20 per cent and 32.5 per cent on income between 20 and 30 per cent.[59] Companies that are new to the collective agreement and recently signed up for the pension scheme will automatically be covered by ITP1, with the result that a white-collar employee, born before 1978 and covered by the ITP2 (defined-benefit scheme) in a previous employment, will be subject to the ITP1 if he or she transfers to a new employer that only recently entered into the programme.[60]

2.4 Private Pension Schemes

As mentioned earlier in this chapter, the private pension schemes – 'the third pillar' or 'top of the cone' – are of less importance in Sweden than the public and occupational schemes. It is very likely that the significance of private schemes will decrease even more due to recent changes to the direct taxation of contributions.[61] Until 2015, the tax system incentivized payments made to qualifying pension insurances by either individuals or their employers, while allowing a deduction from taxable income up to a certain limit during the years of contributions; upon retirement the savings are to be repaid in the form of a pension annuity on which income tax is ultimately levied.[62] There have only been voluntary private schemes and even though numerous people have participated in such schemes, the overall importance (when it comes to both contributions and benefits) is significantly lower than for public and occupational pension schemes. Most of these third-pillar private pension

---

58 Ibid 41.

59 See Government Inquiry Report SOU 2013:25 362, and 'Försäkringar på arbetsmarknaden enligt lag och kollektivavtal', above n 51, 44.

60 We discuss the possible lock-in problems of these incoherencies later in this chapter; see further 'Försäkringar på arbetsmarknaden enligt lag och kollektivavtal', above n 51, 33.

61 SFS 2014:1468 lowered the deductible amount from 12,000 SEK/year to only 1,800 SEK and terminated the tax deductions altogether as of 1 January 2016: see SFS (2015:775) introducing a new Chapter 59 Section 1a in the Swedish Income Tax Act (SFS 1999:1229).

62 Chapter 59 and Chapter 28 Section 3 Swedish Income Tax Act (SFS 1999:1229).

schemes have been subject to pension benefits or payments at 55 years of age, with payments accelerated over a shorter, mainly five-year period of time.[63] As a matter of fact, due to the recent changes regarding tax deductions, there are no incentives for individual employees to make any further contributions to private pension schemes, but rather to manage their savings, investments and mortgages.[64]

2.5 Promoting Work over Pensions – Recent Developments in the Swedish Tax System

Income from salaried employment or pensions is closely related to the effects of income taxation and the payment of social contributions. To a significant extent this correlation has been ignored in the more general discussion about incentives for prolonged working life. The Swedish income tax system is based on the neutrality principle, which means that economic decisions should not be taken on the ground of a tax provision, and therefore pension and employment incomes are taxed together and progressively, based on the total amount earned each year. However, to stimulate activity,[65] Sweden introduced a tax incentive in 2007 for salaried employment: the *earned* income tax credit, allowing lower individual income tax on activity income than on pension income.[66]

Moreover, employees and self-employed workers were also entitled to an even more generous tax credit if they postponed their retirement until after 65. In 2016 the basic allowance – a basic deduction before taxes are paid – was increased for pensioners older than 65. This provision resulted in a lower income tax for all elderly persons, irrespective of whether their income is from work, pensions or a combination of the two.

Social security fees for employees and active workers over 65 years old were decreased substantially in 2007, which was meant to stimulate

---

[63] The schemes vary between different providers. For further discussions see Government Inquiry Report SOU 2012:28 445–7, 493.

[64] Swedish tax law provides for some other incentivized investment systems, none of which have a retirement perspective of 'locked up' invested money for delayed distribution during retirement.

[65] This is on the assumption that taxes induce behaviour, an idea that is not uncontroversial. Some reflections about this statement can be found in an overview of economic research studying the incentive effects of welfare systems on retirement decisions, Conny Olovsson, 'Comment on the European Commission's Green Paper towards adequate, sustainable and safe European pension systems', European Policy Analysis (SIEPS 2011:3).

[66] Chapter 63 Section 3a Income Tax Act.

employability of the elderly.[67] After the 2014 change in government and majority at Parliament, some reforms have been carried out, among others based on one study showing that the incentive did not achieve the promised effects and was limited to a small section of the active population (self-employed males).[68]

An effect of the previous tax system was that it was more advantageous for the employer to let employees go with pension compensation and then re-employ them as 'pensioners' before the actual age of retirement (65).[69] This has changed with the new government and the law is currently neutral in this regard. Just how the rules will encourage employees to retire later remains disputable, however, and the preparatory works to these changes are not supported by extensive literature.[70]

The 2007 tax incentive for employment, the *earned* income tax credit, allows lower individual income tax on activity income than on pension and social security income.[71] The earned income tax credit is very valuable to any person working, whether full-time or combining part-time work with part-time social security or even full pension. In other words, already in 2007, and for tax purposes, the choice to work was very well rewarded. This credit breaks the neutrality principle because work income is taxed favourably in comparison with social security income.

This is a highly sensitive subject in Sweden. Many retired individuals consider pensions to be postponed wages and that pension income should be treated as a wage rather than a social security benefit. This is especially relevant with regard to pension systems created by collective agreements. The benefits are not funded by tax or mandatory social contributions; every benefit is typically the result of a trade-off – wages directly or pensions later – concluded by the trade unions and the employers' federations at the bargaining table.

An important aspect of progressive income taxes is the eventual disincentives created by thresholds when marginal tax is increased. Apart from the activity-related tax allowances, which have been both favourable and unfavourable to employment income (and not social insurance

67 Swedish social security law (SFS 2000:980). 31.42 per cent is the standard rate, which was decreased to 10.21 per cent for employees over 65 in 2007. In addition, employers pay 24.26 per cent on pension costs (SFS 1991:687).

68 Lisa Laun, 'Om förhöjt skatteavdrag för äldre och sänkta arbetsgivaravgift för äldre' (2012) IFAU Rapport 2012:163.

69 This is referred to as the 'salary-exchange' (*löneväxling*).

70 Government Inquiry Report SOU 2013:25 187ff.

71 Chapter 67 Sections 5–9 Income Tax Act (1999:1229).

benefits and pensions), the marginal tax could discourage older employees from continuing to work while receiving a pension (from public and/or occupational schemes). While the main income tax is approximately 32 per cent on almost any income, the marginal tax is increased by another 20 per cent at a relatively low level (approximately 46,600 EUR of annual income) and another 5 per cent at 67,000 EUR of annual income), resulting in a marginal income tax of far more than 50 per cent.[72] As is discussed above, for individuals aged 65 or more, these levels are slightly increased due to the recent enforcement of a higher basic tax deduction.[73] This preferential treatment of people 65 years old and older supports, at least to some extent, an increased willingness to continue working – in combination with income from pension. Still, because the thresholds are comparatively low, a lot of people who combine work and pension are likely to face marginal income taxes exceeding 50 per cent; one can argue that this is likely to make continued work less appealing. At the other end of the scale, there is a 'poverty threshold' for low-income retirees who are dependent on social welfare (here, the extra old-age housing allowance) for their living standard. These individuals will have very little, if any, financial gain from continued or prolonged work.[74]

3. DISCUSSION: PROLONGED WORKING LIFE – INCOHERENCIES AND CONFLICTS OF INTEREST

In the following we look at a number of outstanding issues related to the coherence of pension schemes, public as well as occupational, and attempt to create a better understanding of the importance of relating all pillars of the pension scheme to taxes and social contributions. While lawmakers and industrial partners might have different views on the details of old-age pensions, the overarching aim of constructing solid systems which could manifest in intra-generational relations, trust and

---

72 The levels vary in details but the principle of the thresholds remains the same from year to year, 65 Chapter 5 Income Tax Act (1999:1229).

73 In practice this means that 65-year-olds will be taxed progressively on annual income above 49,400 EUR and even more on annual income above 69,200 EUR. Calculations can be found at: www.skatteverket.se/privat/sjalvservice/svarpavanligafragor/beloppprocentsatser/privatbeloppfaq/narskamanbetalastatliginkomstskattochhurhogarden.5.10010ec103545f243e8000166.html, accessed 29 March 2016.

74 Government Inquiry Report SOU 2012:28 21.

loyalty over many years and provide decent retirement benefits without jeopardizing financial stability or economic growth and with a reasonable balance between individual contributions and final benefits, is common to all parties.

As noted, reasons abound for providing structural incentives to prolong working lives. The most prominent of these reasons relates to demographic developments – dramatically increased life expectancy over the last few generations together with improved health status in the population – less hard manual labour as a result of industrial development and, mainly related to this development, increasing financial pressure on the welfare state in general and pension schemes in particular.

As mentioned in the presentation of the three pillars (or the cone) of the Swedish pension system, there are efforts in the schemes to provide for prolonged working life, not least through flexible retirement ages, but to some extent these efforts are not coherently applied to the different pillars and are not necessarily enforced through the provisions on income taxation. Our discussion involves three major issues that emerge from or within the Swedish pension scheme, which could also serve as interesting examples for other jurisdictions – not least as a result of the international attention garnered by the Swedish system that was introduced in the late 1990s.

3.1 Prolonged Working Life – A Common Interest for Occupational and Public Pension Schemes?

The current Swedish public earnings-related retirement scheme allows a flexible retirement age decided upon by the insured (the employee). The scheme regulates a flexible retirement at (still) 61 years of age. Previous – and also most recent – generations of pensioners have had relatively adequate pensions that provide at least 60–75 per cent of previous income when all three pillars are accounted for.[75] However, due to demographic developments and the continuously decreasing numbers of hours worked in a lifespan, future projections indicate significantly lower pensions – if that pace of recent development is maintained.[76]

Incentives to promote a longer working life must focus on economic, social and emotional aspects to be successful. There are indications that the current occupational pension schemes – as they are currently constructed and very much in contrast to the overall aim of pension policy –

75 See Section 2.3 in this chapter.
76 Further in Government Inquiry Report SOU 2012:28 479.

might stimulate more premature retirement than is required for a structurally sustainable working life.[77] Conflicting interests emerge from the different parts of the pension system. Because most occupational systems do not include or collect contributions after 65 years, prolonged working life would not represent further contributions and correspondingly higher future benefits. This is a situation which does not support prolonged working life.[78] Furthermore, collectively agreed work-end solutions, also in cases of redundancy or in other situations, can limit the incentives to continue labour.[79] Packages with partial or full 'early retirement' are often provided to employees over 60, primarily in more general collective agreements, but also in individual arrangements at workplace level.[80]

Constituting a somewhat necessary or reasonable 'escape' for employees and employers, these arrangements might indeed be associated with significant problems, from a general point of view. Not only might the individual retiring employee face a partially decreased overall income during the scope of retirement, but the overall intention to promote prolonged working life as a more normative but not compulsory feature might be undermined. Furthermore, it is likely that the legitimacy of the system could be compromised when some are released from work but others are 'forced' to carry on. Loyalty and trust, within and between generations, are fundamental to the pension schemes on a broader scale; therefore the implications for the future preservation of the system could be significant. The very idea to promote older workers' social security rights might end up being counterproductive and questionable in the light of a sustainable pension scheme. Notwithstanding all this, the possibility for management and employees to come to individual solutions in contrast to an overall policy must be respected. The three-pillar pension scheme plays a very important role in creating such incentives. It is our conclusion that the coherence of the first two pillars – the public pension scheme and the occupational pension scheme – should be significantly improved, with an overall aim of enforcing the idea of a delayed retirement age. In addition, we would encourage the industrial partners

[77] Government Inquiry Report SOU 2012:28 15–24 but also 297ff.

[78] The effects for different income layers are problematized in Government Inquiry Report SOU 2012:28 308ff.

[79] See Government Inquiry Report SOU 2012:28 316–20.

[80] Ibid. However, the Discrimination Act limits the possibility to exercise less favourable treatment in relation to age, and collective agreements are not per se excluded from such scrutiny. See Labour Court decision AD 2011 No. 37 (*Scandinavian Airlines System*, age-discriminatory redundancy selection under collective agreements).

that are concluding the collective agreements on pension to emphasize prolongation of working life. For all the public and most of the occupational pension schemes, the opportunity to accrue pension rights, even at higher ages, while delaying the payment of the benefits (beyond 65 or even 67 years) should be explored and the tax consequences should be taken into account for a more coherent and correct appreciation of net income and financial incentives – with an aim of prolonging working life and balancing increased life expectancy.

Labour market policy-makers – legislators and industrial partners – as well as individual actors should also emphasize the value of facilitating an active work life for elderly employees, through managerial efforts and adjustments on the part of the 'greying' staff. This could be based on individual, or collective, contractual arrangements, facilitating for example changes in workload or accommodated work situations – in combination with adjusted benefits and payments. In our opinion, the current structure in some of the occupational pension schemes – most significantly PA 03 (state sector), under which defined benefits are related to the final years of employment – is highly problematic in this regard, both for employers and employees. Employees are encouraged, or incentivized, to maximize income during these highlighted years, while the extra earnings after the 'ordinary' retirement age normally do not contribute to further pension benefits under the occupational schemes. The more recent provisions under PA 16 (for state employees born 1988 or later), allow continuous payment of pension rights and the abandonment of defined-benefits support, providing more opportunity to be flexible and reduce or change employment, even at the end of working life.

A differentiation of worktime and work efforts might have to be accounted for in many employments if productivity decreases at higher ages; this differentiation needs to be in place much more than is the case today. An elderly employee, who could reduce his or her work efforts – and remuneration – in order to stay on full- or part-time for another ten years, will be highly reluctant to do so unless reasonably compensated in the pension scheme – and most likely also in salary. Occupational pension schemes with defined benefits based on the last five years of employment would be devastating for anyone contemplating a part-time work reduction or a more significant change in employment (to a less-well-paid position) after, say, 60 years of age, even if the aim of the changes is to enable prolonged working life.[81]

---

[81] The issue of part-time retirement has recently been scrutinized in a partly empirical study; see Carin Ulander-Wänman, 'Swedish collective agreements and

In our opinion, and considering this situation, the state sector collective agreement on part-time retirement[82] is a somewhat misguided application that stands in sharp contrast to the general idea of prolonged working life. The scheme allows state employees to reduce their working time by 50 per cent at the age of 61 and still receive 80 per cent of their previous gross salary, while receiving full compensation in relation to the occupational pension scheme.[83] The part-time agreement could – but does not necessarily – facilitate a prolonged working life by making the final years of active working life less burdensome.[84] Because workplaces normally covered by this agreement often entail less physically demanding work, this scheme should be considered a generous, extra employee remuneration – which is indeed likely to constrain productivity-oriented compensation in public workplaces.

The question of flexible and diversified retirement age is closely related to the previous discussion on prolonged working life as an overarching aim of future retirement. Reasonableness and flexibility will have to be applied in relation to retirement age and it is hoped it will be possible to combine retirement age with flexible working conditions, both within and between workplaces. It is apparent from the presentation of the different parts of the pension schemes – especially those for occupational pensions – that this flexibility is not fully and consistently taken into account. In a more flexible labour market, changing job and workplaces late in life should also be encouraged and facilitated – not least by the occupational pension schemes, especially if a new position in another workplace could help prolong the overall productive period of life. Leaving a position at any age is a big step for most employees, but

employers' willingness to hire and retain older workers in employment' (2016) 6(2) Nordic J Working Life Studies 61–79. Ulander-Wänman refers to the ambitions of the schemes for prolonging working life.

[82] These rules apply to state employers who are represented by the Swedish Agency for Government Employers (*Arbetsgivarverket*). The state actors that employ large numbers of blue-collar workers, such as the postal service, are represented by other employer organizations (in that case *Almega*).

[83] 'Avtal om delpension för arbetstagare hos staten', cirkulär 2003:A 4 12 November 2003.

[84] To our knowledge, no data are available to support the idea that this part-time reduced working time actually has a positive effect with regard to extension of working life. It is more likely to be seen as a part-time retirement benefit exercised by individuals who could otherwise work full-time for another few years. The numbers of such part-time retirees who actually continue to work after 67 are, to our knowledge, very limited.

perhaps even bigger for people approaching retirement age. The accompanying uncertainty, especially about the effects on occupational pension schemes, will likely constitute a barrier for many older persons; this in turn could create less sustainable working conditions and thereby increase older employees' incentive to leave at an early or ordinary pension age.

A consequence of a defined-benefit programme could be a reduced turnover of staff. This could be perceived as beneficial by some and controversial by others for the business – and for efforts to promote prolonged working life. Employees are likely to be less inclined to leave a workplace where the occupational pension benefits are calculated based on the final few years of service before retirement.[85] With a defined-contribution scheme, the contributions have been collected and paid (by the employer) during the years of employment and, generally, invested in pension funds based on the individual choice of the employee. There is also the important issue of transportability of occupational pension plans between employers/sectors. As a rule, the incentives for prolonging working life are only explicitly communicated (and exercised) in the public pension scheme and are not coherently enforced in the occupational schemes. Together with the abolition of tax incentives that encourage employers to employ pensioners over 65 years old, the situation is very likely to create overall disincentives for both flexible and prolonged working life.[86] Based on the insights of this paper, it is our conclusion that an overall perspective on retirement and working capacity can be applied to eliminate financial disincentives for flexibility between different workplaces.[87] It is very likely that employees who have already turned 60 are less open to dramatic changes in their working situation and thus are less inclined to change employers, and current information indicates that older workers' mobility is hampered by age-discrimination and ageist attitudes among employers and managers.[88] Arguments put

---

85 Ebony de Thierry et al. (2014), above n 30, 663–4. The article has a UK perspective, but as many Swedish occupational schemes used to have similar features, and still use these for older employees, the same outcome of reduced labour market mobility in old age is likely to be established in Sweden, too.

86 Government Inquiry Report SOU 2013:25 239ff.

87 This position does find some support in the Government Inquiry Report SOU 2013:25, where the strengthening of tripartite discussions for the establishment of sustainable pension ages in occupational pension schemes is proposed.

88 Ali M Ahmed, Lina Andersson and Mats Hammarstedt, *Does Age Matter for Employability? A Field Experiment on Ageism in the Swedish Labour Market* (Linnéuniversitetet 2011).

forward include claims that older workers lack comprehensive knowledge and the ambition to learn new tasks, and that health-related issues decrease skill and capacity. Employees and others in the workplace can also have preconceived notions about older workers' lower ambition and capacity to be flexible at work, and believe that older workers will not be able to 'make the grade'.[89]

3.2 Diverse or Flexible Retirement Age – The Pension System and Taxation

The current 'normative' Swedish pension age is somewhat diverse, taking into account the flexible pension age in the earnings-based public pension scheme (starting at 61) and extending to the employment protection legislation, which sets a retirement age of 67 years. However, 65 is still the preferred pension age in provisions on income tax, pension contributions and most occupational schemes, as well as in other social security legislation. At 65, long-term sickness benefits, work injury and accident insurance, unemployment insurance and other long-term social security benefits cease. It is also the age at which basic pension can be claimed and the special basic tax allowance for the elderly begins. Apparently, this provides for significantly disparate positions on pension age, and should not necessarily be understood as flexibility.

Another option is early retirement through the pension system. Persons can retire from the age of 61, but they must pay for this option themselves through actuarially calculated lower pensions. A 61-year-old leaving the labour market for retirement will lose the earned income tax credit (*jobbskatteavdraget*) and will not qualify for favourable treatment of the elderly regarding the special basic tax allowance (*förhöjt grundavdrag för personer över 65*). Historically, generous early retirement schemes for deserving individuals who could leave hard manual labour before the obligatory pension age constituted some sort of flexibility; however, eligibility was dependent on public decisions on a case-by-case basis and was somewhat disconnected from public – and occupational – pension schemes. It is our opinion that future flexibilization of pension schemes should not look back to those provisions and that a better solution would be to integrate flexibilization in a balanced and sustainable public pension scheme and correlate it to provisions in the occupational schemes in the different collective agreements.

---

89 There is emerging literature on the subject, and the issues have also been recently addressed by Government Inquiry Report SOU 2012:28 499ff.

Pension structures in collective agreements generally provide for some flexibility, allowing early retirement which would be paid partially or fully by the individual through a reduced pension. Subsidized early retirement, on a structural basis, is less common. The most significant example is the part-time early retirement agreement in the government state sector.[90] A healthy worker at the age of 61 may choose to reduce working time from 100 per cent to 50 per cent, while receiving an 80 per cent wage and earning a pension within the collective agreement system, just as if working full-time. Such a person has a work income and will benefit from the earned-income tax credit. Because the marginal income tax is almost 60 per cent for many state employees, the difference between full-time work and early part-time retirement will be negligible, thus establishing a very modest financial incentive to continue full-time work. Flexibility in this regard – or reduced production – is basically provided to the employee 'free of charge' but is paid for by the employers. And, it is obviously not in line with the overall ambition of prolonged working lives for sustainable pensions.

3.3 Concluding Remarks

The establishment, enforcement and taxation of the various pension schemes in Sweden are of great importance for sustaining the welfare state as such. Regulation and taxation reveal and address highly sensitive intra-corporate, collective and intra-generational balances in Swedish society. The normative – but not compulsory – aspects entailed in one part of the pension scheme might be counteracted by other parts, or by the application of income tax provision. In this chapter we have explored how an overarching and well-established political ambition to convince employees to prolong working life can be circumvented, partly by provisions on occupational pensions in collective agreements and partly by statutes on income tax. The Swedish pension system is largely divided into different important 'pillars' with different origins and purposes. Both political representatives and society in general perceive that the ambition of the 'first pillar' or 'base of the cone' to provide for a sustainable system also includes a prolonged working life.

Our conclusion is that the strength of the Swedish public pension scheme, with its clear connection to accrued rights (although still mainly a pay-as-you-go system), flexible pension age and incentives for a prolonged working life, forms a very valuable example for many other

90 'Avtal om delpension för arbetstagare hos staten', cirkulär 2003:A 4.

welfare states where demographic development and limited financial growth put pressure on the balances of the scheme. However, we also find that the significant occupational pension schemes, which cover almost 90 per cent of the employees in Sweden, exhibit some contradictory features that neutralize or at least reduce the potency of the public pension scheme's normative ambition to prolong working life. Because these different occupational schemes are by no means subject to regulatory measures, but on the contrary are a 'commodity' in the hands of the industrial partners who conclude collective agreements, the possibility of combining public and occupational ambitions in this regard is limited, at least in the short term. With the recent common understanding of the impact that occupational pension schemes are likely to have on most retired persons' future income, a thoughtful and more explicit coordination of public and occupational pension schemes would be most welcome in the effort to strengthen the sustainability of the overall pension programme in Sweden. Such a development could also constitute a valuable example and inspiration for other countries confronting similar demographic and economic situations. It can be a model for countries that urgently need to reform historically under-financed, pay-as-you-go systems and to eventually coordinate those with occupational or private pension schemes for the prolongation of working life and improved intra-generational balance.

We also find that the marginal effects of income tax on income from pension *combined with* income of employment could reduce incentives to prolong working life, at least in mid- and high-income occupations, because a combination of continued work and payment of accrued pension benefit is likely to elevate income levels far beyond the threshold for 52 per cent or even higher income tax – despite the increased marginal tax thresholds for people above 65 years. The taxation effects of 'double income' – from both occupational pension and employment after the traditional retirement age might significantly hamper employees' enthusiasm for continuing work in advanced years, because the marginal tax is likely to strike hard even at relatively modest income. Even more flexible occupational pension schemes, which could delay the payments of the accrued benefits, would make it possible to limit this obstacle and make continued work a more generous alternative. As we have touched upon, it is of vital importance to ensure that there are no disproportionate burdens of increased taxation for those who choose to work longer.

All in all the Swedish pension system, with its three-pillar or layered structure, appears to be very robust. It generally encourages employment beyond traditional pensionable ages. However, the overarching normative ambitions of the system could be emphasized further through improved coordination between the different schemes (public and occupational) and better balanced in relation to income taxation. Nevertheless, recent developments in the (PA 16) occupational schemes represent a stronger coherence with the public scheme.

11. Migrant pensioners – taxation and healthcare issues in the EU

Cécile Brokelind and Martina Axmin

1. INTRODUCTION[1]

In the context of the Norma Elder Law Research Environment, this chapter identifies and analyses selected problems linked to the economic situations of pensioners on the move. The decision to retire, the decision to move to another country to reunify with a family or the decision to enter a healthcare centre can all be related to the individual's economic situation.[2] In the European Union (EU), and in contrast with other parts of the world, the legal framework supports mobility of workers, service providers and citizens across borders, but does not harmonize the economic rights arising from welfare states. In other words, pensioners are free to move, but the economic consequences of their decision to move can be discouraging. This is the subject of this chapter, which demonstrates how the lack of neutral treatment of mobile and non-mobile pensioners may influence the decision about where to retire – in conflict with EU law and ambitions.

Within the preventive legal dimension in the multi-dimensional model for elder law that Doron developed in the US, the elderly should be enabled to design their own lives, control decisions pertaining to a time

1 This work was carried out within the Norma Elder Law Research Environment (www.jur.lu.se/elderlaw) funded by Ragnar Söderberg's Foundation and the Marianne and Marcus Wallenberg Foundation.

2 For an overview of economic research on the incentive effects of welfare systems on retirement decisions, see C Olovsson, 'Comment on the European Commission's Green Paper towards adequate, sustainable and safe European pension systems' (2011) 3 Swedish Institute for European Policy Studies, SIEPS, European Policy Analysis 5. The Swedish Government has published a study in Swedish on 'Longer life, longer working life' (Government Inquiry Report SOU 2012:28), studying several factors – among others the economic situation – that influence the decision to retire.

when their condition will deteriorate and thus remain independent as long as possible.[3] In accordance with this theory, the individual should be empowered to choose activity and plan for independence upon ageing. In respect of the EU, however, the existence of diverse protective welfare systems may bias this independence.[4] In general, poor health, demanding working conditions and economic reasons – such as fear of decreasing pensions – have been shown to provoke early retirement.[5] The theory is that encouraging EU elderly to remain active in the labour market and independent from the welfare state should not depend upon economic factors. However, this is not in line with our findings, as will be explained hereafter.

The economic situation of a pensioner can depend upon a variety of factors, ranging from the accumulation of pension rights during working life to the domestic income tax treatment of pension. The lack of neutral tax treatment of pension and employment income may bias the decision to retire, which raises issues in terms of equal treatment under EU law. An additional layer of difficulties lies in the lack of harmonization in the EU for both tax law and social security law. Each Member State finances its welfare with its own funds; these funds vary considerably from one state to another, sometimes even encouraging 'social welfare tourism'. From a social security law viewpoint, EU law does coordinate some matters, but the situation of a pensioner with a low pension still is

[3] I Doron, 'A multi-dimensional model of elder law' in I Doron (ed.), *Theories of Law and Ageing: The Jurisprudence of Elder Law* (Springer 2009) 66.

[4] Several social science and medical sciences find that economic incentives have an impact on the decision to retire. Scientists find that if benefits programmes are equally or more beneficial than work, individuals voluntarily readily leave working life. See K Nilsson, 'To work or not to work in an extended working life? Factors in working and retirement decisions' (Fil Dr Med Faculty thesis, Lund University 2013) 331–2. See also the Swedish Government Inquiry Report SOU 2012:28 'Longer life, longer working: Preconditions and barriers to older people working longer' (*Längre liv, längre arbetsliv: Förutsättningar och hinder för äldre att arbeta längre*). In the Government Inquiry Report SOU 2013:25, the Government suggests that tax rules align on the general recommendation that the recommended age for pension follows life expectancy, which is not the case now (Swedish Income Tax Act 1999:1229 Chapters 28 and 52).

[5] See for instance C le Clainche, 'Les déterminants des âges de départ à la retraite: une comparaison France/Suède', Institut de recherches économiques et sociales (2009) 36. http://archive.cfecgc.org/e_upload/pdf/le_clainchejanv09.pdf, accessed 1 November 2015.

problematic in respect of mobility because he or she risks being a burden on the host's welfare system.

Moreover, EU Member States provide a number of tax incentives for individuals to save for pensions during working life, resulting, for instance, in a beneficial tax treatment of occupational pension income upon receipt. However, the symmetric tax treatment of contributions to pension schemes and of benefits paid upon retirement is not guaranteed when pensioners move from one Member State to another.[6] This conflicts, however, with the Treaty of Functioning of the European Union (TFEU), which guarantees the elderly's right to mobility.[7] According to the EU Commission, greater flexibility in job mobility improves the adjustment capacity of economies and unleashes the full potential of the single market, which could bring significant benefits for all citizens. For this reason, mobility needs be organized during the period of constitution of pension rights as well as during retirement.[8]

The choice to retire either here or there and becoming dependent upon the states' welfare in terms of pension systems may therefore be biased – for better or worse – by economic factors and institutional differences; this can also prove true for states other than EU Member States. Our chapter shows that tax rules and EU social security rules may hamper mobility. The concrete example of Sweden is interesting, because (as exposed earlier in this book[9]) this country provides for a high welfare standard and relatively high pensions, financed through one of the worlds' highest individual income taxes, and thus taxes pensioners moving out of Sweden at the source to limit tax base erosion. Furthermore, as explained in Chapter 13, EU coordinated rules on social security ensure that migrant workers are entitled to social security benefits only within certain limits, among others excluding potentially inactive migrants.[10] EU law therefore acknowledges the relationship between the constitution of pension rights during working life and the right to pension

---

6 For an overview of the problems linked to the institutional differences, see G Staats, 'Personal pensions in the EU' (2015) 24 Kluwer EC Tax Rev 144.

7 Article 20 TFEU (citizen rights to free movement); Article 45 TFEU (free movement of workers); Article 48 TFEU (aggregation of contribution periods across EU); Article 63 TFEU (free movement of capital).

8 Matching economic migration with labour market needs in Europe and free movement of workers and labour market adjustment. Recent Experiences from OECD Countries and the European Union (Joint OECD–EU report September 2014).

9 See Inghammar, Brokelind and Norberg, Chapter 10 in this book.

10 Mattsson, Axmin and Holm, Chapter 13 in this book.

or social security benefits (minimum pensions). The question is therefore whether, in the EU, migrant pensioners enjoy equal treatment when exercising their freedom of movement as provided for in primary EU law.

2. MIGRANT PENSIONERS: WHO ARE THEY, AND WHAT ARE THE CONSEQUENCES WHEN THEY MIGRATE?

2.1 Statistics

In order to grasp the extent of the pensioners' economic problems when they move across borders, it may be interesting to know where they move. The case of Sweden is interesting as the Swedish Pensions Agency (*Pensionsmyndigheten*) keeps track of pensions paid to non-residents; this information is publicly available. According to this authority, 6.8 per cent of pensions were paid to retirees living outside Sweden in 2015. The average monthly amount of the pension paid to these retirees living (that is tax resident) outside Sweden is around 300 EUR per month, and the statistics show that around 4 million EUR are paid yearly from state pensions in the first pillar to non-Swedish residents.[11] The largest groups of migrant pensioners benefiting from this public pension (approximate figures) reside in Finland (50,000), Germany (17,000) Norway (11,000), Denmark (9,000), the US (6,000), Spain (6,000), Greece (5,000), France (3,300), the UK (3,000), Austria (2,700), and so on, with an overall total of 143,564 pensioners in 2015.[12]

The higher number of Swedish migrants in the other Nordic states in relation to other countries and low average monthly payments of public pensions could be explained by the fact that migrant workers came to Sweden (especially from Finland where Swedish is also spoken) to work; they constituted pension rights during their working lives in Sweden and then moved back to Finland upon retirement.[13] The high number of

---

[11] The information relates to the 'life certificates' filled in by retirees entitled to Swedish pensions. In 2015 there were 143,564 beneficiaries living outside Sweden, out of 2,116,486 retirees in total. See the statistics at www.pensionsmyndigheten.se/levnadsintyg15.html, accessed 15 November 2015.

[12] Ibid 2.

[13] In Germany, for instance, only 1 per cent of pensioners receiving state pension are established abroad; see R Himmelreicher and W Keck, 'Transnational ageing as reflected in Germany's pension insurance' in V Horn and C

migrants to the US may be explained by Sweden's history, as a large part of the population emigrated there to escape poverty.[14]

It should be noted, however, that the number of Swedish pensioners who remain residents of Sweden for tax and social security purposes but who live abroad, on a part-time basis, is officially unknown. Some indications can be found that around 50,000 Swedes live in France, for instance, whereas only 3,332 have officially transferred their residence there.[15] Similarly, around 1,000 Swedes move to Spain each year, yet only 6,000 Swedish retirees are officially resident in Spain, and it is likely that this outflow started more than six years ago. In other words, the pensioners temporarily moving out of Sweden could greatly outnumber those who will not return to Sweden, and to the best of our knowledge no official statistics are available on this group.

From the state perspective, the situation of pensioners moving abroad can be analysed as follows. Firstly, the state partially financed the constitution of pension rights: part of the pension contribution was tax-deducted by the individuals while working as well as by their employers. When pensioners retire in the same country, this financial burden is compensated by the income taxes levied by the state on pensions; this is not possible for pensioners who move out, unless an exit tax is levied on pensions paid abroad. Secondly, the exiting pensioners may have strong purchasing power during the first years of retirement, which will be lost for the state that they have left. Indeed, the second and third pillars of the pension systems usually offer a maximum replacement of income in the beginning of the retirement period.

From the individual perspective, the exit to another state creates a potential situation of double taxation: once in the state where the pension rights were accumulated, and once again in the new residence state where the pension is received.

Schweppe (eds), *Transnational Aging: Current Insights and Future Challenges* (Routledge Press 2015).

[14] For details on how Swedes moved to the USA at the beginning of the twentieth century, see J Bohlin and A Eurenius, 'Why they moved – emigration from the Swedish countryside to the United States, 1881–1910' (2010) 47 Explor Econ Hist 533.

[15] See for instance, www.sparsamskatt.se/lander/frankrike, accessed 15 November 2015. The number of retirees in France is an official statistic from the Pension Authority.

2.2 Immigrant Pensioners: What Pension Rights?

Within the EU, free mobility should be guaranteed. The TFEU has always contained provisions granting free movement for the economically active and the right to free movement has always been a fundamental part of the EU and the internal market. The introduction of a European citizenship expanded the free movement of non-economically active persons.[16] Non-economically active Union citizens in general have gradually been granted rights to move, reside and receive equal treatment within the EU. This development was codified in Directive 2004/38.[17] According to the Directive, Union citizens other than workers have a right to residence under two conditions: they must have sufficient resources to support themselves and their family members so they will not become a burden on the social assistance system of the host Member State during their period of residence and they must have comprehensive sickness insurance in that state.[18] However, recent case law from the Court of Justice of the European Union (CJEU) shows that there is a shift back to requiring economic activity and self-sufficiency as a precondition for free movement.[19]

According to Swedish rules, immigrant pensioners coming to Sweden are entitled to some elderly care and healthcare, even though the constitution of their pension rights may look quite different from that of an exiting Swedish pensioner. Swedish welfare grants a guarantee pension to the elderly (above 65 years old) who are not entitled to any other pension income (accumulated during employment years and through an employer's contribution), but a full amount (around 800 EUR per month) requires that the pensioner has lived for 40 years in Sweden. According to the Swedish Government, in 2011 there were 800,000 beneficiaries of this guarantee pension, which represents 40 per cent of all pensioners; 80 per cent of these beneficiaries are women.

The amount of Swedish state pension decreases by one fortieth for each year of life spent outside Sweden between 16 and 64 years of age,

---

16 Article 21 TFEU.

17 Directive 2004/38/EC of the European Parliament and of the Council of 29 April 2004 on the right of citizens of the Union and their family members to move and reside freely within the territory of the Member States, amending Regulation (EEC) 1612/68 and replacing Directives 64/221/EEC, 68/360/EEC, 72/194/EEC, 73/148/EEC, 75/34/EEC, 75/35/EEC, 90/364/EEC, 90/365/EEC and 93/96/EEC, OJ 2004 L 158/77.

18 Article 7 Directive 2004/38.

19 See Mattsson, Axmin and Holm, Chapter 13 in this book for more details.

except in certain situations (EU migrants).[20] Pensioners moving to Sweden without their own pension rights from abroad thus do not enjoy the full benefit of this welfare measure, although other forms of welfare may be available. For example, a pensioner on a small pension or no pension at all may be entitled to maintenance support for the elderly (*äldreförsörjningsstöd*) and/or a housing supplement (*bostadstillägg*).[21]

In a case before the Swedish Migration Court of Appeal, the question concerned whether a Union citizen, registered as resident in Sweden and granted the abovementioned benefits, was to be considered an unreasonable burden on the Swedish welfare system, in which case he would be deprived of his right to residence in Sweden.[22] The Swedish court found that this was not the case.

Although there might be a shift in the case law concerning the right to free movement for non-economically active persons, Directive 2004/38 acknowledges older persons as a specific group. If a person has reached the age for entitlement to old-age pension in a Member State and has been working in that state for the preceding 12 months, that person may be granted permanent residence after three years of residence.[23] The rules for residence are connected to the entitlement to social security benefits.

EU law in the field of social security provides for the coordination but not the harmonization of social security schemes. This means that each Member State is free to determine the details of its own social security system, including the determination of benefits to be provided, the conditions of eligibility, how these benefits are calculated and the level of contributions to be paid.[24] EU law provisions, in particular

---

20 An Act of 2005 (SFS 2005:728) introduced a possibility to help 'circular migrants' who obtain a political refugee status and permanent residence permit to access Swedish guarantee pensions under certain circumstances.

21 The Swedish Code of Social Security, Chapters 74, 99–103.

22 MÖD 2011:19. See also T Erhag, 'Changing normative patterns in statutory old-age pensions' in A Numhauser-Henning and M Rönnmar (eds), *Normative Patterns and Legal Developments in the Social Dimension of the EU* (Hart Publishing 2013) 246.

23 Articles 16 and 17 Directive 2004/38.

24 See https://research-content.glassdoor.com/app/uploads/sites/2/2016/02/GD_FairestPaidLeave_Final.pdf, accessed 10 February 2016, for a comparison of the various social security benefits excluding pensions.

Regulations No. 883/2004[25] and No. 987/2009[26] (replacing Regulations No. 1408/71 and No. 574/72 since 1 May 2010), establish common rules and principles that must be observed by all national authorities when applying national law. These rules ensure that the application of the different national legislations respects the basic principles of equality of treatment and non-discrimination, and that persons exercising their right to free movement within the EU are not adversely affected by the application of different national legislations.

With regard to pensions, the EU Coordination Regulations cover old-age pensions, survivors' pensions and invalidity pensions. In general, only statutory schemes are coordinated. In contrast to how short-term benefits such as sickness benefit and unemployment benefits are borne by one Member State, the financial charge of an individual's pension may be shared by two or more Member States. Coordination rules thus exclude pensions from the main principle of one single state.[27] Therefore, when an individual is entitled to a pension from more than one Member State, each of these states must pay the pension costs related to periods completed under their respective legislations. Thus an individual may receive pensions from several Member States. There is no 'transfer' of pension rights to the pension system of another Member State.[28] The reason for diverging from the main rule lies in the considerable costs that may be involved in paying long-term benefits. It was found undesirable to require the state in which a person reaches pension age to bear the whole cost of that individual's pension.[29]

Furthermore, coordination rules on pensions provide for the calculation of pensions[30] and they also prevent overlapping benefits.[31] Finally, the coordination rules provide for aggregation of periods.[32] When the right to benefits in a Member State is conditional upon the completion of insurance, employment or residence, the periods completed in another

---

25 Full title: Regulation (EC) No. 883/2004 of the European Parliament and of the Council of 29 April 2004 on the coordination of social security systems, OJ 2004 L 166/1.

26 Full title: Regulation (EC) No. 987/2009 of the European Parliament and of the Council of 16 September 2009 laying down the procedure for implementing Regulation (EC) No. 883/2004 on the coordination of social security systems, OJ 2009 L 284/1.

27 Articles 50–53 Regulation 883/2004.

28 European Commission, SEC(2010)830 final 3.

29 F Pennings, *European Social Security Law* (Intersentia 2010) 179.

30 Article 52 Regulation 883/2004.

31 Articles 53–5 Regulation 883/2004.

32 Articles 6 and 51 Regulation 883/2004.

Member State shall be taken into account as though they were periods completed under the legislation of the state responsible for the benefit.

In a nutshell, pensioners migrating from an EU Member State to Sweden enjoy a limited right to Swedish welfare in terms of social security coverage, and the extent of their pension rights depends on their situation before migration. To some extent, this may hamper free mobility, especially as the Swedish cost of living may be higher than that of the origin country. Furthermore, as we shall see, migrant pensioners may also face obstacles upon exit from their origin country.

3. EXIT TAX RULES ON PENSIONS

3.1 Withholding Taxes

Most states tax individuals on a worldwide basis when they are resident for tax purposes, according to their ability to pay, and also tax non-residents on a source basis. This means that migrant pensioners may end up paying tax on their pension income in both the exit state as non-residents and in the host state, because they are liable to tax on their pension income on a worldwide basis. This is the worst-case scenario: juridical double taxation. However, this situation can be mitigated thanks to bilateral tax treaties. These conventions usually allocate the right to tax migrants in only one state, but they can also give the contracting states shared rights to tax the migrant's income; there is no harmonization in that respect.[33]

From a Swedish domestic tax law perspective, pensioners who remain on the population register (*folkbokföring*) are taxed as residents, and after they have moved, they have to register in another state, where they become resident for tax purposes. In this situation, they become non-resident in Sweden and all their Swedish income is liable to source taxation in Sweden (SINK).[34] Because the Swedish pension system incentivizes savings for retirement, while taxing the yield of these

---

[33] The OECD has drafted a model convention, according to which pensions paid in consideration of past private employment are taxed in the beneficiary's residence state only (Article 18). However, pensions paid for past public employment are taxed only in the other state (the state from which the pension was paid) (Article 19.2.a), unless the beneficiary is a national of the residence state; in that case, the residence state can tax only the pension income (Article 19.2.b).

[34] Swedish law on non-resident income taxation. Lag (1991:586) om särskild inkomstskatt för utomlands bosatta (SINK); SFS 2013:952 ändring i lagen (1991:586).

savings at a lower rate than standard capital income and deferring taxation of pensions until retirement, Sweden has always expressed its concern over protecting its own tax bases, and in this respect, the need to confine the deferral to resident taxpayers.[35] Sweden therefore applies source taxation on pensions paid abroad through a withholding tax at an effective rate of 20 per cent to ensure the taxation of pensions in Sweden.[36] This means that the choice of place of residence determines the final economic outcome for pensioners – even without the double taxation issue.

Indeed, the tax treatment of Swedish sourced income can be dramatically different, as a resident is taxed on a *net* basis at a progressive rate of 30 per cent up to 57 per cent; in contrast, a non-resident is taxed on a *gross* basis at a standard rate of 20 per cent.[37] So already at this point, and depending upon the possible deductions from the gross basis (interest rate for a mortgage for instance), choosing between staying in Sweden or leaving upon retirement for economic reasons is biased.[38] The same holds true for many other states in that they treat residents and non-residents quite differently. The next step is to know how the host state will treat the incoming pensioner, and how juridical double taxation relief will be achieved.

3.2 Mitigating Double Taxation of Pension Income: The OECD Model Treaty

Members of the Organisation for Economic Co-operation and Development (OECD) are invited to negotiate their bilateral (or multilateral) tax treaties on the basis of the OECD Model Treaty (OECD MT), which

---

[35] See the preparatory works for pension taxation in Government Inquiry Report SOU 2000:11 246, Government Inquiry Report SOU 2002:47 311ff.

[36] Government Inquiry Report SOU 2002:47 354.

[37] For 2016, individuals over 65 years old pay municipal income tax at a rate of around 30 per cent on net income up to 47,000 EUR, and the income above that limit is taxed at an additional 20 per cent rate (state tax) up to 65,000 EUR, and then an additional 5 per cent above that limit, for a total marginal income tax of 55 per cent on income above 65,000 EUR. Swedish Income Tax Act SFS 1999:1229. For more details, see Inghammar, Brokelind and Norberg, Chapter 10 in this book.

[38] This present chapter does not take other taxes than income taxes into consideration. However, the fact that most host states presented in this chapter levy tax on inheritance and wealth should not be underestimated when considering the weight of taxes in the decision to retire abroad.

tends to be followed as a kind of 'soft law'.[39] According to this model, the elimination of double taxation is regulated through the allocation of taxing rights to one state only. Indeed, pensions of past private employment should be taxed in the residence state only (Article 18 OECD MT), while social security payments unrelated to previous employment and pensions of past public employment and public pensions should be taxed exclusively at the source (Article 19-2 OECD MT).[40] This recommendation is not followed to the letter in double tax treaties, however, and there are situations where both states share the right to levy tax. Furthermore, because pensions are not defined clearly in the text of the Model Treaty, the internal law qualification shall prevail in case of differences, and may lead to double taxation.[41]

Furthermore, the OECD model treaty also provides that states are entitled to reserve the exclusive right to tax public pensions at source, depending upon the *nationality* of the beneficiary (Article 19-3 OECD MT). Therefore, nationals who were employed in one state and retire in the other state usually pay tax at source in the state where they carried out their professional activity. However, the state financing the public pension completely loses its right to tax at source the pensions paid to a national of the other state. This tends to be especially important for states where immigration of working forces was promoted to mitigate the negative demographic effects of fertility decline.

What happens, then, after the pensioner moves to the new state? When source taxation occurs, and juridical double taxation results from the application of two taxes on the same pension income, the residence state must provide for relief from double taxation arising from the application of source tax and domestic residence tax – unless the two states' double tax treaty provides for taxation in one state only.[42] The residence state, therefore, must decrease its own tax on residents accordingly in proportion to the tax levied at source (Article 23 B OECD MT). When the host state tax is lower than the source state tax, the relief for double taxation is limited, and the economic situation of mobile pensioners deteriorates. In other words, the incentive to move to states with lower tax rates than that of the source state is limited when the double tax treaty allows split

---

[39] OECD Model Treaty July 2014: www.oecd-ilibrary.org/taxation/model-tax-convention-on-income-and-on-capital-condensed-version_20745419.

[40] OECD Model Treaty July 2014, Commentaries on Article 19 para 2.

[41] For a comparison of the Danish and Dutch practices, see B Wiberg, 'Will we see a change in tax treaties between European Countries concerning taxation of occupational pensions?' (2012) 52 IBFD European Taxation 445.

[42] OECD Model Treaty July 2014, Commentaries on Article 18 paras 9ff.

taxation rights, or when the exit state has the full right to tax pensions at source. Thus the taxation applied by the host state can be crucial for the mobile pensioner's tax situation, as well as his/her nationality.[43]

3.3 Divergent Tax Treaty Practices

Interestingly, a number of double tax treaties derogate from the OECD model convention and authorize the source state to levy a tax at source for private pensions as well, especially when the constitution of pension rights was subsidized by the state in which deductions from income tax were granted. For instance, Germany and the Nordic states traditionally negotiate to include the right to tax pensions at source in their bilateral treaties, either as a general rule for all pensions or at minimum for social security payments. The Netherlands' new bilateral tax treaties also provide for source taxation.[44] However, none of the Nordic countries has succeeded in negotiating with France to allow source taxation for private employment pensions, for instance.[45]

Considering the case of Sweden, and the Swedish mobile pensioner's perspective, official statistics (see above at Section 2.1) tell us that pensioners mainly move to Finland, Germany, Norway, the US, Spain, Greece, France or the UK for retirement. The study of the double tax treaties shows quite different outcomes for each of these emigration states.

Under the Nordic tax treaty,[46] Sweden is allowed to tax state pensions and occupational pensions from public and private past employment at source, but the residence state may also tax pensions after relieving the Swedish tax levied at source. In this situation, the 20 per cent SINK

---

[43] Indeed, it is not uncommon that state pensions or pensions for past public employment are taxed in the state where the pensioner is a national; OECD MT Article 19.2.

[44] B Starink, 'Source versus residence state taxation of cross-border pension payments: Trouble shared is troubled halved' (2016) 44 Kluwer Intertax 6.

[45] M Balling and N Winther-Sørensen, 'Legal and economic general report' in R Påhlsson (ed.), *Taxation of Pension*, Yearbook for Nordic Tax Research (DJØF Publishing 2007) and E Reimer and A Rust (eds), *Klaus Vogel on Double Taxation Conventions* (4th edn, Kluwer Law International 2015) comments under Article 18 para 54.

[46] Nordic Multilateral Tax Treaty SFS 1996:1512. Articles 18.1 and 26.4 allowing incoming pensioners to Sweden to receive a basic allowance of 2,000 EUR on their foreign private and public past employment pensions. The minimum pension is taxed only in the source state, except for Finnish state pensions, which are always tax exempt according to Article 26.3.

Swedish tax will be fully relieved, but only to the extent that the other Nordic states levy tax on pension income at a rate higher than 20 per cent. This would most likely be the case for Denmark and Norway, but not for Iceland or Finland.[47]

In other words, the taxation at source of pensions in Sweden may have restrictive effects on movement, in a way similar to that of exit taxation. In the double tax treaties where Sweden withholds its exclusive right to tax state pensions at source on some specific items (*folkpension*), pensioners may have an incentive to move out of Sweden for tax purposes when the host state's effective tax rate on pensions is lower than 20 per cent.[48]

The double tax treaties concluded by Sweden with Spain,[49] France,[50] Germany,[51] Greece[52] and Austria[53] follow the mainstream OECD recommendation. Hence, occupational pensions from *private* past employment are taxed only in the pensioners' residence states. Accordingly, a domestic tax rate on pensions lower than the tax in Sweden provides incentive to move for tax purposes. Indeed, compared to Sweden, most EU Member States provide a lower level of effective taxation on pensioners.[54] This can be explained by the fact that resident taxpayers benefit in the host state from a lower progressivity of income tax than in Sweden;

---

[47] For a description of the Nordic tax systems, see www.nordisketax.net/.

[48] These include treaties with Greece and the Nordic countries, and the former UK double taxation treaty. While few pensioners move to Switzerland, the double taxation treaty also provides for credit of taxes in Switzerland for public pensions and social security payments; Double Tax Treaty (SFS 1987:182) of 7 May 1965 Articles 19 and 24.3.

[49] Double tax treaty with Spain, Förordning (1976:5) Article 18.1 for private pensions.

[50] Double tax treaty with France SFS 1991:673 Article 18 for all pensions except public pensions paid to a Swedish national falling under Article 19§2b and Article 21 for ATP and *Folkpension*.

[51] Double tax treaty with Germany SFS 1992:1193 Article 18.1, and 18.2 for state pensions with a subject-to-tax clause for the exemption in the source state.

[52] Double tax treaty with Greece SFS1963:497 Article 14, not covering ATP, however, this is subject to source taxation in Sweden.

[53] Double tax treaty with Austria SFS 2011:1350 Article 15 for private employment pensions. Article 16 provides source taxation only for public employment pensions.

[54] The OECD publishes this information. See for instance, the table of the official and marginal personal income tax rates for the OECD members at https://stats.oecd.org/Index.aspx?DataSetCode=TABLE_I7, accessed 10 February 2016.

they can also take advantage of incentives (lower tax rates for family situations or old-age ability to pay, no social security fees, larger basic allowance).[55]

Furthermore, the double tax treaty with Spain deviates on a specific point.[56] Swedish pensioners who have moved to Spain pay both the Swedish source tax (SINK 20 per cent) on guarantee pension or any social security benefits and on individual retirement schemes (*pensionsförsäkring*) in addition to the Spanish tax for residents (progressive) on the very same amounts for the same tax year. Instead of granting a tax credit for the Swedish source tax (SINK), Spain negotiated to keep their right to tax residents, at the full income tax rate, and Sweden agreed to provide for a reverse credit of the source tax (SINK) in respect of the Spanish tax paid on Swedish pensions. This means that Swedish pensioners moving to Spain are double-taxed on their pensions during the interval that Sweden makes them wait for the reverse credit. This double tax treaty is not common; usually, the right to tax is not split and the risk of juridical double taxation is quite limited. When negotiating new treaties, Sweden tends to adhere to this principle, as for instance in the 2015 Swedish/UK double tax treaty, which provides for taxation of pensions only in the state from which the pension is paid, and there is no longer any question of imputation of the source tax on the residence tax.[57] This simplifies the situation for mobile pensioners, and unlike the situation in Spain, pensioners do not have to fill in tax returns in their new residence state or wait longer for the Swedish SINK tax to be offset against the domestic income tax in the residence state.

Additionally, the income qualification of the income can have a decisive impact on the tax treatment of the beneficiary. Sometimes, the minimum and guaranteed state pensions fall under Article 19 (pensions arising from past public employment) and are sometimes treated separately, allowing only the source state to tax. The qualification arises from the interpretation of the double tax treaty by reference to domestic law (OECD MT Article 3.2). For instance, the Swedish Supreme Administrative Court decided in 2003 that the French–Swedish tax treaty's Article

---

[55] For a study of EU Member State pensions, see for instance European Parliament, IZA research report 42, 'Pension systems in the EU – Contingent liabilities and assets in the public and private sector' (2008). Finland, Norway, Denmark and Spain apply tax rates for pensioners which are comparable to those in Sweden, but this is not the case in France, Germany, the UK or Austria.

[56] Double tax treaty with Spain Articles XVIII.2 and XXI5.5.

[57] See for instance, the double tax treaty with the UK Article 18(1)(b)(ii) Government Bill Prop 2015/16:17 56ff.

18 (pensions from past private employment) and Article 19 (pensions from past public employment) did not specifically cover pillar 1 income and guarantee pensions paid in Sweden. In contrast, the payments under the former Swedish pension system (ATP) fell under Article 21 of the tax treaty in question ('other income'), and were taxable only in the beneficiary's residence state. Sweden was not allowed to levy the source tax that was applicable to other income, such as occupational pensions.[58]

Notably, the French tax authorities tend to treat the Swedish supplementary pension (tax deducted partly upon constitution) as 'capital insurance' and not as employment income, and hence do not tax this income in France.[59] This demonstrates that double non-taxation of pensions can also be achieved in specific situations.

In respect to the US, the double tax treaty[60] mainly follows the OECD recommendation, and allows the residence state only to tax pensions from past private employment income, whereas pensions paid by state resources remain taxable only in the source state. A number of deviations can be of interest here. American citizens receiving pensions from past public employment in Sweden are not liable for the SINK tax at all; nor can Sweden tax a pension, 'paid by the U.S. Government to Swedish citizens and residents (and those beneficiaries entitled to survivors' benefits), if the relevant individual was hired prior to 1978 by the U.S. Government to work for the United States Embassy in Stockholm or the United States Consulate General in Gothenburg and was covered under the United States Civil Service Retirement pension plan' (Article 20.4). A series of provisions also ensures the mutual recognition of pension funds settled in one of these states, to the benefit of the pensioner of the other state, which is quite uncommon in the double tax treaty practice.

We can conclude that the impact of the provisions in double tax treaties is significant for the economic situation of migrant pensioners, and equally important as the legal qualification for tax purposes of the income received in the host state. Receiving pensions in a lump sum or annuity may change the qualification of income and hence its tax treatment. The variety of solutions negotiated by states in the different bilateral agreements reveals a potential for unequal treatment, even

---

58 RÅ (Regeringsrätten årsbok) 2003 ref 20; see also *Internationell Handledning* (Skatteverket 2010) 611 (Swedish Tax Agency comments on double tax treaties).

59 Double tax treaty with France Article 19.

60 Double tax treaty with the US SFS 1994:1617 Articles 19 and 20.

sometimes on the basis of nationality,[61] against which some remedies in EU tax law are available for EU migrants; this is discussed in the next paragraph.

4. FREE MOVEMENT OF PENSIONERS IN THE EU: TAX LAW ISSUES

4.1 Tax Base Erosion Linked to Migrant Pensioners

Long before deciding to move upon retirement or even knowing that they will do so, individuals take decisions on how to constitute pension rights, and these decisions can have far-reaching economic consequences. Let us study one example. National tax systems tend to provide for some incentives to constitute additional pension rights (pillar two and pillar three), either directly on behalf of the individuals (third-pillar pensions) or as individual retirement schemes in addition to the domestic occupational pension (second-pillar pensions). These incentives build on the premise that the pensioner will remain in the same state that financed pension rights, so they are not designed to cover cross-border situations with the risk of opening the door to free-riders. The CJEU has had some occasions to apply the prohibition on hindrances to the free movement of workers (Article 45 TFEU) and the freedom of capital (Article 63 TFEU), in cases where some national tax provisions reserved the tax incentive for domestic pension schemes and refused tax deduction of contributions in cross-border situations.[62] While the Court found the restriction justified on the ground of public policy reasons (keeping the 'temporal' cohesion of the tax system) in one early case, the latest

[61] The double tax treaties signed by Sweden with Austria (SFS 2011:1350 Article 16), France (Article 19) Germany (SFS 1992:1193 Article 18.2) and the UK (former tax treaty SFS: 1983:88) reserve the right to tax pensions from past public employment (and even the minimum state pension) for the source state, unless the beneficiary is also a national of the other (residence) state. In other words, Sweden taxes exiting Swedish citizens only at source, and this reverse discrimination is not forbidden in EU law; however, an indirect discrimination may result from the exercise of cross-border retirement as will be seen further.

[62] *Bachmann* C-204/90 EU:C:1992:35, *Wielockx* C-80/94 EU:C:1995:271; *Safir* C-118/96 EU:C:1998:170; *Danner* C-136/00 EU:C:2002:558; *Skandia* C-422/01 EU:C:2003:380; *Turpeinen* C-520/04 EU:C:2006:703; *Commission v. Denmark* C-150/04 EU:C:2007:69; *Commission v. Belgium* C-296/12 EU:C:2014:24.

decisions clearly depart from this line of reasoning and find that a heavier tax burden for mobile workers is not in line with EU law.[63]

As a follow-up of this case law, the European Commission issued a communication in which discriminatory treatment of contributions to foreign pension schemes and tax issues related to cross-border transfers of pension capital were described as the two main barriers preventing provision of second-pillar pensions across the EU.[64] In line with this communication the Commission also initiated nine infringement procedures against Belgium, France, Spain, Portugal, Ireland, Denmark, Sweden, the UK and Italy.[65] Both Denmark and Belgium litigated and lost their case at Court, while the others amended their internal laws.[66]

The CJEU found that the Danish and Belgian rules denying the right to deduct payments to foreign pension schemes discouraged both mobility and taking up of employment in other Member States – a violation of EU law. Both states tried to justify this breach by explaining that the temporal link between the tax deduction of pension contribution and the forthcoming right of a state to tax income arising from this deducted pension contribution was disrupted upon mobility, because double tax treaties allocated the right to tax the occupational pension in the residence state of the pensioner.[67] However, the CJEU dismissed this argument, finding that when mobile pensioners come to Denmark and Belgium, both states have the right to tax their occupational pensions, irrespective of how much or how little tax these individuals paid upon constitution prior to immigration. Therefore, these states did not succeed in arguing that the loss of tax revenue for exiting pensioners and the lack of follow-up over an individual's lifetime due to cross-border mobility justified these restrictive tax rules.

---

63 For an in-depth study of this case law, see C M Grassi, 'Taxation of cross-border supplementary pensions: Still an obstacle to the free movement of workers in the European Union?' (2015) 55 IBFD European Taxation 19; L De Broe and R Neyt, 'Tax treatment of cross-border pensions under the OECD Model and EU law' (2009) 63 IBFD Bulletin for International Taxation 89.

64 Communication from the Commission to the Council, the European Parliament and the Economic and Social Committee – The elimination of tax obstacles to the cross-border provision of occupational pensions COM(2001) 214 April 2001.

65 P Schonewille, 'Pan-European pensions move a step nearer' (2007) IPE, available at http://ec.europa.eu/taxation_customs/resources/documents/taxation/personal_tax/pensions/ipe_mar2007.pdf, accessed 1 December 2015.

66 *Commission v. Denmark*, above n 62, and *Commission v. Belgium*, above n 62.

67 *Commission v. Denmark*, above n 62, para 71.

In addition, the loss of tax revenue is linked to the double tax treaties (in line with Article 18 of the OECD MT) allocating the right to levy tax to the pensioner's residence state. The assumption is that tax treaties between states reflect a give-and-take in a bilateral situation, and that the tax base erosion is balanced by the right to tax immigrant pensioners who deducted their pension contributions in another state. Thus if migration flows were balanced and of equal importance on both sides of the border, there would not be any loss of tax revenue for states, and no need to refuse the deduction of contributions to foreign pension schemes. Furthermore, in their bilateral arrangements, some states even accept the deduction of occupational pension contributions paid to schemes in the other state.[68] The bilateral agreements therefore create a difference in treatment between mobile workers depending on their place of work, but the CJEU does not require horizontal equal treatment and respects the different outcomes for tax purposes arising from bilateral tax treaties.[69]

Some states have terminated their double tax treaties, thus ushering in double taxation of mobile pensioners from other states, but also limiting tax base erosion when the balance of inbound/outbound pensioners is not maintained.[70] Other states, such as Sweden or Finland, have negotiated exclusive rights in their double tax treaties to tax pension income at source as explained in the previous section, which also can cause problems for the application of the TFEU.

4.2 Source Taxation in EU Tax Law of Pensioners on the Move

The TFEU provides for equal treatment of migrant workers, primarily in the host state but also in the emigration state, thus preventing exit taxation for individuals.[71] In the landmark case *de Lasteyrie*, the CJEU condemned a provision of French tax law, which taxed notional capital gains on shares upon emigration, while non-mobile taxpayers did not

---

[68] See for instance *Commission v. Denmark*, above n 62; this right was allowed for Danish taxpayers with pension funds in the UK, the Netherlands and Sweden.

[69] *D v. Inspecteur van de Belastingdienst/Particulieren/Ondernemingen buitenland te Heerlen* C-376/03 EU:C:2005:424.

[70] Denmark has terminated its bilateral tax treaties with France and Spain, among other reasons because of the rule according to which Danish pensions are taxed in these countries only.

[71] Article 39 TFEU (free movement of workers) Article 21 TFEU (free movement of EU citizens).

have to pay it.[72] This payment was suspended upon lodging of guarantees equivalent to the value of the shares, and applied only to emigrant taxpayers. The Court found this different treatment to be restrictive to taxpayers' freedom of establishment, as it was not proportionate to the aim of the measure to protect French tax bases from erosion generated by taxpayers' temporary transfer of residence for tax planning reasons.

In light of this case law, it is possible to consider paying a withholding tax on pensions as an exit tax – in so far as it is levied only on exiting pensioners. The TFEU forbids rules that treat two taxpayers in comparable situations differently, and the CJEU has traditionally accepted that even if residents and non-residents are normally not in a comparable situation, they are nevertheless compared when both obtain their income from a similar source (that is, all income originates in the same Member State).[73] However, since pensioners are not workers, only the free movement of citizens (Article 21 TFEU) can be invoked when a restrictive taxation of pensioners is challenged at court, unless their pension rights arise from occupational income, in which case the disputed tax rule has to be tested against Article 45 TFEU.[74]

In the CJEU *Turpeinen* case,[75] a Finnish national moved to Spain upon retirement, deriving her whole income from Finnish pensions. According to the double tax treaty between Spain and Finland, only Finland had the right to tax such income. Finland, just like Sweden, taxed non-resident pensioners at a flat rate similar to SINK, exceeding in certain circumstances the tax due under the progressive rate applicable to pensions paid to residents. Thus the claimant was put at a disadvantage because of the exit. The CJEU applied Article 21 TFEU and found the claimant in a comparable situation to that of a resident taxpayer, since 'the retirement pension paid in Finland constitutes all or almost all of their income, non-resident retired persons such as Ms Turpeinen are, objectively speaking, in the same situation as regards income tax as retired persons resident in Finland who receive the same retirement pension'.[76] Therefore the legislation at issue was declared to be in breach of the right of European citizens to move and reside freely within the EU (Article 21 TFEU).[77]

---

[72] *Hugues de Lasteyrie du Saillant* C-9/02 EU:C:2004:138.

[73] *Finanzamt Köln-Altstadt v. Schumacker* C-279/93 EU:C:1995:31.

[74] *Kohll and Kohll-Schlesser* C-300/15 EU:C:2016:361.

[75] *Turpeinen*, above n 62.

[76] Ibid, para 31.

[77] In *Kohll and Kohll-Schlesser*, above n 74, Opinion of AG Campos Sanchez-Bordona EU:C:2016:86, AG Campos Sanchez-Bordona invited the

The CJEU also scrutinized the Swedish legislation in the *Hirvonen* case.[78] Here, a Finnish pensioner who had worked in Sweden and who moved back to Finland upon retirement had taken a loan in Finland on which she paid interest. According to the Nordic tax treaty applicable at the time, Sweden had the exclusive right to tax this pension, and Mrs Hirvonen had no taxable income in Finland from which she could deduct the interest. Therefore, the Swedish tax for non-residents (SINK, see Section 3.1 in this chapter) was applied at a rate of 25 per cent (then) with no right to deduct the interest charge. However, Sweden allows non-residents in a situation comparable to that of resident taxpayers to be treated as such, and thus allowed Mrs Hirvonen to be taxed on a progressive scale[79] and deduct the interest charge. However, she challenged this decision at court, and asked for the interest charge to be deducted from her non-resident tax bill, in order for these costs to be taken into consideration at least once somewhere. The CJEU stated that since her situation as a non-resident of Sweden (even without the right to deduct the interest there) was more favourable than if she had been treated as a resident of Sweden, her rights were not infringed. The CJEU therefore ruled that the refusal to grant non-resident taxpayers the same personal deductions as those granted to resident taxpayers under the ordinary tax regime does not constitute discrimination contrary to Article 21 TFEU, *when they are not subject to a greater overall tax burden* than that placed on resident taxpayers and on persons in a similar situation whose circumstances are comparable.

In a 26 May 2016 case, *Kohll & Schlesser*, a Luxembourgian taxpayer receiving pensions from his former private employment in the Netherlands contested that he was refused the benefit of a domestic tax credit (limited to 300 EUR), reserved for pensions paid from Luxembourg because only domestic paying institutions are able to tax the pension at its source. Had the pension been paid by a Luxembourgian former employer, he would have received a payslip on the basis of which tax would be paid, and would have enjoyed the tax credit. In other words, according to Article 45 TFEU, pensioners receiving foreign pensions may not be taxed more heavily than pensioners receiving domestic pensions.

CJEU to apply Article 45 TFEU to occupational pensions, but as both rules provide for a similar level of protection, the extent of the mobility rights should not be different.

78 *Hirvonen* C-632/13 EU:C:2015:765.

79 Swedish Income Tax Act SFS 1999:1229 Chapter 65: 30 per cent up to 45,000 EUR and 50 per cent on the net income above this threshold for 2015 taxable income.

In this interesting case, the CJEU applied both Articles 21 and 45 TFEU (the first one for guarantee pensions and the second one for occupational pensions), and found a restriction to both freedoms. No justification ground was upheld by the CJEU, which found that neither the social policy of supporting the vulnerable elderly nor the need to ensure the effectiveness of fiscal supervision were valid arguments. Following AG Campos Sanchez-Bordona,[80] the CJEU also found that the different treatment of mobile pensioners may not be justified by the need to prevent tax base erosion, as there was no direct link between the tax credit and the taxation of pensions in general.

In brief, this case law shows that source taxation of pensions is not unproblematic in the EU, and even if it solves the problem of tax base erosion for states that previously subsidized pension rights through deduction from taxes at the moment of constitution of pensions, the overall situation of mobile pensioners has to be dealt with in each individual situation in order to comply with EU law. Member States would be in a difficult situation justifying a higher tax level on emigrant pensioners than on the domestic population.[81]

A pending case at the CJEU, also referred by a Finnish court, deals with this issue of comparison.[82] According to Finnish tax law, resident pensioners are liable to an additional tax of 6 per cent on pension income in excess of 45,000 EUR after pension income deductions. In other words, the domestic income tax may end up being higher than the tax on a similar amount of employment income. This supplementary tax was meant to collect tax revenue from pension income recipients with greater financial ability to pay taxes, and to narrow differences of tax rates applicable to employment income and pension income, as a way to convince workers to postpone retirement – because pension income would be taxed higher than occupational income. An individual taxpayer claimed that this tax violates the prohibition of age discrimination.[83] Should the CJEU find these texts applicable, the next question would be whether pensioners and active taxpayers are in a comparable situation for assessing the ability to pay individual income tax. Some arguments in favour of this position can be found in the structure of the tax system:

---

[80] *Kohll and Kohll-Schlesser*, above n 74, Opinion of AG Campos Sanchez-Bordona.

[81] De Broe and Neyt (2009), above n 63.

[82] *C* C-122/15 (ongoing) Opinion of AG Kokott EU:C:2016:65.

[83] Article 21 of the EU Charter on Fundamental Rights; Article 19 TFEU and Directive 2000/78 of 27 November 2000 establishing a general framework for equal treatment in employment and occupation, OJ 2000 L 303/16.

part of one's pension income can be considered as postponed employment income. If so, could this different treatment be justified for an objective reason of public interest, such as the incentive to work more and postpone one's retirement?

AG Kokott remains within the scope of the Employment Equality Directive and does not study the issue of the ground of age discrimination, as it was not raised by the referring Court. She suggests that Finnish domestic tax law is in line with EU law, as taxation of pensions does not fall within the scope of application of Employment Equality Directive Article 3(1). The AG also concluded that the EU Charter's prohibition of age discrimination is not applicable because the disputed Finnish provision does not implement any EU law provisions.[84]

This case law indicates that EU Member States may tax at source an emigrant pensioner, both under internal law and under double tax treaty conventions, provided that the individual's overall tax burden after exit is not heavier than that of a non-mobile pensioner in a comparable situation, that is, for pensions arising from similar sources. In other words, Sweden may tax its exiting pensioners at source (SINK) only to the extent that migrant pensioners are not taxed more than non-mobile pensioners. Due to the diversity of bilateral scenarios (see Section 3.2 in this chapter), we cannot rule out that in some situations the Swedish 20 per cent withholding tax (SINK) that is applicable for non-resident pensioners enjoying pensions paid from Sweden will be lower than if the pensioner had stayed in Sweden and had been taxed as a resident (for instance, as no personal tax deductions are available in Sweden for non-residents).[85] In this situation, a restriction on free movement of EU citizens (Article 21 TFEU) could be at hand, on the basis of which individuals may challenge domestic laws, irrespective of whether this right to tax arises from double tax treaties.[86]

Furthermore, the CJEU case law indicates that workers' mobility requires EU Member States to offer tax incentives for the constitution of pension rights in non-discriminatory fashion, as well as equal treatment

---

84 Cf also the pending case (to be delivered in November 2016) *de Lange* C-548/15.

85 In *Bouanich* C-265/04 EU:C:2006:51, the CJEU left the referring Court (Sweden) free to assess which situation was more or less favourable for the individual.

86 However, a situation of juridical double taxation arising from the allocation of taxing rights in double tax treaties is not covered by EU law; see *Gilly* C-336/96 EU:C:1998:221.

for resident taxpayers receiving foreign pensions; these requirements limit the Member States' ability to combat potential tax base erosion.

All in all, the balance to be struck between the individual's right to mobility and the Member States' rights to limit tax base erosion and keep a sustainable financial pension system lies on a fine line and the ultimate decision on the matter is left to the CJEU.

5. THE ENTITLEMENT TO HEALTHCARE FOR PENSIONERS

5.1 The Specific Coordination Rules Concerning Healthcare

The lifetime contributions to a tax system would be expected to grant some rights to access to care upon retirement, when individuals' need of medical assistance is greater and their income lower. However, as far as the EU is concerned, rules are not harmonized but rather coordinated; this means that mobility still poses some potential obstacles to the access of welfare benefits of other EU Member States. In addition to facing a complex and non-transparent set of rules, the most exposed economically mobile pensioners in need of care may face refusal in the host state. This section identifies the situations where this could happen.

The coordination Regulation No. 883/2004[87] foresees issues on access to healthcare in cross-border situations for pensioners who are receiving pensions but are not simultaneously pursuing any economic activity. The main rule for determining the state responsible for an economically active person's social security is the *lex loci laboris* principle (the employment state) in combination with the single-state rule.[88] The regulation aims at ensuring that both Union citizens and third-country nationals who travel or reside in another Member State are entitled to healthcare when necessary.

However, the CJEU has concluded that EU law cannot guarantee an insured person who moves to another Member State that the new state will be neutral in terms of social security. Therefore, differences in the social security schemes of the Member States with respect to the level of protection against the risk of sickness cannot be regarded as a restriction of the right to move and reside freely within the EU. Such differences are

---

87 Regulation (EC) No. 883/2004 of the European Parliament and of the Council of 29 April 2004 on the coordination of social security systems, OJ 2004 L 166/1.

88 Article 11 Regulation 883/2004.

the result of the lack of harmonization of European law in this field.[89] The purpose of special rules for pensioners is first to identify the state responsible for providing a pensioner with healthcare (including long-term care), and second the state responsible for the costs related to the healthcare benefits. The state responsible for providing healthcare does not have to be the state that is liable for the costs. As a rule, pensioners are subject to the legislation under which they receive a pension. To a large extent the pension reflects contributions made to the system and therefore the coordination rules provide a way to specify that the state responsible for the pension is also responsible for the healthcare costs.

Regarding pensioners' entitlement to healthcare, the regulation distinguishes three different situations: (1) the pensioner receives pensions from two or more Member States and resides in one of the states from which he or she receives a pension and also has a right to healthcare; (2) the pensioner has no right to healthcare under the legislation of the state of residence; and (3) the pensioner receives a pension or pensions under the legislation of one or more Member States other than the state of residence and has a right to healthcare in the state of residence.

In the first situation, when the pensioner resides in one of the states from which he or she receives a pension, that state is liable for both providing and paying for the healthcare. For instance, a pensioner entitled to pensions from both Sweden and Italy and who resides in Sweden is granted access to healthcare in Sweden based on residence; the pensioner is thus entitled to healthcare in the state of residence. Therefore, Sweden is the competent state to provide healthcare, but also the competent state to pay for the costs related to these benefits. The pensioner is thus entitled to healthcare in Sweden at the expense of Sweden.

In the second situation, the pensioner is not entitled to healthcare under the legislation of the residence state because the state entitles healthcare to residents on the basis of prior contributions to the system. Nevertheless, the pensioner may receive healthcare for himself or herself in that state, on condition that he or she would be entitled to healthcare in at least one of the Member States competent in respect of the pensions. So if the pensioner would have been entitled to healthcare in the state of pension *if* he or she resided there, then the pensioner is also entitled to healthcare in the new state of residence. The benefits shall consequently

89 See for example, *JA van Delft and Others v. College voor zorgverzekeringen* C-345/09 EU:C:2010:610.

be provided by the state in which the pensioner resides.[90] The state responsible for the healthcare costs, however, is the state responsible for the pension.[91] A pensioner moves from Sweden to Germany. She has worked only in Sweden and receives a Swedish pension. In Germany the pensioner is thus not entitled to a pension. If she had not moved to Germany and still resided in Sweden, she would have been entitled to healthcare in Sweden. As a result, she also is entitled to healthcare under the German legislation where she now resides. The costs are borne by Sweden, however, since the pensioner receives a pension from that state. Without the coordination rules, the pensioner would thus not have been entitled to healthcare in her new state of residence.

If the pensioner described above is entitled to healthcare under the legislation of two or more Member States, the healthcare costs shall be borne by the Member State to whose legislation the person has been subject for the longest period of time. So if the pensioner instead receives pensions both from the United Kingdom and Sweden and now resides in Germany, the coordination specifies the state where she has been insured for the longest period as the responsible state for the costs of the healthcare. The pensioner has been insured for the last ten years in Sweden. Before moving to Sweden, she was insured in the United Kingdom for 30 years. Since the United Kingdom is the state where she has been insured for the longest period, the United Kingdom is the competent state and shall therefore pay for the healthcare costs. The CJEU's case law interprets this prerequisite as meaning the legislation to which the pensioner has been subject for the longest time in respect of pensions.[92] A clear link can be seen here between the rights to pension and the entitlement to healthcare.

Finally, in the third situation the pensioner resides in a Member State with a national healthcare system; this means that the right to healthcare is based on residence, and no pension is received from that state. A pensioner has moved to Sweden to reunite with his daughter and grandchildren who already live in Sweden. The pensioner has never worked in Sweden and receives a pension from Germany. However, the pensioner does not receive a pension from Sweden, so Sweden does not have to bear the healthcare cost. The cost of the healthcare provided to pensioners covered by this situation, shall instead be borne by the Member State that pays the pension. Without this provision, Member

---

[90] Article 24 Regulation 883/2004.

[91] Article 24.2(a) Regulation 883/2004.

[92] *F van der Helder and D Farrington v. College voor zorgverzekeringen* C-321/12 EU:C:2013:648.

States with national healthcare systems, such as Sweden, would not be reimbursed by the state that pays the pension, because the pensioner is already entitled to healthcare on the basis of residence.[93] In the example above, the cost shall thus be borne by Germany, although the pensioner is entitled to healthcare in Sweden as a consequence of being resident there.

The choice of pointing out the state of pension has been criticized for being outdated. This choice was made long ago when the social security coordination applied only to economically active persons and the national healthcare insurances around Europe were closely linked to employment. Today, most of the European healthcare systems provide universal coverage. Moreover, for non-economically active persons, the legislation of the Member State of residence is applicable as the main rule in respect of other social security benefits. Therefore, many are asking whether it is time to let the state of residence carry healthcare costs.[94]

What we can see here is that the state of residence has to bear the costs for healthcare for pensioners *if* the pensioner also receives a pension from that state – no matter how low that pension might be. For this reason the coordination rules have also been criticized for not taking the size of the pension into account when the responsible Member State is ultimately determined. This triggers an unfair distribution of the financial burden of healthcare.[95] The original draft for Regulation No. 883/04 actually proposed a rule where the costs were divided on the basis of the length of the insurance period (similar to the rules concerning calculation of pensions).[96] However, the Member States could not agree on this proposal.[97]

With these scenarios in mind, and considering the criteria for determining the Member State that will bear healthcare costs for the migrant pensioner, we can draw this conclusion: generally speaking and irrespective of where pension rights were accumulated, migrant pensioners' access to healthcare in the EU is secured. However, the system does not

---

93 See S Roberts, B Schulte, C Garcia de Cortazar, T Medaiskis and H Verschueren (eds), *Think Tank Report 'Healthcare for Pensioners'* (trESS, European Commission/Ghent University 2009) 13.

94 A Pieter van der Mei, G Essers and C Douven, 'Pensioners and the financing of cross-border health care: Bottlenecks in the fields of European social security law and international tax law' (2011) 2 Eur J Soc L; and Roberts et al. (2009), above n 93.

95 Pieter van der Mei, Essers and Douven (2011), above n 94.

96 See Article 20 of the original proposal of the Commission COM (1998) 779 final.

97 Roberts et al. (2009), above n 93.

provide any incentive to accept inbound pensioners with no previous pension rights, as the host state may not obtain any compensation from the state of origin. This – together with the requirement in the Residence Directive of having comprehensive sickness insurance – may hinder mobility of pensioners with limited means.

5.2 Contribution Paid by Pensioners

As mentioned above, the rules determining the applicable legislation are also relevant in identifying the state where the pensioner shall pay social security contributions. In the absence of harmonization, each Member State has the power to determine how to organize their social security system. However, according to the coordination rules, a person may be covered by only one social security system. The main rule for this in the regulation is the state of employment.[98] An insured person is only required to pay contributions in that state. A pensioner has made contributions during his or her working life into the social security system in the state of employment. If the pensioner has worked in several countries, contributions have been made into more than one system. The coordination rules therefore provide a way to specify the state where contributions have been made as the state responsible for the healthcare costs. However, after ending work a pensioner may also be required to pay compulsory insurance contributions to cover healthcare. As a consequence, the coordination rules cover the levying of contributions on pensioners.

According to Article 30 of Regulation No. 883/2004, the Member State responsible for the healthcare cost may request deductions in respect of contributions for sickness benefits. In the *Rundgren* case,[99] the CJEU held that the connection between the competence to provide pensions and the obligation to bear the healthcare cost is incidental to an actual competence in respect of pensions. In the case, the Finnish Tax Appeals Board found Mr Rundgren liable for paying contributions to the Finnish social security system calculated by reference to his annual income, although he only received pensions from Sweden and had no other income. The reason for the Board's decision was that Mr Rundgren had not confirmed that he did not have a potential right to a Finnish pension.

---

98 Article 13 Regulation 883/2004.
99 *Rundgren* C-389/99 EU:C:2001:264.

However, the CJEU held that healthcare costs cannot be borne by a Member State that has only hypothetical competence in respect of pensions.

The entitlement to receive healthcare in the new state of residence is contingent upon the pensioner's registration in that state.[100] The CJEU has ruled in *van Delft*[101] that a registration in the new state of residence must be carried out to ensure that the pensioners are in fact entitled to healthcare in that Member State. That being so, in the absence of registration in the new Member State of residence, an insured person cannot receive healthcare in that state. However, that does not in any way affect the existence of such a right and hence the corresponding obligation of contribution in the Member State responsible for paying pensions and the healthcare cost. Pensioners cannot choose to remove themselves from the application of the regulation in order to avoid the obligation of paying contributions in the Member State responsible for payment of their pensions. Thus, the requirements established by the coordination rules for pensioners and their entitlement to healthcare are mandatory. A pensioner must pay contributions in respect of healthcare in the Member State responsible for the healthcare costs.

6. CONCLUSIONS

The developments described here indicate that individual income tax and the design of social security systems may weaken economic situations of the elderly, especially when two or more systems are applicable to one taxpayer's income. Both wealthy and less wealthy pensioners face similar issues of the lack of a common system and the need to identify the rules that apply. These factors render cross-border situations complicated and sometimes cause juridical double taxation; they can threaten social security coverage and trigger cash flow problems for mobile pensioners, in conflict with their legitimate expectations.

Older persons may be said in one sense to have stronger protection than other persons who are not economically active. An older person who is entitled to a pension fulfils the criteria of self-sufficiency and there are specific rules in Regulation No. 883/2004 for determining the Member

---

[100] Article 24 Regulation (EC) No. 987/2009 of the European Parliament and of the Council of 16 September 2009 laying down the procedure for implementing Regulation (EC) No. 883/2004 on the coordination of social security systems, OJ 2009 L 284/1.

[101] *Van Delft*, above n 89.

State that shall bear the costs for healthcare. For older persons, the issue of sickness insurance is important when moving to another Member State, because this insurance is a prerequisite for acquiring the right to reside in another Member State for a period longer than three months. On the other hand, a pensioner with a small pension may not have a right to free movement because he or she risks being a burden on the host's welfare system.

Moreover, when Member States use taxes to finance the constitution of pension rights for individuals, they try to find legal solutions to limit tax base erosion that may occur when beneficiaries move out for retirement in another Member State. The state of origin loses revenue from the taxation of pensions in that state. Indeed, while current international tax practice allows the residence state of mobile pensioners to tax the pensions, and even if some Member States have negotiated to keep their power to tax the pensions paid to exiting pensioners at source, states may still face problems in respect of this different treatment as infringing upon the fundamental EU principle of equality.

As explained earlier, the overall tax burden of mobile pensioners should not be greater than that of non-mobile pensioners in relation to the state of origin and even to the state of residence. Therefore, taxpayers are allowed to compare and find out where they can pay less tax and make the best of their mobile years for economic purposes. As shown in this chapter however, this may be easier said than done due to the complexity and lack of transparency of these rules.

Some underlying issues have not been treated in this section, and may need further investigations dealing with other types of taxes, with regard to their potential impact on the economic situation of mobile pensioners. Very few Member States of the EU have abolished succession or gift duties, or wealth tax. These taxes may prevent pensioners from staying too long in these states, and incentivize a return back in the state of origin before they die (as could the new EU regulation on applicable law with regard to successions[102]). The influence of such taxes on pensioners' mobility is left here as a topic for further research. In addition, studies remain to be carried out to understand how efficient economic incentives

---

[102] Regulation No. 650/2012 of the European Parliament and of the Council of 4 July 2012, on jurisdiction, applicable law, recognition and enforcement of decisions and acceptance and enforcement of authentic instruments in matters of succession and on the creation of a European Certificate of Succession, OJ 2012 L 201/107.

actually are, how aware mobile pensioners are of their rights, and how interested they are in these incentives.

12. Legal approaches to private and public responsibilities for elder care

Hanna Pettersson and Mirjam Katzin

1. INTRODUCTION[1]

Privatization and deinstitutionalization of elder care is a common trend throughout Europe. Ageing populations, combined with diminished public financial resources, have created a situation where family care is emerging as an increasingly common solution to the needs of elderly people, regardless of welfare state typologies. Convergence in the organization of welfare is increasing across Europe, among other things because of the ongoing restructuring of the 'Nordic' model, characterized by universalistic welfare.[2] Private financing and production of elder care and mediation by market mechanisms are becoming more common not only in classical welfare societies such as Sweden but also in countries where elder care already relies to a large extent on private subjects.[3] This type of privatization is accompanied by the transfer of care work performed, and responsibilities borne, from the public sector to the families and relatives of older people.

This chapter examines legal aspects of this development in one of the Nordic welfare state countries: Sweden. Swedish elder care is organized by municipalities, and publically funded to a large extent; furthermore, the right to elder care is not related to economic needs. Unlike many other countries, Sweden has historically striven to make elder care a

[1] This work was carried out within the Norma Elder Law Research Environment (www.jur.lu.se/elderlaw) funded by Ragnar Söderberg's Foundation and the Marianne and Marcus Wallenberg Foundation.

[2] Blanca A Deusdad, Charles Pace and Anneli Anttonen, 'Facing the challenges in the development of long-term care for older people in Europe in the context of an economic crisis' (2016) J Soc Serv Res 144.

[3] D Brennan, B Cass, S Himmelweit and M Szebehely, 'The marketization of care: Rationales and consequences in Nordic and liberal care regimes' (2012) J Eur Soc Policy 377.

public responsibility to the greatest extent possible – an ambition that is increasingly being reduced to precisely history. According to estimations from recent years, around 70 per cent of the total elder care work in Sweden is performed by relatives.[4] While this may not approach the level in the US – where costs of unpaid care work were estimated in 2009 to be three times the amount of government spending on caregiving[5] – Sweden's current elder care ambitions are far from those of the past.

Informal care provided by family members has always been a significant part of elder care in Sweden. However, the workload on families caring for elderly relatives has increased during the last decade, as part of the downsizing of municipal elder care and increased emphasis on private responsibility for welfare. The physical and psychological burdens of caring for relatives are well noted in research. Although the increase in family caregiving during the past decade has occurred for all groups of people, it is the daughters – especially daughters of people with lower education and income level during their lifetimes – who bear the heaviest burden and suffer the most negative consequences as a result of their caregiving. Family care, therefore, must be said to have structural dimensions when it comes to class and gender.[6]

When compared to men's health, women's health is more adversely affected by family caregiving,[7] and care for older relatives also results in greater negative effects on the wellbeing and everyday life of women. Women more often find care work to be physically or mentally challenging; they find it harder to make time for leisure and seeing friends; and they take more sick leave from their regular jobs.[8] Taking on a care responsibility also has negative effects on the caregiver's economic situation and relation to the welfare system. It is common that a caregiver uses paid or unpaid leave, such as vacation days or compensatory leave, from a regular job to take single days to care for older relatives.[9] In addition, family caregiving has consequences for the caregivers' access to

---

4 Ann-Britt Sand, 'Anhöriga som kombinerar förvärvsarbete och anhörigomsorg' (Nationellt kompetenscentrum Anhöriga, Kunskapsöversikt 2010:1).

5 National Alliance for Caregiving and AARP, 'Caregiving in the United States 2009' (2009).

6 Petra Ulmanen, *Omsorgens pris i åtstramningstid* (Institutionen för socialt arbete, Stockholms universitet 2015) 86.

7 Ann-Britt Sand, *Anhörigvård: arbete – ansvar – kärlek – försörjning* (Studentlitteratur 2002) 88–90.

8 Ulmanen (2015), above n 6, 77.

9 Marta Szebehely, Petra Ulmanen and Ann-Britt Sand, 'Att ge omsorg mitt i livet: hur påverkar det arbete och försörjning?' (Working Paper/Department of Social Work, 2014:1) 5.

the welfare system. In the social insurance part of the Swedish welfare model, unpaid care work is not regarded as a merit and does not give access to merit-based benefits. The social insurance system is focused on participation in the wage labour market, and thus care for older relatives, which is performed alongside or instead of paid employment, does not provide access to important parts of the welfare system such as sickness insurance or pensions.

In recent years, the municipal responsibility to support family caregivers has been strengthened in the Social Service Act.[10] Through these changes in regulation, a pattern can be detected: families are given more responsibility for the welfare of older persons and the expectations on society have taken on more of a secondary nature. This chapter will examine the course of this development.

Apart from municipal support for caregivers, Swedish law also provides a time-limited right to leave from work and a right to social insurance benefits for employees with a temporary need to provide care for a close relative. However, this right is limited to situations involving very serious health problems, where the life of the relative is assessed as being seriously threatened without care. Less than 2 per cent of the group giving care to older relatives at least once a month have received kin-care allowance (*närståendepenning*).[11]

The municipal support system, the right to leave and the social security kin-care allowance have no formal connection to older people or elder care. Anyone with a severe illness can be the subject of care, regardless of age. The person performing the care does not have to be a biological relative. If a person is willing to leave work to care for someone who is seriously ill, that is considered as demonstrating the existence of a close personal relationship between the two persons; this is the criterion for defining the care.[12] As we will see, however, the legal provisions in question were created and have usually been discussed within a context of elder care and ageing. This is also reflected in case law, where most cases regarding kin-care allowance concern adult children who provide care for their elderly parents.

This chapter concerns legal approaches to the Swedish development towards increased family responsibilities for elder care. We have studied legislation and preparatory works on long-term and short-term family care from the 1970s and onward, as well as case law on short-term

---

10 Socialtjänstlagen (2001:453).

11 Szebehely, Ulmanen and Sand (2014), above n 9, 5.

12 Government Bill Prop 1987/88: 176 *om äldreomsorgen inför 90-talet* 100.

family care. What are the differences and parallels when it comes to long-term and short-term family care and their regulation? In particular, we take an interest in the ongoing negotiation of boundaries between public and private responsibilities that is reflected in legislation and politico-legal discourse on these matters. These perceptions are constantly renegotiated and influenced by prevailing ideologies and ideas about society, the individual and the family.

By tracking legislative developments and reasoning on long-term and short-term family care, respectively, we attempt to understand the historical background of this situation.[13] What ideological choices have been made regarding public and private responsibilities for elder care, and when? How have the financial responsibilities for elder care been regarded during different time periods? How have societal conditions – such as strained public finances, and the amount of elder care actually performed by relatives – been handled by the legislative bodies? To what extent has concern with gender (in)equality played a role in legislative processes?

2. HISTORICAL BACKGROUND

2.1 Elder Care Extension and Downsizing

Swedish public elder care underwent extensive development from the 1960s onward, and elder care was thought of as a public responsibility. This was expressed in the Social Service Act of 1980, which is based on the fundamental idea of independence of the individual in relation to the family, in both economic and practical terms. This idea was also manifested in the government inquiry report on family caregiving (The Committee on Family Care, *Anhörigvårdskommittén*, Ds 1981:15, SOU 1983:64). The Committee envisioned a society that would eventually manage all care of older people through a public system, with efforts of relatives only as a temporary solution until public elder care was sufficiently expanded. However, the report of the Committee did not result in any legislative changes.[14] The discourse at the time thus did

---

[13] This chapter draws on Mirjam Katzin, 'Tillbaka till familjen: privat och offentligt ansvar i den svenska äldreomsorgen' (2014) 37(2/145) Retfaerd 37–53, and Hanna Pettersson, 'Döden – en privatsak? Socialförsäkringsrättsliga perspektiv på ansvarsfördelning vid närståendevård' (manuscript).

[14] Ann-Britt Sand, *Äldreomsorg: mellan familj och samhälle* (Studentlitteratur 2007) 142.

describe family caregiving as a problem, especially for women, because it affected their possibilities to be active in the labour market and choose their own life paths. Legislators thought that the problem would be solved in the long run by increasing public elder care, but also through a better support system for family caregivers – support which would also include economic compensation for family-supplied care.[15]

The 1980s, however, brought about a significant change in the discourse regarding elder care. A lower ambition level was adopted for the welfare state, motivated by and through economic crises, coupled with a changed ideology with respect to the boundary between the public and the private sphere and a critique of what was seen as an overgrown welfare bureaucracy. This brought about downsizing in the elder care sector and a discourse based on keywords such as 'choice' and 'individualism' became stronger.[16]

In 1992, a large reform of the welfare sector (*Ädelreformen*) moved the responsibility for elder care from the state and counties to the municipalities. Helene Brodin claims that it simultaneously enabled significant cuts in elder care, and was the institutional shift that matched the ideological change in the view of elder care as an increasingly private responsibility. The downsizing that the *Ädelreform* brought about, Brodin says, was an expression of the reprivatization discourse that wished to reformulate the need for elder care from being a public problem to a private one.[17] The cuts in public elder care accelerated during the 1990s, with cuts mainly in institutional care but also in home-care services.[18] Anneli Anttonen describes the development in terms of the two parts of the welfare state. The reconstruction of the welfare state has mainly affected social services more than social insurances. This relates to ideological changes and has meant that care burdens have partly moved back to the family.[19]

---

15 Ulmanen (2015), above n 6, 72.

16 Katharina Tollin, *Sida vid sida: en studie av jämställdhetspolitikens genealogi 1971–2006* (Atlas Akademi 2011) 104–6.

17 Helene Brodin, *Does Anybody Care? Public and Private Responsibilities in Swedish Eldercare 1940–2000* (Umeå Universitet 2005) 104.

18 Sand (2007), above n 14, 44–5.

19 Anneli Anttonen, 'Den sociala servicestaten som feministiskt kampgrepp' in Marta Szebehely and Rosmari Eliasson-Lappalainen (eds), *Vad förgår och vad består? En antologi om äldreomsorg, kvinnosyn och socialpolitik* (Arkiv 1998) 82–6.

2.2 Support to Long-Term Family Caregivers

The discourse of long-term family care, in Swedish legislation, has primarily been formulated around the municipal obligation to provide support for family caregivers. In 1998, a municipal responsibility was established to provide special support to family members and other relatives who care for chronically ill or older people. The new rule entailed a voluntary commitment by the municipalities, which also had significant influence over the form and content of this support.[20] The starting point for the investigation preceding the legislative change was an altered economic situation for the municipalities, created by an economic crisis. This new situation was supposed to be resolved through a more integrated care system, in which relatives would receive a more important role, at the same time as elder care remained a public commitment. In the investigation, family carers are also described as a new category that previously was not recognized, because elder care policy had focused only on public care. The extent of family care is described as 'surprising' in the report. Support from the municipality to family caregivers is thus supposed to recognize the work that is already done by relatives, but is also intended to integrate relatives in the elder care system to a greater degree, with a reference to limited municipal resources.[21]

Through a legislative amendment in 2009, support to family caregivers became a mandatory municipal task. In the report from the department prior to the amendment, family care is described as 'the basis' of the elder care system, which means a further shift in the importance that family caregivers have for the legislator. Relatives are supposed to take the whole responsibility for older persons in need, or at least a shared responsibility.[22] Paradoxically, the legal responsibility is not changed, but remains with the municipalities. The fact that family caregiving is a voluntary commitment is not described as a problem, as caring for relatives is assumed to be something 'natural' and 'positive' for most people.[23]

Regulation of the municipal obligation to provide support for care-giving family members has thus not changed the legal situation regarding the family's or the municipalities' obligations to care for older people. However, the fact that family caregivers are now a subject category in the

---

[20] Government Bill Prop 1996/97:124 133.
[21] Government Inquiry Report SOU 1994:139 *Ny socialtjänstlag* 321–9.
[22] Government Report Ds 2008:18 10.
[23] Government Report Ds 2008:18 10, 14, 49.

law, entitled to receive special support, is a clear sign of the increasing importance of family caregivers in elder care.

2.3 Support to Short-Term Family Caregivers

Short-term family care benefits can be given for a maximum of 100 days per person in need of care[24] at a level corresponding to the sickness benefit that the caregiver would have received if s/he had been prevented from working by illness;[25] this benefit is currently 80 per cent of the person's income, up to a set level of income. When a caregiver receives short-term care benefits, the right to leave work is automatic and cannot lead to a legally valid dismissal, transfer to new tasks or reduction of employment benefits.[26]

The right to family care benefits requires that the person cared for is 'severely ill'.[27] As we shall see, this is usually interpreted as meaning that there must be an imminent threat to the care recipient's life.

The legislation on short-term family care benefits is not exclusively applicable to care for elders; anyone with a 'severe illness' can be the subject of care. However, the legislation was created and has subsequently been treated as part of a context of elder care. A majority of court cases in this category concern care for an older person. It can also be noted that the caregiver is usually a child of the person receiving care. However, the recipient of short-term care benefits does not have to be a child or even a relative; in the legislative process it was stated that anyone who is willing to abstain from paid work in order to care for a severely ill person must be assumed to have a close relationship with the person in question.[28] The short-term care allowance and the related right to leave were introduced in 1989, as part of a greater revision of the legal framework on elder care. Revisions since then consist mainly of lengthened maximum time periods for short-term family allowance.

The first proposal for regulation that resembles the current rules on the right to leave and receive social security benefits in connection with a close person's illness was presented in 1979, in the context of medical-ethical issues regarding death and terminal care.[29] This proposal did not result in actual legislation. However, in 1983, the matter was discussed

24 Socialförsäkringsbalken (2010:110) 47:8.
25 Socialförsäkringsbalken (2010:110) 47:14.
26 Lag (1988:1465) om rätt till ledighet för närståendevård.
27 Socialförsäkringsbalken (2010:110) 47:3.
28 Government Bill Prop 1987/88:176 100.
29 Government Inquiry Report SOU 1979:59 *I livets slutskede* (End of life).

by a new inquiry, from a new perspective. The Committee on Family Care (*Anhörigvårdskommittén*), which delivered its final report in 1983, had been appointed on the basis of parliamentary discussions regarding support for relatives who cared for 'the sick, the elderly and the disabled' in their homes. The high employment rate of both men and women was making it difficult to participate in such care work, which was the reason that leave with intact job security and the right to return to work for caregivers was considered.[30]

The Committee proposed a general right to unpaid leave of up to 30 days for short-term care. This was twice as much as the leave rights already provided by several collective agreements. The right to leave would apply in cases of 'severe illness', but also in situations where a person was temporarily or briefly cared for at home in anticipation of hospital or nursing home care; during a temporary break in such institutional care; and when convalescent.[31]

In 1989, six years after the proposal of the Committee on Family Care, legislation was finally put in place for short-term family care allowance and the right to leave – though only in relation to 'severe illness'. Thirty days would be the maximum total amount of time – not 30 days per year, as suggested by the Committee on Family Care. This limit was justified by reference to consulting bodies, according to which the proposals from the Committee of Family Care could have far-reaching labour market consequences, and that a more limited time-frame should first be evaluated.[32] The government bill on the legislative changes took a starting point in (among other things) the report of the Committee of Family Care, and treated elder care in the 1990s in a broad perspective. Again, a main feature was the ambition to facilitate elder care in the homes of elderly people. This was presented as a question of autonomy and freedom of choice for older people.[33]

The criteria for entitlement to short-term family care allowance remain largely unchanged since the introduction of the legislation. However, some adjustments to the regulation have been made. In 1994 the maximum amount of time with family care allowance was extended from 30 to 60 days per care recipient, and in 2010 this was increased to 100 days per care recipient. The first extension of the number of days was made for 'both humanitarian and economic reasons'; the allowance was

---

30 Government Inquiry Report SOU 1983:64 *Ledighet för anhörigvård* (Leave for care of relatives) 21.

31 Ibid 85.

32 Government Bill Prop 1987/88:176 97–8.

33 Ibid 176, 1, 23–4.

not claimed by many people, and the extension was not predicted to entail large costs.[34] The subsequent extension to 100 days was not related to elder care or to the situation of the elderly, but rather to concerns about (the few) cases where the ill person was young and had small children.[35]

3. FUNDING OF ELDER CARE

As we see it, Swedish elder care is in conflict over whether the responsibility for the costs of elder care should be placed on the individual or on society. This is connected in turn to different societal interests and is inevitably linked to questions of justice and distribution.

3.1 Elder Care in an Economic Discourse

The report of the Committee on Family Care contains a clear discourse about strained public finances. The increasing number of elderly people over 80 years of age is mentioned as an additional burden for the economy. The report also stresses that the elderly should be able to live at home rather than in elder care institutions for a longer time, for both humanitarian and economic reasons. This is mentioned repeatedly – not only in the sections regarding long-term family caregivers, but also when discussing short-term care.[36]

Because of this situation of restricted public finances, the Committee found that it was not possible at the time to provide a right to economic compensation in every situation where short-term family care could be appropriate. However, there was a belief that these aspects of the social security system could be expanded in the future through reforms. The form of care that should be prioritized in a first phase was terminal care given at home, which was also assessed as being relatively easy to define.[37]

As for support to long-term family caregivers, the main reason given for introducing municipal responsibility for support was that family care,

---

[34] Government Bill Prop 1993/94: 100 *Förslag till statsbudget för budgetåret 1994/95*, Annex 6 43–4.

[35] Government Bill Prop 2008/09: 194 *Vissa socialförsäkringsfrågor mm* 22–3.

[36] Government Inquiry Report SOU 1983:64 83, 85, 91.

[37] Ibid 97. Cf Government Inquiry Report SOU 1987:21 *Äldreomsorg i utveckling. Slutbetänkande av äldreberedningen* 137, where a new committee makes the same assessment, but concludes that there are still no economic resources for such a reform.

despite being a voluntary commitment, was considered to have become more burdensome for relatives. The governmental investigation of 1994 stated that this was a consequence of the major 'restructuring' of elder care that had taken place, which was in turn presented as necessary in light of the development of the Swedish economy following an economic crisis in the early 1990s.[38] The efforts of relatives were recognized as an important (economic) resource to be protected – if relatives reduced their care responsibility, it would result in increased public costs. It was therefore important that the support was preventive, so that caregivers were not worn out by their caring responsibilities.[39]

In a departmental report from 2008, the restructuring of elder care towards greater private responsibility was described as unavoidable. Family care, as the starting point, was something positive. However, for the individual providing the care, it could become a burden if sufficient support was not given.[40]

3.2 Public Support for Long-Term and Short-Term Caregivers

Municipalities have the right, in accordance with the principle of local autonomy, to decide how support to family caregivers should be organized. The support that is offered often comprises various forms of respite care for the older person – during a shorter or longer period older people may be staying elsewhere than in the home. In recent years, conversation groups for caregivers have become increasingly common, as well as various training programmes. Knowledge is limited about the impact of these different forms of aid.[41] The support may also be given as financial compensation. However, a change in the economic compensation for informal care can be noted over time. The number of relatives *employed* was at its highest in the 1970s, when about 24,000 family caregivers were employed to care for their relatives. Today, this figure is not even a tenth of that number. Instead, other kinds of subsidies are paid for, such as *care benefits*, which are paid directly to the dependent and which only indirectly benefit the caregiver. The amounts of these benefits are often much lower than a salary for a caregiver and vary between 3,000 SEK and 6,000 SEK a month, which is significantly lower than a corresponding salary for a formally employed elder care worker (although this salary is also low). Furthermore, the number of dependents receiving care

---

38 Government Bill Prop 1996/97:124, 39.
39 Ibid 132–3.
40 Government Report Ds 2008:18 12.
41 Sand (2007), above n 14, 111–14.

benefits is substantially lower today, which means that economic compensation to family caregivers is increasingly rare.[42]

In a departmental report from 2008, economic support was briefly mentioned as one of the alternatives for municipal support to family caregivers, but it was stated that support should be considered mainly to have a symbolic value and serve as an encouragement and recognition of the family's efforts. The words *recognition*, *respect*, and *encouragement* recurred repeatedly in the texts studied. Individuals who were caregivers were supposed to need, above all, society's appreciation of them and what they do, and being given a position. As family caregivers are seen to have the primary responsibility for older persons, social services should consider the needs of the family as a whole rather than just those of the individual requiring care.[43]

Short-term family care, on the other hand, was first proposed as a reform to support the relatives of people who were approaching the end of their lives. In 1979, when the first proposal was made – but which did not result in actual legislation – it was actually assumed to entail increased costs, rather than the opposite. In an official report, relatives were described as the natural psychological support for the dying patient. While this support could lead to a decreased workload for public healthcare, it was also predicted that it would create new demands on professional healthcare workers, who would need to give instructions to relatives when necessary, and be prepared to offer psychological support to relatives in their time of crisis. This would require health professionals to undergo appropriate training. As we can see, the proposed right to leave and social security benefits was aimed at improving the situation of dying people and their relatives, rather than at lessening the burden on the public healthcare system.[44]

When short-term family care benefits were introduced in 1989, the legislative process preceding adoption of the scheme was permeated by a cautious approach to public spending. In 1983 and 1987, different official inquiries had concluded that short-term care benefits for the relatives of people at the end of life would be introduced as a first step, to be followed up by short-term care benefits for relatives in other situations where additional care and support were required – such as during convalescence or while awaiting a place in hospital or another public-care institution. Even though there was no certainty that such reforms would

---

42 Sand (2010), above n 4, 42–3.
43 Katzin (2014), above n 13, 45.
44 Government Inquiry Report SOU 1979:59 143–6.

actually entail increased public costs, the inquiry from 1983 recommended evaluation of the economic consequences arising from the first step of family care benefit reforms before further steps were introduced.[45]

4. PUBLIC OR PRIVATE RESPONSIBILITY?

The 1990s saw changed regulation and a new discourse on the position of long-term family care. A more positive approach emerged, presenting family care as 'natural'. Long-term family care has moved from being regarded as an important complement to public elder care in the 1990s to being presented in recent years as the foundation of elder care. As for short-term family care, no equivalent changes are evident in the legislative discourse or in the legal provisions. In relation to the legislation on support for short-term family caregivers, the Swedish government has always declared that elder care is and must remain a public responsibility – and this is the reason often cited in case law for denial of short-term family care allowance.

4.1 Development of the Discourse Concerning Public and Private Responsibilities

4.1.1 Long-term care support

The investigation in 1994 of support for long-term caregivers claims that a new perspective on elder care is needed, which places family members' care more at the centre of attention. This new approach is expected to lead to more effective ways to address elder care needs by creating an 'integrated' care system based on cooperation between public and private spheres.[46] In the Ministry of Social Affairs' report made prior to the strengthening of the legislation in 2009, there was a further shift in the discourse regarding the division of responsibilities – from public to private. The report stated that although family care should still be voluntary, the foundation of elder care should be seen as care given by relatives and not by the public. Relatives were expected to take full responsibility – or at least a shared responsibility. The municipalities' care was described as a 'complement' and as a support for relatives.

45 Government Inquiry Report SOU 1983:64 97; see also Government Inquiry Report SOU 1987:21 137.

46 Government Inquiry Report SOU 1994:139 329.

Other important support functions should be based on 'signs of appreciation', such as 'feel-good' activities, which could include access to therapeutic massage, podiatry, recuperative breaks and get-togethers for family caregivers.[47]

Repeating and emphasizing the fundamental importance of the role of family caregivers in elder care, then, is a way to justify support for caregivers. However, especially in the report of 2009, family caregiving is also described as something inherently positive and desirable, and even something that should increase. Care for older people is described as a private matter which society should support when needed, while this statement – paradoxically – is emphasized parallel to the statement that elder care is primarily a public responsibility. The family is portrayed as something fundamentally positive, without problematization, and caring relationships within the family are described as qualitatively better than caring relationships established within professional elder care. Furthermore, informal care is *supposed* to be desired by older persons as well as caregivers. Therefore, there is no need to shift responsibility from families to the public; the existence of family caregiving is not a problem to be solved, but is instead generally unproblematic and natural, according to the legislative documents. The regulation of caregiver support marks in that sense that the responsibility for meeting the needs of older people is now considered a family matter. The public should support families when relatives either cannot or do not want to give care.[48]

Thus family care is described in later legislative documents as natural for most caregivers and caretakers, and something that carers willingly provide. Yet it is also stressed that family caregiving should be a voluntary commitment. The paradox – that is, the increasing need for family care owing to decreased municipal resources for elder care, coupled with the claim that family care of older relatives should remain voluntary – is not seen as a problem, because family care is assumed to be something natural and positive.[49] However, the studies of Marta Szebehely show that family care is in fact not desired by older persons in need of care. Nine out of ten say that they prefer public care to being taken care of by a family member.[50] Szebehely's studies call into question these legislative assumptions about family caregiver volunteerism.

---

47 Government Report Ds 2008:18 10, 36, 49.

48 Katzin (2014), above n 13, 46.

49 Ibid 48.

50 Marta Szebehely, 'Omsorgsmönster bland kvinnor och män – inte bara en fråga om kön' in Evy Gunnarsson and Marta Szebehely (eds), *Genus i omsorgens vardag* (Gothia 2009) 41–2.

4.1.2 Short-term care support

The government bill preceding the introduction of support for short-term family care emphasizes that the responsibility for providing service and care to older people and 'people with disabilities' belongs to municipalities and county councils. Deficiencies in care should not make relatives and other persons close to the person in need of care feel compelled to take on care work. The efforts of relatives and other close persons must be voluntary, and should be a complement to care work performed by 'society'. Therefore, the right to care leave and family care allowance should not apply in cases where the care recipient is awaiting hospital care or undergoing convalescence.[51]

Initially, the short-term care allowance required that care must be carried out in the home rather than at a health or elder care institution. This requirement was abolished as early as 1992 because it had been interpreted as incomprehensible. However, the regulation emphasized that removing this requirement should not be interpreted as a deviation from the original principle: the care work of relatives should serve only as a complement to the care that society is responsible for providing.[52]

4.2 Case Law: Social Insurance Benefits for Relatives Who Take on Public Responsibilities?

As mentioned above, the preparatory works on short-term care benefits emphasize both the importance of not transferring public responsibility for elder care to relatives, and the need to take several different circumstances into account when assessing the right to short-term care allowance. In judgments by higher courts on short-term care allowance, the latter point of departure is absent, whereas the former is repeatedly cited as a ground for not granting short-term care allowance.

In a few cases, denial of allowance can be explained by the fact that care has been given under circumstances that were proposed as, but never actually made, grounds for short-term care benefits by different government inquiries. This applies to cases where care has been given to a person who is at home while awaiting care in a hospital or another public-care institution, or recovering after medical treatment. However, such circumstances do not automatically mean that the person in question is not 'severely ill'.

---

51 Government Bill Prop 1987/88:176 99-100. Cf 1988/89:SOU 6 73–4.

52 Government Bill Prop 1991/102:106 17.

One such case from 1990 concerns a 39-year-old daughter who helped her ill mother, who was suffering from severe dementia, while awaiting further support from public healthcare.[53] The mother had not yet received a place in a nursing home, so she had moved temporarily to a new home closer to that of her daughter. The move had increased her confusion and caused aggression and anxiety. She was assessed by a doctor as 'mentally ill' and in need of virtually continuous attention during the daytime. As long as no other type of care could be arranged, the mother was in need of constant care by her daughter, according to the medical certificate. She was unable to take care of herself, to an extent that put her life in danger.

The daughter was denied short-term care benefits on the ground that the mother's condition was not life-threatening. The highest court that was responsible for these legal issues at the time – the Insurance Court of Appeal – referred to statements from the preparatory works that social service or healthcare deficiencies must not lead to relatives feeling obliged to provide care; private short-term care should be voluntary and serve as a complement to different types of public care. The fact that not receiving care would pose an imminent threat to the mother's life was not taken into account.

In another case from 1990, a middle-aged man caring for his father was denied short-term care allowance – less surprisingly, because the son did not put forward any evidence suggesting that his father had life-threatening health problems.[54] The father, who suffered from dementia and had greatly reduced mobility, had been awaiting a place in hospital following the illness and hospitalization of his wife, who had previously functioned as his caregiver. The son argued that the purpose of short-term care allowance was to enable relatives to assist those close to them in difficult situations and to be an important complement to public elder care services. Here, the Court once again referred to the statements from the preparatory works that relatives should not have to take on public responsibilities.

A more recent judgment from 2014 concerns a very similar situation. In this case, a middle-aged woman was helping her mother.[55] The mother who had several serious health conditions and had broken her arm, needed assistance to use the medical equipment necessary for being able to breathe, drink and eat. Here, as well, the ordinary caregiver – the mother's husband – was hospitalized, and therefore could not assist. A

---

53 Case from Försäkringsöverdomstolen: FÖD 2669/90.

54 Case from Försäkringsöverdomstolen: FÖD 1244/90.

55 Kammarrätten i Göteborg Case No. 3656-14.

doctor had certified that the mother needed the assistance of a relative in this situation. The courts that assessed the case acknowledged the need for assistance, but concluded that there was no significant or imminent threat to the mother's life and therefore no right to family care allowance could be claimed. Once again, by reference to the preparatory works, it was stated that public authorities have the responsibility to provide the care and assistance that is needed. The purpose of family care allowance was to give families the opportunity to be together in difficult times.

These two cases demonstrate how provision of elder care, even if considered a public responsibility, often depends in practice on relatives. In both cases mentioned here, the need for family care arose when the normal caregiver – a spouse, also elderly and in both cases afflicted by health problems of his/her own – became unable to perform care work for his/her ill spouse.

Finally, in a case from 2013 a daughter claimed the right to short-term care allowance for accompanying her 88-year-old mother to hospital and taking part in the planning of her future care.[56] According to a medical certificate the mother had several physical health conditions, as well as dementia, which was worsened by her deteriorating domestic situation. The certificate also affirmed that the mother's condition would be better served if she was with relatives.

In this case, unlike the ones discussed above, it was clear that assistance with the hospital visit had been requested from the public home-care service, but that it had been denied due to a lack of resources. The Court concluded – in line with previous judgments – that relatives should not have to perform care work that is a public responsibility, and denied the daughter family care allowance because there was no imminent threat to the mother's life.

Thus, family care allowance is routinely denied when relatives perform care work that is considered a public responsibility, even in cases where the care institutions responsible declare themselves unable to assist. The ambition not to 'force' care work on relatives is in line with the general ambitions of the Swedish welfare state, but becomes somewhat ironic in cases where circumstances entail that care work is, and in some cases apparently must be, performed by relatives. Because the legally enforceable right to demand that public health and service institutions fulfil their responsibilities is very limited, it could be argued that – according to the preparatory works of the legislation – such circumstances should be taken into account when determining the right to family care allowance.

---

56 Kammarrätten i Jönköping Case No. 1195-13.

5. ELDER CARE AS A GENDERED QUESTION

As we have seen, family care is a predominantly female task. After declarations of gender equality goals in the 1980s, this matter has seldom been discussed in the preparatory works of the legislation on support for family caregivers. According to our view, this contributes to rendering the nature of care work – that is, its nature as precisely work – invisible.

5.1 Feminist Perspectives on Care

Questions about care work, such as who should take responsibility, how it is distributed and compensated and what the consequences are for care responsibilities, have long been regarded as key feminist issues.[57] A basic problem has been that this category of work, in a traditional societal understanding of the concept, does not include the unpaid care that takes place within the family. The special qualities of care work are difficult to capture in a definition of work based on a male norm. This leads to care being undervalued in different ways.

The concept of work has traditionally been understood in terms of male life structures, placed outside the home, in a public sphere. Care work has other qualities; it is usually performed in a private sphere and is associatively linked to family bonds and love. This tends to make care work invisible or undervalued. By paying attention to work carried out in the home, the existing dominant conceptions of work can be extended to include the unpaid caring work traditionally done by women.[58] The feminist sociologist Kathi Weeks states that one of the reasons that care is not widely recognized or valued as work is that it is based on emotional involvement in an everyday practice – by working with managing emotions to achieve a particular social effect – which is something that traditionally belongs to the private and the female sphere. She believes, however, that care is based on an 'active emotional effort',

---

[57] See for example, Chantal Mouffe, *Deliberative Democracy or Agonistic Pluralism* (Institute for Advanced Studies 2000); Hima Shamir, 'The public/private distinction now: The challenges of privatization and of the regulatory state' (2014) 15(1) Theoretical Inq L 1–25; Martha Fineman, 'The vulnerable subject: Anchoring equality in the human condition' (2008) 20(1) Yale J L and Feminism 8.

[58] Kathi Weeks, 'Life within and against work: Affective labor, feminist critique, and post-Fordist politics' (2007) Ephemera 233.

which is something that requires skill and should therefore be treated as work. Like all social practices it is constitutive of the person doing it, which contributes to the naturalization of women as 'emotional beings'. To act caringly is a practice that forms the subject and becomes part of the personality, in an interaction between personality, practice and gendered expectations. Therefore, it may be more difficult to see the *work* in care.[59] With the development of the welfare state, care responsibilities have increasingly been taken over by the public. However, formal care is also predominantly a female and undervalued (low-paid) type of work. It is problematic to distinguish between formal and informal care in qualitative terms, because such a division is based on the notion that informal care – in other words, care provided by family members – is necessarily better because it is carried out with 'love'. However, formal care must also be based on emotional involvement. It is important to keep track of both aspects: informal care work also includes work, and formal care work is also based on consideration.[60]

When one claims that women choose to care for relatives, on an unpaid basis 'out of love', it is on the premise that there is an innate authenticity of the feeling in a way that rarely occurs in men. Weeks notes, however, that there is no such thing as an 'unmanaged heart'.[61] Feelings do not independently appear but are a product of a socialization process, although they are obviously perceived as true for those who have them. As many feminist theorists have noted, the private sphere is full of political power relations that set the pattern and guide our behaviour, although in each case there can be elements of freedom of choice.[62]

5.2 Gender Equality in Relation to Support to Caregivers

In the 1983 report of the Committee on Family Care, both short-term care and more permanent family care were discussed as a gender equality issue. It was assumed that family care had 'always' been a female task,

---

[59] Ibid 240–41.

[60] Clare Ungerson, '"Betalning för omsorg" – europeiska tendenser och feministiska dilemman' in Marta Szebehely and Rosmari Eliasson-Lappalainen (eds), *Vad förgår och vad består? En antologi om äldreomsorg, kvinnosyn och socialpolitik* (Arkiv 1998) 102.

[61] Weeks (2007), above n 58, 244.

[62] Åsa Gunnarsson and Eva-Maria Svensson, *Genusrättsvetenskap* (Studentlitteratur 2009) 207–10.

and that women would probably continue to have primary responsibility for such work, both privately and 'in society's so-called health care sector'.

Despite the limited belief conveyed in this report with respect to achieving fundamental changes to gender structures, there was an ambition to increase gender equality by introducing a right to leave for family care. Many women left employment after being denied leave to take care of relatives. As a result middle-aged women – a dominant category among family caregivers – could find it difficult to return to the labour market. Men, on the other hand, appeared to prioritize waged work and the role of family provider, but they were also denied leave for family care more often than women. The Committee made the assessment that a right to leave for family care would give women greater opportunities to keep their jobs and also increase the status of care work, which in turn should also make it easier for men to take time off work for family care.[63]

Studying the legislative works on support for long-term family caregivers reveals a development between the report of 1994 and the amendment of 2009. In the first report, it is stated that it is 'unrealistic' to hope for further efforts from relatives in the future. Relatives are not going to take on care responsibilities 'unreflectingly', since family roles and gender roles are supposed to change.[64] The report from 2009, on the other hand, suggests a return to a collective family concept in the context of elder care. What is striking in the legislative documents studied is the naturalization and individualization of family care. Gender and other social structures surrounding care are seldom mentioned. Instead, in several instances caring relations are described as 'unique' and 'non-homogeneous'.[65] However, family caregiving is surrounded by societal structures, and this enables the unpaid work of caring for older relatives to be unequally distributed. The lack of problematization of these societal structures tends to hide the unjust effects of placing increased elder care burdens on families.

The individualization discourse leads to a decontextualization of older people's care needs from conditions that are linked to gender, class and ethnicity. Helene Brodin claims that today the argument that women, for 'natural reasons', are better caregivers is not viable. The fact that it is mainly women, who for social reasons feel the need to act as caregivers,

---

[63] Government Inquiry Report SOU 1983:64 92–3.
[64] Government Inquiry Report SOU 1994:139 330.
[65] See for example, Government Bill Prop 1996/97:124 131.

is instead hidden behind an individualized rhetoric, where the distribution of caring responsibilities is assumed to be a consequence of individual choices. This idea masks both a socialization process where women take on larger caring responsibilities and a lack of sufficient and good public alternatives to family care.[66]

One striking aspect is that elder care is seldom discussed in the context of gender equality politics. Ulmanen draws the conclusion that even though the amount of family care given to older persons by middle-aged children, especially daughters, has increased, this has not been seen in the general discourses on the subject. In the discourse on gender equality and care, the focus has been on childcare and the need for parents. When it comes to the discourse on family care, this has primarily focused on family caregivers within the family – that is to say spouses, and their needs and situations.[67]

6. CONCLUSIONS

Family care for older people has increased in recent decades and gained a new role in the Swedish elder care system. The political ambitions have changed since the 1970s, when family care was supposed to gradually become redundant. In the 1980s, this goal remained, even though strained public finances had now emerged as a threat to the ongoing advancement of the welfare state. However, there was still belief in welfare state progress. Not only was elder care supposed to gradually become an exclusively public responsibility, in terms of both financing and actual care work, short-term family care was to be economically remunerated in several situations where older people could need extra support from people close to them. Even if it cannot be completely excluded as an implicit motive, these future reforms were not at all described as aiming to transfer public responsibilities for elder care to relatives. Instead, the reforms seemed to aim to increase quality of life for elderly people with health problems and for their relatives.

In the 1990s, long-term family care was seen as a solution to temporary economic problems of the welfare state. As for short-term care, the idea of expanding the scope of the legislation to new situations – such as family care while the elderly waited for public care – was no longer mentioned. Instead, case law on short-term family care started to appear, and the courts were clear that short-term family care benefits

66 Brodin (2005), above n 17, 203–5.
67 Ulmanen (2015), above n 6, 70.

should not be used to finance private care work that was actually part of public responsibilities. As we have seen, this is still a central principle of short-term family care case law.

More recently, an ideal of long-term family care as something positive and desirable has emerged. The discursive shift has occurred on two levels: on one level is the downsizing of elder care as an answer to an economic crisis, and on the other is a changed view of the family, and ideas about what should belong to the public and private spheres.

It could be argued that there is a discrepancy within the legislation, between the Social Services Act's claim that elder care is a public responsibility and the same Act's regulation on support for family caregivers. The claim that family care should be a voluntary commitment is repeated again and again in the studied material. On the other hand, the fact that family caregivers now exist as a category in the law is a sign of the continued and future existence of family caregiving. It becomes clear that due to downsizing in the public-care system, the legislation on support for family caregivers is part of a process in which family care is becoming increasingly important as a part of the elder care system and in fact less and less voluntary.

The economic crisis discourse goes hand in hand with reduced ambitions for the welfare state when it comes to older people in need of care. The statutory public responsibility is still there, but the actual level of elder care is lower, family care is more frequently taken for granted and the municipalities increasingly consider the family unit as the subject to help, rather than the older individual. Municipal elder care is seen as a complement, sharing the responsibility for older people's needs in a 'partnership' between the family and publicly financed care. In accordance with this discourse, it becomes reasonable to provide support to the family unit rather than the individual.

This, however, is not reflected in short-term family care legislation or case law. It must be said that the legal rules in question have no direct potential to transform the division of care work between professionals and relatives. Perhaps this is part of the reason that courts instead reinforce the invisibility of care work performed by relatives, arguing that their work should be a public responsibility – even in cases where this responsibility is clearly not taken.

The policy documents contain little discussion of issues such as gender, class and ethnicity, even though studies show that due to socialization processes and societal expectations, these factors are important in understanding the actual distribution of care responsibilities and work. Gender is addressed only in the relatively optimistic reasoning of the 1980s documents, and short-term family care benefits are presented as a tool for enabling women to combine waged work and family care, as well as an instrument designed to legitimize men's participation in family care work, even if they are family providers.

The fact that these aspects are usually not handled in the policy process means that they will not influence the legislative solutions to problems detected in relation to family care. In that way, the discourse 'excludes' problems and political solutions based on an understanding of the social reality that surrounds family care. By describing family caregiving as natural and families as unquestioningly positive, unjust structures and distribution of unpaid care work are legitimized. This naturalization is explained by theories indicating that the general perception of care is an emotional exercise rather than work. The lines of conflict that manifest themselves in the discourse also show how, in order to seem reasonable, the support models developed in the legislative documents – designed primarily to provide recognition and 'feel-good' activities for caregivers – are dependent on certain discursive conditions. They rely on individual explanation models, a premise that most caregivers want to give family care to the extent that they do, and a negligence of the economic problems that could be connected to extensive family caregiving.

A reading of the legislative processes shows that increased family care could be understood as a transition from one welfare model to another, where a partial reprivatization of elder care has taken place. The emergence of special support systems for caregivers reflects and reinforces the change. Providing support to caregivers becomes a way of 'greasing the wheels' of the transition to private care.

It is clear from our study that care work is undervalued. This relates to its association with feminineness. Most importantly, care work is not seen as work but rather as a 'natural' female activity. The regulation on support for caregivers has partly given recognition to family caregivers and their situation. However, the social structures surrounding care work are not recognized; nor are many of the difficulties that caregivers face. Care work is unpaid or underpaid, a fact that primarily affects women, especially those from a non-Swedish, working-class background. According to the discourse of recent years, family care is seen as a welfare resource with economic dimensions, which is supposed to solve an economic crisis for the municipalities. However, the caregivers themselves are not compensated economically for their work, within the support system for family caregivers. On the contrary, unpaid caregiving is replacing publicly financed care.

13. Perspectives on solidarity in social security, healthcare and medical research

Titti Mattsson, Martina Axmin and Emma Holm

1. INTRODUCTION[1]

The European Union (EU) has declared itself a highly competitive social market economy.[2] This declaration gives rise to the question of how to combine social principles with principles of a market. The topic is highly relevant due to the massive demographic change that is taking place in the Union and the expected social, economic, budgetary and political consequences. In this chapter, we are particularly interested in how the principle of solidarity distributes, in a coordinated way, both authority and obligations to the Member States and older EU citizens. Solidarity is a term that usually refers to the feeling of unity and belonging between people or the unity of a group or a nation that is based on community of interests, objectives, and standards.[3] The principle of solidarity is essential to the notion of a social Europe and has also been central to EU legislation as well as case law in many areas.[4] It is referred to in various objectives of the EU, such as the promotion of solidarity among Member States and among generations, and is a guiding principle for the Union

---

[1] This work was carried out within the Norma Elder Law Research Environment (www.jur.lu.se/elderlaw) funded by Ragnar Söderberg's Foundation and the Marianne and Marcus Wallenberg Foundation.

[2] Article 3.3 Treaty of the European Union (TEU).

[3] See for example, Merriam Webster, www.merriam-webster.com/dictionary/solidarity, accessed 8 December 2015.

[4] Articles 2, 3.3, 21 and 80 TEU. See also Catherine Barnard, 'EU citizenship and the principle of solidarity' in Michael Dougan and Eleanor Spaventa (eds), *Social Welfare and EU Law* (Hart Publishing 2005).

and the Member States when acting on the global level.[5] The principle of solidarity is also reflected in the EU Charter of Fundamental Rights – particularly in Chapter IV of the Charter, which is aptly titled 'Solidarity'. The chapter includes various social rights, such as the entitlement to social security benefits, social assistance and healthcare.

The notion of solidarity in the EU context has had an impact on academic debate, especially since the entry into force of the Lisbon Treaty. Various scholars have been concerned about the impact of EU law on national solidarity,[6] whereas others have been more occupied with whether solidarity exists at EU level and if so, how the normative content of such a transnational solidarity can be defined.[7]

The principle of solidarity is also a concept that is well known in the context of national welfare models in general. The very idea of solidarity presupposes belonging to a closed group or community committed to sharing social goods. A welfare state, in very simple terms, constitutes a community where the belonging of the citizen is based on nationality, residence or employment. Although different welfare models can be distinguished in Europe, most national systems contain several benefits based on the principle of solidarity and not related to any form of earnings through previous employment. Examples of such benefits are family benefits, guaranteed pension and healthcare. The latter two are of particular importance for the elderly population.

Traditionally, the European Member States have seen their welfare systems as 'free' from EU law. However, since the introduction of Union citizenship in the mid-1990s, the EU legislator and the Court of Justice of the European Union (CJEU) have gradually moved away from focusing solely on workers' rights to free movement and benefits in the new host state. It has been said that a certain degree of financial solidarity must be upheld between nationals of a host Member State and nationals of other Member States as regards social benefits, and that any restrictions to free

---

5 See for example, Malcolm Ross and Yuri Borgmann-Prebil (eds), *Promoting Solidarity in the European Union* (Oxford University Press 2010).

6 See for example, Tamara Hervey, 'Social solidarity: A buttress against internal market law?' in Jo Shaw (ed.), *Social Law and Policy in an Evolving European Union* (Hart Publishing 2000); Gráinne de Búrca (ed.), *EU Law and the Welfare State: In Search of Solidarity* (Oxford University Press 2005); and Michael Dougan and Eleanor Spaventa (eds), *Social Welfare and EU Law* (Hart Publishing 2005).

7 See for example, Michael Dougan and Eleanor Spaventa, '"Wish You Weren't Here …": New models of social solidarity in the European Union' in Dougan and Spaventa (2005), above n 6; and Andrea Sangiovanni, 'Solidarity in the European Union' (2013) 33 Oxford J Legal Stud 213.

movement must be made in accordance with the proportionality principle.[8] As will be described below, however, recent case law from the CJEU shows that there is a shift back to economic activity and self-sufficiency as preconditions for free movement and social benefits.

An example of this concerns access to certain solidarity benefits covered by Regulation 883/2004 on coordination of the social security systems of the Member States.[9] These benefits are called special non-contributory benefits or hybrid benefits. In national legislation they are intended to supplement social security benefits, such as an extra supplement to retired persons with low old-age pensions.[10] These benefits are residence-based and have some features similar to those of social assistance benefits, which are normally excluded from the scope of the Regulation. Their specific character has led to a solution where – in contrast to the Regulation's main principle on work-state affiliation – the benefits are always granted in accordance with the legislation in the state of residence and may not be exported to other Member States.[11]

Access to available healthcare is an important issue for older persons. The healthcare systems in Europe are also an example of an area where most national systems have benefits based on solidarity and that are not related to any form of earnings through previous employment.[12] The principle of solidarity is recognized by the EU as one of the values shared by the Member States for healthcare.[13] Another common characteristic regarding the European healthcare systems is health as a territorial right. Healthcare has traditionally been financed and provided for those residing within the state. Today, the European Member States offer a universal right to healthcare for those residing within the territory of the state, based on solidarity. Resources are being redistributed in accordance

---

8 *Grzelczyk* C-184/99 EU:C:2001:458.

9 Regulation (EC) No. 883/2004 of the European Parliament and of the Council of 29 April 2004 on the coordination of social security systems, OJ 2004 L 166/1.

10 For example, the Swedish elderly maintenance support (*äldreförsörjningsstöd*) and housing supplement for pensioners (*bostadstillägg för pensionärer*).

11 Article 70 Regulation 883/2004. See Hervig Verschueren, 'Free movement or benefit tourism: The unreasonable burden of Brey' (2014) 16 Eur J Migr Law 159.

12 Anna Christensen and Mattias Malmstedt, '*Lex loci laboris* versus *lex loci domicilii* – an inquiry into the normative foundations of European social security law' (2000) 2 Eur J Social Security 71. Another example is guaranteed pensions.

13 The Council of the European Union, 'Conclusion on common values and principles in the European Union health systems' (2006) OJ C 146/3.

with the principle of solidarity within the territory of the state. However, as we shall see, the EU rules on cross-border healthcare challenge this principle.

Furthermore, the principle of solidarity has always been a fundamental motivation for allowing research on humans, to develop more advanced and efficient healthcare. The argument is basically that that there is a general obligation as a member of a community to contribute to the health and wellbeing of the whole.[14] The EU has a major role to play in supporting and coordinating research and innovation in Europe. This includes research for the active ageing part of the 2020 EU Strategy, and during recent years research has expanded significantly in the areas of age-related health problems and ageing.[15] The solidarity principle is the main argument for allowing research on human beings where the objective is to build better healthcare for older populations and future generations.

However, application of the solidarity principle is challenged during crisis and upheaval. Europe is currently undergoing both of these, in the form of rapid demographic changes, greater mobility and economic difficulties. The question arises how these societal changes challenge European legal systems originally based on solidarity. One crucial challenge is assuring sufficient solidarity and inclusion for non-economically active older persons. Intergenerational conflict is often referred to as one of the possible outcomes of the demographic trend. At the same time, one of the goals of the EU is to promote solidarity between generations.[16] The principle of solidarity is thus considered to be a core value in European social welfare systems and one of the core values shared by the Member States. At the same time, another characteristic of European social welfare systems is the right to benefits as a territorial right. What we can now see is European integration leading to increased mobility, for example for retired and older persons. This

14 See for example, John Harris, 'Scientific research is a moral duty' (2005) 31 J Med Ethics 242.

15 During the period of the seventh framework programme for research and technological development (FP7), with a total budget of over 50 billion EUR for the period 2007–13, a lot of research was funded in the areas of active and healthy ageing, including technological innovation to support independent living of older citizens; electronic inclusion and e-health; solutions for longer working lives; and research into new treatments of diseases more common in elderly populations. See 'The EU contribution to active ageing and solidarity between generations' (EU 2012) 10: http://ec.europa.eu/social/main.jsp?catId=738&langId=en&pubId=6920&visible=1.

16 Article 3 TEU.

integration process challenges the traditional conceptions of solidarity. Today European societies are facing considerable pressure on their social welfare systems due to decreasing financial resources and demographic changes with increasing proportions of persons above 65 years of age.

This chapter aims to investigate the principle of solidarity from the perspective of social security, healthcare and medical research with this European development in mind, and to analyse the situation in legal terms with a focus on older people. We discuss the ways in which increased mobility challenges the European legal systems that were founded on solidarity and what remains of the original ideas of the principle as a basic component of the European welfare regime.

2. SOCIAL SECURITY BENEFITS – SOLIDARITY IN RELATION TO NON-ECONOMICALLY ACTIVE UNION CITIZENS

2.1 The EU Legal Framework on the Right to Entry and Residence

Starting out as first and foremost economic community, the European integration has expanded its cooperation to new fields over the years, such as the social dimension of the internal market. In December 1989 a Community Charter of Fundamental Social Rights of Workers was adopted. The Social Charter was purely a declaratory measure, however, focused on the economically active. The 1993 Treaty of Maastricht was an important development towards a closer-knit EU. The Treaty also introduced the notion of EU citizenship, which entitles every Union national to certain rights – including the right to move and reside within the territory of the Member States. The next development towards the completion of the internal market was the entering into force of the Lisbon Treaty in 2009, which made the Charter of Fundamental Rights from 2000 legally binding. In the Treaty of Lisbon in 2009 it was laid down that the EU is based on a social market economy.[17]

Workers have in principle an unconditional right to reside in a host state and be treated equally with the new host state's own nationals. The boundaries for the rights of non-economically active persons were discussed in the case law of the CJEU shortly after the insertion of provisions on Union citizenship in the Treaty. Although existing directives concerning the free movement of non-actives contain requirements

[17] Article 3.3 TEU.

on sufficient resources in order not to become a burden on the new host state, the Court established the direct effect of the new treaty provision. It was also stated that Union citizens legally residing in another Member State were entitled to equal treatment in relation to benefits, regardless of their economic activity.[18] Even those who did not fulfil the Directive's requirements on sufficient resources could not automatically be deprived of the right to reside. According to the Court the secondary legislation – stating that the burden must be unreasonable – 'accepts a certain degree of financial solidarity between nationals of a host Member State and nationals of other Member States, particularly if the difficulties which a beneficiary of the right of residence encounters are temporary'.[19]

The Member States were permitted in other cases to uphold conditions aimed at showing that the Union citizen had demonstrated a certain degree of integration into the society of that state, for example having resided in a state for a certain period of time, but only as long as such conditions were deemed to be proportionate.[20]

Issues regarding Union citizens' right to entry and residence in other Member States are now regulated in Directive 2004/38 (the Residence Directive).[21] For Union citizens other than workers, requirements on self-sufficiency and comprehensive sickness insurance must be fulfilled, in order not to become an unreasonable burden on the social assistance system of the host state. In addition, the right to equal treatment is limited for this group. The Directive gives no guidance as to the types of benefits that constitute social assistance. Nor has the Community legislator given any guidance as to the priority between the Residence Directive and Regulation 883/2004.[22] Elderly persons constitute a significant share of non-economically active Union citizens.[23] The issue of legal residence

---

[18] *Martínez Sala* C-85/96 EU:C:1998:217.

[19] *Grzelczyk*, above n 8, para 44.

[20] See for example, *Bidar* C-209/03 EU:C:2005:169 paras 56–63.

[21] Directive 2004/38/EC of the European Parliament and of the Council of 29 April 2004 on the right of citizens of the Union and their family members to move and reside freely within the territory of the Member States amending Regulation (EEC) No. 1612/68 and repealing Directives 64/221/EEC, 68/360/EEC, 72/194/EEC, 73/148/EEC, 75/34/EEC, 75/35/EEC, 90/364/EEC, 90/365/EEC and 93/96/EEC, OJ 2004 L 158/77.

[22] M Coucheir, M Sakslin. S Giubboni, D Martinsen and H Verschueren, Think Tank Report 2008 'The relationship and interaction between the coordination Regulations and Directive 2004/38/EC' (trEss, European Commission/Ghent University 2008) 3.

[23] ICF and Milieu Ltd, 'A fact finding analysis on the impact on the Member States' social security systems of the entitlements of non-active intra-EU

is thus of particular importance. Notably, receiving an old-age pension in accordance with Regulation 883/2004 may lead to the fulfilment of the condition of self-sufficiency. However, the pension levels vary between the Member States and the pensioner may be forced to rely on social assistance benefits in the new host state.

2.2 Applicable Legislation and Solidarity-Based Benefits

In order to ensure free movement of workers, it was early deemed necessary to establish a system of coordination of the different national social security systems within the EU. Social security systems are traditionally based on the idea of territoriality – demanding that the person has worked or lived in the state in question or is a national of that state.[24] In a cross-border situation within the Union, this could have a negative effect for the persons concerned. Article 48 of the Treaty therefore states certain principles of coordination, which are further developed in Regulation 883/2004. The Regulation provides a method for identifying the Member State social security system that will provide coverage for a migrating person. Coordination means that each Member State still determines the national provisions on social security, but that certain national provisions might be disregarded in cross-border situations, namely provisions with a discriminatory effect. Examples of such provisions are conditions regarding residence, which may not be upheld against a person working in a Member State, and where the Regulation provisions stating that the social security legislation of the state of employment is to apply.

The first secondary legislation concerning social security coordination was adopted back in 1958, in Regulation No. 3. In 1971, this regulation was replaced by the infamous Regulation 1408/71. At that time, free movement within the Community was reserved for the economically active. The social security systems of the original EC Member States were based on employment, so it was natural to choose the state of employment – *lex loci laboris* – as the main rule for applicable legislation.[25]

With time, it became apparent that the rules on applicable legislation sometimes leave migrating persons in limbo. *Ten Holder*[26] concerned a

---

migrants to special non-contributory cash benefits and healthcare granted on the basis of residence' (2013) 200.

24 Christensen and Malmstedt (2000), above n 12, 69.

25 Ibid 76.

26 *Ten Holder* C-302/84 EU:C:1986:242.

woman who had worked in Germany and lived in the Netherlands. In accordance with the *lex loci laboris* principle, she became entitled to German sickness benefit. After a while, the benefits in Germany expired, since they were time-limited according to national legislation. Due to her residence the woman was entitled to benefits in the Netherlands, in accordance with the national provisions. However, since the rules on applicable legislation in the Regulation were considered to be exclusive, the Member State of residence was not allowed to grant benefits. This was an expression of the single-state principle established in the Regulation.

In order to remedy this situation a new rule was inserted in the Regulation, stating that a person for whom the legislation of a Member State ceased to be applicable should be subject to the legislation of the state in which he or she resides, in accordance with the provisions of that legislation alone. The legislation of the state of residence, *lex loci domicilii* was thus introduced as applicable legislation. A person who had ceased working could now be granted benefits from the state of residence in accordance with its legislation, instead of being stuck in the system of the state of employment without any actual right to benefits there. The new rule was given a wide interpretation. Even those who had ceased working, for example due to child-rearing, were considered subject to the legislation of the state of residence as opposed to the legislation of the previous state of employment.[27]

The *lex loci laboris* principle came to be challenged further when new Member States with residence-based systems joined the EU and more residence-based benefits were introduced in national legislations. Another important factor was the general shift in EU law from free movement for workers to free movement for all Union citizens. The insertion of rules on Union citizenship in the Treaty in the 1990s meant that Regulation 1408/71, with its primary focus on economically active persons, began to seem outdated; it was replaced by a new regulation in 2004.

One of the main novelties in the successor, Regulation 883/2004, is thus that it applies to all Union citizens who are or have been covered by a Member State's social security system. The *lex loci domicilii* principle is also more generally formulated, stating simply that persons for whom the other rules on applicable legislation do not apply, shall be subject to the legislation of the Member State of residence.

---

27 *Kuusijärvi* C-275/96 EU:C:1998:279. See also *Elsen* C-135/99 EU:C:2000:647 and *Kauer* C-28/00 EU:C:2002:82, where the women in question were considered to have a link to the previous state of employment.

Non-economically active persons may thus be entitled to residence-based benefits, such as special non-contributory benefits and healthcare, when moving to a new Member State. The increased importance of the *lex loci domicilii* principle is also demonstrated by the need to define clearly the concept of residence; this definition is found in the implementing Regulation 987/2009. A number of factors must be considered when determining whether a person is residing in a Member State; ultimately it comes down to the person's intention.[28] The issue of legal residence in accordance with other EU rules is not mentioned. Notably, being covered by the legislation of a Member State due to residence in that state grants a right to equal treatment in that state, in accordance with Article 4 of Regulation 883/2004.

In conclusion, Regulation 883/2004 seems to provide possibilities for non-actives to receive some solidarity-based benefits in other Member States. As for the elderly, the special non-contributory benefits are of particular importance, since they aim at providing a minimum level of subsistence. A majority of the special non-contributory benefits provided by the EU Member States are related to old age/death or disability.[29] For some pensioners, getting access to such benefits may be crucial to be able to live in the new host state.

2.3 Solidarity Revised? Recent Case Law Concerning Non-Economically Active Union Citizens

The fear of social tourism seems to have increased in recent years, leading to Member States wanting to restrict the possibilities for non-actives to receive benefits.[30] Lately, the Court in particular has been faced with cases concerning restrictions on the right to non-contributory benefits, which according to Regulation 883/2004 shall be granted by the state of residence. As mentioned above, non-actives may be covered by the legislation of the state of residence and claim equal treatment as regards benefits covered by the Regulation. By imposing conditions on legal residence in order to receive such benefits, some Member States have tried to avoid payment of such benefits to non-actives from other Member States. The question has arisen whether this is compatible with EU law. In recent case law, the limits of solidarity between the Member States in this regard have been put to the test.

---

28 Article 11 Regulation 987/2009.

29 ICF and Milieu (2013), above n 23, 203.

30 Ibid 199.

The *Brey* case concerned a German man who left Germany and moved to Austria with his wife. He received a small retirement pension and applied for an Austrian benefit called compensatory supplement (*Ausgleichszulage*), which is included in Regulation 883/2004 as a non-contributory benefit.[31] According to Austrian law, the granting of such a supplement presupposed fulfilling the conditions on lawful residence as stipulated in the Residence Directive, namely having comprehensive sickness insurance and sufficient resources to avoid having to request social assistance benefits or the compensatory supplement. The question arose whether the fact that a person applied for this special non-contributory benefit actually meant that he became a burden on the social assistance system in the meaning of the Residence Directive. The Court found that the benefit at issue, although covered by Regulation 883/2004, was indeed to be regarded as social assistance. The Court then stated that according to its case law[32] there was nothing to prevent the granting of social security benefits to non-actives from being made conditional upon those citizens meeting the necessary requirements for obtaining a legal right to residence in the host state. However, although the fact of a non-active person being eligible to receive compensatory benefit, in light of his low pension, could be an indication that the person does not have sufficient resources not to become a burden, the national authority must make an overall assessment of the specific burden the granting of the benefit would cause.

As the Court emphasizes, the right to freedom of movement is the general rule and the conditions on legal residence in the Residence Directive must be construed narrowly and in compliance with the proportionality principle. The mere fact that a person receives social assistance is not sufficient to show that he or she constitutes an unreasonable burden on the social assistance system. A general condition excluding non-active Union citizens from receiving a particular social security benefit, such as the Austrian rule in question, did not enable the authorities to make an overall assessment.

In the *Dano* case the Court was again faced with the issue of right to residence in relation to special non-contributory benefits.[33] It concerned a Romanian citizen who resided in Germany with her child. She had never worked, had no education and did not plan to search for work in Germany. The question was whether it was allowed for Germany to

---

31 *Brey* C-140/12 EU:C:2013:565.

32 For example, *Martínez Sala*, above n 18, and *Trojani* C-456/02 EU:C:2004:488.

33 *Dano* C-333/13 EU:C:2014:2358.

uphold a national provision excluding the granting of a special non-contributory benefit to persons who had entered Germany to claim social assistance or whose right to residence stemmed only from seeking employment.

In the *Dano* case, the Court stated that the principle of equal treatment in Regulation 883/2004 does indeed apply in relation to special non-contributory benefits. Still, the Court argued that Member States must have the possibility of refusing to grant social benefits to economically inactive Union citizens who exercise their right to freedom of movement solely in order to obtain another Member State's social assistance – even when they lack sufficient resources to claim a right of residence. To deny the Member State that possibility would mean that persons who do not have sufficient resources to provide for themselves in the new host state would receive these resources automatically, through the grant of a special non-contributory cash benefit which is intended to cover the beneficiary's subsistence costs.

The *Brey* and *Dano* cases are difficult to reconcile; in the former case the Court did not accept legislation that automatically excluded non-actives, but in the latter it made no such objection.[34] One may wonder if the fact that Mr Brey was a pensioner and had some means of his own had an impact on the Court's decision not to accept a general exclusion from the right to benefits. Ms Dano was a non-economically active Union citizen in a stricter sense. On the other hand, a pensioner's dependence on the benefit cannot be expected to be short-term.

The later judgment in the *Alimanovic* case, concerning persons who had worked for a short while in the host state, shows that the Court adheres to the principles established in *Dano* by stating that no assessment of the individual person's situation has to be made.[35] The cases show that once again, economic activity is a precondition for equal treatment. Member States do indeed have the possibility automatically to exclude non-active persons, such as pensioners, from the right to certain solidarity-based benefits covered by Regulation 883/2004. The rules in the Residence Directive seem to play out quite clearly in the rules of the Regulation. For elderly persons this issue is particularly relevant because

---

[34] For in-depth analysis of the cases see Niamh Nic Shuibhne, 'Limits rising, duties ascending: The changing legal shape of Union citizenship' (2015) 52 CML Rev 889 and Daniel Thym, 'The elusive limits of solidarity: Residence rights of and social benefits for economically inactive union citizens' (2015) 52 CML Rev 17.

[35] *Alimanovic* C-67/14 EU:C:2015:597.

special non-contributory benefits are often supplements to old-age pensions. Pensioners with small pensions will thus have difficulties moving to a Member State with higher costs of living. The discretion of the Member States when it comes to granting such benefits to non-actives will be wide and the issue of solidarity seems to have been set aside in the later case law of the Court.

3. CROSS-BORDER HEALTHCARE – UNDERMINING SOLIDARITY WITHIN THE STATE?

3.1 European National Health Systems and EU Law Impact

The legal development and case law concerning social security benefits is also relevant in relation to healthcare benefits. A question that needs attention here involves the significance of the legal development described for the healthcare sector in the EU. As part of the social welfare state, each healthcare system has been developed in its own historical, social, political and cultural context, and the EU Member States vary considerably in the organization of their healthcare systems. Nevertheless, although different types of healthcare systems can be observed in Europe, Member States have systems implying a certain redistribution of resources on a collective level in accordance with the principle of solidarity. All of these systems have a more or less redistributive element based on national solidarity. In the literature, various concepts of typologies have been put forward to describe the differences among European healthcare systems. One common and frequently used distinction is based on how the systems are financed: social health insurance systems and national health systems.[36]

Social health insurance systems, also called the Bismarck model, are financed by insurance premiums or contributions, whereas national health systems, or the Beveridge model, are publicly financed through general taxation. Furthermore, among social health insurance systems, a distinction could be made between systems that provide benefits-in-kind and those that reimburse healthcare costs.[37] In a benefits-in-kind system the payment is made directly by the insurance fund to the care provider. In a

---

36 Elke Jakubowski and Reinhard Busse, *Health Care Systems in Europe – A Comparative Study* (European Parliament 1998). See also Susanne Grosse-Tebbe and Josef Figueras (eds), *Snapshots of Health Systems* (WHO 2005).

37 See for example, the MISSOC database, where comparative data of the healthcare systems in EU is presented: www.missoc.org/INFORMATIONBASE/

reimbursement system, the insured person often pays for the care in advance and is then refunded by the insurance fund.

Member States have traditionally seen healthcare – a part of their welfare system – as an area 'free' from EU law. The original Treaty of Rome gave no explicit competence to the Community institutions in the field of health. At that time, it was clear that the Member States had exclusive competence to organize their healthcare systems. An explicit legal basis was introduced at the beginning of the 1990s and today the Treaty provides that Member States' responsibilities include health management and allocation of the resources assigned to them.[38]

3.2 Cross-Border Healthcare – Development and Content

Although the Treaty provides that Member States' responsibilities include health management and allocation of the resources assigned to them, secondary legislation concerning cross-border healthcare has been adopted in the form of Regulation 883/2004 – the legislation on coordination of social security benefits. The healthcare provisions in this regulation include administrative rules governing cooperation between the social security institutions of the state responsible for the costs and the state which provides the healthcare; for example, the state that pays the pension is also responsible for costs related to healthcare. However, the Regulation also contains provisions concerning cross-border healthcare, or the right to obtain healthcare during a temporary stay in a Member State other than the state of affiliation. In the latter case, obtaining care in another Member State requires authorization. In other words, authorization is required from the home state in order for citizens to be reimbursed for the costs of care received abroad.

Regulation 883/2004 requires the home state to pay the medical costs incurred while in another Member State in two situations. One situation is where an insured person needs emergency medical treatment during a stay in another Member State. The patient is then entitled to healthcare as though he or she were an insured resident in that state (Article 19).

Another situation in which the home state is obliged to pay medical costs is when a person is authorized to go to another Member State to receive appropriate treatment there (Article 20). Two conditions must be fulfilled for authorization. Firstly, the treatment in question shall be among the benefits provided for by the legislation in the competent

---

COMPARATIVETABLES/MISSOCDATABASE/comparativeTableSearch.jsp, accessed 25 November 2015.

[38] Article 168.7 Treaty on the Functioning of the European Union (TFEU).

Member State. Secondly, the state cannot provide the insured person with treatment within a medically justifiable time limit, taking into account his or her current state of health and the probable course of illness. Many judgments of the CJEU have been concerned with the mobility of patients and the possibility of receiving prior authorization for obtaining treatment abroad. For a long time, this was the only way to receive healthcare in another country. The Member States were pleased with the authorization procedure because they had the last word in deciding which treatments would be reimbursed.

In 1998, the CJEU decided to extend the scope of healthcare integration under the free movement of services. Since then there has been a chain of case law granting the freedom to individuals to receive health services in a Member State other than the state in which they are affiliated for health purposes. In the *Kohll*[39] and *Decker*[40] cases, the CJEU ruled that in some cases the condition of authorization is contrary to the Treaty. The authorization could constitute an obstacle to free movement. Medical treatments, according to the CJEU, are to be considered as services and fall within the rules of free movement. For the first time, an individual was able, under certain circumstances, to seek treatment beyond national borders and have it reimbursed by the home country. Previously, the European healthcare systems had been connected only through the coordination rules. Social rights such as healthcare could now be obtained on the basis of the Treaty and on the provisions of the right to free movement. This challenged the social boundaries of the welfare states.

The *Kohll* and *Decker* cases created legal and administrative uncertainty. The cases concerned the Luxembourg healthcare system, which operates on a reimbursement basis. Some Member States argued that the judgments were confined to social health insurance systems where an insured person is entitled to reimbursement of costs incurred for medical treatment. According to these Member States, the judgments thus did not apply to national healthcare systems. Systems that did operate with a reimbursement mechanism were uncertain whether the judgments applied only to non-hospital treatment or if treatment at hospitals was also regarded as a service.[41]

---

39 *Kohll* C-158/96 EU:C:1998:171.

40 *Decker* C-120/95 EU:C:1998:167.

41 Jason Nickless, 'The internal market and the social nature of health care' in Martin McKee, Elias Mossialos and Rita Baeten (eds), *The Impact of EU Law on Health Care Systems* (Peter Lang 2002).

In both *Geraets-Smits and Peerbooms*[42] and *Vanbraekel*,[43] the CJEU found that the provisions on the free movement of services also applied to medical treatment provided in hospitals. In the latter case, the Advocate General argued that 'services which, on the one hand, are an integral part of the public healthcare system, in the sense that they are established and organized by the state, and, on the other hand, are financed by public funds, must be excluded from the provisions on freedom of movement'.[44] Similar arguments were brought forward by the Advocate General in *Geraets-Smits and Peerbooms*.[45] However, the CJEU concluded that there was 'no need to distinguish between care provided in a hospital environment and care provided outside the environment'.[46]

In the *Müller-Fauré and van Riet* case[47] the referring national court emphasized the characteristics of the Dutch social health insurance system. The system is benefit-in-kind, based on agreement between the sickness fund and care providers, and one of the referring questions was whether such a system could be a possible justification to a restriction on the fundamental principle of freedom to provide services, that is whether the provision on free services was applicable to such a system as the Dutch one. The cases concerned a request from two Dutch nationals to be granted reimbursement of medical costs incurred in Germany and Belgium. Some Member States maintained that entitling insured persons to go to a Member State other than the state in which they were insured would create adverse consequences in priority-setting for medical treatment and management of waiting lists. If patients could shorten their waiting time by obtaining medical treatment in other Member States without prior authorization, and for which the competent institution was not obliged to assume the costs, the financial balance of the system would be threatened and the resources available for more urgent treatment would be severely depleted.[48] The CJEU reconfirmed the need of Member States to be able to plan and overview the administrations of hospitals. However, a refusal to grant prior authorization, based solely on

---

42 *Geraets-Smits and Peerbooms* C-157/99 EU:C:2001:404.

43 *Vanbraekel* C-368/98 EU:C:2001:400.

44 *Vanbraekel*, Opinion of AG Saggio C-368/98 EU:C:2000:271, para 21.

45 *Geraets-Smits and Peerbooms*, Opinion of AG Ruiz-Jarabo Colomer C-157/99 EU:C:2000:274, para 49.

46 *Geraerts-Smits and Peerbooms*, above n 42, para 53, and *Vanbraekel*, above n 43, para 41.

47 *Müller-Fauré and van Riet* C-385/99 EU:C:2003:270.

48 Ibid, paras 53–60.

the ground that there are national waiting lists that do not take into consideration the patient's medical status, could not be considered as a properly justified restriction on freedom to provide services.

In *Watts*[49] a third type of system – a national health scheme – was examined. The CJEU held in *Watts* that even if healthcare under the British legislation is free of charge and financed by taxation, the patient is entitled to reimbursement of the difference between the costs of equivalent treatment in a hospital covered by the British system up to a total amount invoiced for the treatment provided in the host Member State. The fact that reimbursement is sought from a national health system does not mean that the rules on freedom to provide services, guaranteed by the Treaty, are not applicable.

The CJEU has thus repeatedly found that regardless of the way in which the European healthcare system operates, medical treatments are to be considered as services and thus fall within the rules of free movement. The condition of an authorization could constitute an obstacle on the rules of free movement. Member States have had problems accepting that healthcare may be provided in another Member State without prior authorization. Member States' healthcare systems are based on the principle of territoriality. In addition, Member States have maintained that issues concerning social security do not fall within the scope of the rules of free movement.[50] The principle of territoriality is seen by the Member State as a guarantee for quality of the healthcare. Member States consider it impossible to guarantee the quality of healthcare if patients are free to receive care and medical goods in other states. Another reason for applying the principle is that a right allowing patients freely to choose treatments or products would lead to higher costs, and the responsible health institution would be unable to reimburse the costs. Member States have to plan the number of hospitals, as well as their geographical distribution and organization. In order to do so, states need to know approximately how many patients will make use of their healthcare systems.

The case law of the CJEU referred to above has led to a dual system of reimbursement for cross-border healthcare. The coordination rules are no longer the only way for a Union citizen to obtain healthcare in another country: there is also the Treaty-based freedom of services.

---

49 *Watts* C-372/04 EU:C:2006:325.

50 *Kohll*, above n 39, para 16, *Geraets-Smits and Peerbooms*, above n 42, para 51 and *Vanbraekel*, above n 43, para 39.

Not only have the Member States had problems accepting that healthcare may be provided in another Member State without authorization, but also national administrative procedures have made it difficult to obtain cross-border healthcare.[51] Therefore, Directive 2011/24[52] (the Patient Mobility Directive) was adopted to ensure patient mobility in accordance with the principles established by the CJEU.[53] The Directive sets out a framework for cross-border healthcare in the EU. According to Article 1 of the Directive, the aim is to facilitate access to safe, high-quality cross-border healthcare and promote cooperation on healthcare between Member States, in full respect of national competencies in organizing and delivering healthcare. The principles of universality, access to good quality care, equity and solidarity shall thus also be respected with regard to patients from other Member States.[54]

3.3 Aspects of Solidarity

Healthcare has traditionally been provided for those present in the Member States' territory. As a consequence, the right to benefit from a healthcare system is basically linked to a duty to contribute to that system, either in the form of contributions or through taxes. In an expression of solidarity, a citizen may be obligated to contribute more to a system than he or she will receive from that system. The territory of a state reflects the outer limit of that solidarity and excludes those living and working outside the state's border.

An exception from the territoriality principle concerning healthcare can be discerned in Regulation 883/2004 and the special rules concerning healthcare for pensioners. The state from which the pensioner receives a pension also has to pay for costs related to healthcare, even when the pensioner resides in another Member State. The reason for having special rules for pensioners is the fact that during his or her working life, the pensioner has made financial contributions to a collectively organized system based on solidarity. The pensioner is thus benefiting from the system to which he or she has contributed, even though this person no

---

[51] Frans Pennings, 'The cross-border health care directive: More free movement for citizens and more coherent EU law?' (2011) 13 Eur J Social Security 424.

[52] Directive 2011/24/EU of the European Parliament and of the Council of 9 March 2011 on the application of patients' rights in cross-border healthcare, OJ 2011 L 88/45.

[53] Ibid 10th recital of the preamble.

[54] Ibid 21st recital of the preamble.

longer resides in that state's territory. It would be inconsistent with the idea of European integration if pensioners – when exercising their right to free movement – were to lose all advantages representing previously paid contributions.

As has been described above, European integration has also led to increased mobility in healthcare. A chain of case law has developed, granting the freedom to individuals to receive health services in a Member State other than that in which they are affiliated for health purposes. However, contrary to the referred rules in the Regulation regarding pensioners and their entitlement to healthcare in a cross-border situation, the patient still resides in the system to which he or she belongs and which ultimately must reimburse the costs. That challenges the traditional conception of solidarity: belonging to a closed group committed to sharing social goods that are redistributed at a collective level within that very system.

The notion of solidarity in the context of European healthcare systems is of utmost importance. It is one of the values shared across the EU about how health systems respond to the needs of the population. However, demographic change is now putting pressure on national healthcare systems. When people get older, their need for medical care increases. Old age is often connected with illness and disability. Due to the demographic trend, a shrinking workforce has to handle increasing healthcare needs for the elderly. At the same time, we can see a development in which Union citizens are being allowed to receive healthcare in Member States other than the home state.

Consequently, the rising cost of healthcare challenges the sustainability of healthcare systems. In the long run this could affect accessibility and availability when it comes to health services and facilities. As is well known, the right to health is an established part of the international human rights canon.[55] The notion of health as a human right requires special attention to vulnerable persons, such as the elderly. States have a special obligation to provide necessary health insurance and health services to those who do not have sufficient means.[56]

---

55 Article 25 the Universal Declaration of Human Rights; Article 12 the 1966 UN International Convention on Economic Social and Cultural Rights; Article 11 the European Social Charter and Article 35 the Charter of Fundamental Rights of the European Union.

56 See General Comment No. 14 on the right to health, which refers specifically in paragraph 19 to the elderly as a vulnerable group.

One could argue that cross-border healthcare actually undermines the principle of solidarity by putting the individual before the group.[57] It benefits those who have the resources to go abroad to receive healthcare and takes resources from vulnerable groups such as the elderly. Others have seen cross-border healthcare as an opportunity. The increased use of cross-border healthcare may be seen as a move towards empowering individuals to turn away from delayed or inadequate healthcare.[58] Indeed, that might be so. However, a change towards more individualization could lead to a decrease when it comes to equal access to healthcare services and thus make already older persons with limited resources even more vulnerable.[59]

4. MEDICAL RESEARCH – SOLIDARITY FROM AN INTERGENERATIONAL PERSPECTIVE

4.1 EU and Medical Research

European societies today are facing considerable and mounting pressure on their healthcare systems due to dwindling financial resources and a demographic shift resulting in larger proportions of persons above 65 years of age. Medical research is closely connected to this demographic development in Europe. The ageing population in the EU and worldwide and diminishing birth rates have led to intensive discussions about the urgency of increasingly cost-efficient and tailored healthcare adapted to meet these changing and expanding needs. One part of those discussions involves demands for increased medical research to find ways of decreasing morbidity and easing disability among older people. In the coming decades, the impact of the demographic development will be at least partly reflected in rising healthcare costs. Spending on health is already substantial in the EU, accounting for 6–10 per cent of gross domestic product (GDP) in the EU Member States and around 8 per cent of GDP in most countries in the Organisation for Economic Co-operation and

---

[57] See for example, Christopher Newdick, 'Citizenship, free movement and health care: Cementing individual rights by corroding social security' (2006) 43 CML Rev 1645.

[58] See for example, Tamara K Hervey, 'The current legal framework on the right to seek health care abroad in the European Union' (2006–2007) CYELS 261.

[59] See further Mattsson and Katzin, Chapter 5 in this book about the applicability of the vulnerability theory for ageing and law.

Development (OECD) countries.[60] Most countries in the EU are concerned about planning future healthcare in accordance with this demographic development, for economic as well as quality reasons. This naturally includes estimating not only the overall demand of healthcare but also the types of healthcare services that will be needed. Predictions are difficult and yet necessary. However, there are strong indications in research and reports that healthcare services face many challenges in the near future due to the ageing population. For example, it is probable that in the near future people will not only live longer but also in better health.[61] On the other hand, it is also expected that falling mortality will be accompanied by an increase in morbidity and disability. So, while health may continue to improve, different causes of morbidity and disability may at the same time become more common, demanding increasing efforts from the healthcare sector. For example, it is expected that the EU population will have much higher levels than today in terms of some disabling conditions such as dementia and musculoskeletal diseases.[62]

The current demographic trends seem to highlight medical research as one solution for finding new tools to deal with the coming situation. The EU is heavily promoting research in the field. For example, Horizon 2020 is the largest-ever EU Research and Innovation programme, with nearly 80 billion EUR of funding available over a seven-year period (2014 to 2020).[63] One medical research method involves the use of so-called 'big data'. There is currently a research trend of heavily increased collection and use of digital health data; this trend is largely driven by technological advancements and improvements in data analysis techniques. These developments are expected to be helpful in

---

[60] The share of healthcare expenditure in 2012 exceeded 10 per cent of GDP in six EU Member States (the Netherlands, France, Belgium, Germany, Denmark and Austria), compared to GDP recorded in Latvia (2010 data), Estonia and Romania (6.0 per cent or less), see Eurostat health care statistics, http://ec.europa.eu/eurostat/statistics-explained/index.php/Healthcare_statistics, accessed 8 February 2016. For OECD statistics, see OECD Health Statistics, www.oecd.org/els/health-systems/health-data.htm, accessed 8 February 2016. In 2013, health spending (excluding investment) as a share of GDP was 8.9 per cent, ranging from 5.1 per cent in Turkey to 16.4 per cent in the United States.

[61] European Commission, 'The 2015 ageing report: European economy, economic and budgetary projections for the 28 EU Member States (2013–2060)' (2015) 3 European Economy 118–19.

[62] Ibid.

[63] European Commission, Horizon 2020: https://ec.europa.eu/programmes/horizon2020/en/what-horizon-2020, accessed 8 February 2016.

dealing with neurodegenerative diseases like dementia. Because of dementia's clinical and biological complexity, some of the studies needed for drug discovery and development of new therapeutic strategies – with the aim of slowing disease progression – seem to require massive amounts of very diverse data.[64] In Sweden, quality registries represent one type of big data that is considered a particularly valuable tool for future health and medical care. The development of registries is encouraged by favourable national patient data regulations and government funding. A national quality registry contains individualized data concerning patient illnesses, medical interventions and outcomes after treatment. The registries can be very useful in research aimed at finding future treatments for older patients or patients with cognitive impairments. Using data from some of the registries may pose some problems, however, from a patient privacy point of view. For example, developing successful healthcare for dementia requires the participation of patients with dementia.[65]

Clinical research directly involves a particular person or group of people, or uses materials from humans (such as samples of tissue). There are two kinds of clinical studies – clinical trials and observational studies. In a clinical trial, subjects receive specific interventions, such as medicine, drugs, devices or medical procedures.[66] The aim is ultimately to determine the safety and efficacy of the intervention. For example, patients may be given a drug or treatment to see whether their blood pressure decreases. In an observational study, no such interventions are made. One such study can be to observe a group of older persons to learn more about the effects of different lifestyles on cardiac health. Both types of medical research are commonly applied. The results of the studies can make a significant difference in the care of future patients by providing information about the benefits and risks of new drugs or interventions. This is where the solidarity principle becomes a central issue.

---

64 E Ronchi, 'Using big data in the fight against dementia' in P Love (ed.), *Ageing: Debate the Issues* (OECD Publishing 2015) 39.

65 However, the increasing use of data from people with limited or no decision-making capacity raises concerns about the limited ways to apply the right of refusal to those without enough cognitive capacity to do so. See for example, T Mattsson, 'Collecting data for quality improvement and research in Swedish health care, and the individual patient's right and ability to protect their privacy' (2016) 2(2) Int J Tech Policy and Law 160–68; and T Mattsson, 'Patient safety at odds with patient privacy? The case of national and regional quality registries for incapacitated elderly in Sweden' (2014) Lex medicinae, Special issue 69.

66 See for example, ClinicalTrials.Gov https://clinicaltrials.gov/ct2/about-studies, accessed 8 February 2016.

4.2 Medical Research for the Common Good

As we have seen in the previous sections, legal systems and courts struggle with the question of the extent to which the solidarity principle should apply within the European social welfare systems, and the ways that this principle should be applied. These issues have important effects on retired and older persons. It appears that the integration process in Europe challenges the traditional conception of solidarity in the social welfare states. These changes call for a discussion of solidarity's significance for research. As we have seen, one part of medical research is clinical research, which is characterized by the involvement of patients. This type of research is dependent on the solidarity of individuals as participants in new medical interventions or drug development. The solidarity principle is also a fundamental reason for allowing – sometimes risky or painful – clinical research on human beings, with the purpose of developing healthcare for the common good and for the next generations. However, participating in medical research based on registries is also founded in solidarity. Persons whose data is used in a medical study most often do not benefit from the results; the benefits are enjoyed solely by future patients. Thus, in general the main argument for participating in medical research rests on the principle of solidarity.

Medical research is a necessary component of helping others with diseases, pain and suffering, and therefore, it is argued, participating in research becomes a moral obligation.[67] In addition, the obligation stems from the benefit we receive from the existence of the social practice of medical research. We continually benefit from others' participation in medical research and therefore should not be 'free-riders' in this system.[68] Europeans, as well as people from many other parts of the world, benefit from living in societies where research is carried out and the benefits of past research are applied. Since we accept the benefits that have been given to us, it is argued that we have a moral obligation to contribute to this social practice that continuously advances our society.

At the same time, the most influential international documents on medical research restrict the participation of persons who are not capable of consenting to being part of a research study.[69] The limitation rules are based on the principle that the wellbeing of the person should take

---

67 John Harris, 'Scientific research is a moral duty' (2005) 31 J Med Ethics 242, 242.

68 Ibid.

69 Declaration of Helsinki, CIOMS etc.

precedence over the interests of science and society.[70] To justify research on persons with dementia or other cognitive impairments demands major consideration and careful reflection. According to ethical standards, such as the Declaration of Helsinki, seeing medical research as a common good cannot by itself justify research based on solidarity reasons. Gathering information for research purposes should only be pursued if it can be done in a research-ethical, acceptable manner. It involves an examination of the balance between the risks to the subject and the scientific value of the study. Therefore, most medical research in Europe needs to pass through an ethical review process. In all European countries, the ethics review legislation demands minimally invasive and minimally risky research procedures on vulnerable groups, and safeguards against wrongful use. Under such circumstances, research on these groups may be justified. The research in these cases is often based on the solidarity principle – the moral obligation to help others and the moral obligation to be just and do one's part.[71]

4.3 Solidarity as One Ethical Standard

As we have discussed in this chapter, demographic changes challenge the solidarity principle in different ways. The question is how medical research is affected. We can all agree that medical research is a necessary component for the future health of EU citizens. For older people to be able to obtain good, quality-assured care in the near future, there is a need for research on specific diseases and injuries suffered by older people, about how the elderly react to drugs and how they experience the care. In addition, the expected rising pressure on health and medical care in general calls for new measures to increase efficiency in the care system and decrease the cost per patient. Similarly, research is needed on the living conditions of older people in the home, of care taking and healthcare delivery at home and for methods to prevent or reduce vulnerability. The list can be made longer. These are the reasons why older people, among others, need to be involved as research subjects.

In medical research, the principle of solidarity is an accepted ethical standard. However, another ethical standard is the principle of integrity. Research integrity may be defined as respecting the ethical principles and professional standards essential for the responsible practice of research that relates to individuals participating in the research. Research may not

---

[70] See for example, Declaration of Helsinki (World Medical Association 2013) para 5.

[71] Cf Harris (2005), above n 67, 247.

be carried out for integrity reasons, even if it is supposed to benefit different patient groups and promote patient safety and security when patients are in contact with health and medical care, and people are willing to share their data for the sake of helping others. The problem is the risk of breach of privacy rights for the very same patients. The line between acceptable and unacceptable use of data must be determined by legislation.

So far, the legislation and practice in Sweden has been an example of a relatively permissive attitude to collecting data about individuals – including incapacitated persons. However, the new EU data privacy laws, comprising the General Data Protection Regulation (GDPR),[72] which governs the use and privacy of EU citizens' data, and the Data Protection Directive, which governs the use of EU citizens' data by law enforcement, will probably change this. The new privacy regulations entering into force in the near future aim to create strong data protection laws for the EU. The GDPR will enable people to better control their personal data and put up legal barriers for using data without the individual's consent. This is a challenge for Sweden, which is known for its many national registries and mandatory collection of data without consent as well as for its registries of incapacitated persons. A possible outcome is that the principle of solidarity will have to bow to the principle of integrity, due to the increasing demands for collecting and using data for research. The situation may cause difficulties for medical research in countries like Sweden, which have had wide access to data thus far. However, this possible tension between the medical interest in good data as a basis for future healthcare and the individual's right to privacy is also an important issue to take into account.

5. CONCLUSION

Demographic changes are transforming the population of the EU. The demographic trends include an ageing population with low birth rates and a rapid growth in the number of older persons – two developments that will put the principle of solidarity to a severe test. Another challenge is the rapidly changing migration pattern. Over the years the pattern of retirement migration around Europe has changed. An increasing number

---

[72] Regulation (EU) 2016/679 of the European Parliament and of the Council of 27 April 2016 on the protection of natural persons with regard to the processing of personal data and the free movement of such data, and repealing Directive 95/46/EC, OJ 2016 L 119/1.

of non-economically active Union citizens are staying or moving to reside long-term in another Member State, for widely differing reasons. This is particularly true for pensioners.

In this chapter we have discussed different effects of this development on the principle of solidarity within the welfare states in Europe. If we apply the concept of solidarity – defined as the unity of a group or a nation that is based on community of interests, objectives, and standards – we can see that there are very good reasons for solidarity to maintain a dominant position as a fundamental principle both within and between the EU Member States. Some degree of solidarity between Member States may be crucial to ensure free movement, in particular for non-active Union citizens. The ethical reasons for justifying solidarity among people as well as states in Europe are also convincing. Access to social benefits in a welfare state is a common good and there is an obligation to help others. Participation in medical research is also considered a moral obligation to do one's part, and is a basis for good future healthcare in Europe.

The solidarity principle is a concept well known in the context of national welfare models in general. The idea of solidarity presupposes belonging to a closed group or community committed to sharing social benefits. In the EU mobility context, the proportionality principle has often been used to balance the interests of the individual Member States in relation to the needs of the individual. For example, a temporary need of social assistance benefits in the host state has not automatically entailed forfeiture of the right to reside.

However, the principle of solidarity is being challenged in Europe. Recent case law from the CJEU shows that there is a clear shift back to economic activity and self-sufficiency as preconditions for free movement and equal treatment in relation to solidarity-type social security benefits. No individual assessment has to be made, which may have particularly severe consequences for those of advanced age and/or with health problems. This shift may be said to reflect a traditional way of applying solidarity: situations where the territory of a state is the outer limit of the solidarity and thus excludes those crossing the state's borders. As regards free movement and access to social benefits, this development may partly be explained by the increased movement of economically inactive Union citizens between Member States. In addition, the economic crisis has affected migration patterns so that some Member States have been put under heavy strain. From a situation with rules upholding a certain degree of financial solidarity between nationals of a host

Member State and nationals of other Member States, as well as proportionality in any restrictions to free movement, the situation has now drastically changed. This development is, of course, in contrast to the European idea of integration.

Another aspect of a shift away from solidarity may be seen in the healthcare field. It can be argued that cross-border healthcare, in the terms of free movement of services, to some extent undermines the principle of solidarity – traditionally understood as putting the individual before the group in a Member State perspective. People with good economic and social situations have more opportunities to seek care abroad, whereas persons without these means find themselves sidestepped. At the same time, one could argue that cross-border healthcare is in line with the European idea of integration.

If we take the example of the Swedish healthcare system; this is a tax funded system where healthcare is provided to the whole population as a benefit-in-kind in accordance with need. Buying healthcare services abroad can be seen as a shift from a collective approach to an individual approach. For example, waiting lists are being set aside when people seek healthcare across the border. Moreover, other parts of the national health system are also challenged due to the changing patterns in healthcare use within Europe. This is illustrated by the complaint system. When it comes to cross-border healthcare, Swedish citizens whose requests for healthcare cost reimbursement have been rejected have a right to appeal to the administrative courts. A corresponding right does not exist when it comes to healthcare provided within Sweden – there is no general right to appeal a decision concerning healthcare, that is, in terms of which treatment is provided and so on. Instead of strengthening common interests and objectives of the European Member States, the current development runs the risk of creating a fragmented union without a strong conception of solidarity.

Finally, medical research is an area where the principle of solidarity plays a significant role with challenges for the coming years. It will most probably be difficult to involve enough patients with the illnesses and disabilities that are expected to become more and more common (but which have limited or no cures today). Their participation is based on the solidarity for future generations but may be questioned because it involves groups with limited decision-making capacity. The forthcoming EU GDPR will also allow limited access to data for groups with mental disabilities, without their consent. Thus, the integrity principle may most likely dominate over the solidarity principle when it comes to the matter of participation by these groups.

14. New legal conflicts in an old legal context: the law of inheritance and its challenges in the twenty-first century in the perspective of the ageing individual

Elsa Trolle Önnerfors

1. INTRODUCTION[1]

The purpose of the inheritance law is a legal matter of constant discussion and interest – and especially so for elderly people.[2] About 80 per cent of the roughly 90,000 persons who pass away in Sweden each year are 65 years or older.[3] There is often an assumption that elderly people accept death as an 'inevitable and natural event'.[4] It is easier and the 'right time' to die in old age, at the end of life when a person's life goals are completed. But as society changes, so do the attitudes about death. Increased longevity has led to expectations among the ageing population that the lifespan will be stretched: death is no longer 'appropriate at 65, 75 or even 85'.[5] Ageing does not automatically

[1] This work was carried out within the Norma Elder Law Research Environment (www.jur.lu.se/elderlaw) funded by Ragnar Söderberg's Foundation and the Marianne and Marcus Wallenberg Foundation.

[2] For a definition of old or elderly people, see Ann Numhauser-Henning, 'An introduction to elder law and the Norma Elder Law Research Environment' in Ann Numhauser-Henning (ed.), *Introduction to the Norma Elder Law Research Environment: Different Approaches to Elder Law* (The Norma Research Programme 2013) 27–8.

[3] Statistics Sweden, 'Lägsta antalet döda sedan 1977', www.scb.se/sv_/Hitta-statistik/Artiklar/Lagsta-antalet-doda-sedan-1977/, accessed 1 April 2016.

[4] Glennys Howarth, '"Just live for today". Living, caring, ageing and dying' (1998) 18 Ageing Soc 673.

[5] Ibid 687.

liberate people from fear of their own death as well as the deaths of others. It is a constant challenge for the legislator to balance different interests and meet the demands for an inheritance law that can function in contemporary society. In addition to regulations for inheritance, most jurisdictions provide protections for the surviving spouse, cohabitant, minor children and other dependents of the deceased in terms of welfare state measures. In this chapter, these protection systems will not be discussed. Instead, this chapter concentrates on the arguments in current legal debates, and issues such as inheritance rights of the surviving spouses and cohabitants, the legal status of forced heirship versus testamentary freedom, the use of wills, and finally, the effects of the new EU regulation on international succession. Characteristics for Swedish inheritance rights will be highlighted but comparisons with other legal systems will also be made.

2. THE CONDITIONS OF INHERITANCE LAW IN A NEW SOCIETY

The family law implications for elder law are numerous. In the autumn of a person's life, one inevitable aspect of family law is, of course, inheritance law, and the questions an ageing individual raises about what is going to happen with one's assets after one's decease. The death of a person creates a new situation. From time immemorial, societies have had to respond to and deal with the deaths of its members: 'where people live in society, there will be rules concerning succession'.[6] Although the deceased person disappears from the society, he or she leaves both body and assets behind. Therefore, there is a need for funeral rites as well as rules for the transfer of the estate of the deceased. On an individual level, planning for death, whether it is expected or not, is one of the oldest matters of law, and a perennial topic of discussion. When a person prepares for his or her own death in advance, the person has the possibility to create the opportunity for a peace-filled end of life, and is able to relieve the bereaved of some decision-making burdens. Death planning can comprise such measures as making a will and planning for

---

[6] Christoph Castelein, 'Introduction and objectives' in Christoph Castelein, René Foqué and Alain Verbeke (eds), *Imperative Inheritance Law in a Late-Modern Society* (European Family Law Series Vol 26, Intersentia 2009) 2.

the funeral as well as decision-making in advance to donate organs.[7] Professor Israel Doron has presented a multidimensional model for elder-law issues. In this model, inheritance law can be placed in the so-called 'protective dimension', which has an individualistic as well as a preventive perspective. In the protective dimension, elder law relates not only to the protection of the elderly; it also focuses on the abilities of ageing individuals to decide for themselves and design their own lives. Inheritance law can be one such legal planning tool that the elderly can use to make their own decisions and manage their own lives.[8] Inheritance law gives an opportunity for an ageing individual to take care of a surviving spouse as well as children even after one's own decease. One could regard 'proper death planning (as) a final gift to loved ones'.[9]

The restraint that history places on inheritance rights is evident, and is often used as an argument for not making more legal reforms than absolutely necessary.[10] Sometimes, inheritance law is regarded as a legal order given by nature, history or a higher power, and it seems as if the regulations are almost impossible to change. New laws of inheritance are seldom issued, but two of the Nordic countries have recently reformed their inheritance regulations. New laws of inheritance came into force in Denmark in 2008 and in Norway in 2015.[11] When it comes to family law, several reforms have been made in Sweden during the past 50 years. This is the case with matrimonial law as well as the rights of parents and children. However, one branch of family law is almost unaffected when it comes to legal reforms: the law of inheritance. The foundations of inheritance law were laid almost a 100 years ago and have changed very little since then. In Sweden, the Inheritance Code dates from 1958, and many of the provisions in the code originate from even older laws.[12]

The question of who is entitled to inherit the estate of the deceased is timeless, and apparently so is the answer: the family of the deceased.

---

[7] Israel Doron, 'A multi-dimensional model of elder law' in Israel Doron (ed.), *Theories on Law and Ageing: The Jurisprudence of Elder Law* (Springer Verlag 2009) 67.

[8] Ibid 60 and 66–7.

[9] John F Wasik, 'Lifting from others the burden of your own death: Proper death planning is a final gift to loved ones', New York Times (14 May 2014).

[10] Anna Singer, 'Blodsband, släktskap, försörjning eller kanske kärlek? Om arvsrättens grund och funktion i det postmoderna samhället' in Thomas Eeg (ed.), *Samfunnsutvikling og arverettslige utfordringer* (Cappelen Damm 2013) 103.

[11] Inheritance legislation, Denmark: Arveloven 2008 (515 06.06.2007) and Norway: Lov om arv m. m. (LOV-1972-03-03-5).

[12] Inheritance Code (*Ärvdabalk* 1958:637).

Inheritance rights in almost all countries are based on consanguinity and/or marriage. But to say the least, the concept of family has changed in the past 50 years, especially when it comes to the form and function of a family.[13] For a long time, the role of the family was to reproduce, provide for the family members and protect them in times of misfortune. The most important function of the family today is perhaps to give a feeling of affinity.[14] In the case of Sweden, this has led to a situation where the inheritance law in many ways is out of step with the times. Since the beginning of the twentieth century, the society has changed to a great extent, and this has, of course, affected ways of living in several different aspects.

First of all, the average length of life has increased during the last century. In 2014, life expectancy in Sweden was 84 years for women and 80 years for men.[15] This increased longevity and an ageing population make new demands on contemporary inheritance law, especially in times of financial crisis and impaired social security systems. It is sometimes a delicate task for the elderly to balance the wish to help family members during their lifetime (with financial support in the form of gifts and loans, for example) with the effort to save money for their old age.[16] As life expectancy increases, people will also inherit at older ages. Nowadays, the children of the deceased are often in their fifties or sixties when their parents pass away. For this reason, inheritance can be a potentially important retirement income source, and many heirs express that they will probably use their future inheritance to fund their own retirement. According to a recent global report, seven out of ten of those who are expecting a future inheritance say that the inheritance will fund their retirement to some extent. One out of ten states that the inheritance will fund their retirement entirely.[17]

Another consequence of this longevity is that people tend to be older when they divorce and remarry. Today half of all marriages in Sweden and elsewhere in the Western World ends in divorce, and remarriage is frequent in all age groups. In the US, for example, the divorce rate for

---

13 Masha Antokolskaia, *Harmonisation of Family Law in Europe: A Historical Perspective* (European Family Law Series Vol 13, Intersentia 2006).

14 Singer (2013), above n 10, 99–100.

15 For further reading, see Scott, Chapter 2 in this book.

16 Jacqueline L Angel, *Inheritance in Contemporary America: The Social Dimensions of Giving across Generations* (Johns Hopkins University Press 2008).

17 *The Future of Retirement. Life after Work?* HSBC Report 2013 22 and 27.

Americans over the age of 50 has doubled since 1990.[18] The so-called nuclear family, with two parents married to each other until parted by death and family members remaining in stable positions for all their lives, is no longer in sole control. Separations have become more frequent and families consisting of 'my children, your children and our children' are not uncommon. Marriage among the elderly has its own set of problems when it comes to inheritance law, for example the protection of the lifetime accumulation of wealth of both partners and the concern of adult children from previous relationships. The remarriage of an older parent does not always bring out the best in adult children, especially when the children fear that the new spouse is only marrying the parent for the money.[19] These family structures with a remarried elderly parent, a new step-parent and adult children and stepchildren are perhaps more susceptible than others to clashes over inheritance and family assets, especially when there is an absence of planning or a valid will.[20]

Another tendency in the society of today is that the number of couples living together as cohabitants has increased during the last decades.[21] This also affects the inheritance law; inheritance legislation in many countries does not grant intestate succession rights to cohabitants. One could ask if cohabitants' rights to inherit from each other are of lesser importance than the rights of a married couple in the society of today. Family constellations and conditions nowadays do not look like the families that the legislator had in mind in the 1950s, and the present inheritance law is not designed for alternative families in many cases. In this aspect, inheritance laws face several challenges in the years to come.

---

[18] Susan Gregory Thomas, 'The grey divorcés', Wall Street Journal (3 March 2012). www.wsj.com/articles/SB10001424052970203753704577255230471480276, accessed 1 April 2016.

[19] Joanna Lyn Grama, 'The "new" newlyweds: Marriage among the elderly, suggestions to the elder law practitioner' (1999) 7 Elder L J 380 and 389.

[20] Naomi Cahn and Amy Ziettlow, '"Making things fair": An empirical study of how people approach the wealth transmission system' (2015) 22 Elder L J 332 and 348–9.

[21] See for example, Göran Lind, 'The development of cohabitation and cohabitation law in the Nordic countries' in John Asland, M Brattström, G Lind, I Lund-Andersen, A Singer and T Sverdrup (eds), *Nordic Cohabitation Law* (European Family Law Series Vol 37, Intersentia 2015) 6–8.

3. THE INHERITANCE RIGHT OF THE SURVIVING SPOUSE OR COHABITANT

Marriage, and the legal rights that come with it, does not have exactly the same implications in all societies. Even though marriage, of course, is a social institution, it cannot be fully understood if its legal and cultural context is excluded. The legal consequences of marriage have been regulated in many different ways over time and in different countries. The surviving spouse is often protected by the matrimonial regime and by intestate inheritance law. Even though most European countries classify the surviving spouse as an intestate heir, one thing that differs the most between different legal systems is the extent of the inheritance right of the surviving spouse.[22]

From the Middle Ages until modern times, the interests of the family and kin were of greater importance than the inheritance right and protection of the surviving spouse. In the case of Sweden, as well as the other Nordic countries, this can be explained by the fact that these countries depended on farming and self-sufficiency until the late nineteenth century. When a farmer died, the rest of the family needed to keep the farm and the land within the family in order to survive in the rural society. The surviving widow was protected by other legal solutions, such as the dowry.[23] With a starting point in the first half of the nineteenth century and for the 100 years to come, reforms to strengthen the legal position of the surviving spouse were introduced in many European countries. These reforms led slowly but steadily to an increased equality between men and women in inheritance law.[24] In the case of Sweden, a more modern form of inheritance rights was introduced in the 1920s. The dowry was abolished and the surviving spouse was given a limited inheritance right in cases where the couple did not have any children.[25]

The succession in Swedish inheritance law has always been based on the genetic relationship between the deceased and the heirs. The fundamental idea is that closer relatives inherit before more distant relatives.[26]

---

22 Castelein (2009), above n 6, 12–17.

23 For further reading on spouses' property and inheritance rights in the early modern Sweden, see Maria Ågren, *Domestic Secrets: Women and Property in Sweden, 1600–1857* (University of North Carolina Press 2009).

24 Jens Beckert, *Inherited Wealth* (Princeton University Press 2004) 90–99.

25 Margareta Brattström and Anna Singer, *Rätt arv. Fördelning av kvarlåtenskap* (4th edn, Iustus 2015) 23.

26 The group of relatives with intestate succession rights in Sweden was narrowed in the 1920s. In 1928, the Parliament decided to abolish the right of

In the Inheritance Code, the deceased's relatives are classified into three levels of succession. Other persons close to the deceased, for example cohabitants, stepchildren, foster children, first cousins and friends, will only inherit if they are mentioned as a beneficiary in a will.[27]

The improvement of the inheritance rights for the surviving spouse was one of the more striking changes of inheritance law in Europe during the twentieth century.[28] An example of this development could be seen in a major reform of the Swedish law of inheritance in the late 1980s. At this time, the general opinion was that the legal reforms that took place in the 1920s no longer offered sufficient protection for the surviving spouse. In addition to this, the regulation that obliged children to pay maintenance for their elderly parents had been abolished in 1979.[29] From the legislator's point of view, focus was now on the surviving spouse whose legal rights had to be strengthened. It was now stated that if the deceased was married, the main rule was that the estate should go to the surviving spouse. If the deceased and the surviving spouse did not have any common children, or if there was not a will that stipulated otherwise, the surviving spouse inherited the estate with full ownership. If the couple had common children, the estate was still transferred to the surviving spouse, but in this case not with full ownership but with the right for the

---

inheritance for first cousins and more distant relatives. The same year, a Swedish state fund, the Swedish Inheritance Fund (*Allmänna arvsfonden*), was established. When a person in Sweden dies without a written will and no living spouse or close family, his or her property is transferred to the fund. The purpose of the fund is to support non-profit organizations and other volunteer associations help improve conditions for children, young people and the disabled; see www.arvsfonden.se/om-arvsfonden, accessed 1 April 2016. The only other country except Sweden with a state-governed inheritance fund is Iceland; see Peter Lødrup, *Nordisk arverett: en sammenlignende studie av dansk, finsk, islandsk, norsk og svensk rett med drøftelser av harmoniseringsmuligheter og reformbehov* (Nord Series Vol 3, Nordiska ministerrådet 2003) 258.

27 The first class of heirs is the descendants of the deceased, for example children, grandchildren and so on. The second class includes the parents of the deceased, as well as siblings and their descendants. If there are no heirs in the first class, this class will inherit the estate. The third and last class consists of the deceased's grandparents and their children, for example uncles and aunts. According to the law, each class has to be 'empty' before continuing to the next one, and the estate is divided in equal shares between the heirs in every class (Inheritance Code (*Ärvdabalk* 1958:637) Chapter 2 Sections 1–4).

28 Castelein (2009), above n 6, 13.

29 Government Bill Prop 1978/79:12 about maintenance for minors and divorcees (*Regeringens proposition om underhåll till barn och frånskilda m.m.*) 74.

surviving spouse to dispose of the estate freely for the remainder of his or her life. The spouse was not allowed to will away the estate, but was free to spend all the assets if he or she so desired. The children's inheritance rights in these cases were to be postponed until the time of the surviving spouse's death.[30] The same tendency, with stronger inheritance rights for the surviving spouse and postponed inheritance for children, can be seen in many other European countries as well, for example Belgium and Holland. This development can be characterized as a paradigm shift within intestate succession law when it comes to the most important heir: focus has changed from the children to a preference for the widow or widower. The inheritance rights of the surviving spouse have become stronger while the inheritance rights of the children are delayed until the death of the surviving parent. This, of course, strengthens the economic situation for many elderly. For example, the surviving spouse is not forced immediately to sell off the home or property in order to disburse the children's inheritance. In addition, married couples are committed not least to an economic partnership that continues after death. The bulk of their common estate is often accumulated during the marriage.[31]

Another significant social tendency in the Western World is that more and more couples, in all age groups, live together without being married. In Sweden this is the case as well, and since the 1960s cohabitation has become increasingly common. A growing part of the population is choosing not to get married. Today, about 40 per cent of all couples that live together do so as cohabitants. Individuals born in the latter part of the twentieth century, who have formed families after it became more common to cohabit, tend to marry later and to a lesser extent. Of those born in 1975, only half were married at age 35.[32]

Nowadays, cohabitation is widely and socially accepted in most parts of the Western World. Legally, the distinctions between spouses and cohabitants are less and less frequent.[33] Sweden was one of the first countries to create a special legal set of rules and regulations for cohabitants. The first form of legislation (with a rather limited scope) for cohabitants came into force in 1974, and the present version dates from 2003.[34] The Act applies to two unmarried persons of the same or

30 Inheritance Code (*Ärvdabalk* 1958:637) Chapter 3 Sections 1 and 2.

31 Castelein (2009), above n 6, 15–16.

32 Statistics Sweden, *Generations through the years – a demographic description of those born during the 20th century*, Report 2014:2.

33 Lind (2015), above n 21.

34 Act on the joint dwelling of unmarried cohabitants (*Lagen om sambors gemensamma bostad* 1973:651); Cohabitees Act (*Sambolagen* 2003:376).

different sex, living permanently together in a relationship and sharing the same household. The law is intended as a protection regulation for the financially weaker party, and no registration of the relationship takes place.[35] The field of application of the Cohabitees Act is rather limited though. The Act only regulates what happens when cohabitants separate, and does not say anything about what happens if a cohabitee dies.

A problem here is that cohabitants, unlike married spouses, do not inherit from each other by default according to Swedish inheritance law. It is a general public misunderstanding that cohabitants have the same legal rights as married couples, but this is not the case. Cohabitants do not inherit from each other under the law. This is irrespective of whether or not they have common children. The lack of inheritance rights for cohabitants is still an unknown legal fact for many, and comes as a shock in some cases. Many live in the belief that the Cohabitees Act gives them some sort of marital status, and the legal rights that come with it – but this is not the case, and perhaps the Cohabitees Act presents a picture of false security. A survey from 2012 shows that about 40 per cent of all cohabitants in Sweden know what will happen with their assets and their domestic economy if they separate or if one of them dies. This means that 60 per cent are not aware of the legal consequences entailed by a dissolved relationship. Only 14 per cent of the cohabitants had made a will and 12 per cent had made an agreement about their assets.[36]

Inheritance rights for cohabitants in the Swedish law of inheritance are, and have been, a much-debated legal matter. In the legislative history of the second Cohabitee Act from the late 1980s, the matter of inheritance rights for cohabitants was a topic for discussion. This was a time when marriage still was the norm for cohabiting. The predominant opinion regarded marriage as an active choice, which granted the married couple more legal rights. Cohabiting, on the other hand, was more of a temporary and 'loose' way of living. The government bill for the new Act stated that there was no need for a general inheritance right for cohabitants, but it would be suitable to let cohabitants inherit from each other if the couple had lived together for a long time.[37] However, that argument was dismissed in the Parliament. If the couple had lived together for so long, they would have had a lot of time to reconsider their

---

35 Cohabitees Act (*Sambolagen* 2003:376).

36 'Sambor lever i falsk trygghet' (Länsförsäkringar 26 June 2012), http://nyhetsrum.lansforsakringar.se/2012/06/26/sambor-lever-i-falsk-trygghet/, accessed 1 April 2016.

37 Government Bill Prop 1986/87:1 about the Marriage Code etc. (*Regeringens proposition 1986/87:1 om äktenskapsbalk m.m.*).

way of living. If they did not want to get married, but still wanted to live together, they could make a joint will. Thus, in the 1980s, the general opinion of the Parliament was that there was no need for inheritance rights for cohabitants, and the legislator was content with this. Since then, no more bills have been presented to the Swedish Parliament on this matter. It was not discussed in the government bill for the present Cohabitee Act of 2003, for example.

The question of inheritance rights for cohabitants has also been in focus for a working party within the Nordic Council of Ministers. In 2003, the working party stated that legislation in the Nordic countries is similar, and that there is no need for harmonization. None of the Nordic countries has a system where a cohabitant has the same legal rights as those of a married person or a person in a registered partnership. The rights that go with the marriage, require a marriage.[38] In recent years, a new inheritance law in Norway extended cohabitants' rights of inheritance. Cohabitants who have (or are expecting) a child together have the same right of inheritance as married spouses. The same applies for cohabitants who have lived together for at least five years.[39] Outside the Nordic countries, inheritance rights for cohabitants have been a legal fact in many jurisdictions for years. In Croatia, Slovenia and Kosovo, for example, inheritance rights for the surviving cohabitant were enacted in the 1970s. Similar rights were introduced in New Zealand and Australia in the 1980s.[40] In the US, 11 jurisdictions recognize the doctrine of common-law marriage. The laws of these states allow both parties to the common-law marriage to inherit from each other under state intestacy laws when either spouse dies without a will.[41]

Despite the lack of new and improved inheritance laws in Sweden, there is still a political interest in inheritance matters. Each year, several proposals concerning inheritance are issued from the members of the Swedish Parliament. These often propose the same rights of inheritance for both married couples and cohabitants. But the proposals are always rejected for the same reason: the legislator does not want to create a system with a relationship that looks like a marriage but which is of

---

38 Lødrup (2003), above n 26, 133–4.

39 NOU 2014:1 *Ny Arvelov* 46.

40 John Asland, 'Balancing interests – How much freedom of testation?' in Katharina Boele-Woelki, Jo Miles and Jens M Scherpe (eds), *The Future of Family Property in Europe* (European Family Law Series Vol 29, Intersentia 2011) 235–7; NOU 2014:1 *Ny Arvelov* 48.

41 NOU 2014:1 *Ny Arvelov* 48. For further reading, see Göran Lind, *Common Law Marriage* (Oxford University Press 2008).

lower dignity.[42] If cohabitants are to inherit from one another, they must make a will. That leaves Sweden with a legal solution implying that a married couple must make a will if they do not want to inherit from each other, while cohabitants need to draw up a will if they want to inherit from each other. This can be seen as an odd arrangement, since most people today consider these to be the same kind of relationship.

4. THE 'TO BE, OR NOT TO BE' OF FORCED HEIRSHIP

The conception of the freedom of disposition by will, familiar as it is in modern England and the US, for example, is not by any means universal.[43] Complete testamentary freedom is the exception rather than the rule in many countries. Forced heirship laws are most prevalent among civil law jurisdictions, which often have restrictions on the testator's possibility of disposal. Characteristic for Sweden, as well as the other Nordic countries, is the use of the statutory share of inheritance for children.

In Sweden, the first provisions about the children's right to a statutory share of inheritance appeared during the Middle Ages. This coincided with the new practice of disposing of property and estates by making a will. The main purpose of the medieval will was to make donations for pious and charitable purposes, such as gifts to churches and convents. The medieval Swedish rules of inheritance, however, were based on the view that family came first when possessions were to be distributed: property, in particular real estate, was to be kept within the family. The family was a unit, and the inheritance right was based on social and economic ties between the parents and the children. Children depended on the inheritance from their parents for their support and survival in the agricultural society. As far as possible, the legislator as well as the courts supported the idea that a child had a right to inherit at least something from his or her parents. Ever since the Middle Ages there have been

---

42 Government Bill Prop 2002/03:80 A New Cohabitees Act (*Ny sambolag*) 25.

43 In the US, Louisiana is the only state with a statutory inheritance share for children (up to 23 years of age). For further reading on testamentary freedom versus the support obligations of parents, see Elisabeth Travis High, 'Tension between testamentary freedom and parental support obligations: A comparison between the United States and Great Britain' (1984) 17(2) Cornell Int L J.

limitations on testamentary freedom in Swedish law when it comes to the children's share of the deceased parent's estate.[44]

Nowadays in Sweden, the statutory share of inheritance is limited to half of the deceased parent's estate, which is then divided among the children: 50 per cent if there is only one child, 25 per cent per child if there are two children and so on. This provision in Nordic inheritance laws differs from, for example, the succession laws in England and many of the states in the US, where, as mentioned above, the principle of testamentary freedom is the fundamental idea. The statutory share is without parallel in England, for example, where the Wills Act established the doctrine of testamentary freedom in 1837. According to the Wills Act, which still remains the basis for the current law, a person (the testator) should be free to determine how his or her property is distributed on his or her death by making a will that sets out the intentions of the testator. A testator can make an unfettered distribution of his or her entire estate, and is entitled, with some exceptions, to disinherit any and all of his or her children.[45] Nowadays, the testamentary freedom is restricted by subsequent enactments[46] and can be limited under certain conditions.[47]

---

44 Elsa Trolle Önnerfors, *Justitia et prudentia. Rättsbildning genom rättstillämpning: Svea hovrätt och testamentsmålen 1640–1690* (2nd edn, Institutet för rättshistorisk forskning 2014) 251–7.

45 The first Statute of Wills in England was enacted in 1540 during the reign of Henry VIII. The Act allowed owners of real estate and personal property to bequeath their assets upon death. In 1837, the Wills Act replaced the Statute of Wills. Slightly reformed over the years, the Wills Act is still in force in England and Wales. Roger Kerridge, 'Testamentary formalities in England and Wales' in Kenneth G C Reid, Marius J De Waal and Reinhard Zimmerman (eds), *Testamentary Formalities* (Oxford University Press 2011) 308–9 and 312.

46 For example, the Inheritance (Family Provisions) Act from 1938 and the Inheritance (Provision for Family and Dependants) Act from 1975. For further reading on the latter see Paul Matthews, 'Comparative law – United Kingdom' in Christoph Castelein, René Foqué and Alain Verbeke (eds), *Imperative Inheritance Law in a Late-Modern Society* (European Family Law Series Vol 26, Intersentia 2009) 137–43. For further reading on testamentary freedom and adult offspring, see Biran Sloan, 'Testamentary freedom and caring about adult offspring in England & Wales and Ireland' in Katharina Boele-Woelki, Jo Miles and Jens M Scherpe (eds), *The Future of Family Property in Europe* (European Family Law Series Vol 29, Intersentia 2011).

47 The Inheritance (Family Provision) Act from 1938 gives the courts the possibility to make provision for certain classes of persons based on testator's failure to make reasonable provision for them. This includes, for example, the surviving spouse (as well as cohabitants and civil partners) and minor children in some cases; see Rebecca Probert, *Family and Succession Law in England and*

Most jurisdictions in the US have enacted statutes that prohibit a testator from disinheriting a spouse. The majority of states recognize the right of a surviving spouse to claim a share in the deceased partner's estate regardless of any statements made in a will.[48]

Thus, in Sweden the statutory share of inheritance is the absolute right for a child to inherit from their parent. This is the share of the inheritance that can never be willed away from the direct heir. A child is entitled to receive his or her statutory share, even if the parent has decided by way of a will that the remainder of the estate should wholly or partially pass to some other person. If a person who has children disposes of all of her or his remainder of the estate by a will, the children can nevertheless demand their right in court.[49] However, the children can accept the will, of course, and decline their legal portion. This also applies to the surviving spouse's inheritance rights. Thus, common children cannot demand any kind of statutory share on the death of the first parent. As mentioned above, the common children are defined as heirs with a postponed right to inherit, because they have to wait for the surviving parent to pass away to receive the inheritance from the first deceased parent. Children of the deceased person from a previous marriage, on the other hand, have the right to claim their share of the inheritance immediately. This can lead to difficulties, for example for the surviving spouse, who is perhaps forced to sell off real estate or other property in order to disburse the inheritance of children from the deceased's previous relationships.

Family conditions in Sweden have thus changed considerably since the beginning of the twentieth century, and the number of children not growing up with both their parents has increased. For those born up to 1935, the death of a parent was the most common reason for not growing up with both parents in Sweden. The proportion of those who grew up with both parents was highest for those born in 1955. For Swedish children born in 1985, the parents' separation was by far the most common reason for not growing up with both parents.[50]

Wales (3rd edn, Wolters Kluwer 2013) 25–6. For further reading see Joseph Dainow, 'Limitations on testamentary freedom in England' (1940) 25 Cornell L Rev 337.

48 The ability to disinherit a spouse depends on the state's individual laws. For surviving spouse rights in different states in the US, see www.surviving-spouse-rights.com, accessed 1 April 2016.

49 The Inheritance Code (*Ärvdabalken*) Chapter 7 Section 3.

50 Statistics Sweden, above n 32.

Already in 1981, a group of experts in family law suggested in a Swedish Government Inquiry Report that forced heirship for children should be abolished. The experts asserted that this kind of forced heirship had no function in a modern society and was out of step with the times.[51] But the Parliament stated that the legislative question regarding an abolishment of the statutory share had been raised too early. In addition, Sweden wanted to preserve a similar legal identity along with the other Nordic countries on this matter. Once again, arguments based on history and tradition were used.[52] Today, the reference to the Nordic legal identity is of lesser importance. Both Norway and Denmark have recently reformed their laws of inheritance, and have imposed restrictions on the extent of the statutory share of inheritance.[53]

The *raison d'être* of the statutory share of inheritance has been a constant subject of discussion for the last decades. Many pros and cons have been formulated around the forced heirship issue. To whose interest should the legislator give priority: the surviving spouse, which in most cases is an ageing individual, or the younger generations to come? In many cases, the children of the deceased are adults and self-supporting at the time of death of the parent. With this in mind, one could ask why children still have an absolute right today to inherit from their biological parents. The opponents stress that a principle of legislation should be that freedom of action is the main rule. A retired and elderly person, who has worked all of his or her life, must be free to dispose of his or her property, even after death. In accordance with this, it is often stated that the statutory share conflicts with a person's right of possession according to the European Convention on Human Rights as well as a state's constitution.[54]

Furthermore, an abolishment of forced heirship would in many cases strengthen the rights and the economic conditions for the surviving spouse. Today, it is sometimes hard to justify why intestate succession

---

51 Government Inquiry Report SOU 1981:85 Marriage Code (*Äktenskapsbalk*) 206–12.

52 Government Bill Prop 1986/87:1 79–80.

53 Marianne Holdgaard, 'Konsekvenser af ændringerna i dansk arvelov – balancen mellem længstlevende og livsarvingernes interesser' in Utviklingen i nordisk arverett – tegn i tiden, nordisk arverettskonferanse 24 October 2012 (2013) 517 TemaNord 111.

54 See for example, Viola Boström and Bertil Strömberg, 'Laglotten – ett irrationellt inslag i svensk rätt' (2012–13) 1 Juridisk Tidskrift. For examples of recent proposals from members of the Swedish Parliament (*Riksdag*) with demands for the abolition of the statutory share, see 2015/16:795, 2012/13:C242, 2012/13:C327 and 2010/11:C207.

law should prefer adult non-dependent children above the surviving spouse as the most important heir to the deceased. Why should adult children be able to make a claim for provision from the estate of a parent when they are obviously capable of maintaining themselves? In Swedish inheritance law, for example, a child of the deceased can always claim the statutory share, even if the child is an adult, has not been heard of for years or has had no contact with the deceased biological parent. Unfortunately, family unity is not always present in real life.

The advocates for upholding the forced heirship on the other hand often emphasize that the statutory share is a symbol for the unity of the family and the solidarity of the family members, in other words the family ties. It is perfectly proper for a testator to be required to make adequate provision for his or her dependants, and most countries in the world permit wills to be varied where they would leave dependants destitute. The forced heirship is also a fair protection for children from a previous marriage or relationship. Freedom of testation would perhaps imply that these children would not inherit anything from the biological parent. The forced heirship can in this aspect guarantee a fair distribution of the deceased's estate and balance the interests among the heirs.

5. THE POINT OF WILLS

Wills are one of the oldest forms of legal documents; they existed already in Ancient Egypt. Although the will is steeped in history and tradition, it is also perhaps the most personal legal document an individual ever creates. Making a will is a unique experience for each testator, and can be described as a process by which a person makes a disposition of his or her assets. But at the same time the testator also confronts mortality and assesses the accomplishments and disappointments of his or her life.[55] Even if wealth transmission is of great concern for senior citizens, the will is more than just a legal document used to transmit probate wealth upon death.[56] Making a will often moves the testator to reflection and

---

[55] Karen J Sneddon, 'The will as personal narrative' (2012) 20 Elder L J 2 359 and 368.

[56] In the US, the inheritance system is often irrelevant for how property is transferred at death. A recent study shows the wealth transmissions in many cases are carried out in other ways than by a will or a trust in the inheritance process. See Cahn and Ziettlow (2015), above n 20.

contemplation.[57] One could describe the will-making experience as 'a *memento mori* as well as a routine law-office transaction'.[58] The thought of making legal arrangements relating to one's own death is not always pleasant, though. This is often the case with ordinary wills as well as so-called 'living wills'. In a 'living will', a person can leave instructions for end of life care and specify the actions that should be taken for his or her health at a stage when he or she is no longer able to make decisions due to illness or incapacity. Surveys show that approximately only 20 per cent of Americans have engaged in any form of advance care planning and, even among older Americans, the process is frequently delayed until an acute illness creates sufficient pressure to act.[59]

When it comes to intestate inheritance law, it is often stated that the law constitutes the unwritten will of a person who dies intestate. For that reason, it is important that the legislator formulates the succession law so that it reflects the testament that an average testator would have left. Thus, families that are 'well functioned' often regard a will as an unnecessary measure; the succession law is sufficient for their needs. Surveys in Sweden show that only about a quarter of the population make a will in their lifetime. It is hard to get an exact figure since wills in Sweden do not have to be officially registered. An often-stated reason for not making a will is that a person is satisfied with and relies on the statutory rules in the inheritance law. In comparison, statistics for England show that for about 42 per cent of all deaths the deceased left estates with a will of some kind.[60] In the US, many Americans die intestate, but among the elderly today, about 70 per cent in the age group 70–85 years say that they have made a will.[61] Still, one can ask why so many avoid making a will and other preparations for the unavoidable. Perhaps it is because most of us find it quite uncomfortable to confront the thought of death. It is not something that a person wants to think about on a daily basis or discuss with one's family or partner over

57 Karen J Sneddon, '*Memento mori*: Death and wills' (2014) 14 Wyoming L Rev 211.

58 Sneddon (2012), above n 55, 375. '*Memento mori*' translates as 'remember you must die' or 'remember that you are mortal'. See also Sneddon (2014), above n 57, 222–8.

59 Barbara A Noah, 'In denial: The role of law in preparing for death' (2013) 2 Elder L J 1. For an overview of the 'living will' in Germany, see Alexandra Maschwitz, '"Living will" under German Civil Law Code' in Katharina Boele-Woelki, Jo Miles and Jens M Scherpe (eds), *The Future of Family Property in Europe* (European Family Law Series Vol 29, Intersentia 2011).

60 Kerridge (2011), above n 45, 316–17.

61 Angel (2008), above n 16, 21 and 64.

breakfast. A recent Swedish study shows that many elderly have never discussed their forthcoming death with their family or partners. Paradoxically, the same persons stated that it would have been easier for them if their own parents had expressed something – about arrangements of funerals for example. One explanation can be that the elder generations were raised not to talk about death with family and relatives.[62] Money and discussions about financial matters can also be a sensitive and uncomfortable subject of conversation, perhaps especially for the generations who were born during the first half of the twentieth century. For many of them, money and inheritance are topics that parents do not discuss openly with the children.[63] Another recent study from the US shows that in most cases, the deceased's family react with appreciation when the deceased has made any type of advanced planning for death, whether or not the planning has resulted in a formal will.[64]

If an individual dies intestate the provisions in the inheritance law will make assumptions about how he or she would want to distribute his or her property. Some of these assumptions may be correct; others may result in a distribution of property in a manner far different from the deceased's wishes. Although the intestacy laws will determine who will inherit the property and in what shares, the law does not determine who will receive a specific item of property. For example, the law may state that the two children, a daughter and a son, will each take one-half of the estate, but it will not specify that the daughter should receive a particular piece of furniture and the son should receive a particular piece of jewellery.[65]

Married or not, often the best solution is to make a will. Even if one spouse is seriously ill or is much older, it is often a mistake to think that the other spouse will live longer. Even if the heirs are getting along fine at the moment, no one knows what will happen in the future. The unexpected will often happen, and therefore it is wise to plan accordingly. A will can often prevent disputes among the relatives of the deceased: 'family harmony is the most commonly overlooked aspect of inheritance planning'.[66] Inheritance and money have a tendency to cause problems, and inheritance conflicts can sometimes be the final straw for

---

62 Magnus Broström, *Äldre människors föreställningar om den egna framtiden, döendet och döden* (Linköping Studies in Arts and Science No. 612 2014) 128–9.

63 Angel (2008), above n 16, 58–9.

64 Cahn and Ziettlow (2015), above n 20, 331.

65 Sneddon (2012), above n 55, 400–405.

66 Angel (2008), above n 16, 22.

challenged families, with members vowing never to speak to one another again. Throughout history, one of the most common reasons for drawing up a will has been a wish to avoid unnecessary conflicts among the children on the disposition of the estate. Another thing one can learn from history is that it is better, as much as is possible, to determine the distribution of one's own estate and not leave the task to the heirs. If the assets are not divided up in equal shares in a will, it can be a good idea to explain why, whatever the reason. Maybe one child is doing well financially while another child is having a tougher time.[67]

In Sweden, as in most other countries, there are form requirements with respect to a will. Normally, the will has to be a written document, signed by the testator in the presence of (normally) two witnesses. The testamentary formalities serve as a safeguard against forgery. But in Sweden, unlike many other legal systems, there is no requirement for the will to be officially registered, and this can cause problems. In some cases, wills are never found; the testator perhaps never mentioned to the immediate family that he or she had made a will. In other cases, a disappointed heir finds a will and destroys it, and no one will ever know that there was a will to begin with.

In recent years there has been an increase in the number of legal disputes launched regarding inheritance issues in Sweden. Cases of disputed wills at the Swedish courts have increased by nearly 80 per cent in recent years.[68] This number is most likely the tip of an iceberg, since many inheritance disputes are settled outside the courtroom. How can the increase be explained? Every case is different, of course, but some underlying factors can be identified. This pattern can partially be explained by the fact that families today are more complicated than they used to be. The high divorce rates in recent decades have created many second and third families, who do not always agree about what should happen when someone dies. The real estate market of today is a second explanation. Due to current house prices, virtually every homeowner who dies leaves an estate large enough for the heirs to fight over. A third explanation is that people live longer, often with extended periods of mental decline at the end of their lives, and are therefore more vulnerable to influence and confusion when it comes to wills. As many heirs become

---

67 Önnerfors (2014), above n 44, 259–60.

68 The number of disputed wills in the Swedish courts was a little less than 150 in 2000. Ten years later, in 2012, the total amount was about 260. Maria Crofts, 'Så slipper du bråk om arvet', *Dagens Nyheter* (Stockholm 21 October 2013).

increasingly aware of errors of form in wills, for example, they turn to the courts to contest the will and claim their legal rights.

6. THE CONSEQUENCES OF THE NEW EU REGULATION ON INTERNATIONAL SUCCESSION

Until recently, questions of inheritance in most European countries have been determined by the citizenship of the deceased. For example, Swedish inheritance law was applicable when a Swedish citizen died, irrespective of where the estate was situated, in Sweden or elsewhere. The increasing mobility within the EU has led to a growing number of people crossing the borders. Nowadays, it is not uncommon that people live, work and own property in other Member States. In 2015, the circumstances for nationals living abroad changed drastically when a new EU regulation on jurisdiction, applicable law, recognition and enforcement of decisions and acceptance and enforcement of authentic instruments in matters of succession came into force in August 2015.[69] The Regulation gives, among other things, (almost all of) the EU Member States the same international civil law regulations on inheritance.[70] Instead of being covered by the inheritance laws of the home country, the law applicable to the succession shall be the law of the Member State in which the deceased had his or her habitual residence at the time of death.[71] The determination of the deceased's habitual residence can be complex in some cases. The authorities involved shall make an overall assessment of the circumstances of the life of the deceased at the time of his or her death as well as the years preceding the decease. An important factor is the duration and regularity of the deceased's presence in the state concerned, and, of course, the reasons for the presence: just to work temporarily or to settle down permanently? The new regulation will affect the succession to the estates of deceased Swedish citizens who have moved abroad after their retirement, and for that reason were not

---

[69] Regulation (EU) No. 650/2012 of the European Parliament and of the Council of 4 July 2012 on jurisdiction, applicable law, recognition and enforcement of decisions and acceptance and enforcement of authentic instruments in matters of succession and on the creation of a European Certificate of Succession, OJ 2012 L 201/107.

[70] Denmark, the United Kingdom and Ireland are not taking part in the adoption of the Regulation, and are not bound by it or subject to its application (Regulation (EU) No. 650/2012, preamble (82) and (83)).

[71] Article 21 Regulation (EU) No. 650/2012.

living in their native country at the time of death.[72] More and more Swedish pensioners move abroad in their old age. According to the Swedish Agency for pensions, almost 7 per cent of all pensions in 2015 were paid to pensioners who lived outside Sweden.[73]

It is important to bear in mind, though, that the new regulation also enables individuals to organize their succession in advance by choosing the law applicable to their succession. Individuals can choose the law of their own nationality to apply to the succession as a whole. The choice has to be expressed and included in a declaration in the form of disposition of property upon death.[74] However, so far few seem to know about the new regulation. This can lead to several legal complications because the inheritance laws of the respective Member States of the EU differ significantly. Among other things, some Member States favour freedom of testamentary disposition, while others provide for compulsory heirship. For example, in the case of Spain – home to about 90,000 Swedes – heirs can inherit debts, which is not the case in Swedish law.[75]

Inheritance tax and the obligation to register wills also differ significantly from state to state. Sweden has a nearly 700-year tradition of taxing inheritances and bequests, and had some of the highest tax rates in the world. But for one tax it is a zero-tax country: since 2004 there is no inheritance tax.[76] Prior to December 2004, legal heirs and beneficiaries of wills in Sweden were subject to inheritance taxation according to the laws stipulated in the Inheritance and Gift Tax Ordinance. Sweden had one of highest inheritance tax rates at the time of the abolition. In some cases, it was as high as 70 per cent of the capital in larger estates.[77] But

---

[72] Preamble (23) and (24) Regulation (EU) No. 650/2012.

[73] Swedish Pensions Agency (*Pensionsmyndigheten*), 'Nu förenklas levnadsintygen för de 143 564 pensionärer som bor utomlands', www.pensionsmyndigheten.se/levnadsintyg15.html, accessed 1 April 2016. For further reading see Brokelind and Axmin, Chapter 11 in this book.

[74] Article 22 Regulation (EU) No. 650/2012.

[75] Svenskar i Världen, 'Alltfler svenskar bor utomlands – idag 660 000', www.sviv.se/wp-content/uploads/2015/06/660-000-svenskar-bor-utomlands-pressmeddelnde-21-juni-2015.pdf, accessed 1 April 2016.

[76] Government Bill Prop 2004/05:25 Abolished Inheritance Tax and Gift Tax (*Slopad arvsskatt och gåvoskatt*).

[77] Act 2005:194 Exemption from Inheritance Tax and Gift Tax (*Lag om undantag från arvsskatt och gåvoskatt*); Gunnar Du Rietz, Magnus Henrekson and Dan Waldenström, 'The Swedish inheritance and gift taxation, 1885–2004' in Magnus Henrekson and Mikael Stenkula (eds), *Swedish Taxation: Developments since 1862* (Palgrave Macmillan 2015).

after a proposal in 2003, the government decided to repeal the inheritance and gift tax for spouses and cohabitants from 1 January 2005 out of recognition of the fundamental unfairness of the tax. The loss of income was financed by other means, for example green taxes. The Swedish inheritance tax, or rather the lack of it, can be compared, for example, to Germany, where only close relatives get to pass on any money untaxed, or Spain, where the tax-free amount allowed by the state is tiny, although the local regulations can vary quite a bit. Some countries have followed in Sweden's footsteps when it comes to abolishing inheritance tax: Austria (2008) and Norway (2014).[78] However, in most European countries inheritance tax is still a fact.[79] Until 2015, Swedes living in those countries were bound only by Swedish law, and paid nothing when inheriting wealth. But from August 2015, it is of vital importance to know that a person's domicile determines inheritance tax. Therefore, one must be aware of the laws that apply in the country of one's residence. This is not only a matter of taxes; other countries' laws of succession, for example, may have very different rules for how relatives inherit.

7. CONCLUSION

Inheritance law is based on a common understanding of inheritance and property in our society, and the legislator transfers these views into legal rules. Even though inheritance law is seldom reformed, the process of modernization is crucial. For the last half-century, there has been a development towards a more open and flexible society in many ways. When the social and cultural context of our society changes, so do the conditions for inheritance and the law has to respond to changing family structures. In the years to come, more and more people are likely to live in what the legislator would regard as non-traditional families. The law does not always keep up with the changed conditions. Which function and purpose should inheritance law have in the future? Do marriage and consanguinity still form the best basis for the right to inherit? The present Swedish Inheritance Code is made according to one standard and therefore has to be applied as a single model for a wide variety of situations. It lacks the flexibility to deal with the circumstances in a specific case: did the spouses have a good/bad relationship that lasted for

---

78 In the US, the states of Louisiana, New Hampshire and Utah do not have any inheritance tax.

79 For an outline of taxation of inheritance in the US, Germany and France, see Beckert (2004), above n 24, 167–204.

a long/short period of time? Do the family members live in harmony? Are family members rich or poor? Are the deceased's children minors or adults?

A question that the legislator has to ask is if there is really still a need for forced heirship today. If the answer is yes, who should be given rights such as the statutory share and how should such rights be determined? Are the needs of minor and still-dependent children and the surviving spouse or partner of greater importance than the inheritance rights of adult children? Should perhaps social affinity and emotional ties be given greater importance, not only in society but also in the law? The automatic right for specific categories of heirs to receive a statutory share of the deceased's estate is a strong point, but at the same time it is a weakness. Forced heirship is a 'blind mechanism, not open or flexible, but closed and fixed. It does not offer any possibility to adapt to the circumstances of need or contribution.'[80]

It is an impossible task to find a legal inheritance solution that will satisfy everyone everywhere. History has shown that there is a strong need for individuality when it comes to laws of succession. The legal situation in Europe as well as in the US implies that every legal order has to have a regulation that meets the needs of the specific society. For example, the EU is not about to harmonize inheritance law. This was clear when the new EU succession reform came into force in 2015. The reform did not alter the inheritance laws of the different Member States, and that was never the purpose of the new regulations: it only determines which law should be applicable.

For most of us, it is neither easy nor pleasant to talk about inheritance and death. Perhaps today's society prefers to suppress the fear of death rather than confronting it. But acknowledging mortality is not altogether a bad thing. Planning for death should be regarded as an opportunity rather than a tragedy. Mortality is part of the human condition, so we better plan for it. A death in the family, especially when it is the last parent, can expose a lot of unresolved and painful issues. Without written directives, family members may not know the testator's true intentions. This is one of the reasons why, early on, one should complete what is perhaps the most important planning of one's life. For safety's sake: make a written will, keep it updated and in a safe place. Some things are not best avoided and should be dealt with head on rather than leaving the

[80] René Foqué and Alain Verbeke, 'Towards an open and flexible imperative inheritance law' in Christoph Castelein, René Foqué and Alain Verbeke (eds), *Imperative Inheritance Law in a Late-Modern Society* (European Family Law Series Vol 26, Intersentia 2009) 217.

closest family to face the consequences of one's own lack of foresight. Death planning may be one of the most difficult things a person will ever have to do, but at the same time it is the final and very important act of self-determination. It is an inevitable fact that death is certain, but its hour is uncertain: *mors certa, hora incerta*.

15. Dementia and autonomy

Eva Ryrstedt

1. INTRODUCTION[1]

The elderly as a group are increasing in numbers throughout the world. At the same time, although elderly individuals[2] often seem physically healthier than the elderly of only a few years ago,[3] a nominally higher number are likely to suffer from dementia.[4] Being old does not automatically mean having reduced cognitive function, or as expressed by

[1] This work was carried out within the Norma Elder Law Research Environment (www.jur.lu.se/elderlaw) funded by Ragnar Söderberg's Foundation and the Marianne and Marcus Wallenberg Foundation.

[2] Being older is defined in various ways. Sometimes the age of 60 functions as the dividing line. It is predicted that the group of older people, defined in this way, will rise from today's 900 million to about 2 billion individuals by 2050. Furthermore, by 2050, the need for support for daily activities in developing countries is predicted to quadruple: www.who.int/features/factfiles/ageing/ageing_facts/en/, accessed 9 April 2016. In many developed countries the dividing line goes at 65 years of age: www.who.int/healthinfo/survey/ageingdefnolder/en/, accessed 9 April 2016. See, for the opinion that an age measured in numbers is not the whole story, Jonathan Herring, *Older People in Law and Society* (Oxford University Press 2009) 2–3. See also for the view that what an elderly person is, is debated and best defined in context, Ann Numhauser-Henning, 'An introduction to elder law and the Norma Elder Law Research Environment' (2013) 3 Eur J Soc L 235. The context here is created by being afflicted with dementia.

[3] Proposal for a decision of the European Parliament and of the Council on the European Year for Active Ageing (2012) COM(2010) 462 final 2.

[4] Dementia is defined by the World Health Organization (WHO) thus: 'Dementia is a syndrome – usually of a chronic or progressive nature – in which there is deterioration in cognitive function (that is the ability to process thought) beyond what might be expected from normal ageing. It affects memory, thinking, orientation, comprehension, calculation, learning capacity, language, and judgement. Consciousness is not affected. The impairment in cognitive function is

Rowe and Kahn, ageing does not always induce illness;[5] nevertheless it is natural that cognitive disabilities[6] are quite common in this group.[7]

Another issue also in this context is whether elder law is just another part of disability law.[8] In my view that is not the case. Instead, the part of elder law dealing with cognitive disabilities is an entity much in itself.

---

commonly accompanied, and occasionally preceded, by deterioration in emotional control, social behaviour, or motivation. Dementia is caused by a variety of diseases and injuries that primarily or secondarily affect the brain, such as Alzheimer's disease or stroke.' See www.who.int/mediacentre/factsheets/fs362/en/, accessed 9 April 2016. See also Elissa L Ash, 'What is dementia?' in Charles Foster, Jonathan Herring and Israel Doron (eds), *The Law and Ethics of Dementia* (Hart Publishing 2014) 3. However, even if proportionally younger persons in high-income countries now need help with basic activities such as eating than was the case some 30 years ago, the decline is not substantial. Nor has the prevalence of less severe limitations in function changed to any greater degree; see www.who.int/features/factfiles/ageing/ageing_facts/en/index1.html, accessed 9 April 2016.

[5] John W Rowe and Robert L Kahn, 'Human ageing: Usual and successful' (1987) 237 Science 143, 143. See also Liam Foster and Alan Walker, 'Active and successful aging: A European policy perspective' (2015) 55 (1) Gerontologist 83, 84–5.

[6] *Disability* is defined in Merriam-Webster as 'incapacitated by illness or injury; also: physically or mentally impaired in a way that substantially limits activity especially in relation to employment or education'; see www.merriam-webster.com/dictionary/disabled, accessed 9 April 2016.

[7] Gary Sinoff and Natalia Blaja-Lisnic, 'Advance decisions and proxy decision-making in the elderly: A medical perspective' in Charles Foster, Jonathan Herring and Israel Doron (eds), *The Law and Ethics of Dementia* (Hart Publishing 2014) 97. See also the Report of the United Nations High Commissioner for Human Rights, Economic and Social Council E/2012/51 www.un.org/ga/search/view_doc.asp?symbol=E/2012/51, accessed 17 April 2016. See further Claudia Martin, Diego Rodriguez-Pinzón and Bethany Brown, *Human Rights of Older People: Universal and Regional Legal Perspectives* (Springer Science and Business Media 2015) 106–8.

[8] See for a discussion, Doug Surtees, 'What can elder law learn from disability law?' in Israel Doron, *Theories on Law and Ageing: The Jurisprudence of Elder Law* (Springer Verlag 2009) 95 and 103. However, 'disability law' can be used as a lens to evaluate the impact that almost any law has on members of the disability community, thus making it applicable to most areas of law: 'How will the development of the law in this area affect members of the disability community differently than non-members?'; ibid 94. It is also argued that elder law is going through a phase of redefinition and that now it is more about the planning for later life. See Lawrence Frolik, 'Later life legal planning' in Israel Doron, *Theories on Law and Ageing: The Jurisprudence of Elder Law* (Springer Verlag 2009) 11.

Firstly, as indicated above, being elderly is not equivalent to being disabled. Furthermore, even when addressing an elderly person with a cognitive disability such as dementia, we are talking about a person who has lived most of his or her life as a cognitively able person. This means that all decisions, all life choices – the forming of a family and so on are made by a person who is cognitively able, up until this period of his or her life. Thus, it seems reasonable to draw the conclusion that this category of individuals needs to be treated in a special way.

Nevertheless, in the absence of a specific regulation on elderly persons with a cognitive disability, disability law in general can be applied, at the same time that rights aimed at disabled persons and rights aimed at elderly persons may be taken into account.

Throughout the world, there is an ideological quest for autonomy, legal capacity and making one's own choices, regardless of any disability; dementia is included in the realm of disabilities. This quest is founded on different international instruments, with the first and foremost being the UN Convention on the Rights of Persons with Disabilities. At the same time the need for protection is highlighted. The right way to resolve what first appears to be a conflict is widely debated. Perhaps the way to do this, as I argue, is through support in order to reach a flexible balance.[9]

In this chapter, I address the various international documents that are relevant to the rights applicable for persons suffering from dementia. I also address the international doctrine in the field. In doing so, I problematize how autonomy and independence, including own choices and legal capacity, may be understood and achieved for a person afflicted by dementia; even as protection is provided, the problem of balancing autonomy, independence and the need and use of support must be dealt with.

In the next Section, I address the different applicable international documents. Thereafter, I discuss how autonomy and protection are understood and how support can be used to reach a balance between the two. In Section 4, I use Sweden as an example, illustrating national legislation evolving in part from substituted to supported decision-making.

---

[9] See Terry Carney, 'Guardianship, "social" citizenship and theorising substitute decision-making law' in Israel Doron and Ann Soden (eds), *Beyond Elder Law*: *New Directions in Law and Aging* (Springer Verlag 2012) 4. Cf also Larry Polivka and Harry R Moody, 'A debate on the ethics of aging: Does the concept of autonomy provide a sufficient framework for aging policy?' (2001) 6(4) J Aging Identity 223–37; and Israel Doron, 'A multi-dimensional model of elder law: An Israeli example' (2001) 28(3) J Aging Identity 242–59.

Even if concepts such as elderly, disabled, or elderly disabled are understood on their own, the line between them is blurred and it is possible to draw many conclusions cross-wise about these concepts. This is evident when discussing different human rights for these groups; therefore, I begin the discussion by examining human rights for both the elderly and the disabled.

2. HUMAN RIGHTS

2.1 Some International Documents

While no international conventions specifically aimed at elderly persons exist, there are different international obligations including the elderly.[10]

Firstly, old age is mentioned in the Treaty on European Union, Title I, Article 3:3, where solidarity between generations is stressed.[11]

In addition there is the Charter of Fundamental Rights of the European Union, now a part of the Treaty. Articles 21 and 25 are the most important ones in this context. Article 21 expresses a protection against discrimination, for example due to disability or old age. Article 25 rather generally expresses that elderly persons have the right to live a life of dignity and independence. Elderly persons are also granted the right to participate in the social and cultural life.[12]

Among the international obligations that address elderly persons is the European Social Charter, entered into by the governments that are members of the Council of Europe. The most interesting article for the

---

[10] Cf Ann Numhauser-Henning, 'An introduction to elder law and the Norma Elder Law Research Environment' in Ann Numhauser-Henning (ed.), *Introduction to the Norma Elder Law Research Environment – Different Approaches to Elder Law* (Norma Research Programme, Faculty of Law, Lund University 2013) 25. Cf further Israel Doron and Benny Spanier, 'International elder law: The future of elder law' in Israel Doron and Ann Soden (eds), *Beyond Elder Law: New Directions in Law and Aging* (Springer Verlag 2012) 126–133, with further references. See also Alan Neal, 'Active ageing and the limits of labour law' in Frank Hendrickx (ed.), *Active Ageing and Labour Law: Contributions in Honor of Roger Blanpain* (Intersentia Publishing Ltd 2012) 43–5. See also Israel Doron and Itai Apter, 'The debate around the need for an international convention on the rights of older persons' (2010) 50(5) Gerontologist 586, 586–7.

[11] See europa.eu/eu-law/decision-making/treaties/pdf/consolidated_versions_of_the_treaty_on_european_union_2012/consolidated_versions_of_the_treaty_on_european_union_2012_en.pdf, accessed 17 January 2016.

[12] Ibid.

context discussed in this chapter is Article 15, in which persons with disabilities are granted certain rights, irrespective of age, in order to safeguard the rights of independence, social integration and participation in the life of the community. Furthermore, Article 23 states: 'Every elderly person has the right to social protection.' Further on this is explained with: 'to enable elderly persons to choose their lifestyle freely and to lead independent lives in their familiar surroundings for as long as they wish and are able'.[13]

The UN Declaration on Human Rights[14] also addresses old age as such in Article 25(1), where it is stated that one reason for a right to security is old age.

Even though old age in itself is not a disability, many elderly persons are afflicted by disabilities such as dementia. In such cases, documents regarding human rights for disabled persons are, of course, applicable. An important convention for elderly persons with dementia is thus the UN Convention on Rights for Persons with Disabilities.[15]

The quest for autonomy, legal capacity and own choices is first and foremost founded on that convention. The notion of protection is also stressed – against exploitation, violence and abuse together with the demand for reasonable accommodation to promote equality and eliminate discrimination. Moreover, support is commanded to assist the disabled person in executing his or her legal capacity. The support is clearly stated to be construed in a way that prevents abuse according to international human rights law.

The UN Principles for Older Persons also deserve mention here.[16] These principles emphasize, for example, dignity and security, fairness and freedom from exploitation and abuse.

However, there is no convention as such aimed at the elderly, nor is there a convention aimed at elderly disabled persons. The need for a new convention aimed at human rights for the elderly has been debated. Doron gives an account of two main reasons to create such a convention, as well as two reasons against, founded in the opinions from a few years back. The reasons in favour of a convention are that the international law situation is lacking and that such a convention would be both important

---

13 See www.coe.int/en/web/turin-european-social-charter/charter-texts, accessed 10 April 2016.

14 See www.un.org/en/universal-declaration-human-rights/, accessed 17 April 2016.

15 Ratified by Sweden in 2008, SÖ 2008: 26.

16 See www.ohchr.org/EN/ProfessionalInterest/Pages/OlderPersons.aspx, accessed 19 January 2016.

and effective in strengthening the position of elderly persons in general. One reason against such a convention is that international conventions seldom seem to alter much, and may even be detrimental to the situation. Furthermore, another reason against the idea is that in reality, international documents already cover the field.[17] The arguments Hall uses in disputing why the elderly need a dedicated area of law – elder law – may also be used when discussing the establishment of a convention on human rights for the elderly. Hall finds the notion of the dedicated area of law controversial, due to the paternalism that is embedded in it. If elderly persons are perceived to be vulnerable as such, this gives way to an ageist presumption. Furthermore, the elderly comprise a heterogenic group. However, Hall finds that the value and validity of the law and ageing are not totally impaired – and thus require a focused theoretical approach.[18] Thus, there seems to be consensus about the need for specific rules directed at the elderly; perhaps these rules would be ideal content for an international convention and in follow-up national regulation.[19]

2.2 The UN Convention on Rights of Persons with Disabilities

2.2.1 Autonomy

Autonomy includes self-determination. Without self-determination, there is no autonomy. Independence is often included as a concept in

---

[17] Doron and Apter (2010), above n 10, 586, 588–9.

[18] Margaret Isabel Hall, 'Equity theory: Responding to the material exploitation of the vulnerable but capable' in Israel Doron, *Theories on Law and Ageing: The Jurisprudence of Elder Law* (Springer Verlag 2009) 107. See also Hall, '"Old age" (or, do we need a critical theory of law and aging?)' (2014) 35(1) Windsor Rev Legal Soc Issues 1. For an example of the theory of vulnerability developed by Martha Albertson Fineman, who describes vulnerability as something that is a part of all humans, see M Fineman, 'The vulnerable subject and the responsive state' (2010–11) 60 Emory L J 251 and also Mattsson and Katzin, Chapter 5 in this book.

[19] Cf Israel Doron, 'On a journey to a new international human rights convention for the rights of older persons' in Ralph Ruebner (ed.), Teresa Do and Amy Taylor (co-eds), *International and Comparative Law on the Rights of Older Persons* (Vandeplas Publishing LLC 2015) 32. See also Eilionóir Flynn, 'International discourse on ageing – The journey towards a convention' in Ralph Ruebner (ed.), Teresa Do and Amy Taylor (co-eds), *International and Comparative Law on the Rights of Older Persons* (Vandeplas Publishing LLC 2015) 35–54; and Ervin Nina, 'Towards an international legal instrument to promote and protect the rights and dignity of older persons' in Ralph Ruebner (ed.), Teresa Do and Amy Taylor (co-eds), *International and Comparative Law on the Rights of Older Persons* (Vandeplas Publishing LLC 2015) 55–64.

autonomy.[20] This use of the concepts is very clear in the UN Convention on Rights of Persons with Disabilities. In Article 3, the individual right to autonomy is addressed; the right to individual autonomy entails a right to make choices of one's own and to be independent. Further, Article 12(2) states that persons with disabilities are to have legal capacity on the same grounds as other persons.[21] This full legal capacity includes both legal capacity to act and the ability to hold rights.[22] As articulated in the Comment to Article 12, 'unsoundness of mind' is one of several discriminatory labels. None of these constitute legitimate reasons to deny anyone legal capacity. Thus deficits in mental capacity cannot be used to justify the refusal of legal capacity.[23]

2.2.2 Protection

The UN Convention on Rights of Persons with Disabilities further states, in Article 16, that state parties are to take all measures to protect persons with disabilities from exploitation, violence and abuse. Many different measures may be used to fulfil the right to protection. The enumeration in Article 16 is not absolute; the list ends with 'other measures' – so it might be anything that is needed to protect persons with disabilities. Furthermore, the right to protection applies both within and outside the home. Taking measures to protect a person with a disability is not enough, however. In addition to what is stated in Article 16, Article 17 provides for the equal right to respect for every person's physical and

---

[20] However, there is not a total equivalence between legal capacity and self-determination. Self-determination is a concept that is both prosaic and broader than legal capacity. Even if self-determination is always included in legal capacity, legal capacity is not always included in self-determination. A person may lack legal capacity, but his/her wishes may be determining nevertheless: see Eva Ryrstedt, 'Ställföreträdare och självbestämmande' (2016a) 4 Tidskrift utgiven av Juridiska föreningen i Finland (JFT) 395, 396; cf also Eva Ryrstedt, 'Dementa äldre personer; vem ska bestämma?' (2016b) 1–2 JFT 179, 196–7.

[21] Even though Terry Carney (2012), above n 9, 8–9, suggests quite a variety of what this article implies.

[22] General Comment No. 1 (2014) on the Convention on the Rights of Persons with Disabilities, Article 12: Equal recognition before the law. By the Committee on the Rights of Persons with Disabilities, http://tbinternet.ohchr.org/_layouts/treatybodyexternal/Download.aspx?symbolno=CRPD/C/GC/1&Lang=en, accessed 17 January 2016, under 12.

[23] General Comment No. 1 (2014) on the Convention on the Rights of Persons with Disabilities, Article 12: Equal recognition before the law. By the Committee on the Rights of Persons with Disabilities, http://tbinternet.ohchr.org/_layouts/treatybodyexternal/Download.aspx?symbolno=CRPD/C/GC/1&Lang=en, accessed 17 January 2016, under 13.

mental integrity. Article 5 expresses a duty for the state parties to take appropriate steps to ensure that reasonable accommodation is achieved to promote equality and eliminate discrimination.

2.2.3 Autonomy and protection through support?

The right to autonomy and legal capacity in Articles 3 and 12(1) and (2), respectively, the right to protection in Article 16 and the right to respect in Article 17 in the UN Convention on the Rights of Persons with Disabilities are not arranged in a hierarchy. On the contrary, these rights exist in their own right and are to be fulfilled simultaneously. This means that the right to be autonomous is to coexist with the right to protection, and also with the right to respect.

The notion that support is key to the coexistence and thus balance between autonomy and protection is evident in the wording of Article 12(4) in the UN Convention. The article recognizes that to exercise autonomy, persons with disabilities may need support. This support must be designed in a way that safeguards persons from abuse according to human rights law. It is further stated that the safeguards shall ensure that the measures taken in regard to legal capacity respect not only the rights, but also the will and preferences of each person. The safeguards are also to be free of conflicting interests and should protect against undue influence. Furthermore, they must be proportional and adapted to suit each person. They also have to be put in place for as short a time as possible and be reviewed regularly by an authority or judicial body that fulfils requirements on competence, independence and impartiality. The safeguards shall not only be proportional and adapted to suit each person, but must also be proportional to how the measures affect the person's rights and interests. There is also an obligation, stated in Article 16(4) to ensure that appropriate forms of gender- and age-sensitive assistance and support are given. Article 5 expresses a duty for the state parties to take appropriate steps to make sure that reasonable accommodation is achieved to promote equality and eliminate discrimination.

The result of the rights given in the convention is that the legislator, as well as the bodies or persons supplying support to persons with disabilities must perform a balancing act if persons with disabilities shall be able to exercise the rights of autonomy, but also have their right to protection fulfilled. Supporting persons with disabilities in exercising the rights of autonomy is spelled out in Articles 3 and 12, and at the same time supporting persons must make sure that those in need of support are protected, as regulated in Articles 12(4), 16 and 17.

3. UNDERSTANDING AUTONOMY, PROTECTION AND SUPPORT FOR THE ELDERLY WITH DEMENTIA

3.1 Autonomy for All

Just like human rights documents, doctrine reveals the ideological perspective of autonomy.[24] A view of elderly persons suffering from dementia as being autonomous agents is developing[25] and autonomy has been defined as 'the right to be treated as independent beings, even in the presence of diminished capacity'.[26] The importance of identifying laws on autonomy as civil rights matters, and not just as something of moral or ethical importance, has also been emphasized.[27]

When discussing the right to autonomy, one way to start is with this question: Why do we need a special regulation to give the rights everyone else has to persons who deviate in some way from the norm? Is there any other path to take? Surtees advocates the application of the universalism model to the elderly instead of the human (or civil) rights model, as the minority group model is also called.[28] In the human rights model the question regarding the physical environment could be: 'Has this individual been discriminated against by the design of this building?'[29] In the universalism model the corresponding question would instead be: 'Has universal design been used to create a building that

[24] Maintaining and retaining mental capacity is also one of the seven major priority themes listed in 'A road map for European ageing research' (FUTURAGE October 2011), which is a mapping of future research areas. This mapping is closely connected with the European Pact for Mental Health and Well-Being, launched at an EU mental health conference in 2008.

[25] M B Kapp, 'A therapeutic approach' in Israel Doron, *Theories on Law and Ageing: The Jurisprudence of Elder Law* (Springer Verlag 2009) 38.

[26] Ann M Soden, 'Foreword' in Israel Doron and Ann Soden (eds), *Beyond Elder Law: New Directions in Law and Aging* (Springer Verlag 2012) vii.

[27] Nina A Kohn, 'A civil rights approach to elder law' in Israel Doron and Ann Soden (eds), *Beyond Elder Law: New Directions in Law and Aging* (Springer Verlag 2012) 29.

[28] Surtees (2009), above n 8, 101, 104–5. See further for universalism Jerome Bickenbach, Somnath Chatterji, E M Badley and T B Üstün, 'Models of disablement, universalism and the international classification of impairments, disabilities and handicaps' (1999) 48(9) Soc Sci Med 1173. See also Richard K Scotch and Kay Schriner, 'Disability as human variation: Implications for policy' (1997) 549 Annals Am Acad Pol & Soc Sc 148.

[29] Surtees (2009), above n 8, 101.

minimizes the effect of individual variation?'[30] The main difference between the models is thus the respective model's starting point – either in the minority group and its rights, or in the human being as having different traits.[31] Thus, depending on how it is done, the building of the social environment may mean a creation of disability. The same can be said about the creation of a physical environment and the existence of social norms.[32]

3.2 The Need for Protection – Must It Entail a Paternalistic View?

When a person is dependent on others for things such as care, they risk being hurt.[33] Consequently, the doctrine is striking in that it takes a strong starting point in the notion of protection.[34] However, in many cases protection as a human right is not articulated as such. Instead, it is more or less taken for granted in explaining adult guardianship, as Doron notes – when a person has been deemed as being incompetent to be in charge of his or her legal rights, possessions and decision-making power, these are transferred to a guardian.[35] It is also argued that as dementia

---

30 Surtees (2009), above n 8, 101.

31 Surtees (2009), above n 8, 101.

32 Surtees (2009), above n 8, 98–9.

33 Tom Hickey and Richard L Douglass, 'Neglect and abuse of older family members: Professionals' perspectives and case experiences' (1981) 21(2) Gerontologist 171, 174.

34 See for example, Therése Fridström Montoya, *Att leva som andra genom ställföreträdare – en rättslig och faktisk paradox* (Iustus 2015). Montoya stresses the aim of protection in the institution of administrator, 310 and 356. See also Government Bill Prop 1987/88:124 om god man och förvaltare, 132. See also Ryrstedt (2016b) above n 20, 200. See also Titti Mattsson, Linus Broström and Mats Johansson, 'Vilka personer saknar förutsättningar att ge informerat samtycke till att delta i forskning? En rättslig och etisk diskussion rörande etikprövningslagens regler och tillämpning' (2014) 1 Förvaltningsrättslig Tidskrift 171, 181. See also Ryrstedt (2016b) above n 20, 200 and 203. See also Eva Ryrstedt, 'Får jag inte bestämma något själv? En studie av kvarstående beslutanderätt hos dementa äldre' (2014) 3–4 Socialvetenskaplig Tidskrift 343–6. Cf further Marijke De Pauw, 'Interpreting the European Convention on Human Rights in light of emerging human rights issues: An older person's perspective' (2014) 8 Hum Rts & Intl Legal Discourse 236, 247–8.

35 Israel Doron, 'Mental incapacity, guardianship, and the elderly: An exploratory study of Ontario's consent and capacity board (2003) 18(1) Can J Law and Soc 131, 131, with a reference for the basis of the definition Abuse in Guardianship of the Elderly and Infirm: A National Disgrace (Subcommittee on Health and Long Term Care, One Hundredth Congress 1987) 1. See also for

gets worse, the legal capacity of a sufferer weakens. The ability to make decisions or be rational when following a line of reasoning is thus affected. The person will reach a point at which society will find it necessary to effect protection, also from the person him- or herself. This protection is then stated in terms of the best interests of that person,[36] which in turn also has been described as a reason behind guardianship.[37] The application of an objective view on measures taken for the elderly person will entail that the elderly person has to understand a decision, and its consequences, to be attributed the right to make that decision.[38] Even in a mediation scenario regarding a certain person's situation, a party to the mediation must have capacity to negotiate and make decisions, as well as enter into agreements that are in the person's best interests. The mediation will often be deemed inappropriate otherwise.[39]

Consequently, the wishes of a person suffering from dementia are often interpreted in the context of what is perceived to be in the best interests

---

example, José Miola, 'Proxy decision-making' in Charles Foster, Jonathan Herring and Israel Doron (eds), *The Law and Ethics of Dementia* (Hart Publishing 2014) 149; and Lawrence A Frolik and Richard L Kaplan, *Elder Law in a Nutshell* (6th edn, West Academic Publishing 2014) 235.

36 Anna Mäki-Petäjä-Leinonen and Kati Juva, 'Of sound mind? Dementia and aspects of assessing legal capacity' (2015) Eur J Health L 13–15. Cf also Mattsson, Broström and Johansson (2014), above n 32, 176 and 181; cf also Ryrstedt (2016b), above n 20, 23.

37 M M Raivo, A P Mäki-Patäjä-Leinonen, M L Laakkonen, R S Tilvis and K H Pitkälä, 'The use of legal guardians and financial powers of attorney among home-dwellers with Alzheimer's disease living with their spousal caregivers' (2008) 34(12) J Med Ethics 882, 882 with further reference to Anna Mäki-Petäjä-Leinonen, *Legal Status of a Person with Dementia* (A-series No. 241, Finnish Lawyers' Association 2003) 367–75. However, many elderly persons are susceptible to self-neglect, exploitation and abuse, due to being personally or socially vulnerable, regardless of whether they are cognitively capable; Hall (2009), above n 18, 107–8.

38 Ryrstedt (2016b), above n 20, 199. See further Mäki-Petäjä-Leinonen and Juva (2015), above n 34, 14. Cf also British Medical Association and the Law Society, *Assessment of Mental Capacity: Guidance for Doctors and Lawyers* (BMJ Books 2004) 3–4. Cf also NJA 1994, p. 108 and sec 8 in NJA 2010, s. 648. See further Ryrstedt (2016a), above n 20, 397, n 15. Cf also Ryrstedt, above n 34, 329, 332, 334 and 344.

39 Robyn Carroll and Anita Smith, 'Mediation in guardianship proceedings for the elderly: An Australian perspective' (2010) 28 Windsor Yearbook Access Just 53, 53, 56–7. See also Ann M Soden, 'Family matters: Some emerging legal issues in intergenerational and generational relations' in Israel Doron and Ann Soden (eds), *Beyond Elder Law: New Directions in Law and Aging* (Springer Verlag 2012) 108–9 with further references.

of the elderly person, established in an objective way. Such an interpretation is often done by person(s), who are cognitively able, mainly from other perspectives than the elderly person him- or herself.[40] The objective best-interests approach is thus a paternalistic view.[41] In applying such a view we treat the elder person in much the same way that we treat children, who to some extent are also seen as participants.[42]

The legal representative is another factor that creates parallels between the treatment of children and elder persons; often this representative is a family member. This makes the establishment of the content of the best-interests principle rather intricate. The family member may well have his or her own interests, in hidden conflict with the elder person.[43] The issue of discrepancy in the principles and the practices of participation can also have similarities with how such participation for children is treated.[44]

When respecting the wishes of elderly persons with dementia in the decision-making process on specific matters, the degree to which these wishes are taken into account indicates the degree of self-determination that is achieved. Self-determination is what constitutes autonomy, so the adherence to these wishes corresponds directly to autonomy.[45] Such opinions can, of course, be hard to decipher and interpret,[46] but

---

[40] Ryrstedt (2016b), above n 20, 199.

[41] Doron (2003), above n 33, 131, 139. See also Carney (2012), above n 9, 4 and Soden (2012), above n 37, 101.

[42] For the treatment of children see Anna Hollander, 'Att tillvarata barnets rätt och bästa, Om det komplexa uppdraget att företräda barn i rättsliga processer' in Anna Hollander, Rolf Nygren and Lena Olsen (eds), *Barn och rätt* (Iustus förlag AB 2004) 58 with further references.

[43] See Eva Ryrstedt, 'Civil rights of the elderly in a family law setting' in Ann Numhauser-Henning (ed.), *Introduction to the Norma Elder Law Research Environment – Different Approaches to Elder Law* (Norma Research Programme, Faculty of Law, Lund University 2013) 81, 83–4.

[44] See Titti Mattsson, 'A right to active ageing for all? On the status of the elderly in social services and health care' in Ann Numhauser-Henning (ed.), *Introduction to the Norma Elder Law Research Environment – Different Approaches to Elder Law* (Norma Research Programme, Faculty of Law, Lund University 2013) 93. See further for children's participation for example, Titti Mattsson, 'Participation and flexibility for all? A study of modern family structures and children's rights' in Ann Numhauser-Henning and Mia Rönnmar (eds), *Normative Patterns and Legal Developments in the Social Dimension of the EU* (Hart Publishing 2013) 117.

[45] Ryrstedt (2016b), above n 20, 200.

[46] Tove Harnett and Håkan Jönson, 'Sill och potatis till den ena och entrecote till den andra? Individanpassning och likvärdighet på särskilda boenden för

expression of opinions may be conducted without verbal communication, through showing pleasure, distress or emotional response.[47] The respect of an incompetent person's opinions may also be part of a subjective best-interests test, even if the decisions as such are substituted.[48] When accepting the wishes of elderly persons with dementia and attempting to achieve protection, an alternative to taking the paternalistic view may be to assess decisions in terms of potential harm or in terms of the behaviour or wish being uncharacteristic compared to the individual's behaviour in his or her earlier life.[49] The way a person has lived his or her life previously thus seems to be a perspective with which we can compare the current wishes of that person, to determine what is in his or her best interests.[50]

Deducing what a person wishes, taking into account the standpoints earlier in life, is thus a way to create a kind of subjective best-interests test. In using such a test, we may remove ourselves from the paternalistic view and move towards a more autonomous perspective, while at the same time the right to protection is upheld. This also leads to the conclusion that support in this non-paternalistic way could be the solution to achieving the balance between autonomy and protection – as outlined in the next section.

äldre' (2014) 21(3–4) Socialvetenskaplig Tidskrift 249. See also Tova Harnett and Håkan Jönson, 'That's not my Robert! Identity maintenance and other warrants in family members' claims in mistreatment in old age care' (2010) 30 Ageing Soc 627, 629 and 644.

47 Department for Constitutional Affairs, 'Mental Capacity Act 2005 Code of Practice' 5.40. See also Michael Dunn, 'An ethical overview' in Charles Foster, Jonathan Herring and Israel Doron (eds), *The Law and Ethics of Dementia* (Hart Publishing 2014) 128.

48 Jonathan Herring, 'Losing it? Losing what? The law and dementia' (2009) 21(1) Child and Family L Q 3, 12. See for the view that the Mental Capacity Act 2005 (in England and Wales) seeks to maximize the exercising of autonomy, Aisling Boyle, 'The law and incapacity determinations: A conflict of governance?' (2008) 71 Modern L Rev 433. See also Department for Constitutional Affairs, 'Mental Capacity Act 2005 Code of Practice' 5.22 and 5.40.

49 Cf Herring (2009), above n 46, 3, 7. See further on the view on the contemporary or the former life, arguing precedent autonomy, Ronald Dworkin, 'Autonomy and the demented self' (1986) 64 Suppl 2 Milbank Q 4. See also Hugh Series, 'Best interests determination: A medical perspective' in Charles Foster, Jonathan Herring and Israel Doron (eds), *The Law and Ethics of Dementia* (Hart Publishing 2014) 85.

50 Cf Dunn (2014), above n 45, 128. See further Herring (2009), above n 46, 59–65.

3.3 Support to Create Balance Between Autonomy and Protection

It has been questioned whether protection against all harm can be considered to override autonomy, or if persons suffering from illnesses such as dementia should be able to make bad choices, as the rest of us sometimes do.[51]

Autonomy and protection coexist – or are perceived to be existing in conflict[52] – in both the UN Convention on the Rights of Persons with Disabilities and the international doctrine. There is a difference, however, due to the articulated right to autonomy and protection in the convention. When autonomy is addressed in the doctrine, there is often a requirement that the person must be legally capable, or at least must be able to understand the decision. Even if the decisions of a person with dementia are to take precedence, this applies only as long as the decision is valid; thus the paternalistic perspective is evident.[53]

According to this view it is clear that the dividing line between the right to autonomy and the right to protection is perceived as being determined by the individual's capabilities, much in the same way as has been done for a long time. The sharp dividing line between capacity and non-capacity in the law has been articulated by Herring.[54]

In considering the case of a person with borderline capacity, concern may be raised regarding a certain behaviour or wish.[55] However, blurring the line between competence and incompetence will make the threshold between the two states easier to negotiate than when competence is established in accordance with certain criteria regardless of the action at hand.[56] The way to do this may, for example, be to weigh the grade of

---

[51] Carney (2012), above n 9, 4.

[52] Cf Vivianne Dörenberg and Brenda Frederiks, 'The legal position of vulnerable people in the future: Improving or going backwards' (2012) 19 Eur J Health L 485, 496.

[53] Mäki-Petäjä-Leinonen and Juva (2015), above n 34, 13, 15. Cf also British Medical Association and the Law Society (2004) 3–4 and Rosie Harding, 'Legal constructions of dementia: Discourses of autonomy at the margins of capacity (2012) 34(4) J Soc Wel and Fam L 425.

[54] Jonathan Herring, *Vulnerable Adults and the Law* (Oxford University Press 2016) 45, drawing on J Herring and J Wall, 'Autonomy, capacity and vulnerable adults: Filling the gaps in the Mental Capacity Act' (2015) 35(4) Legal Studies 698. Compare and contrast Hall (2009), above n 18, 108, who argues that the dividing line between capacity and incapacity often is not clear, but instead gradual.

[55] Herring (2009), above n 46, 3, 7.

[56] Cf ibid 3, 28.

competence against both what harm may come to the individual in carrying out the action and whether or not the actions are uncharacteristic compared to the individual's behaviour in earlier life.[57] This assessment seems to be quite different from the more common notion of competence being assessed in relation to the understanding of a certain action and its consequences. However, as Herring advocates, this does not mean that the solution suggested here cannot start out with the comprehension of an action and its consequences.[58]

Sometimes appointing an administrator (guardian) seems to be the only option to give protection to someone with a cognitive disablement. On the other hand, such a decision can also lead to abuse of the administrated person's civil rights and his or her autonomy.[59] Administratorship is an institution designed to protect incapacitated adults by way of a surrogate decision-maker.[60] Still, justifying the use of administratorship requires evidence that a person's wellbeing will be improved through administratorship.[61] There might also be a certain danger in the use of protection itself. As Herring puts it, elderly persons have a human right to be protected from abuse – but the measures the respective state has instituted may pose threats in and of themselves to the rights of autonomy.[62]

In this context, it is argued that we need a legal fiction of incapacity to answer the question of when the state is entitled to limit an individual's right to make independent decisions. However, it must be taken into account that the state's incursion can be both beneficial and supportive. The determination of a person's legal incapacity lies in prevailing values, knowledge and the political and economic situation at the time. The concepts of legal capacity and legal incapacity will evolve in the same

---

57 Ibid 3, 8–12 and 28, with further references.

58 Ibid 3, 9–10, with further references.

59 Yuval Melamed and Israel Doron, 'Guardianship of people with mental disorders' (2007) 65 Soc Sci Med 1118, 1118.

60 Jennifer L Wright, 'Guardianship for your own good: Improving the well-being of respondents and wards in the USA' (2010) Int J Law Psychiatry 350, 350.

61 Jennifer L Wright, 'Protecting who from what and why, and how? A proposal for an integrative approach to adult protective proceedings' (2004) 12 Elder L J 53 79. See also Wright (2010), above n 58, 350, 351.

62 Jonathan Herring, 'Elder abuse: A human rights agenda for the future' in Israel Doron and Ann Soden (eds), *Beyond Elder Law*: *New Directions in Law and Aging* (Springer Verlag 2012) 175.

way as social values.[63] However, Sabatino and Wood argue that under the UN Convention on the Rights of Persons with Disabilities, incapacity is not a legitimate concept. Instead, supported decision-making is the focus of the convention.[64]

When discussing how to achieve autonomy for elderly persons and the implications that are present in the concept, it is important to embrace Nancy Dowd's suggestion – to focus on the development of the different stages and processes of the elderly.[65] Thus, the process is very much about empowerment and potential; as expressed by the EU, in order for the elderly to remain active as workers, consumers, carers, volunteers and citizens, they need to be empowered.[66] Ann Numhauser-Henning also talks about empowerment when she stresses that support is the key, and then not only where employment is concerned. Support is also needed to ensure that the elderly can be part of a community and family activities. This is considered to promote active ageing across all aspects of life. Independence is thought to be the solution and active ageing means offering better support to older people in all areas of life.[67] The importance of empowerment and emancipation is also stressed by Doron: 'that the challenge elder law faces in the future is to transform itself from a social control mechanism of a therapeutic state and a therapeutic jurisprudence into an emancipating, empowering, integrating assertion in an aging society'.[68] In Doron's multidimensional model, autonomy is

63 Charles P Sabatino and Erica Wood, 'The conceptualization of legal capacity of older persons in western law', in Israel Doron and Ann Soden (eds), *Beyond Elder Law: New Directions in Law and Aging* (Springer Verlag 2012) 36 with further reference to E Wood, 'History of guardianship' in M Quinn (ed.), *Guardianship of Adults: Achieving Justice, Autonomy, and Safety* (Maryland Institute for Continuing Professional Education of Lawyers Springer Series on Ethics, Law, and Aging 2005) 17.

64 Sabatino and Wood (2012), above n 61, 51 with further references.

65 Nancy Dowd, 'Conceptualizing elder law' in Ann Numhauser-Henning (ed.), *Introduction to the Norma Elder Law Research Environment – Different Approaches to Elder Law* (Norma Research Programme, Faculty of Law, Lund University 2013) 12. Dowd refers to the use of such a developmental focus for children and refers for a general view to Nancy Dowd (ed.), *Justice for Kids: Keeping Kids Out of the Juvenile Justice System* (New York University Press 2012).

66 *The EU Contribution to Active Ageing and Solidarity between Generations*, Brochure (Publications Office of the European Union 2012) 3. See also Numhauser-Henning (2013), above n 10, 23.

67 Numhauser-Henning (2013), above n 10, 23.

68 Israel Doron, 'Preface' in Israel Doron, *Theories on Law and Ageing: The Jurisprudence of Elder Law* (Springer Verlag 2009) ix.

represented by empowerment.[69] The connection between support and autonomy is argued by Kohn, Blumenthal and Campbell as empowering persons with disabilities.[70] Support thus seems to be the key to empowerment, and thus to autonomy, legal capacity and making one's own decisions.

This need for support is also expressed by Martha Albertson Fineman in her theory of vulnerability. Fineman stresses that all individuals are vulnerable at some time during their lifespan.[71] It is the state's responsibility to give individuals access to the different societal institutions, such as healthcare.[72] To be autonomous, individuals need the state's support to make choices.[73] The extent of the support that is needed depends on the individual's situation.[74] Individuals vary in their resilience in relation to vulnerability – and such resilience is dependent on the individuals' access to support. By giving support the state thus ensures a decrease in vulnerability.[75]

However, contrary to the quest for autonomy and the view held by the UN Convention on the Rights of Persons with Disabilities, a clear shift has taken place from substituted decision-making to supported decision-making, and this is evident in national legislation and international doctrine. Here, a kind of a universal truth is held: when one is incapacitated, one needs to have decision-making powers transferred to

---

[69] I Doron, 'A multi-dimensional model of elder law' in Israel Doron, *Theories on Law and Ageing: The Jurisprudence of Elder Law* (Springer Verlag 2009) 60 and 70. See further I Doron 'A multi-dimensional model of elder law: An Israeli example' (2003) 28(3) Ageing Int 242.

[70] Nina A Kohn, Jeremy A Blumenthal and Amy T Campbell, 'Supported decision-making: A viable alternative to guardianship?' (2012–13) 117 Penn St L Rev 1111, 1112–14.

[71] See Fineman (2010–11), above n 18. Compare and contrast Israel Doron, *Theories on Law and Ageing: The Jurisprudence of Elder Law* (Springer Verlag 2009) 60 and 70. See further Doron (2003), above n 67, 242.

[72] Fineman (2010–11), above n 18, 251, 256–7.

[73] Fineman (2010–11), above n 18, 251, 260. See also Martha Fineman, '"Elderly" as vulnerable: Rethinking the nature of individual and societal responsibility' (2012) Emory Legal Studies Research Paper No. 12–224 101, 123.

[74] See Fineman (2010–11), above n 18, 251, 266, 268 and 269.

[75] Ibid 251, 269. See also Håkan Jönsson and Titti Mattsson, 'Likvärdighet och äldreomsorg – en introduktion' (2014) 3–4 Socialvetenskaplig Tidskrift 240, 241, about two versions of equality. For a critique of the concept of vulnerability see Hall (2009), above n 18, 107–8 and Herring (2016), above n 52, 5.

another person.[76] The dividing line is thus between persons with and persons without legal capacity. When legal capacity prevails, but the person still needs help, supported decision-making has become more common. The Swedish legislation is an example of such a view.

4. FROM SUBSTITUTED DECISION-MAKING TO SUPPORTED DECISION-MAKING – AN EXAMPLE

During the last decades of the twentieth century, a move was seen in Sweden from substituted decision-making in situations where a person has a cognitive disability, but still is able to make his or her own decisions, towards more supported decision-making. This was achieved through the development of the administratorship concept and through use of the so-called 'good man' (*god man*) institution. An administrator takes over the subject's decision-making powers and acts in his or her place. Nowadays, however, when appointing an administrator, the court can and must limit the appointment to what is necessary. This means that a person may retain his or her legal capacity to act in certain areas of life, even if other areas are put under the care of an administrator.[77]

Getting help from a good man does not in itself mean that the supported person loses his or her legal capacity to act. If the person's health condition means that he or she no longer has legal capacity to act, however, the good man may act on behalf of him or her. If this is not the case, and the good man is only there to support and help, the Swedish legislation applies supported decision-making.[78]

A new development means that the person needing support will have rather extensive possibilities to influence the selection of his or her administrator or good man.[79] The reasoning behind this new development seems to be the power that this would presumably give the elderly person

---

[76] See for example, Doron (2003), above n 33, 131, 131. See also Mäki-Petäjä-Leinonen and Juva (2015), above n 34, 13, 15. See further Herring (2009), above n 46, 3, 3.

[77] Children and Parents' Code, Chapter 11 para 7. See further Torbjörn Odlöw, *Ställföreträdare för vuxna; kamrer eller handledare?* (Jure Förlag AB 2005) 232–4.

[78] Children and Parents' Code, Chapter 11 para 5. See further Odlöw (2005), above n 75, 234–7.

[79] Children and Parents' Code, Chapter 11 para 12.

needing support.[80] Looking at this piece of legislation from the outside, it certainly seems to be a huge step towards autonomy. However, looking at it from the inside is another matter altogether: there is increased risk that the wrong person will be chosen, a person who will act to the detriment of the dementia sufferer's interests. This risk is also associated with current insufficiencies in the monitoring of the administrator and the good man.[81] Furthermore, when a person is suffering from a cognitive disability like dementia, it is not certain that the person will receive information in a way that makes him or her able to make an informed decision.[82] Thus, a dementia sufferer's decision about whom he or she wants to act as administrator or good man could be influenced by someone who aspires to the position. This new legislation opens up for a family member to be designated by elderly persons with dementia, which in itself may pose a problem. It means that family members act as the administrator or the good man even more often than today. The individual perspective in the family can make the appointment of a family member as administrator or good man problematic. Nowadays, conflicting interests are quite common in families.[83] This may depend on the general developments in society, but also on the development of the family as such; for example, the nuclear family consisting of a couple and their common children is no longer always the norm.[84]

5. CONCLUSIONS

However, when all is said and done there seems to be a change taking place in how guardianship laws are being designed; we are moving from a focus on protection to a focus on autonomy.[85] On the other hand, such a view will uphold the perceptions of autonomy and protection as different and conflicting concepts. Instead, the relation between

---

80 Government Bill Prop 2013/14:225 *Bättre förutsättningar för gode män och förvaltare* 1, 32–3.

81 Compare and contrast Fridström Montoya (2015), above n 32, 324, who argues for the use of family members as good men.

82 See Ryrstedt (2016a), above n 20, and Ryrstedt (2016b), above n 20, 179, 200.

83 See for the individual perspective, Eva Ryrstedt, *Bodelning och bostad: Ekonomisk självständighet eller gemenskap* (Juristförlaget i Lund 1998) 383–429. See also Ryrstedt (2016b), above n 20, 179, 183–4.

84 See Ryrstedt (2016b), above n 20, 179, 183–4.

85 Lawrence M Solan, 'Legislative style and judicial discretion: The case of guardianship law' (2012) 35 Int J Law Psychiatry 464, 464.

autonomy and protection may be phrased as aiming at a balance, which can be achieved through support given to the elderly individual; the support may then be directed towards both autonomy and protection. Support will thus be the means that makes balance, by creating flexibility in the extent of the support necessary.

As argued by Fineman according to her vulnerability theory, support is a prerequisite for vulnerable persons' attainment of autonomy.[86] However, when support is influenced by the supporting person's views – whether professional or private – autonomy will be reduced. Such an impact is perhaps inevitable to some extent, because the supporting person always will have views (often internalized ones). The problem is enhanced when the person providing support has his or her own interests in the different actions taken by the elderly person. For support to be empowerment, it must be provided by someone without subjective interests and without a paternalistic approach.

The view of support as the solution for achieving autonomy results from the fact that support can also fulfil the need for protection. Nevertheless, if autonomy and protection are to be balanced, it is paramount that support is given by someone without any interests in the decisions taken. In addition, support would need to be designed with a well-functioning control system to ensure that no abuse is taking place and that the views of the elderly are properly acknowledged.[87]

Supported decision-making can become more complex in cases where the elderly individual suffers from an advanced case of dementia, in that it can be difficult to interpret the person's wishes. In addition to using all available means to carry out such an interpretation, it is also possible to take into account how the person in question led his or her life until the onset of dementia. Those two sets of wishes and ways to live have also been advocated as part of a subjective best-interest test,[88] and the consideration of the behaviour in earlier life has enabled a new view for understanding capacity in relation to the taken or desired action. Legal

---

[86] Fineman (2010–11), above n 18, 251, 269.

[87] As has been advocated by Naomi Karp and Erica Wood, 'Guardianship monitoring: Promising state and local court practices to protect incapacitated older adults' (2008) XXXII ASA 22, 26 regarding well-functioning guardianship which is dependent on the monitoring. They stress the positive and negative impacts that guardianship may have on elderly persons with a cognitive disability, on the one hand in giving protection to the individuals, and on the other hand in diminishing the fundamental rights of the elder person.

[88] Cf Dunn (2014), above n 45, 128. See further Herring (2009), above n 2, 59–65.

capacity can then be constructed as entailing and accepting decisions by the person with dementia, as long as the decisions are not uncharacteristic compared to the individual's previous life and do not lead to harm for the individual carrying out the action.[89]

Considering not only the current wishes of a dementia sufferer but also how he or she has led his or her life puts focus on the individual so that protection is formed with this individual as the starting point.

[89] Cf Herring (2009), above n 46, 3, 10–12 and 28, with further references. However, Herring seems to find this principle to be applicable only to a person who has borderline capacity.

Index